Hitler's Mountain

# Hitler's Mountain

*The Führer, Obersalzberg and the
American Occupation of Berchtesgaden*

ARTHUR H. MITCHELL

McFarland & Company, Inc., Publishers
*Jefferson, North Carolina, and London*

LIBRARY OF CONGRESS CATALOGUING-IN-PUBLICATION DATA

Mitchell, Arthur, 1936–
Hitler's mountain : the Führer, Obersalzberg and the
American occupation of Berchtesgaden / Arthur H. Mitchell.
p.     cm.
Includes bibliographical references and index.

ISBN-13: 978-0-7864-2458-0
ISBN-10: 0-7864-2458-3
(illustrated case binding : 50# alkaline paper) ∞

1. Hitler, Adolf, 1889–1945—Homes and haunts—Germany—Obersalzberg Region.
2. Obersalzberg Region (Germany)—History.
3. Berchtesgaden (Germany)—History.   I. Title.
DD247.H5M528   2007        943.086—dc22        2006033189

British Library cataloguing data are available

On the cover: An American soldier views the burning Berghof,
May 1945 (National Archives)

Manufactured in the United States of America

McFarland & Company, Inc., Publishers
Box 611, Jefferson, North Carolina 28640
www.mcfarlandpub.com

To Liam Mitchell Peeples and
Virginia Gray Peeples

# Acknowledgments

The genesis of this book dates to my first visit to the magnificent alpine setting of Berchtesgaden, Germany, in 1996. My friend and colleague Joseph Siren, who had spent many youthful years there, had often urged me to make this trip with him. Since then Joe has been my constant resource person on matters German and military. In Berchtesgaden I met Florian Beierl, Iris Melcher and David Harper, who have provided all kinds of grassroots assistance. I have also had the generous help of many American soldiers who shared their experiences with me. I am particularly grateful to Sherman Pratt, Lloyd Ramsey, Russ Cloer, Isadore Valenti, Jack Agnew and David Daub (who even edited a chapter for me) and the Society of the Third Infantry Division. In Paris I greatly benefited from Alain Godec's knowledge and contacts concerning the role of the French Second Armored Division during the war. My gratitude extends to Col. Maurice Courdesses and Charles Pegulu de Rovin of the Archiv Leclerc (Memorial du Msarechal Leclerc de Hauteclocque) in Paris. Angelike Obermeier and Reinhard Horn of the Bavarian State Library provided valuable assistance.

I am indebted to a cadre of translators—Sharon Folk and Ted Kennedy for French (*Merci beaucoup*) and Joe Siren, David Heisser and Allan Greenberg for German (*vielen Dank*). My North Quincy friend and first intellectual mentor, Jim Watson, has been a valued critic of all my writing. As always, my old teammates and confreres, Tom Bingay, Jack Downey and Tom Greland, provided suggestions and measured encouragement. In Ireland Charlie Callan, Frank Darcy, Kevin O'Byrne, Padraig O'Snodaigh, Chris Woods and Rayner Lysaght have given me the benefit of their advice. Merrill Horton of the Salk faculty provided rigorous editing of a chapter. Not for the first time, my wife Marie encouraged me to get on with the work.

It has been a pleasure doing research in a variety of archives—the Bavarian State Archives in Munich, the National Archives in College Park, Maryland, the Military History Institute in Carlisle Barracks, Pennsylvania, the Library of Congress in Washington, D.C., the U.S. Military Academy at West Point, New York, and the Public Record Office in London. The staffs of all of these centers greatly facilitated my research. I am also grateful for the assistance provided by Walter Meeks and Vicki Hester of the Third Infantry Division Museum at Fort Stewart, Georgia. Sherrill Pinckney, Marvin Light, Edwin Merwin—librarians all—at the Salkehatchie Campus of the University of South Carolina always responded cheerfully to my mountain of requests for all kinds of materials. The staffs at the University of South Carolina inter-library loan office and at Auburn University are deserving of a Library

Iron Cross or at least a Good Conduct Medal for all the help they provided. As on previous occasions, Milton Harden gave me the benefit of his rock-solid computer expertise. Andrew Thomas came forward with timely help in constructing a map for the Berchtesgaden area. The Research and Productive Scholarship program of the University of South Carolina helped fund my research and travel on two occasions and for that I am grateful.

Since the events of the Second World War figure so largely in twentieth century history, I hope my students have derived some benefit from my many expositions based on my research. I suspect they will be more impressed by the book than by my talk.

With an exciting story to be told and with all this kind of help, how could I write a bad book? If it turned out that way (which I hopefully doubt), all the errors, omissions, confused language and more are my responsibility alone.

# Contents

Acknowledgments                                              v
Preface                                                      1
Introduction: Der Mann und der Berg                          3

One: Vagabond to Führer                                      7
Two: Berghof                                                 25
Three: Festung                                               48
Four: Occupation and After, 1945–2005                        144

Notes                                                        183
Selected Bibliography                                        199
Index                                                        211

# Preface

Adolf Hitler was a mountain man, not in the sense that he liked to climb the heights or trek through mountain paths, but that he found in terrain towering above mundane flatlands a place of secure detachment and reinforcement of inner convictions. As an indication of his political skill, he was able to employ this predilection in carving out a public personality of great impact. At the peak of Hitler's power in the late 1930s Arnold Toynbee noted that in the case of the *Anschluss* with Austria the Führer demonstrated an "uncanny manipulation ... from his wizard's cave at Berchtesgaden."[1] Hitler's connection with the Obersalzberg lasted to the end of his life—and beyond.

The ultimately most destructive yet dynamic event in the heart of European civilization in the twentieth century was the consolidation in power of the Nazi Party in Germany in the 1930s. The focus and guiding light of this movement was Adolf Hitler. The astounding success this man achieved in gaining the trust, support and loyalty of the mass of the German people was due, in large measure, to its perception of the Führer as a man of devotion, determination and effectiveness, but strongly related to this were Hitler's claims to be a visionary and prophet. For the latter purposes he needed a persona, a mystique that would appeal to the pronounced strain of romanticism in German political consciousness. He found it with his identification with the German mountains.

From the early 1920s Hitler attached himself to Berchtesgaden and the Obersalzberg in the Bavarian Alps, a connection which lasted until his death in 1945. This relationship was central to both his personal and political identification. It provided him with a specific connection to Germany that otherwise was lacking in a person without roots, family, education or conventional profession, one whom Hermann Göring, in the wake of defeat, declared was just a vagabond from the cafes of Vienna. Hitler often declared that the Berghof, his villa on the Obersalzberg, provided him with isolation and calm which stimulated inspiration, but it also allowed him free rein for his preferred bohemian lifestyle.

The public image of the Führer in the mountains was so strong that when Germany was facing total defeat at the end of World War II there was a general consensus among Allied military leaders that Hitler, given his Wagnerian mentality, certainly would retreat to a "National Redoubt" in his beloved mountain fastness. This turned out to be the greatest hoax of the war, but is evidence of his extraordinary impact on the public mind. Occupation of Germany resulted in the U.S. Army's taking control of the Berchtesgaden area. The immediate process of de–Nazification was completed without difficulty, but the fifty years that the American military was there ultimately put off the issue of how the reformed German government would deal with the legacy of Hitler and his physical identification with Berchtesgaden and the Obersalzberg. By erecting a "documentation center," in reality a museum of the Nazi Party, adjacent to the site of Hitler's Berghof, the German government imposed this historical burden on the Obersalzberg, not on Munich, the "birthplace" of the Nazi movement, or on Berlin.

These are some of the matters that are addressed in this book. The range is wide, but the focus always comes back to the evil genius who was supported by the bulk of his people to the bitter end. The man and the mountain had become one and, sixty years later, they remain so.

Arthur H. Mitchell
November 2006

# Introduction:
# Der Mann und der Berg

At the end of the 20th century a variety of journalistic assessments were made about what had occurred during that time within European civilization—what were the best novels, movies, personalities, greatest inventions, major events, etc. In the category of who was the most murderous, the greatest monster of the 20th century, Adolf Hitler won hands down, with Joseph Stalin a close second.

Hitler's first achievement was in gaining control of the most dynamic people in Europe, perhaps in the world, and then mobilizing them for not just conquest but extermination of millions of people, to the lasting shame and reproach of the German people. After more than half a century, this condition and stain has only gradually diminished.

The impact of the film based on Thomas Keannelly's account, *Schindler's List*, vivid scenes of huge smokestacks spewing out fumes from bodies of victims of the Holocaust, was brought home to me while driving from Berchtesgaden to Salzburg (surely Hitler territory), with a young German editor, who said to me, "We did that!?," meaning, "Did we Germans commit these monstrous crimes?" I replied, "Yes, you did." And then I felt sad and regretful about intruding on the burden of generations of German people who carry the weight of the atrocities committed by Hitler, the Nazis and their legions of supporters in the dozen years from 1933 to 1945.

At the same time, despite sometimes feeling almost overwhelmed by thinking and writing about this horrific episode, I felt that I was really not minding someone else's business. The people of the United States have, one way or the other, been tied up in the determining events within Europe and European civilization in the 20th century. Furthermore, Americans have demonstrated their own capacity for racism, violence and mass murder. On the other hand, the Americans, along with their Russian allies, were the people who destroyed the evil Nazi murder machine and drove its mad dog dictator to suicide.

Yet here I was, traveling to Berchtesgaden four times and for the same number of years spending almost all of my research time on a study of Hitler, the Obersalzberg and the American occupation of Berchtesgadener Land. I was brought up listening to people often talking about World War II, the war against the Japanese, the Nazis and Hitler. Like many other people too young to have served in the war, I developed a great interest in military history, particularly about the conflict between 1939 and 1945. Friedrich Nietzsche, another deranged German, once said that war is for men what childbirth is for women. But then he never was in a war. I spent my time in the U.S. Army in the late 1950s hoping there would not be one.

The proliferation of television channels has created the opportunity to deluge our people with heaps of military history, but the emphasis seems always to be World War II, the good war with a clear-cut outcome—total victory. What comes across from the likes of the History Channel is not simply graphic and stimulating presentation of stirring events, but gross editorial distortion and, ultimately, the glorification of war and military virtues. Wouldn't it be great to be able to claim that you fought in the Battle of the Bulge! We can remind ourselves that this type of television enterprise is a commercial activity to attract viewers and to sell advertising to make money. The effect of all this, however, is to condition another generation of credulous couch potatoes to the excitement, manly courage and glamour of it all, with, of course, lots of stirring music. (Shades of Newt Gingrich watching *Sands of Iwo Jima*, starring non-soldier John Wayne, over and over.) Most of my students much prefer to watch that stuff than listen to me going on about evidence, documents and a balanced presentation of these events. And now the wonders of the U.S. Army's invasion of Iraq! Capitalist, commercial culture is winning hands down. It is depressing and, moreover, dangerous.

Why then have I written about an aspect of the miserable and humiliating event? Having spent thirty years researching, writing and thinking about the people of Ireland, I have gradually come to the happy conclusion that events in that country have led to the state of affairs that I hoped and anticipated would occur—progress towards political consensus and reconciliation, broad- based educational opportunity, economic prosperity and social development. I hope I am right! I remain interested in the Irish diaspora in this country and intend to complete two studies of that great migration.

Several visits to Germany revealed to me that nothing substantial had been written about Hitler and the symbolism of the Obersalzberg and how the Americans dealt with this heritage as the conquering power in south Germany after the war. Here was an opportunity to jump into a whole new area of study and research. If I wasn't going to break some new ground at sixty years of age I wasn't going to do it all. But the pitfalls for me were little knowledge of German history and no facility in the German language. A quickly-assembled, superficial book on the Führer, his house and dogs and all that would be another disservice to historical truth and knowledge of the subject. But I have worked hard to overcome these obstacles and to make this book well-researched yet readable, scholarly (lots of reference notes, etc.) and balanced in its treatment. I hope the reader will find it so.

The first difficulty in this account is that it includes a lot about Hitler that reveals that he was, in some respects, thoughtful, considerate, generous and kind. In many ways, he led a life of simple tastes, deportment and activity. This leads to the central paradox of Hitler. The evidence is overwhelming and conclusive that he was a criminal lunatic who hungered for and achieved the ability to kill and mutilate millions of people. He was a shallow, cold-blooded egotist who, without any moral scruples, used his great powers of persuasion and ruthless organizational ability to carry out his crimes against humanity. In achieving a mass mobilization of evil, he degraded a whole people and, indeed, European civilization itself.

He could not have done any of this if he had not been able to convince a substantial proportion of the German people that what he said he wanted to do for them was good, fair, beneficial and just. He also had to convince them that he was a wholesome and intelligent person, dedicated to their welfare, clear in his vision of what he wanted to do for them and Germany. He succeeded in getting them to see him as a leader they themselves had produced, a democratic figure, of no family standing, privileged background or anything of the sort. Being one of them, he knew, from experience, of their hopes and dreams, fears and resentments. In addition, he succeeded in projecting an image of a strong leader, who had the qualities of determination, inspiration and audacity that they were seeking.

One of the aspects that has often been overlooked in assessing Hitler and his achievements is the sheer professionalism of Hitler as a politician. The focus so often is on the series of brutal actions initiated by the Führer during and under the cover of war. He gained the confidence and support of the mass of the German people by honing his political skills over a period of thirteen years, becoming a quintessential politician. Without any family responsibilities and no other job, he carried on a non-stop political campaign, gradually mobilizing popular support, expanding the party organization and perfecting his oratorical abilities. He held no public office until he became head of the German government. With nothing better to do, he engaged in the game of waiting for the main chance—an event that would discredit the conventional political parties and the existing parliamentary system of government. The Nazis, like a lot of other German political groupings, carried on a sustained agitation about the horrors of the Versailles treaty and the burden of reparations, but by the late twenties the political impact of these had diminished with the abandonment of reparation payments and a willingness of the former adversaries of Germany to adjust and eliminate some of the provisions of that *Diktat*.

The big break for Hitler and the Nazis came with the Depression, a product of the United States of America. The stupendous impact of the American-generated economic fiasco on Germany is almost always underestimated by historians, many of whom have been bound up in studying exchanges of diplomatic documents. At this critical juncture there was Hitler, a known if exotic public figure, with a well-organized political machine and a clear if controversial program. There was a way out of catastrophe for the German people.

Once Hitler attained dictatorial control of the German people he gradually led them to the abyss, but they cheered him on almost all of the way. He promised he would once again make them strong, proud and prosperous. In substance, he delivered on these promises by the late 1930s. Yet he had a lot more on his agenda of which they knew little, and when they found out it was too late to stop him. One of the staggering aspects of the period of war, death and destruction into which he led his people and the rest of Europe is that virtually until the end he retained the support and confidence of a majority of German people. His many achievements in the 1930s led many people to have a strong, grateful attachment to him as well as the belief that his "genius" would provide a way out of the trap of a losing war that threatened to engulf Germany.

When Hitler was bidding for their support, the German people had to make an assessment not just of the Nazi Party and what it proposed to do about their problems, but of Hitler himself. Being a completely experienced politician of the people, he knew how to appeal to them, and this was crucial to his success. The image of Hitler as a dedicated, clean-living man of simple tastes was not just propaganda but reality. Yet, as time was to show, there was the other side of him—a man planning unlimited conquests, mass murder and total domination of nations. The people saw only the strong leader; what he was planning was outside their time, place and vision.

So there was a bad Hitler and a good Hitler. It is a common phenomenon among pathological killers and various other kinds of sick and disturbed people that they require some rationale to demonstrate to themselves and those around them that they are not just brutal, nasty murderers. Over and over Communist propaganda presented Joseph Stalin as a plain, simple, dedicated leader of the Soviet people. Although unlike Hitler he did smoke and drink, the image was also the reality. Yet we know that Stalin had an almost unlimited desire to kill and punish. Mafia gangsters are noted for having close, loving family attachments, and they even call their criminal enterprise a family. It is not unusual for bad people to try to justify themselves, at least in their own eyes, as having good qualities. Moreover, in a dog-eat-dog world, they argue, they simply get in the first bite.

Hitler justified his criminal agenda on the basis of deeply held convictions: the Jewish curse must be eliminated in Germany and Europe, Germany rightly should dominate Europe and should be a world power. Stalin had what he saw as an ideological foundation for his brutal activities, something Hitler respected. When one of his lackeys dismissed Stalin as a mere bank robber, Hitler responded that Stalin had not robbed banks for himself but for his cause. It takes one to know one.

Just as Stalin was not a Russian, so Hitler was not a German, but, rather, a blow-in from Austria who spoke the language with a funny accent. (The Russian people were baffled by Stalin's speech when for the first time, after the German invasion of 1941, they heard his voice on the radio.) Hitler was a drifter, a bum from the cafes of Vienna (as Göring, in the end, described him), the type of wretched, indolent and conceited "artist" to be found hanging around the fringes of great cities.

His service in the German army in the first European war was the basis for establishing his credentials as a German patriot. Fearing the restrictions (and more) that marriage would impose on his unlimited desire for freedom of activity, he also felt that marriage was not going to help him gain public acceptance as a real German. Ranting in Munich beer halls helped, but there were a lot of people at that. What he needed and wanted was a gimmick, an image, a statement about who he was and what he was about. He found this in a place that was distinctively his own. Being an excellent political actor and one who had plenty of imagination and flair, he settled on a domicile with a dramatic setting. Up in the great Bavarian mountains he could retreat for refreshment, for thought and planning. The alpine location was most appealing to many German people. Up on his berg he could define himself as a healthy, natural sort of man who relished the simple pleasures of life—climbing the hills, tramping the paths, although, in fact, he kept that activity to a bare minimum. But it was the image, the appearance, that counted. There he had the undisturbed freedom to develop his great plans. The man was on his mountain. Going to the mountain for inspiration has a long historical resonance.

During the dozen years that Hitler ruled Germany he spent an extraordinary amount of time away from the capital and at his country retreat—surely more than any other major political leader. When faced with total military defeat there was the general assumption in Germany and abroad that he would withdraw to his beloved Berghof in the Alps for a proper Wagnerian finish to it all.

Recognizing that leaving Berlin would remove him from whatever political authority remained in Germany, he did not head for the mountains, but bunkered down in the capital. The capture of Berchtesgadener Land was a task for the U.S. Army, but lengthy occupation of the area meant that it was the American government that would have to deal with this aspect of the physical heritage of Hitler, the Nazis and a mad episode in German history. After half a century, this burden was handed to the authority which rightly bore historical responsibility—the government of a re-united Germany. These are some of the matters that this book examines.

# CHAPTER ONE

# Vagabond to Führer

In the 1930s one of the most famous private residences in the world was located above the town of Berchtesgaden, high in the Bavarian Alps. It was on the Obersalzberg that Adolf Hitler put down his personal roots in Germany. He first visited the place in the spring of 1923, before his attempted putsch in Munich, and he repeatedly returned there until the end of his life. He spent so much time there that Berchtesgaden became the second capital of the Reich. Towards the end of World War II Nazi propaganda claimed that this would be the center of their final stand, in the mountains; indeed, a Wagnerian "Twilight of the Gods." This threat sent Allied forces on a mad rush to capture the area. For the next fifty years the U.S. Army occupied the place, effectively putting a lid on Hitler's association with it. In the wake of the U.S. military withdrawal from Germany, the Hitler hot potato was finally handed over to the German government in 1995. Amidst considerable controversy, it has constructed a "documentation center," which opened in October 1999, beside the ruins of the house of the greatest monster of the twentieth century.

This is a study of the political events that took place in that setting from the 1920s through the aftermath of the U.S. Army's returning control of Hitler's Obersalzberg to the German government in 1995. It is also an attempt to access the symbolic significance of the Berghof and Hitler's assumed identification with that locality within the context of Nazi ritual, propaganda and myth. In addition, it seeks to address the wider matter of self-identity and public perception in relation to place, setting and life style of political figures. What is the importance of the identification of FDR with Hyde Park, JFK with Hyannisport, LBJ with his Texas ranch? Does it matter if George Bush, with his preppy New England background, assumed a forced identity with Texas, dropping his g's, etc.? What is the significance of a mountain and a great man—Moses, Jesus, Mohammed? The image of the Führer up on the Obersalzberg had a powerful impact on the imagination of the German people. Not for nothing, Hitler claimed to be the best actor in Germany.

## The Wanderings of Young Adolf

Berchtesgaden is a picturesque town of about four thousand located in the Bavarian Alps one hundred and ten miles south-east of Munich and a dozen miles south of Salzburg, Austria. The Berchtesgadener Land juts into Austria and overlooks the city of Salzburg. The protrusion is framed on three sides by the Steinernes Meer and two mountain chains—the Hagengebirge and the Watzmann, whose principal peak is almost 9000 feet high. The principal natural resource of the area is salt, hence Obersalzberg, "upper salt mountain." Wood-carving also was a traditional occupation.

During the nineteenth century the Wittelsbachs, the royal family of Bavaria, built a series of castles in the Bavarian Alps; the most notable builder being Ludwig II, "Mad Ludwig," whose castle at Neuschwanstein ("new swan rock") has famously provided the model for the centerpiece for the magic kingdom of Disneyland. The castle he built nearest to Berchtesgaden, a copy of Versailles, looms over the moody Chiemsee, near Prien, forty-five miles away, on the autobahn to Munich. A more modest endeavor of the Wittelsbachs is a royal residence facing the Berchtesgaden market square.

The little town perched on a hill-side remained relatively isolated until a railroad was built there in 1910, which later extended to the Königssee, a mystical blue-green lake bordered by mountains. On the eve of the Hitler era the town had a population of about 2500.

Above the town on the north-east slope of the Hoher Goll was the village of Obersalzberg, which had great vistas of the surrounding mountains, the Salzburg plain and the magnificent mountain lake of the Königssee. The setting is striking: "In the gap of the mountains to the north, at the foot of the Gaisberg, there nestles the old diocesan town of Salzburg. On days when the Alpine Wind is blowing the castle and the little town can be seen with the naked eye ... to the left of the Obersalzberg there looms the mastiff of the Untersberg, whose changing colors evoke a different atmosphere every day. Still further to the left the eye then wanders over to the Watzmann and the giant mountains which surround it, and which finally appear to move closer in a wide arc and culminate in the Hoher Goll behind the Obersalzberg." In the early years of the twentieth century the locality had six inns, a children's sanatorium and eleven villas.[1]

The U.S. Army military government's Civil Affairs unit in the Land a year after the war provided a succinct description of the area:

> The Landkreis Berchtesgaden is situated at the extreme southeastern corner of Bavaria, forming a spur projecting into Austrian territory by which it is, roughly speaking, surrounded on three sides. It is one of the beauty spots of Germany, famed for its mountain and lake scenery; for this reason it has always attracted

Hitler on the Obersalzberg, mid–1930s. (Library of Congress, Heinrich Hoffmann collection)

Berghof in the late 1930s. (Bavarian State Library, Munich)

streams of holiday visitors, persons of means from other parts of Germany who built themselves houses here for summer or for permanent residences; and last but not least the "Führer" and his coterie of high-rank party leaders established themselves under guard of the SS in luxurious and costly buildings, above and underground, on the slopes of Obersalzberg, a mountain overlooking the town of Berchtesgaden. It was world-wide known that in this tranquil Bavarian retreat Hitler chose his vacation office and home and thereupon the name of Berchtesgaden sprang into press reports and prominence all over the world as the seat of the impregnable fortress of the "Führer."[2]

The area, with its magnificent scenery and pure air, became both a summer and winter resort in the early years of this century. The German explorer Alexander von Humboldt declared that the valley was the most beautiful spot on earth. Among those who built villas in the location were Carl Linde, the inventor of the refrigerator, and Dr. Artur Eichenenbruen, who developed the aspirin. In this period a guest house was built on the Obersalzberg. Among the guests at the Zum Turken were Thomas Mann and his daughter Erike as well as conductor Wilhelm Furtwängler. The family of Sigmund Freud vacationed in the area, usually at Schonau near the Königssee, in the 1920s. There are some parallels between Sigmund and Adolf. They both came to Vienna, which they said they hated, and they both enjoyed the hills around Berchtesgaden. Often when he was there, Freud led his children on mushroom hunting expeditions in the hills. Several of Freud's short expository books were written during his summer alpine sojourns. It was there in 1929 that he wrote he wrote *Civilization and Its Discontents*. Surely by that time he must have heard of another Austrian who made his residence there in the late 1920s, the rising racist, super-nationalist politician Adolf Hitler. For whatever reason, after 1929 Freud no longer spent summers in the Berchtesgaden area, preferring to vacation in Austrian resorts.[3]

Hitler was not from Bavaria and did not become a citizen of the German state until 1932. He was born in 1889 at Braunau am Inn, Austria, on the border with Germany, where his much older father was a customs inspector. He grew up in Linz twenty miles from the German frontier in the most Germanic part of the Hapsburg realm. Thus, he was a southern German. His surviving siblings were an older half-brother, Alois, Jr., who fled from the family home at an early age, an older half-sister, Angela, and a younger full sister, Paula. In his semi-biographical screed of the mid–1920s, *Mein Kampf*, he mentions no siblings; in his view, he was an only child of misfortune—life was a struggle. Although he was an ambitious, egotistical and solitary person, he nevertheless maintained some sort of a relationship with his siblings, financially helped his sisters when he had the means and provided for all of them in his will of 1938 and for his sisters in that of 1945.[4]

According to his sister Paula, Adolf "challenged [her] father to extreme harshness and got his sound thrashing every day. He was a scrubby little rogue, and all of his attempts to thrash him for his rudeness and to cause him to love the profession of an official of the state were in vain." Hitler recalled that once he stopped responding to whippings, his father no longer resorted to corporal punishment. Hitler was an indifferent student. Dr. Eduard Bloch, the family physician, later recalled that at the age of twelve Hitler apparently was guilty of *Sittlichkeitsvergehen*, a sexual indiscretion or indecent assault, and was severely censured. He changed schools the next year and, now sixteen years of age in 1905, two years after the death of his father, he ended his formal education. He turned to his principal interest, painting. He also walked through the nearby hills, seeking artistic inspiration. One observer recalled that "he was seen there delivering speeches to the rocks of the country side in the most energetic tone of voice." His younger sister Paula remembered that at this time he "very often" delivered long harangues to their mother and herself—the budding orator. His doting mother bought him an expensive Heitzmann grand piano and paid for lessons. After loafing around for two years, in his distorted version of events he claimed that "poverty and hard reality" forced him into action. In 1907 he ventured to Vienna to fulfill his ambition to become an artist, but his hopes were dashed when he was twice rejected for admission to the Vienna Academy of Fine Arts. His mother died in December 1907 without Adolf ever telling her of his failure to be admitted to the academy. Now he was an orphan.

Despite his later claims of hardship, he received an orphan's pension, money from his mother's estate and additional funds he had "borrowed" from a childless aunt in Spital; he also could anticipate receiving a modest legacy from his father's estate when reaching the age of twenty-four, in 1913. When in 1911 his widowed sister Angela discovered he had largely stripped their aunt of her savings, she forced him to transfer his orphan's pension to his sister Paula. His hard times seemed to have been entirely self-imposed.[5]

## Adolf Arbeiter

During the five and a half years that Hitler lived in Vienna he supported himself, after he had dissipated his family money, by painting post-cards and larger paintings, working on construction sites and at various odd jobs, including shoveling snow, carrying luggage, and running errands. Although he always was publicly respectful to Hitler, Hermann Göring—after Hitler was dead—referred to him as "that vagabond from a Viennese cafe." Twenty years later the German historian Erich Kuby declared that Hitler was nothing less than "a gangster, prepared for the worst, a shady figure from the underworld of Vienna, which was his spiritual home."

From the beginning of his political career he made great play of his brief experience as a worker on construction sites. It is not unusual for politicians and others to exaggerate their rise from humble origins, "being brought up the hard way," but Hitler went far beyond the usual embellishments. In 1920 he told a Nazi Party meeting, "I am a working man, made of workers' flesh and blood." The next year in a letter to party comrades, he declared that when he arrived in Vienna, he "became a laborer on a building site and during the next two years did every conceivable type of casual labor." But, he claimed, he had worked his way up: "I became an architectural draughtsman and painter and by the age of 21 I was almost completely independent." In his political screed *Mein Kampf*, published in 1925, he referred to "Five years in which I was forced to earn a living, first as a day laborer, then as a small painter; a truly meager living which never sufficed to appease even my daily hunger."[6]

Later, as Führer, he further dramatized his manual laboring experience. In May 1933, addressing the inaugural convention of the German Labor Front, which the Nazis had formed by destroying the independent trade unions, he proudly declared, "Due to the unique course of my life I am perhaps more than anybody else in a position to understand all social classes, because I was right in the center of life, because in a whim or perhaps by virtue of its providence fate simply threw me into the large mass of people.... I myself worked for years as a construction worker and had to earn my living." At this time he told an assemblage of Seimans factory workers, "Like you, I came up from Labor," claiming that he had "neither stocks, bonds nor bank account." Indeed, he was a man of no property, as his chalet in Bavaria was in his sister Angela's name.[7]

The worker image was driven home in a party "ideological catechism": Question—

"What professions has Adolf Hitler had?"; answer: "Adolf Hitler was a construction worker, an artist and a student." The Nazi German Labor Front proclaimed Hitler as the "first worker of the nation."[8]

Years later, in one of his late-evening monologues, he told his military staff about the poverty he suffered in his Vienna years. "Who knows?" he opined; "If my parents had been sufficiently well-to-do to send me to a School of Art, I should not have made the acquaintance of poverty, as I did. Whoever lives outside poverty cannot really become aware of it, unless by overthrowing a wall." This situation, however, had its positive side: "The years of experience I owe to poverty—a poverty that I knew in my own flesh—are a blessing for the German nation. But for them, we'd have Bolshevism today." None of the assembled staff dared to ask the obvious question: Why was he poor? What about earnings from work? Obviously based on his self-imposed hard times when he was in his late teens and early 20s, he privately described himself in 1938 as a "proletarian."[9]

Although he did not go in for Mussolini's bare-chested participation in the Italian harvest-time "battle for wheat" or Stalin's occasional digging in a garden plot in the Kremlin, the Führer demonstrated that he too was a horny-handed son of labor. At the initiation of one public works—the famous autobahn system—a pile of two cubic feet of sifted soil awaited his ceremonial turning of the first cut. Spade in hand, the Führer proceeded to tackle the whole pile. Unlike the over-educated effete leaders of the declining Western democracies, here was a man who from hard experience knew how to handle a shovel.[10]

Hitler's "five years of misery in Vienna" was captured by the German journalist Ignatius Phayre in 1936 when he was Hitler's guest at his Bavarian home: in Vienna Hitler "had hunted odd jobs as a common laborer, a carpenter, or house painter, with a little money picked up at intervals by drawing Christmas cards in a sentimental vein. In quiet tones will Hitler recall his dreary tramps with the workless hordes past the noble mansions of the Ringstrasse." Robert Ley, head of the German Labor Front, celebrated Hitler's time as a manual laborer: "The Führer himself was a worker for long years and learned from experience how tiring it is to work in the sun from morning to night, or in wind and rain, in frost or heat." Eduard Bloch, his family doctor in Linz, believed that Hitler's later stomach trouble came about "largely as a result of bad diet while working as a common laborer in Vienna." In 1942 Hitler declared that one of the bonds between Mussolini and himself was that "at the same period Il Duce and [he] were both working in the building-trade."[11]

In fact, he probably only worked in construction for about a month, from November to December 1909, with some occasional work later on. Because he had no training for the work, he was classed as an assistant worker, probably working as a hod carrier. He obviously found the physical labor involved most demanding and, apparently after two weeks at this work, he said some of fellow workers threatened to toss him off a scaffold when he argued with them about Marxism, international socialism and German nationalism and refused to join their union. After a few weeks of unemployment, he said, he was forced to return to this kind of work, which he implied did not last long. This time he probably cleaned up a building site after the other workers had finished for the day. There is no documentary evidence concerning any of this employment, but its essentially casual nature could account for the lack of any surviving records. Reinhold Hanisch, who was a close companion immediately after this time, observed that he never saw Hitler do any hard work or did he ever mention having worked as a building laborer. Moreover, he said, at that time Hitler was too weak and run-down for that kind of labor: "Builders employ only strong and husky men." Due to the lack of evidence and the fact that those who knew him at the time did not recall him mentioning this activity, Ian Kershaw in his 1998 biography of Hitler has concluded that Hitler's claim to have been a construction worker "is almost certainly fictional." After this abortive work experience, Hitler did occasional pick-up jobs—beating carpets, carrying luggage, shoveling snow. At the time of his triumphant arrival into Vienna on occasion of the *Anschluss* of 1938, upon entering a grand hotel Hitler noted that long before he had shoveled snow at its entrance. This extremely casual employment is typical of footloose, wayward young men.

Years later Hitler privately expressed very negative views about blue collar workers, whom he saw as an indolent mass that cared only for eating, drinking and sex (young Adolf was not interested in any of these). He recalled his experience of contact with construction workers: "I do not know what horrified me most at that time: the economic misery of my companions, their moral and ethical coarseness, or the low level of their intellectual development." Reinhold Hanisch later said that Hitler did not know any real workers, only the drifters, misfits and beggars he associated with. As for those in the men's hostel, Hanish declared, "Only loafers, drunkards and the like stay for a long time in such a home." In 1933 Hanisch wrote an article for a Vienna newspaper entitled "Hitler as a Beggar in Vienna."[12]

Hitler's fawning supporters sometimes differed in their estimate of his "working man" image. In 1933, when Hitler was supervising the reconstruction of the chancellery in Berlin, Albert Speer was surprised to find that "it was very evident that he felt at home on site," easily climbing around the work stagings, and that Hitler quickly established an easy and familiar relationship with the building workers. The day before the official opening of the building Hitler had a special reception there for the workers and their wives.[13]

Taking him at his word concerning his youthful employment in the construction trade and seeking to mock his artistic pretensions, some of Hitler's opponents later demonstrated an unintended snobbery. In 1933 Bertolt Brecht wrote "The Song of the Housepainter Hitler," and Hitler's connection with this occupation was widely believed. As well, he sometimes was said to have been a paperhanger (visions of the one-armed paperhanger). Although probably he had been neither, Nazi propagandists used these accusations to show that he had been a working man, a man of the people.[14]

Hans Georg Ludecke, who first met Hitler in 1920 and who then traveled extensively in the United States, in the late 1930s argued that "to deride Hitler as a former 'housepainter,' the standard belittling sobriquet flung at him by the world Press, is absurd and unfair." Ludecke declared, "With equal justice one might call any American youth a waiter for the rest of his life because he earned his way through college by waiting on table." Although not enrolled in a university, Hitler "remained an earnest student of history and life." At the same time an English admirer of Hitler, A.P. Laurie, declared that the common observation that Hitler was "only a house painter" and that he had "no education" reeked of pure class snobbery. He pointed to the example of the "poor Scottish student" doing farm work in the summer to pay his way through university, which was "our equivalent to the finest type of European peasant, who produces a Mussolini, and a Hitler, and the small farmers of America who produced an Abraham Lincoln."

The story of Adolf *der Arbeiter* had a long life. In a book published in 1934, Michael Fry stated that Hitler had occasionally worked as a bricklayer. German people did not forget the claims made about the Führer's involvement in the building trade. Towards the end of the war the joke went around the Reich that Churchill upon inspecting Longworth House on St. Helena Island, the residence in exile of Napoleon, commented "It will do; the occupant can do his own decorating." In its obituary on 2 May 1945, the *Times* of London declared that during his Vienna years Hitler earned a living as an "assistant to a housepainter and by selling sketches."[15]

After sharing a room with August Kubizek for a year, during which time he failed to gain admission to the Vienna School of Fine Arts, he spent the next two years in marginal boarding houses and worse, by which time he was reduced to wearing a bizarre assortment of cast-away clothing. He then moved to the Mannerheim, a new men's hostel, where he carved out an area for his painting, reading magazines and delivering assorted lectures on architecture, history and politics. Amidst the flotsam of Vienna, he remained in this cozy and inexpensive establishment for three years.

Thereafter he never referred to this residence or to his previous use of doss houses. Albert Speer observed that Hitler could never be lured into providing any detail about his life in this period. To avoid providing any particulars, Hitler would declare that it had been a hard and bitter experience and, thus, he did not want to talk about it. Kurt Ludecke characterized the Hitler of this period as an "urban vagabond," but like many young men of this age bracket Hitler was in the process of finding himself and simply drifting along.[16]

As was his father, Hitler was a confirmed German nationalist and disliked Vienna for its cosmopolitan, substantially non–German population. Already in Linz he had noted the local concern about the encroachment of Czech people into the area. In Vienna it was very much the case of the small town boy coming to the big city, someone from a very German area now living in an extremely polyglot metropolis. Included in this mixture, Hitler later commented, was "the eternal fission-fungus of humanity: Jews and more Jews. To me the city was the personification of incest." In fact, Vienna had the largest Jewish population of any German-speaking city (8.6 percent) and in Brigittenau, the run-down area in which he lived, it was 17 percent. According to William Patrick Hitler, Adolf's father was anti–Semitic. August Kubizek, his boyhood friend in Linz, noted Adolf's growing dislike of Jews when they were together in Vienna. In *Mein Kampf*, Hitler charted his course in Vienna from puzzlement about Jews to his growing hatred of them.[17]

Hitler was an admirer of Karl Lueger, the anti–Semitic mayor of Vienna, but Lueger's opposition to Jews was purely rhetorical. He lacked authority to impose any restrictions on them, and he had Jewish friends. Lueger's death in 1910 left his Christian Socialist Party leaderless. According to Reinhold Hanisch, Hitler got the idea of forming a successor party, which would incorporate anti–Semitism and a leader of great oratorical ability. Hanisch recalled that "for some time" Hitler "was absorbed night and day" with this idea.[18]

Hanisch also remembered the Hitler he knew at that time as one who expressed respect for and appreciation of Jews for their business ability, charitable spirit and resistance to persecution. Moreover, Hitler had satisfactory dealings with Jewish art dealers and several Jews were helpful to him. One of these, Josef Neumann of the Mannerheim, gave him an old long coat, which he badly needed. Beyond that, Hanisch recalled that "Hitler at that time looked very Jewish" which led Hanisch to joke "that he must be of Jewish blood, since such a large beard rarely grows on a Christian chin. Also he had big feet, as a desert wanderer must have." Hanisch, however, was a petty criminal who tried to capitalize on Hitler's notoriety in the 1930s by writing dubious accounts of their brief relationship and by forging copies of Hitler's paintings. He died in a Vienna jail in 1936.[19]

Albert Speer recalled that during World War II Hitler at staff meetings often expressed the necessity to exterminate the Jews, adding that "it's lucky that as [an] Austrian I know the Jews so well." When Hitler was asked about the specific basis of hatred of Jews, he replied vaguely, "It is a personal thing." Did he have a particularly terrible encounter with a Jewish person, possibly a woman, or was he heaping all his frustration on the remarkably successful Jewish community of Vienna? Did he react to the fear that he was "infected" by Jewish blood from his putative paternal grandfather—a rumor which dogged him for years? No one knows, but the flaming anger he directed at Jews remained to the end of his life. This boiling emotion would indicate that indeed it was based on a personal event or events and these happened in Vienna.[20]

During his time in Vienna he was an indolent but acute political observer, soaking up the pan–Germanism of Georg von Schonerer (whose few followers used the "Heil" salute and referred to him as "der Führer"), the political techniques of Karl Lueger, Vienna's popular mayor and professional anti–Semite, the virulent racism of such magazines as *Ostara* and the Social Democratic Party with its extensive organization and impressive processions. As well, he undoubtedly derived some of his vitriolic views about Jews from the polemics of his favorite composer, Richard Wagner, about whom Hitler claimed to have expert knowledge of both his music and writings. August Kubizek recalled that the only organization which Hitler claimed to have joined at that time was the Anti-Semite Union, but a young man as adrift as was Hitler does not join anything.[21]

In 1913, having reached the required age of twenty-four in April, he received the anticipated inheritance from his father, which came to the considerable amount of 819 *Kronen*. A week after he received the funds and with a much-needed new suit of clothes, he set out with a companion for Munich, "a real German city." In 1921 he claimed he made this move the previous year. If he disliked Vienna so much, why did he remain there for five years and why the precipative change? There were two reasons: first, the Austrian army was after him for a year's service; as a German nationalist he shunned this. Secondly, he could not afford to leave the bare subsistence level of the men's hostel for a relocation in an unknown place. In the Munich police registration form he listed his nationality as stateless. In essence, he was a draft-dodger, avoiding military training, for which he was eligible beginning in 1909, his twentieth year. But by 1913 the military authorities were closing in. When he finally reported for a physical examination in Salzburg he was rejected as physically unfit, which says a lot about his physical condition at that time; military authorities are not noted for being very demanding in this regard.[22]

A spoiled child, lazy, dreamy and isolated, his young life was marked by failure, sponging and drift. As was to be said many years later of his nephew, William Patrick Hitler, when he was about the same age, "he was a young man that had not amounted to much." In fact, a lot of young men go through the same pattern of aimlessness. Moreover, Hitler did read, study and observe what was going on around him in those two great cities. In any case, the guns of August 1914 were to bring about a drastic change in his life, one that he welcomed.

## Munich to Obersalzberg

Hitler became firmly attached to his adopted city of Munich for the rest of his life. He once declared, "Here I was truly born, here I started my movement and here is my heart." During the year he spent in Munich he continued to paint pictures, which he sold. According to one account, he also sometimes worked as a cleaner in beer halls, carrying out his duties in a vigorous and cheerful manner. This is most doubtful; his landlady recalled that he seldom left his one room garret. She found him to be, if aloof, courteous and trouble-free. Apparently she and her husband were the only people he corresponded with during his war service. More than twenty years later, when he was chancellor, he told Hans Baur of the kindness of his landlady and he arranged for her to be given a "modest allowance."[23]

With the outbreak of war he immediately enlisted in a Bavarian unit of the German army and served in northern France throughout the war of 1914–18, and was wounded and gassed; among his decorations was the Iron Cross First Class. Although he later expounded about having been one of the many who "served in the trenches," he was not a front-line infantryman, but rather a dispatch carrier, which allowed him to have bunkered quarters and hang around headquarters. Despite this long service, he never rose above the level of lance corporal (private first class), which, given the carnage of that war, seems most unusual. He claimed he declined promotion because he liked the position he held, which, at best, associated him with combat decision-making. There is evidence that he was not promoted because he lacked leadership ability and because of his eccentric personality, which included apparently homosexual activity. But with an Iron Cross First Class, he was a certified decorated veteran of the war, a role which would serve him well in his political career, and it was just about all he had to begin with. He always remained secretive about the circumstances surrounding the award and did not begin to wear the medal until 1927, long after the beginning of his political career.[24]

At the end of the war, not having any other destination, he returned to his division's home base in Munich. While the mass of soldiers quickly left the army, Hitler, with no place to go, stayed put. While there he experienced the "Red Republic" in Bavaria in 1919 and he also returned to painting, with his army comrade Hans Mend selling the paintings in the beer halls and in the streets. Then came a crucial event in his life. Well known among his wartime comrades as an outspoken, indeed fanatical, German nationalist, he was appointed a political education instructor and informant on radical political activity. Karl Mayr, for fifteen months Hitler's superior in the "instruction division," recalled that the reports Hitler submitted "were scrupulously honest, but his style and grammar were lamentable.... His intellect was not higher than that of an eight-year-old child." Mayr also noted that Hitler was "shy and self-conscious. The reason for this was probably the deformity (described in his medical report) that made him unlike other men." As is well known, it was in September 1919 that he encountered the tiny German Workers' Party, over which he soon took command.[25]

With the German army being reduced to insignificance by the Versailles treaty, he finally left the barracks (a barracks rat?) in June 1920 and sub-let a small room and an adjoining hallway in an apartment at 41 Thierchstrasse, a shabby building near the Isar River. The owner of the building, a Herr Erlanger, a Jew who later declared that he had had casual, amicable contact with Hitler, described the room: "The back room in which he slept is only eight by fifteen feet. It is the coldest room in the house.... Now we only use it as a lumber room; nobody will have it any more." Ernst Hanfstängl, one of his earliest supporters, said that Hitler "lived there like a down-at-heels clerk," but this humble abode provided evidence that he indeed was a man of the people.[26]

About this time Captain Truman Smith, U.S. military attaché, recalled the setting in which he met Hitler: "The room in the house where Hitler received him was drab and dreary beyond belief, akin to a back bedroom in decaying New York tenement." Smith provided some generally inaccurate background concerning the aspirant leader of the German people: "Hitler, an Austrian by birth, of humble parentage, practiced as a young man, first in Salzburg, later in Munich, his profession of wall painter, with what success the historian of the movement does not state." Truman was struck by the contrast in Hitler's appearance, noting that "the stocky figure, short cropped black hair and stubby moustache marks him in no way from the German middle-class shopkeeper." On the other hand, there were the "dark eyes, gleaming with fanaticism, intense and unceasing. The eyes, coupled with the voice, for it is as a speaker and agitator before hostile audiences that Hitler is in his element, have brought him to the forefront." Smith noted that "the National Socialists were at first regarded in Berlin as another Munich beer fantasy, and perhaps they would still be inconsequential had it not been for the curious, demagogic personality of their leader." Hitler's powerful oratory, "His derisive, rasping, often angry voice, his feeling for the dramatic, and a veritable genius in sensing the temper of his audience," Smith observed, "carried Munich by storm during 1920 and 1921."[27]

Off the platform, the Hitler of the early 1920s was not an impressive figure. Ernst Hanfstängl recalled that when he met Hitler at that time he was "a minor provincial political agitator, a frustrated ex-serviceman, awkward in a blue serge suit. He looked like a suburban hairdresser on his day off." Not content with this description, Hanfstängl also described the Hitler of this period as looking "like a waiter in a railway station restaurant."[28]

Hitler continued to live in spartan circumstances until his fortunes improved in 1929, when he moved to a large apartment at 16 Prinz Regentenplatz in the best area of Munich. Apparently he kept the little place—it could become a shrine of Nazism if all went well. Although his first place was tiny, he soon acquired a Mercedes convertible in which his chauffeur drove him around Munich. He greatly enjoyed motoring and he did want to be noticed.[29]

Increasingly during the 1920s Hitler was subjected to a great deal of abuse from his political opponents and their publications, who raised questions and made charges about his background, early life, personal life and sources of income. Beginning in 1931 came a new matter of public speculation—his role in the death of his half-niece, Geli Raubal.

By the beginning of 1923 Hitler and his Nazi movement had made only modest progress. On May Day, in a counter-demonstration to the socialists and communists, the SA (Stormtroopers), the military wing of the party, participated in a mass gathering of militant nationalists outside Munich which concluded with a humiliating surrender of arms to the Bavarian police. Robert Murphy, a twenty-eight-year-old acting U.S. consul in Munich, miscalculated when he declared that with this fiasco the Nazi movement was "on the wane." Many people, he declared, "are wearied of Hitler's inflammatory agitation which yields no results and offers nothing constructive." Moreover, "his anti–Semitic campaign made many enemies; the rowdy-like conduct of his youthful following has antagonized order-loving members of the community." Another disadvantage that Hitler had, not noticeable in his public performances, was that he spoke German with a marked Austrian and Bavarian accent. Then again, Stalin spoke a peculiar form of Russian, heavily laced with his native Georgian language.[30]

After the disaster of the Nazi demonstration, Hitler obviously decided to disappear from public view for a while. He headed for the hills to lick his wounds. In mid–May, facing criminal charges, he made his first visit to Berchtesgaden, 111 miles from Munich, but on a rail line that at that time terminated just beyond there at Lake Königssee, a fine tourist destination. He came to visit Dietrich Eckart, a senior member of the little party who was then avoiding a court appearance in Leipzig on charges of defaming the president of the new republic. Konrad Heiden, an early biographer of Hitler, declared that Eckart and Hermann Esser, another original member of the party, chose this location "because from there one could escape quickly and unobtrusively to Austria."[31]

Dietrich Eckart (1868–1923) was a literary man, political plotter and activist in extreme right wing racist circles. Edgar Mowrer described him as "a strange drunken genius." Eckart was involved in the Thule Society, which indulged in Aryan mythology and funneled funds to super-nationalist organizations, such as the *Deutsche Arbeiterpartei*. After a lifetime of gluttony, drug addiction and alcoholism, he expired at the age of fifty-five, but not before passing on to Hitler his potpourri of ideas. There has been speculation that Eckart provided Hitler with entry into mystical powers probed by the Thule Society. Eckart is said to have said of Hitler, "Here is the one for whom I was but the prophet and forerunner," and, more importantly, "We have given him the means to communicate with Them," some sort of supernatural forces. Karl Haushofer, father of "geopolitics," is credited with giving Hitler predictive powers through the revelations of the Vril Society.

During his life, Hitler was to demonstrate a variety of precognition. On the day of the Italian armistice in 1943 but before it was publicly announced, Hitler had a "queer feeling of unrest." He had the same feeling just before the attempt was made to kill him in July 1944.

Adolf dedicated his hodge-podge of biography and political ranting, *Mein Kampf*, to the seer Eckart. In the center of Berchtesgaden there is a cemetery filled with religious grave markers, but one—a plain slab—is for Dietrich Eckart.[32]

During World War II, in one of his almost nightly monologues, Hitler described his first visit to Berchtesgaden. Arriving at night, he made the steep climb ("Did they think I was a goat!") to the Pension Moritz, a large boarding house on the Obersalzberg. The next morning proved a revelation: "What a lovely view over the valley! A countryside of indescribable beauty." His attachment was to last until the end of his life: "I'd fallen in love with the landscape." He also was convinced of the therapeutic value of salt, and the area had an abundance of *Salz*. It became his *Wahlheimat*, his chosen homeland. Living in Munich, had he not heard of the Alps? He was back on the Obersalzberg several times that summer, where he cultivated the name of Herr Wolf. Ernst Hanfstängl says that he had a hard time convincing Hitler to return to Munich in June for an important political occasion.[33]

In November of 1923 he led an attempted seizure of power in Munich and spent the next year in comfortable confinement in Landsberg Prison, thirty miles north of Munich. He was joined by some "voluntary internees," wrote his little book, was flooded with gifts and had unlimited visits by admirers (with at least one visit by his dog). After his release in December 1924 Hitler at first was active in reviving the party, with a re-founding meeting being held in February 1925. Because of his violent language on this occasion, he was banned from public speaking in Bavaria and later in most of the rest of the country (where would he be without the spoken word!). Because of his record of violent actions and statements, he was an obvious candidate for expulsion to his native Austria. Even before his release from prison, however, the Austrian government had revoked his citizenship, thus precluding his expulsion to there. Nevertheless, he proceeded to renounce his Austrian citizenship in April 1925; now he truly was stateless. With the speaking ban, he now was free to spend most of the summer and autumn on the Obersalzberg, staying once again at the Moritz. In 1926 he also spent much time in the area, but, displeased with the politics and management of the new owner of the pension, he shifted his base to the Deutsches Haus in Berchtesgaden. At this time he wrote an expanded edition of *Mein Kampf*, using a cottage, later called the "Kampfhausl" ("cottage of the struggle"), on the Obersalzberg for the writing. While there he also wrote another book, a rambling exposition on foreign policy which repeated much of what was in the first book; because of this, the work was not published.[34]

He lived at the Deutsches Haus, with breaks—for political business in Munich—for two years. "I lived there like a fighting-cock. Every day I went up to Obersalzberg, which took me two and a half hours walking there and back." He also frequented the Dreimaderl-haus, "where there were always pretty girls. This was a great treat for me. There was one of them, especially, who was a real beauty." Beginning in 1926, he became particularly attached to Maria (he called her Mimi) Reiter, a sixteen-year-old girl whose mother had a dress shop on the ground floor of the Deutsches Haus; he was then thirty-seven. Apparently this was Adolf's first girlfriend. For the rest of his life he was to persist in having his closest female relationships with girls—Geli Raubal and Eva Braun—who were hardly out of their teens when he first met them. His relationship with Fräulein Reiter had lasted for two years when he ended it: it was a bad image for a serious politician to have a teen-age "woodland sprite." This was not quite the end of the story—later she claimed that she was Hitler's overnight guest in Munich in the 1930s, apparently one night of love. After the war for many years she lived with Hitler's sister Paula in a cottage on the Waldsee, near Berchtesgaden.[35]

Looking around the chosen neighborhood, Hitler was not pleased with the composition of its population, which he viewed as a mongrel lot. A believer in selective breeding by a racial elite, he was not then in a position to do anything about the matter, and he personally never did anything about it. When he became chancellor he had an SS bodyguard unit on the Obersalzberg which was free to pursue the local Fräuleins. After ten years he noted the difference: "Today there are numbers of strong and healthy children running around the area. It shows that elite troops should really be sent wherever the composition of the population is poor, in order to improve it."[36]

The period of 1925–28 was a fairly lean time for Hitler. With Germany experiencing a period of considerable prosperity, the Nazi Party was at a low ebb. He had been banned from public speaking in most places. This constraint was not lifted until 1927. His income was derived from the sale of his book and payments he received for writing articles for Nazi newspapers. On the other hand, his expenses were low—rent on his tiny apartment in Munich and payments for his lodging in Berchtesgaden.

For tax purposes he claimed that his occupation was that of a writer and his only income was derived from the relatively small sales of his book. Nothing was said about gifts, donations and income derived from other sources. He had no salary from his party position, and thus avoided being its employee, yet he employed a secretary, an assistant and a chauffeur, and in February 1925 he purchased a large automobile. Together with travel expenses, he claimed all of these costs as deductions from income tax. He assured the tax authorities that he lived a simple life: "Nowhere do I possess property or other capital assets that I can call my own. I restrict of necessity my personal wants so far that I am a complete abstainer from alcohol and tobacco, take my meals in the most modest restaurants, and aside from my minimal apartment rent make no expenditures that are not chargeable to my expenses as a political writer."

The tax authorities allowed only half of his deductions, concluding that at least half of his expenses derived from his political activity. This was the beginning of a long *Kampf* between Adolf and the tax men, with Hitler being frequently in arrears in payments. In the end, it all turned out well for him. When he became Reich Chancellor in 1933 he donated his salary to the dependents of party members and policemen who had been killed in the preceding political violence. In response, the tax authorities wiped out the arrears of 400,000 marks that he owed in tax and concluded that he no longer would be subject to taxation. During this period his income rose with the fortunes of the Nazi Party. Although only 3000 copies of *Mein Kampf* were sold in 1928, this soared to over 800,000 in 1933.[37]

During the late 1920s he began to look around for a house in Berchtesgadener Land. His wealthy friends, the Bechsteins, suggested the Sonnenkopfl, but he found that it was too warm and sunny. Then there was a house at Steingaden, but it also had a disadvantage: "If I had taken the Steingaden place, I should have been compelled to become a producer of the famous Steingaden cheese, in order to keep the place up." In 1928 he leased the Haus Wachenfeld, a five-room rustic building on the Obersalzberg that faced the Untersberg, mythically linked with both Charlemagne and Fredreich II, and partially overlooking Salzburg. Albert Speer offers a description: "It had a wide overhanging roof and modest interior: a dining room, a small living room and three bedrooms. The furniture was bogus old-look." Hitler filled it with Nazi-embossed pillows and knick-knacks, presents from admirers. He made various improvements to the property and kept a notarized list of the costs of these. Speer, who said he was often there in the early 1930s, noted that guests were accommodated at a nearby pension, while only Hitler, his mistress Eva Braun, an adjutant and a servant stayed there. He makes no mention of Hitler's half-sister Angela or her daughter Friedl, who probably usually went to the Munich apartment when important visitors were there for the week-end.

Five months after he became chancellor, in June 1933 he bought the place, which included three acres of land. The owner of the property was listed as his sister Angela. As a result, he could claim to own no property. With the dramatic rise of the Nazi Party, largely due to the impact of the Depression, he was receiving large sums from the greatly increased

**Hitler at Berghof, 1933, from left, with Henriette von Schirach, Baldor von Schirach, leader of the Hitler Youth, Erna Hoffmann, and Angela Raubal, Hitler's half-sister. (Bavarian State Library, Munich)**

Hitler with group on Berghof veranda, late 1930s. From left, Albert Speer, Theo Morell, three of Hitler's secretaries, Hitler with young boy, Julius Schaub, Hermann Esser. (Bavarian State Library, Munich)

sales of his book and income from writing articles as well as money from German industrialists.[38]

He now had carved out a place of his own; he was now even a German citizen. Often he waxed lyrical about the Obersalzberg. In 1942 he declared, "When I go to Obersalzberg, I'm not drawn there merely by the beauty of the landscape. I feel myself far from petty things, and my imagination is stimulated. When I study a problem elsewhere, I see it less clearly, I'm submerged by the details. By night, at the Berghof, I often remain for hours with my eyes open, contemplating from my bed the mountains lit up by the moon. It's at such moments that brightness enters my mind." Karl von Wiegand speculated upon this: "Perhaps the snow crowned peaks of the Alps glistening in the moonlight remind Adolf Hitler of the glittering but cold, lonely heights of fame and achievement to which he has climbed. 'I am the loneliest man on earth' he said to an employee of his household." He certainly was a *Abendmensch*, a nocturnal person. He told Speer this was due to the fact that after one of his lengthy evening orations he could not sleep for hours. Even when he was a house guest at the home of Richard Wagner he would not go to bed until 5 a.m. Walter Langer speculated that, filled with fear and secret misgivings, Hitler was afraid to go to sleep, a common pattern of a psychopath. His very late soirees were a continuing strain on invited staffers and guests.[39]

He was not in the mountains for the sunshine: "Those rainy days at Berchtesgaden, what a blessing they were! No violent exercise, no excursions, no sun-baths—a little repose!

... There was a time when I could have wept for grief on having to leave Berchtesgaden."
Nor was he there for the joy of strenuous activity. Unlike Göring, he was not a hunter, sportsman or rock climber. He celebrated the pleasure of wearing lederhosen, which he declared
was "the healthiest clothing." "Abandoning my shorts," he said in 1942, "was one of the
biggest sacrifices I had to make" in pursuing his political career. Among the advantages of
leather shorts was "that one's not afraid of getting them dirty. On the contrary, they're
ennobled by stains, like a Stradivarius by age." Recalling that he was decked out in Bavarian hat, lederhosen and walking stick, Hitler liked to talk about the mountain tours he had
taken in the early 1920s. He recalled that for many of them he was led by a Baroness Abegg,
who "could climb like a goat" but had the tongue of a scorpion, without whom "I'd probably never have been on the summit of the Jenner." Albert Speer, for one, was not impressed:
"From a mountain climber's point of view ... they did not amount to much." In any case,
by the 1930s Hitler preferred less rigorous activities—easy walks, car rides, picnics, boat rides
on the Königssee. In winter he sometimes joined others on a sled ride down the hill.[40]

For a person who so often preached the doctrine of hard physical conditioning, the
only exercise Hitler ever got was to train his right arm to remain outreached for long period
of time, this in order to amaze the masses at Nazi march-bys. He noted that the flabby
Göring could not maintain this position for long. He had no interest in sports and while
in Landsberg prison declined to participate in any games because, as the leader, he could
not been seen as a person of inferior physical performance. On the Obersalzberg he always
refused invitations to swim in Göring's pool. In the later years of the war, with his health
in catastrophic decline, he turned not to physical therapy or a regular regime of exercise
but to an overload of drugs.[41]

Like many other Germans, Hitler was very much caught up in the cult of mountains
and forest. According to one account, when a rock formation was found during the construction of the building on top of the adjoining Kehlstein, Hitler, an enthusiastic student
of Germanic mythology since childhood, decided that this was in the shape of the hand of
Wotan, the ancient god of creation and destruction. Viewing its discovery on his domain
as having prophetic meaning, he had put it in a small display case in the Berghof. He particularly liked the mythical association with Frederick Barbarossa, supposedly slumbering
on a surrounding mountain. He once said to Speer, "You see the Untersberg over there. It
is no accident that I have my residence opposite it." He also liked the fact that his view
looked into Austria, which, he said, was a "draw to the homeland."[42]

Two of his important colleagues have declared that it was not the wonderful scenery
that was the principal attraction of the region for Hitler. To Ernst Hanfstängl Hitler "had
little eye for, and took little pleasure in, the beauty of nature as such.... Although he would
sit brooding over the mountain scenery, it was really only the solitude that fed his thoughts.
The solitude and the sense of power that came from the height, and the fact that he was
able without interruption to plot and plan political moves with his cronies." Albert Speer
made the same observation: "He did frequently admire a beautiful view, but as a rule he
was more affected by the awesomeness of the abysses than by the harmony of the landscape.
It may be that he felt more than he allowed himself to express." In 1934, shortly before he
was killed, Ernst Rohm complained of Hitler, "All he wants to do is sit up in the mountains and play God."

The setting obviously appealed to Hitler's megalomania. He once told one of his secretaries, "In the broad horizons of the land around Berchtesgaden and Salzburg, cut off from
the everyday world, my creative genius produces ideas which shake the world. In those

moments I feel no longer part of mortality, my ideas go beyond mortal frontiers and are transformed into deeds of great dimensions." Elly Danat, a Berghof maid for eight years, recalled Hitler's appreciation of the Alpine views: "The Führer liked to stand on that balcony and look at the mountains. For a long time he would stand there and look. It gave him great pleasure."[43]

Although he liked the fog and drizzle on the Obersalzberg, Hitler had a strange aversion to snow. Although years before he had enjoyed skiing and Eva Braun continued to ski, he now saw it as dangerous. He banned this activity on his estate. Moreover, "What pleasure can there be in prolonging the horrible winter artificially by staying in the mountains?" His dislike of snow greatly increased as a result of the Russian winter of 1941–42, the coldest in one hundred and forty years. He declared at that time, "I've always detested snow ... I've always hated it. Now I know why. It was a presentiment."[44]

Hitler hugely enjoyed the drive from Munich to Berchtesgaden in his large Mercedes convertible. There was always a motorcade, with guests bound for the mountain joining in on the outskirts of Munich. When she was going to the Berghof, Eva Braun traveled with Hitler's two secretaries, departing two hours later. There was an obligatory stop for refreshments at the Chiemsee, "that strangely moody lake," noted Otto Dietrich, "which exercised a great attraction upon Hitler," who claimed that its "blurred tints are so restful to the eye." The party always stopped at the Lambach inn, the attraction of which, said Albert Speer, was the "delicious pastries that Hitler could scarcely ever resist." Speaking about the drives

to the Alps, Otto Dietrich, his veteran press aide, declared, "I do not know how many hundreds of times Hitler drove along this road in an open car, nor what he felt at the sight of those majestic mountains. But it may surely be said that those rides, taken together over two decades, were an important part of his private life."[45]

The first autobahn was built from Munich to Salzburg, which, conveniently, was Hitler's route to the Obersalzberg. As part of his plans for a network of highways through the Alps, a new scenic road branched off the autobahn in the direction of Berchtesgaden.

**Eva Braun at Berghof, 1938. (Bavarian State Library, Munich)**

The advent of the Great Depression drove many people to support the radical program of the Nazis. The increased tempo resulted in Hitler engaging in near–non-stop campaigning. He held no government position, abjured membership in the Reichstag and avoided Berlin, leaving the place to the conventional parties and their leaders to dig their political graves. He devoted himself to the hustings, speaking in almost every city and town, often giving several speeches a day. In the process, he honed his political and personal skills. He developed a reputation for being a plain, modest, good-hearted man—in so many ways "just like everyone else." Kurt Ludecke described the response of many people to the would-be savior of Germany: "They felt no social embarrassment before him. Seeing in him the apotheosis of themselves, they were hypnotized with wonder and hope. Thousands trembled when he spoke, and yet—he was simply one of them." He noted that Hitler "seemed perfectly at home" with ordinary party members "and showed the best of humor." Moreover, "Hitler liked to be amused, to laugh, and showed his utter contentment by slapping his knees."[46]

As did others, Ludecke described the Hitler of this period as having "this typical Austrian *Schlamperei*, this lackadaisical casualness, an 'all-embracing disorderliness.'" With mounting political success, Hitler became better organized, but as he neared his goal of Reich leadership he told his associates he would not become a prisoner of office. "Chancellor or President, I don't intend to be treated like a glass doll packed in cotton-wool, riding only in special trains at fixed times.... I'll keep on doing as I please." He would continue doing those things that gave him pleasure—motoring, flying, dashing from one place to another to meet people and, of course, noted Ludecke, "always returning to his retreat in the mountains, his little chalet on the Obersalzberg ... the only place where he really felt at home."[47]

It was Ludecke who was among the first to refer to the Obersalzberg as Hitler's "magic mountain," and until the end of his life Hitler was often either coming or going there. Until he became head of government he rarely was in Berlin, much preferring the compatible environment of southern Germany. As a result of a massive increase of Nazi support in the 1932 election, there was hectic political maneuvering in Berlin concerning inclusion of the Nazis in government. While thousands of members of the SA, the Nazi militia, poured into the capital, Hitler was at the Obersalzberg, where he made it plain that he would accept the chancellorship and nothing else. He briefly went to Berlin to participate in the political infighting, but when he was denied the leadership of government, he "returned to his 'Magic Mountain' to confer with his Party chieftains." This pattern of behavior did not please Gregor Strasser, one of the earliest Nazi figures: "First the big show of teeth, then back into the mountains with your tail between your legs. Downright monkey-business! And we're left to shovel out the dung. '*Eine tolle Schweinerei!*'" But that was the way Hitler did things—then and later.[48]

CHAPTER TWO

# Berghof

The Nazis in power became the masters of propaganda and manipulation of the German people. The *Volk* were presented with a series of festivals, stirring commemorations and appeals for selfless dedication to the new world that was emerging. There was a barrage of announcements of goals achieved and new ventures launched. Gigantic public works were undertaken with accompanying fanfare. Massively impressive public buildings were designed to demonstrate that this Reich would indeed last a thousand years. What the Nazi regime became, according to Peter Labanyi, was a *Gesamtkunstwerk*—a total work of art. Nazi propaganda, declares Labanyi, "was less didactic than liturgical and narcotic: an appeal to the collective unconscious. The hypnotic intensity of image and rhetoric was raised to a pitch where questions of plausibility became irrelevant."[1]

When Hitler became Reich Chancellor in January 1933 an enormous amount of attention was lavished on him. At the center of Nazi public dramas was the Führer. The culmination of this activity was the stirring scenes of the Nuremberg Rally. Always the spotlight was on Adolf Hitler, man of the people and savior of Germany. To Labanyi, Hitler became "the star commodity of Nazism"; to the performer David Bowie, Hitler was the "first rock star." By this time Hitler had total confidence in his persuasive powers and he had a corresponding contempt for the opponents he had bettered; he once said of them, "With those you cannot even lure a dog from behind the stove."[2]

A major part of the developing Hitler mystique was that of the Führer in the mountains. Once Hitler was in power there was increasing public interest in his mountain retreat. The number of visitors who came to see his house increased massively. Josef Geiss, who wrote the first history of the complex, estimated the average daily crowd at 5000. When Hitler was there, he greeted the visitors at a mid-day walk-by. The happy crowds, Albert Speer observed, left Hitler visibly refreshed. He would personally receive letters and petitions and occasionally invite children to join him on the terrace. One resident of the area recalled that "swarms of people started coming, by train, buses, cars, to tramp up the mountain and stand as close to Hitler's house as they could, chanting rhythmically, 'We want to see our Führer' until he came out. And then they would scream, applaud, sob, laugh hysterically, even fall to their knees." "A throng of intrusive admirers and inquisitive people" pursued him on his walks and some people ripped off pieces of his wooden fence as mementos. There was a flood of postcards and souvenirs showing "*das kleine Haus und der Volkskanzler*," the little house and the People's Chancellor.[3]

Joseph Goebbels, the principal architect of the Hitler Myth, related a moving experience he said he had one day on the Obersalzberg when Hitler was greeting delegations from around Germany. This was before the 1938 *Anschluss* with Austria, and along came a delegation from there. When Hitler beckoned some of them to him they were overcome with emotion, to which the Führer responded similarly.[4]

But problems could be lurking amidst the pilgrims, and obviously there was a need for security. At one point a Swiss theology student, determined to kill Hitler, spent about a month in Munich and Berchtesgaden on this mission, but could not penetrate the Berghof area. Police and soldiers guarded the estate. A 1933 police decree declared, "In the interest of the People's Chancellor's relaxation, the citizens are required to strictly follow the regulations and thereby participate in making the Chancellor's stay at Obersalzberg as pleasant as possible. Under no condition should any unnecessary noise be made in front of the house, i.e., shouting or the use of megaphones. It would also be considered bad manners to constantly follow the Chancellor's move[s] through binoculars." That year the proprietor of the adjoining Zum Turken guesthouse, Karl Schuster, was obliged to sell his premises to the *Sturmabteilung* ("storm troopers"), who used it for a security office.[5]

Until about 1936 Hitler went for walks along the public paths, with only a couple of security guards. It is said that he detested security measures. The year before Pierre Huss, an American journalist who spent eight years in Nazi Germany, was taken by Hitler for a trek through the snow, accompanied only by a "big Hungarian dog" who, Huss was later informed, "could be relied upon to rip to pieces any stranger approaching Hitler unannounced." When Huss inquired about Hitler's lack of security, Hitler asked Huss to throw a snowball in the air. When Huss did so, Hitler whipped out a pistol and hit it with a bullet. This feat was repeated and Hitler claimed an accuracy which surpassed that of his bodyguards. According to his valet Hans Linge, Hitler always carried a small pistol concealed in his trousers, and the Führer was a better shot than many army marksmen. At that time, Hitler told Huss that because Himmler and other Nazi security people were concerned about Hitler's exposure during his short hikes, "I am buying up all these hills and making it forbidden property so that Himmler can quit worrying." The process of the takeover of the Obersalzberg had begun.[6]

As he had in the late 1920s, and despite being head of government, Hitler spent an enormous amount of time on the Obersalzberg. During the summer of 1932, when intense political infighting was taking place in Berlin, Hitler, with apparent insouciance, commuted from the Berg. Except for his first year as chancellor, he was at his mountain retreat from two to six months each year from 1925 to 1936. As Reich Chancellor on most weekends he traveled from Berlin to Munich or Berchtesgaden or both, as a result of which he conducted little government business on Fridays or Mondays, but then he shunned ordinary office routine.[7]

Nazi publicists made a virtue out of his original Obersalzberg residence. One publication declared, "Many people wonder why The Leader has chosen the Obersalzberg of all places for his home. However, anyone who has ever stood up there realizes that there is probably no other place in Germany which despite the mountains all around, offers such a far reaching and unimpeded view of the beauty of the world." A caption to a photograph of Adolf in the Alps declared, "In his beloved mountains. From time to time the Führer visits his 'villa' in the Bavarian Alps for a few hours or days. He has a small wooden house that his sister purchased. There he finds the inner strength for new tasks." Wilhem Bruckner, his long-time adjutant, declared that Hitler was only at the Berghof for "short rest periods" and his work continued, with ideas being "born twice as fast here and decisions reached even faster."[8]

Another Nazi publication became lyrical about the setting: "One who has been there understands that there is probably no place in Germany where, despite the nearness of the surrounding mountains, one has so wide and unhindered a view of the beauties of nature. The Führer lives here in the midst of the beauties of nature, a metaphor for human events. Here he writes his major speeches which affect not only Germany, but give new direction to events in the entire world. Far from the confusion and noise of everyday life, the seeking spirit, surrounded by the vastness of the landscape, finds the right paths for the people and Fatherland. As the mountains remain eternal despite the passing of millennia, so too the work the Führer has begun here will live for millennia in the history of his people."[9]

In the winter of 1935 Pierre Huss was given a personal tour of the Hitler area by the Führer himself, dressed in a "grey golf suit with heavy woolen socks stuck into snow boots and an old felt hat drawn down over his right eye." Leaving what was then the modest Haus Wachenfeld, Hitler led him to a "somewhat forsaken Bavarian-style cafe." Here Hitler was a man of the people: "There, sitting on the hard chairs hewn by peasant hands, Hitler drank hot milk and chatted about mountains and weather and cows with the bearded mountain men who might be having their daily restoratives of schnapps at that moment." The Leader relaxed in "his own close circle of alpine neighbors."

For many years Heinrich Hoffmann had a monopoly on photographs of Hitler, and he certainly made the most of it. In 1934 he published a collection of photos (with text by Wilhelm Bruckner) which featured the *Volkskanzler* relaxing in the hills. Beneath a photograph of a smiling Hitler in civilian clothes sitting on the grass with a newspaper in front of him, the text ran: "Relaxation. Far from the noise and disorder of the cities, here the Führer recovers from the stress of struggle. In the broad meadow near his little house, he reads opponents' newspapers. How he laughs at the tales of his champagne cellars, Jewish mistresses, luxurious villa, and French funding."

Ignatius Phayre, "a personal friend," provided an account for *Current History* of his 1936 visit to Hitler's domain. After Hans Baur, Hitler's personal pilot, delivered the journalist just below the chalet, Phayre was greeted by a familiar figure in unfamiliar garb: there was "the same springy gait I knew so well, with that hearty smile of welcome and a chubby hand raised in the salute.... Bareheaded, and with the unruly 'brownlock' broken loose, Hitler might have been a hired gardener. Clad in an old tweed coat, tightly buttoned and too short for him, and shabby trousers that did not match, he was waving a crooked stick wrenched from a cherry tree."

Phayre's visit was timely: Hitler was staging a party for the *Kinder* of the area. Together with Field Marshal Werner von Blomberg, commander-in-chief of the Wehrmacht, *der Führer* toured around the area inviting young ones to the occasion. A charming scene unfolded: "At four o'clock or so, quite a crowd of his little friends came straggling across the upland meadows." The Leader was in top form: "Never was there a middle-aged bachelor who so delighted in the Company of children." Propaganda Minister Goebbels was on hand to pass out candy to the *Kinder*. A fine item, surely one that was mandatory, for the German press.

Two years later, Phayre provided the readers of the English *Homes and Gardens* with a tour of the Berghof and its grounds, upon which he commented most favorably. Among other things, he noted that Hitler conducted tours of the area "by means of a tripod telescope which he himself operates on the terrace for his visitors."[10]

Joseph Goebbels let no opportunity pass to expound on the simplicity and modesty of the Führer. At the time of one of Hitler's birthdays in the late 1930s Goebbels reported that Hitler fled the celebrations in Berlin to retreat to his alpine house where he could look back and look forward in solitude. Modest man that he was, declared Party media, it was only by chance that the Führer would catch radio broadcasts of the glowing tributes and state-ments of thanks by spokesmen (principally, Goebbels) by the German people.[11]

To many of his colleagues Hitler appeared to be a *Schlamperei*, a disorganized person or one who was not concerned with ordinary routine. His day began late and he spent lit-tle time on ordinary office routine. Reports piled up unread and he would put off decisions until forced to make choices. Officials and others waited for hours to be admitted to his presence. Albert Speer wondered if Hitler ever worked. Konrad Heiden, one of his early biographers, declared of Hitler, "Capable of great physical and mental exertions, he is almost pathologically disinclined to regular work; a magician does not work, and greatness is not achieved by ordered activity." Heiden also noted that despite the fact that Hitler eschewed tobacco, alcohol and meat, "a man who indulges his whims at every moment can hardly be called unassuming." Moreover, for a young man who anticipated a boring office job with horror, as an adult he had "attained his goal as few have done before him—'When I am a man, I shall do what I like all day long.'" The fact that Hitler neither drank nor smoked was seen as admirable by many Germans, a situation that was in sharp contrast to some other prominent Nazis.[12]

Looking back, Otto Dietrich, the Nazi press chief, declared, "In my opinion he led the strangest private life of any man in high political office. He seemed unable to distinguish between his official and his private life.... Regular work and office hours were foreign to his nature. He often said that a single brilliant idea was more valuable than a whole lifetime of conscientious office work." Dietrich lamented, "If he had only understood how to organize his time, if only he had set aside for rest and recuperation a fraction of the days and nights he wasted in boring artificial 'sociability'" then Hitler would not have ended up as a phys-ical and mental wreck. Hitler was, indeed, a bohemian to the end, but one borne down by self-imposed discipline during the war. Speer observed that Hitler, having led the life of an artist "in his undisciplined allocation of time" in the 1930s, was forced by war to observe a much more structured schedule, and "From year to year, his work became more severe and therefore more alien to his personality."[13]

A half century later Herbert Dohring, the Berghof administrator from 1936 to 1943, declared that Hitler only spent two or three hours a day on the affairs of government. In his view Hitler was *Gemütlichkeit*—casual and slack in this regard. Gunter Lohse remembered Hitler as a person who abjured written policies, rarely issued orders and preferred to allow decisions to emerge from his stream of consciousness monologues. Albert Speer noted that Hitler would only get down to work when forced to do so. Although he would retreat to the Berghof weeks before the annual party rallies, he would continuously put off writing his speeches until he ran out of time and "at Nuremberg usually had to stay up nights to make up for the time he had squandered at Obersalzberg." Hitler claimed that he used his mountain retreat to rest up for bursts of physical and emotional activity, particularly for the party rally. During that event he presented the image of a man brimming with energy—greeting delegations as they arrived by train, making nightly visits to them, several speeches, and more. When that was over he would go back to the mountain for another vacation.[14]

Speer concluded that Hitler's avoidance of speech preparation had a method to it: "He let the content of his speeches or his thoughts ripen during these weeks of apparent idling until all that had accumulated poured out like a stream bursting its bounds upon followers or negotiators." This is what Carl Jung probably meant when he wrote that Hitler was let-ting his sub-conscious mind work its way towards his decisions: "Hitler's secret was that he allowed himself to be moved by his own unconscious. He was like a man who listens intently to whispered suggestions from a mysterious voice and then *acts on them*." Otto Dietrich noted that Hitler would spend days and weeks pacing "back and forth in the large rooms he was so fond of," talking on and on about the matters that became the "elements of the addresses he would later deliver in public."[15]

In the early days of the party Hitler had a reputation for disappearing for days and weeks. Later, at important negotiations he sometimes told his colleagues he would be right back and never return. He carried on this way as chancellor. When he found the atmosphere in the chancellery oppressive, he would leave abruptly for the Obersalzberg. There he had total control over his schedule and he was out of reach of the bureaucrats. In the Berghof he could stay up all night and watch movies all day if he felt like it. Night time was his time. Paul Roth, his barber, sometimes was summoned at midnight to give the Führer a haircut, to which Hitler "attached the greatest importance." When luncheon guests, obviously seeking their leader's attention, brought architectural plans, Hitler would abandon all appointments to pore over them; his staff finally imposed a rule on guests: no plans, but the Führer sometimes would look in the vestibule to see if there were any out there. Most of his time was spent talking—at group luncheons, afternoon tea-house sessions, endless conferences and late-night fireside gatherings. His mountain-side abode was also useful for avoiding people that, for one reason or another, he did not want to see, at least for a period of time. Shortly before he launched his invasion of Poland, when he summoned Carl Burckhardt, the League of Nations Danzig representative, to the Obersalzberg, Hitler exclaimed to him, "How happy I am when I am here." When he proceeded to plunge Europe into war, he adopted a more disciplined routine while at his military headquarters, but he still managed to spend a great deal of time at the Berghof.[16]

Hitler's response to the matter of his unconventional worklife was that, as a man of great ambition for the German people, he needed time and solitude to make his sweeping plans. Furthermore, even at his mountain retreat the work of his office continued without substantial interruption. In April 1942 he told the Reichstag, after declaring that no one had a legal right to a vacation, "Since 1933 I myself haven't had three free days in a row." When visiting the Berghof in 1938, British diplomat Ivone Kirkpatrick learned about the Führer's languid lifestyle from some of Hitler's aides and used the information in a wartime broadcast, in which he declared of Hitler's time on the Obersalzberg, "For days and even weeks this idyllic existence goes on. Hitler may claim that it is no holiday, but every German soldier and every German workman would gladly give up his leave for a few days' rest in the enchanting atmosphere of Berchtesgaden."[17]

According to Ernest Pope, an American journalist based in Munich in the 1930s, Hitler used his Obersalzberg house as a base for repeated sorties around Bavaria and, after the union with Austria in 1938, to Salzburg. Throughout the 1930s he spent a week at Bayreuth for the Wagner festival in August. In addition, of course, Hitler also had his apartment in Munich. Pope claimed, "If I had a dollar for every time I have seen Hitler in Munich and his other Bavarian hideouts" he probably could afford to buy a Mercedes.[18]

To maintain the semblance of government, a building for civil and military offices was constructed just outside Berchtesgaden at Stangass. Konrad Heiden commented that "Hitler could not bother himself to go to Berlin, where the threads of business converge; no, the Reich Government had to bother itself to come to the foot of the Obersalzberg." An airstrip for the Führer's flights was built at adjoining Bischofswiesen.[19]

As the Nazi movement grew in the early 1930s Hitler had so many guests for week-ends that tents were erected for them on the grounds. Once in power, he made several improvements to his house, adding a stone patio, a car park and a wing of a few rooms. Then, in 1935 he decided on a complete reconstruction, and he was its principal architect. His objective was to greatly expand the edifice while retaining its original structure. Albert Speer recalled that Hitler borrowed from him all the equipment needed to design a building. Hitler used the professional services of two Munich architects, first Alois Degano, then Roderich Fick.[20]

The result was a structure of thirty rooms, covering four times as much ground as the original building. There was a huge living room (60 by 50 feet) with a marble fireplace and a massive retractable window looking out to the mountains. It also included a large dining room. Hitler's suite opened onto a large balcony. He was relieved to find that the building was not too large for its setting, although he would have preferred an even bigger structure. A long extension from the main building, with rooms for quests, gave the appearance of a forerunner to Days Inn. Ignatius Phayre, a guest in 1936, found his room decorated with Hitler's watercolor paintings from the 1914–18 war. Hitler had plans to build an annex to the Berghof for a library of 60,000 books.[21]

Among the additions were three rooms, one of which, according to one account, was an exercise room, which had a vaulting horse. Another had a door with iron bars and was always kept locked. This room aroused the curiosity of some of the maids, who were told by an SS officer that girls whose racial purity was in question were brought there, stripped and then stretched out on the vaulting horse for purposes of inspection. The maids must have been suitably horrified. In the late 1930s there appeared several books by people claiming to have been close to Hitler. One of these was by Pauline Kohler, who said she had been a Berghof maid for about a year in 1937–38 and declared that she saw maids locked up in the cells and some of them whipped while strapped to the vaulting horse. She further reported that there were five rooms at the top of the house—the "Chamber of Stars"—to which only Hitler and his resident astrologer, Karl Ossietz, had access. The suite included an observatory , astrological library, meditation room complete with crystal ball and a laboratory where Ossietz brewed a special beverage for the Führer known to the staff as "Adolf's Tonic." Ossietz confirmed to Hitler that he would remain ruler of Germany until his death in 1962 at the age of seventy-three. There are interesting claims, but there is no verifiable report of whippings or a celestial penthouse; none of the surviving staff members ever heard of Pauline Kohler.[22]

Whether Hitler believed in astrology remains a matter of conjecture. He clearly believed that he was guided and protected by some spiritual or cosmic force; moreover, he took pride in claiming that no one could know what he was thinking. In the early 1920s he was involved with a group in Munich that did believe in astrology, and he was fully knowledgeable about German mythology, Nordic gods, and the ideas of the Thule society. Heinrich Hoffmann, who was as close to being a friend of Hitler as anyone, recalled that in 1922 Hitler "read a prophecy in an astrological calendar which exactly fitted the events of the putsch of November 1923, and for years afterwards he used to talk about it." Karl Wiegand, who first met him the early 1920s, remembered that Hitler neither denied nor affirmed his belief in astrological calculations. According to Henriete von Schirach, in the early 1930s, Hitler liked to talk about astrology "until Frau Elsbeth Ebertin, an astrologer, whom he visited regularly, predicted his grandiose rise and equally sudden collapse and interpreted the sharp decline of the "r" in his signature as a portent of tragedy." With that, Hitler ceased to talk about astrology.[23]

His library holdings reveal that Hitler read widely in occult, magical and spiritual areas.

If he peered through a telescope at the heavens above the Obersalzberg, this was an interest and activity of many people. Rudolph Hess did believe in astrology, and after his idiotic flight to England in 1941, Hitler ordered a complete crack-down on astrologers and astrology. It has been argued, however, that this action was designed to conceal his own interest in the subject, just as his campaign against homosexuals in the wake of the Rohm affair in 1934 was employed to hide his at least earlier involvement in homosexual practices. When Emmy Göring once asked him if he believed in horoscopes, Hitler, replied, "Horoscopes? No. I am my own horoscope." During the war an astrologer told British intelligence that Hitler was basing his actions on his astrological charts, and, despite opposition, he was employed to follow the Führer's prognostications. To the very end, Hitler convinced himself that there would be a miraculous delivery from defeat, and, upon Joseph Goebbels' suggestion, examined two remarkable horoscopes of his fate and that of the German republic that he had destroyed. The death of Franklin Roosevelt in early April 1945 was seen by Hitler and Goebbels as a providential event, but this occurrence did not save the Reich or their necks.[24]

The Berghof staff recalled Hitler as a considerate and generous employer. Elly Danat, a Berghof maid for eight years, declared that Hitler regularly inquired about her family and at Christmas she received an additional two-months' pay as well as some clothes for her four children. Other members of the domestic staff also noted his thoughtfulness. He made a habit of making the rounds of the estate, having short conversations with its guards and assuring them that he was always available to hear their concerns. Traudl Junge, who joined his secretarial staff in 1942, recalled how different she found the private Hitler to be from his public image of a ranting orator: "He had a soft gentle voice that was full of melody.... And later I found him very charming in the way he behaved in private. And he had a sense of humor. I can't deny that.... I never heard an impolite or angry word. He was always friendly and patient." Leon Degrelle, the Belgian fascist leader, also noted Hitler's private wit: "Anything that might have seemed too solemn in his remarks, he quickly tempered with a touch of humor.... He could be harsh and even implacable in his judgments and yet almost at the same time be surprisingly conciliatory, sensitive and warm."[25]

Hitler's enlarged structure had a new name—the Berghof, "mountain shelter." This modest name was suggested by Joseph Goebbels, a master wordsmith. Josef Geiss has pointed out that the name was inappropriate and misleading. As generally understood, he noted, a *Berghof* indicated "a neat farm building, with the characteristics of a mountain house," but this was a "building of extravagance." This name was used "only to keep up appearances of modesty." With the services of a huge labor force, the work was completed by the summer of 1936.[26]

The new, improved Hitler residence was the object of considerable press attention outside Germany. Writing in the London *Sunday Express* in 1937, Sydney Morrell declared, "From the few official photographs that are allowed to be published, nearly all Germany—outside Berchtesgaden—and most people outside Germany believe it to be a small residence in which Hitler with a few picked friends can find peace and solitude." But all had changed. "Today the Berghof is no longer a mountain hut. It has become a palatial mansion, able to accommodate not merely a couple of guests but forty or more, if need be, in large bedrooms, sumptuously furnished as in a luxury hotel." Moreover, security had been greatly increased, with the surrounding mountains ringed with anti-aircraft guns and "bomb and gas proof cellars ha[d] been built deep under the Berghof in the mountain-side."

Things had also changed in Berchtesgaden: "The little toy town has been repeatedly 'cleansed of undesirable elements'" and detectives spread among the population. The people of the town now rarely saw the Führer, "although they know and have heard enough of the Berghof to become conscious of their possible destiny as the nation's emergency capital if Germany should ever again be fighting for her existence." The town also got a new railway station, a large impressive building, complete with restaurant and beer cellar, which, when completed in 1937, was larger than the main railway station in Athens.[27]

Hitler was proud of his out-sized production of a house; he believed he achieved a "harmony of bigness." "The dimensions of the house made me somewhat afraid it would clash with the landscape," he recalled, but said, "I was very glad to notice that, on the contrary, it fitted very well." The building did have some unique features: the largest retractable window in the world and the largest marble table top made from one piece. For decoration, Hitler acquired some of his favorite paintings, particularly Johannes Vermeer's "The Art of Painting," which was removed from a Vienna gallery in 1942. The paintings of nude women over the fireplace in the great room must have struck some visitors such as Neville Chamberlain as somewhat disquieting.

In Albert Speer's assessment, any school of architecture would have given the building's design a grade of D. "The resultant ground plan was most impractical for the reception of official visitors," he declared; "Their staffs had to be content with an unprepossessing entry hall which also led to the toilets, stairwell and the large dining room." The garage was located under the living room and often "a strong smell of gasoline penetrated the living room." Yet, he concluded, "this very clumsiness gave the Berghof a strongly personal note."[28]

Traudl Junge recalled that there was something disquieting about the house: "The place had a strange, indefinable quality that put you on your guard and filled you with odd apprehensions." The only comfortable room, she said, was the library on the first floor. The best feature was the terrace, "which was immense, full of color, pleasant, with the whole world for a backcloth." James Leasor, who was not there, has commented, "A strange atmosphere prevailed at any house where Hitler was working. Secretaries and aides and adjutants padded about trying to look important, carrying sheafs of paper and brief-cases and files, and talking in whispers as though they were in a church or in some other holy place."[29]

Elisabeth von Stahlenberg, who first visited the Berghof in 1937, was not impressed. She was distressed by "what has been done to the countryside round here. It was so beautiful, but has been built up hideously, concrete roads through the forests." Having passed through two checkpoints and into a barbed wire enclosure, she felt "like being at or rather *in* the zoo." As well, she did not like Hitler's Great Room: "The salon is amazing, like something out of a fairy story, and I don't mean beautiful! It is like a room for a giant. An enormous window, a vast clock with a terrifying bronze eagle crouching over it, a table which has to be twenty feet in length, a sideboard at least ten feet high (it turned out to conceal gramophone records!), huge paintings, tapestries ... and the fireplace (very, very big)."[30]

The house had a staff of fifty, administered from 1936 to 1943 by Herbert Dohring. If Hitler was casual about the affairs of state, he was meticulous about arrangements in the Berghof. Every day Dohring had to see if the chairs were exactly in the right place, "that the curtains were opened perfectly and that the flowers were properly arranged." Hitler followed a rigid routine, not stirring from his room until noon. Dohring also developed a keen sense of the mood of the Führer: "In the morning, if you could hear him whistle to himself, that was the most serious alarm signal." If Hitler came down stairs humming a tune, then all would be well.[31]

In 1936 a small circular building was constructed an easy fifteen minutes' stroll down a gradual slope. This was the Moosland tea-house, a round stone building, which looked to some guests like a power plant or a silo. It contained a central room with six large windows providing a striking view of the Ach River flowing down into the valley and, beyond that, the spires of the white city of Salzburg. The walk down was made after lunch, the main meal in Germany; tea was served and then after some subdued talk Hitler would doze. The return home by himself usually was made by car (by the late 1930s, a Volkswagen); to walk back would have required an uphill trek. His entourage could walk or ride back. According to Ian Kershaw, "Hitler's detestation of physical exercise and fear of embarrassment though lack of athleticism remained acute." During the war and with his health in terminal decline the most he would do is take a short afternoon walk with his dog.[32]

With an expanding domestic staff and security force, a small building for a kindergarten (day-care center) was built behind the Berghof. Adjoining this was another building in which models of the future redevelopment of German cities (one of the Führer's continuing interests) were built and stored. In its basement was a locked room, to which only Martin Bormann and an attendant had keys. Here was secreted Bormann's emergency liquor supply. During war-time strict rationing, additional shipments of booze were called bricks. The Allied bombing of the Obersalzberg on 25 April 1945 created a large pool of liquor in the basement, and, when the American and French troops arrived there on May 5, this probably was responsible for the death of a French soldier who was found floating in the alcoholic pool.[33]

A model farm was also developed, but at an elevation of 3300 feet it was difficult to grow anything outdoors, so large glasshouses were constructed, which supplied Hitler with fresh vegetables year-round, an important matter to a vegetarian. Cattle, pigs and horses were brought in, but with the raw climate, stony soil and short summer season, the farm was a costly venture. Hitler, who took little interest in the farm, was pleased to figure out that the milk produced there was costing him only five pfennigs a liter, which, in fact, was about twenty times what it cost locally.[34]

Hitler told Speer that the construction work had exhausted his personal funds. As usual, he was being disingenuous as he had massive amounts of money available—royalties from his book (six million copies sold by 1940), revenue from the use of his image on postage stamps, which went to a "cultural fund" he controlled, and contributions to the Adolf Hitler Endowment Fund of German Industry (all offerings gratefully received, *mein Herr Krupp*). It has been estimated that Hitler received a grand total of 700 million reichsmarks in corporate payments. Martin Bormann came up with the idea of a deluxe edition of *Mein Kampf* as a compulsory gift to newlyweds, paid for by local governments, with, of course, royalties going to *der Chef*. All of this income was tax-free. Hitler put two million reichsmarks into the secret reconstruction of a palace at Pozen for an eastern Führer's residence. Otto Dietrich, who noted that Max Amann, head of the Nazi publishing house, handled Hitler's finances, held that "In financial matters Hitler was ignorant but generous. As a private person he did not know how to handle his own money, and as head of state he could not manage the government budget." Here was one of the paradoxes about Hitler—a man whose personal needs and expenses were slight, but one who had the compulsion and opportunity to surround himself with luxury in buildings, furnishings and art. The German people were repeatedly told about the simple tastes of their Leader (in German, "Führer"), but not about his extravagances.[35]

The Führer liked to say that he wanted to preserve the pristine state of the area. Trees, birds and animals were to be protected, with winter provisions to be provided. No hunting was allowed, which was inconvenient to the likes of Hermann Göring, Reich Master of the Hunt, who found nearby places to shoot animals. In fact, what Hitler wanted to get rid of was the mountain's human inhabitants. By 1937 all of the original residents were gone and their houses demolished. In their place came an array of government buildings and roads, together with officials, guards, construction workers and party leaders. Expansion of the complex continued until the end of World War Two.[36]

The man in charge of this mini-empire was Martin Bormann, who, by the late 1930s, had usurped the functions of the ineffectual Rudolph Hess as Hitler's right-hand man. Traudl Junge later declared that Bormann was "like the Rubezahl, the legendary bad spirit of the mountain." To the very end, Bormann attempted to impose total control over everyone and every thing on the Obersalzberg, and only Göring and Speer successfully repulsed his efforts to assert authority over their properties. Bormann's house overlooked the Berghof, but from the Zum Turken the staff maintained a look-out to spread the word when Bormann coming down the hill to the Berghof.

Hitler said there should be no coercion in gobbling up the land on the Obersalzberg, but Bormann bullied and threatened anyone who did not cooperate. Most people willingly sold out, on generous terms, with property sales and other taxes being waived. The few that resisted were dealt with by Bormann. On one occasion Hitler told his sister Angela that he was concerned that a neighboring farmer felt he had been cheated out of a thousand marks by one of the property sales. In any case, the property ownership of all of the area, including Hitler's house, eventually was in the name of the head of the party chancellery, one Martin Bormann.[37]

When the Shusters were forced to sell the Zum Turken, they agreed not to settle anywhere else in the area or to reveal that they had been neighbors of Hitler. Some of those who were forced out were happy enough with the matter—they believed they had been well paid and did not mind moving elsewhere. When one resident of the area was later asked if people were angry about having to leave, she replied, "Why should they be? Bormann paid fairly, and people loved Hitler." Others did not agree with this assessment of the situation. Altogether about fifty properties were acquired and the community of Obersalzberg ceased to exist.[38]

The area thus secured was about six square miles. A series of paved roads was built. A complex of barracks, guard posts and other structures was erected out of sight but adjacent to the Berghof. Eventually eighty-seven buildings were included in the *Führergebiet*—the Obersalzberg compound. In 1938 the walk-bys were ended and the entire area was surrounded by wire fencing. Calling it "that industrial oasis in the heart" of the mountains, Otto Dietrich said, "Bormann had built Hitler a golden cage, and Hitler never went outside again."[39]

Dietrich observed the unfolding pattern of construction. "The peaceful idyllic paths through the meadows," he noted, "were transformed into wide driveways and concrete roads." Dynamite blasts rocked the area, but Hitler soon imposed a limitation on this activity: while he was in residence there were to be no explosions before noon—they disturbed his strange sleep patterns. Dietrich saw no end to the uproar: "The pace of the work, the gigantic earth-moving projects, increased rather than diminished with the years."[40]

Bormann's manic building projects did not go unnoticed. The almost-constant construction greatly affected Berchtesgaden, with lorries regularly rolling through the town. One observer commented, "Bormann has created a gold-rush atmosphere. Only he doesn't find any, he spends it." Hitler, who stayed away during periods of intense building activity but eagerly inspected the completed work, liked to give the impression that the impetus for all this came from Bormann, not, of course, from himself. Why, if so much money had not already been spent on it, he would like to blow the whole thing up. Yet he acknowledged the historical importance of the place. In years to come it would be a shrine to himself and his great movement. But, modest man that he was, he claimed, "When it's all finished I'll look for a quiet valley and build another small wooden house there like the first."[41]

To counter the disappointment of some of his followers that they no longer could walk by the Berghof, Hitler, when he was there, often would take a leisurely noon-time drive through Berchtesgaden. Ernest Pope clearly saw the purpose of the sortie: "Adolf knows that his 'Strength-through-Joy' admirers will return to all parts of the Reich to tell their comrades proudly: 'Just think! I actually saw the Führer when I was at Berchtesgaden.'" The English journalist Sydney Morrell only saw withdrawal: "Hitler, ruling Germany from his mountain top in Bavaria, is as remote and inaccessible as a Grand Lama on a peak of the Himalayas."[42]

Albert Speer has described the experience of being a guest at the Berghof: "On the terrace we would stand around informally while the ladies stretched out on the wicker reclining chairs with cushions covered in red and white gingham. The ladies sunned themselves as if they were at some spa, for being tanned was the fashion. Liveried attendants, select SS men from Sepp Dietrich's Bodyguard Regiment, with perfect manners that seemed a shade too intimate, handed around drinks: champagne, vermouth and soda, or fruit drinks.... At the news of Hitler's imminent arrival, the buzz of conversation became more muted, the bursts of laughter cease.... Hitler greets each of the guests with friendly words, asks about everyone's children, personal plans and circumstances."[43]

Elisabeth von Stahlenberg, who was excited to be invited to spend the week-end with her husband at the Berghof in 1937, was disappointed with the occasion. After a plain meal and stilted conversation, about which she said she was "glad when it was over," the guests were shown a film—"we were treated to what seemed like five hours of LaJana"—a musical which had this actress as its star. This was followed by a long session around the fireplace, during which Hitler "went into sort of a trance." She noted in her diary, "The hours dragged." Fortified by some wine, she hung on, but said, "my face was continually stretched by suppressing yawns." Her husband was equally unimpressed: "My God, if the new job means many more of these evenings, I shall request to go back to the old one."

The next day held no surprises. There was a late lunch: "*It was exactly like the previous evening!*" Then a walk to the teahouse, during which Elisabeth was "thrilled by the view." One of the other guests agreed, adding "if you don't have to go there every weekend!" When the group was gathered around a table, Hitler talked of his youth in Austria, "which would have been interesting, but was told so monotonously I found my attention wandering." The group then returned to the Berghof: "The *same* again, plus a different but equally *indifferent* movie." Her conclusion about the event: "The greatest man in the world, possibly *for all time*, and the weekend has been a drag from the moment we arrived. Who would believe it?"

Frau von Stahlenberg made a return visit five years later and noted that nothing had changed, except that as a wartime constraint no films were played, rather hours of Wagner recordings. She observed, "It is peaceful here—but curiously dull.... There's something trivial about the talk of films and actors. The Führer makes jokes about his Ministers and everyone laughs. He tells a few stories about his early life in the army. But it is like an apple without a core.... I once heard Dr. G[oebbels] say how he would do anything rather than stay at the Berghof and I begin to understand why." Hans Baur, Hitler's pilot, related that he sought to avoid these late night sessions, because, among other reasons, the lack of sleep infringed on his flying competence.[44]

Otto Dietrich, the party press chief, recalled the numbing experience of being a guest at the Berghof: "For thinking persons in Hitler's entourage, years of listening to those reiterated discourses represented a considerable burden, which led to their absenting themselves as often as they could, or trying to cut Hitler short—attempts that rarely succeeded." The result was that "in the course of years Hitler used up a great many listeners. I have seen guests come enthusiastically and depart burned out, so to speak."[45]

Another late-rising, nocturnal dictator was Comrade Stalin. If Hitler carried on late night monologues, fortified by tea and wine (for guests), the strain of such gatherings was borne by those invited to the Berghof and, at his military headquarters, by those on his army staff. In contrast, Josif Vissarionovich had the custom of ringing up department heads and party officials at night, which meant that they had to be on hand for aggressive enquiries. On other occasions, Stalin staged (male-only) late-night banquets and drinking bouts, complete, upon command, with spontaneous folk dance performances by the like of Nikita Khrushchev. What a contrast to Adolf's sedate fireside gatherings at the Berghof![46]

Unlike Stalin, Hitler had a love of classical music, particularly the works of Richard Wagner. He once said that if you wanted to understand the Nazi movement you would have to know Wagner. Beginning in 1923, Hitler visited the Wagner family at Bayreuth and, as Führer, spent a fortnight at the Wagner festival. Following the death of Siegfried, the composer's son, in 1931, there were rumors that Hitler had become emotionally attached to Winifred, Siegfried's widow, an English-born woman who strongly supported Hitler and his cause. Nothing came of any romantic relationship, but Hitler became very attached to the Wagner children. Wolfgang Wagner recalled that Hitler invited all the Wagner grand-children to meet with him and "he would listen to us attentively, receptively, and without interruption.... One gained the inescapable impression that, in our company, he sought and possibly found some substitute for the family atmosphere that was denied him elsewhere."[47]

Then there were Hitler's other women friends. With the approval of his half-sister, Angela Raubal, Hitler assumed a dominant role in the life of Angela's daughter Geli from 1927 to her suicide in 1931. He justified his passionate and controlling treatment of the young, vivacious girl on the basis that he was protecting her from a match with unsuitable men; her response was to kill herself.[48]

Soon after this shattering event, Hitler was confronted with a beautiful, cultivated and determined mature woman, already a mother. Magda Quant, divorced from one of Germany's richest businessmen two years before, in 1931 was looking for a cause or at least some excitement. She found this initially with Joseph Goebbels, who had endured years of unhappy relationships with women, when she infiltrated the Nazi propaganda organization. Hitler found her most attractive, and the feeling obviously was mutual, but Hitler was determined to avoid marriage. How to have your cake and eat it too? Hitler sent a message: Magda should marry Goebbels, which would allow her to continue to have a close relationship with Adolf. She agreed to this and they were married in December 1931, with Hitler as the principal witness. Six children followed and Nazi propaganda extolled the Goebbels as the model Aryan family. Goebbels was a fanatical philanderer, but Hitler intervened to keep the marriage together, at least for public purposes. Despite Hitler's deep attraction to her, Magda was an infrequent guest at the Berghof, probably due to the near-constant presence of Eva Braun, Hitler's mistress. Determined to remain faithful to the end to Hitler and his vision of a Nazi future, and with the Russians almost on top of the Führerbunker, on May 1, 1945, she killed her children from the Goebbels marriage and then committed suicide with her husband. Before doing so, she wrote to her son from her first marriage, "That we can end our lives together with him is a blessing for which we never dared to hope."[49]

The year 1931 also marked another important encounter between Hitler and a young woman. After eight years in Germany, Pierre Huss in 1942 believed that for almost a dozen years the center of Hitler's love life was Theresa von Thorn, a petite brunette who "likes to wear her hair in bangs." The daughter of an aristocratic Bavarian family who were early supporters of the Nazis, Theresa was "always there" when Hitler was at his mountain residence. "Even the war has not kept him from her," Huss reported, "and the girl, more than the Alps, is the reason he rushes off to Berchtesgaden at every opportunity." In fact, it was another petite brunette who was Adolf's Fräulein. Eva Braun, the very young Munich photographer's assistant, was not a frequenter of the Berghof until the departure of Hitler's sister Angela at the beginning of 1936. Thereafter, it became her second home and eventually she became the bride for a day of the Führer.

According to Pauline Kohler and Kurt Krueger, two totally unreliable sources, Eva had a perfume fetish—she experimented in developing scents that exactly matched individual personalities. What Elisabeth von Stahlenberg says Eva told her is believable—she wished to be a movie actress and even hoped to go on to Hollywood. When a leading film director was told of this aspiration, he commented, "God Help the German Film Industry." She filled in her time in the mountains by taking colored films of the scenery and sometimes appeared in them, with the Führer occasionally acting as cameraman. In 1945 one of the Berghof maids remembered Eva: "Yes, she lived here often. We did not talk about her. It was understood we were not to mention her name outside. She was young, yes, and beautiful. She was blonde. She loved the cinema. Often we would see the pictures at night in the reception hall."[50]

As Hitler's pilot, Hans Baur often had Eva as a passenger and got to know her quite well. He "found her a simple and charming woman, and [he] liked and respected her." She led a constricted life—excluded from official occasions both at the Berghof and in Berlin. Baur observed that "she was well aware that in the ordinary way she could never hope to be his wife, and that she would have to be content to be his lover; and she certainly did love him." She bore the burden of the lack of any outward acknowledgment of their relationship without complaint and when Hitler returned to the Berghof, which she often called the "Grand Hotel," "she was always cheerful and happy."[51]

Hitler had close relationships with other young women. There was a variety of actresses, most notably Leni Riefenstahl, who through Hitler's patronage rose to became an outstanding film director, producing two of the greatest films of the era—*Triumph of the Will* and *Olympia*. Already she was a notable actress, appearing in a series of alpine nature films such as *Der heilige Berg*, "the Holy Mountain," and *Das blaue Licht*, "The Blue Light," the later of which she also directed. According to Pierre Huss, Leni sometimes claimed that she had slept with Hitler until she was told to shut up. When Bella Fromm in 1933 inquired about her close relationship with Hitler, Leni replied, "Oh, it isn't what you think. He asks me to dinner a couple of times a week, but always sends me away at a quarter to eleven because he is tired." In her memoirs she declared that, despite the rumors, they did not have a sexual relationship. At Hitler's request, in 1938 she made a fifty-minute film about the natural wonders of the Obersalzberg. After she protested to Hitler about the killing of Jews in Poland in 1939, she resigned her position as a war correspondent and thereafter got involved in non-political film projects, principally *Tiefland*, a romance set in Spain. She made her third and last visit to the Berghof in March 1944. Although she never was a party member and claimed to have Jewish friends, when she heard of the death of Hitler, in "a chaos of emotions" she "wept all night."[52]

Two American film directors who worked in Germany during the 1930s both related that Hitler spent a great deal of time visiting film sets and meeting with a variety of actresses. Hitler had two consuming interests in film—as objects of Nazi propaganda and in beautiful women. Frank Wisbar told the U.S. Office of Strategic Services in 1943 about Hitler's great interest in the film industry and the amount of time he devoted to it. Hitler "frequently telephoned him about details of films in production and about even minor characters in the cast." Wisbar got the impression at times "that Hitler devoted about an hour a day to politics and the rest of his time to movie details." Several times Hitler intervened in film production, stopping and shelving films upon appeals of actresses. "This happened so frequently," declared Wisbar, "that it was extremely difficult to manage the girls who were so often guests at the Chancellery since they threatened to complain to Hitler if they did not get the part they wished or the script were not changed to suit their fancy."

Adolf Zeissler had a similar experience. He observed that "when Hitler did not come to the studio in person he frequently telephoned and held lengthy conversations about new films and the cast." Zeissler "often wondered when Hitler had the time to devote to affairs of state because he either spent so much time at the studios, on the telephone or looking at films that there seemed little time left for anything else." As well, Hitler frequently asked him to send actresses to the chancellery; most of the young women thought Hitler was "extremely odd" due to the fact that he spent a great deal of time expounding on his ambitions and achievements: "His chief object in all this was to impress the girls with his greatness and power." One noted actress who certainly found him to be strange was Rene Müller. She told Zeissler that on her visits to the chancellery "she did her utmost to seduce Hitler but in this she never succeeded." On one occasion when they were both naked "she was sure that he was going to have intercourse with her," but he threw himself on the floor, begging her to kick him. With every kick he became more excited and finished the session with a self-sex act. Not long after Rene Müller killed herself, which may or may not have been directly related to what it is said she found out about Germany's Leader.[53]

Although her story undoubtedly is a gross embellishment, if not a total fabrication, Pauline Kohler's account concerning another actress might as well be included. Jenny Jugo was a young film actress who was passed on to Hitler by Goebbels. Kohler claimed that Jenny was Hitler's mistress for several months and he showered her with gifts—including a villa, a small plane, two cars and expensive jewelry. She seemed to have been a headstrong, lively person who liked practical jokes. She once served "Fat Hermann" Göring a rubber sausage, dispatched outrageous telegrams to Hitler in the names of Goebbels or Göring and brought a parrot to the Berghof whom she had trained to declare, "I am the Führer, I am the Führer." She was always late for meals and sometimes locked herself in her room, which disturbed her boyfriend. Hitler had a room fitted out with a stage on which Jenny would perform an artistic dance, better described as a strip-tease act. The performances were filmed and Hitler viewed them at his leisure. It is the case that he liked paintings of female nudes and his extreme fondness for pornography was something noted by several people. At Christmastime a film of one of her performances was shown to the Berghof staff.[54]

According to psychiatrist "Karl Krueger," another most dubious source, in Berlin Jenny showed off the diamond bracelet given to her by Adolf, news of which sent Hitler into a fit of rage: he declared that it was only a gift for an unstated indiscretion. The end of a love affair? Since Krueger claimed to have fled Germany in 1934 and Kohler's supposed time at the Berghof did not begin until three years later, the accounts are surely based on gossip, but there was a Jenny Jugo and she was close to Hitler for a time. In late 1944 the Gestapo discovered that Jenny was hoarding food. Goebbels prevented any prosecution, while Jenny was required to contribute 4000 marks to a fund for aged artists. Otto Dietrich, the Reich press chief, later declared that reports that Hitler had "intimate relations with all these women" were "utterly false." Indeed, Hitler "was no Don Juan; rather, he was a queer sort of monk who rather enjoyed being suspected of many amours—although no one in his immediate circle ever noticed signs of such intimacies." But Hitler led his own private life, and Dietrich, a propaganda hack, was not in a position to know what Hitler did in such matters.[55]

Hitler's principal adjutant until 1941, Hans Hasselbach, recalled Hitler's great interest in the cinema and his role as chief film critic and censor: Hitler "suppressed some of them without much ado, while some had to be changed in parts, and others were promoted by all means available." Isle Werner recalled that when she appeared in a film, "Life Can Be Beautiful," about a young couple who achieved happiness despite poverty and miserable housing, Hitler ordered the film banned. National Socialist Germany did not have a housing shortage and romantic fulfillment could only be achieved by procreation. According to Heinrich Hoffmann, Hitler, noting the critical film comments of Eva Braun and Martin Bormann, "would order cuts and alterations, quite oblivious of the trouble and expenses involved." The propaganda minister was not amused. Joseph Goebbels told Hoffmann that he was "not in the least interested to hear critiques of my films from some stupid little flapper [Eva] or from a glorified butler [Bormann]." The lack of availability of new movies, declared Hoffmann, did not bother Hitler at all: "Hitler delighted to have endlessly repeated those which had pleased him." Seeing the same films over and over again was a trial to many of his guests, but few dared to absent themselves on these occasions.[56]

There were several other women in whom Hitler showed great interest. Inge Ley, the young wife of Robert Ley, head of the German Labor Front, was much admired by Hitler and was often in his company. Described as a "ravishing blond," she was both an actress and a ballerina. Subjected to repeated drunken abuse by her husband, she at least once sought refuge on the Obersalzberg. She left a farewell letter to Hitler, which reportedly depressed him, before attempting suicide in 1943.[57]

Unity Walkrie "Bobo" Mitford, a forerunner of the blonde bombshell, was an early favorite. One of the splendid-looking, head-strong Mitford girls, she provided a high-class English connection. Her hanging about the Osteria Bavaria, Hitler's favorite Munich restaurant, finally paid off and she joined the Hitler retinue. She gave Hitler a gift of an antique pistol. When Leni Riefenstahl asked Hitler about his relationship with Unity, he replied, "I could never have an intimate relationship with a foreigner, no matter how beautiful she might be." Unity's circle of acquaintances in Munich discovered that if she heard them disparage Hitler or the Nazi regime, she would report them to the authorities. Elisabeth von Stahlenberg observed her at the 1936 Nuremberg party rally: "The Mitford girl was there—isn't she everywhere—with her saucer eyes gazing after her beloved." Later, having noted that Unity had sat up front with Eva Braun at one event, Stahlenberg caustically commented, "Tonight Miss England was back in the third row, crying at Hitler's speech and at the singing." Because she followed Hitler everywhere she could, his wearied or perhaps apprehensive entourage gave Unity the name of Mitfahrt—the traveling companion.[58]

Bella Fromm, a keen (and Jewish) observer of the Berlin scene in the 1930s, was told that at the 1937 rally Unity "in her usual ecstasy, dogged Hitler's heels, as last year and the year before, the party badge tossing stormily on her heaving sweater." Fromm believed that Unity was in competition with Eva Braun, who "has given Unity some rather bitter moments. She is terrified that Evi might make headway into the sanctified heart of Adolf." Unity's sister Diana was another Nazi enthusiast and in 1936 married Oswald Mosley, the leader of the English fascist movement, at a ceremony in Berlin attended by Hitler. Unity remained a rabid Nazi Party-time groupie until the commencement of war between Britain and Germany, when she shot herself, dying of her disablement in England eight years later.[59]

While in Spandau prison in 1948, Albert Speer recalled the time when Hitler "was crazy about an American dancer who performed almost unclothed in Munich," whom he invited to tea. Besides Unity, she was "the only foreigner who was ever admitted to his circle." Adolf was apparently serious about his interest in the unnamed performer: he made it "quite plain that he would lay siege to her if it were not for his accursed official position." Ernest Pope observed that in the late 1930s Hitler was fond of the performances in Munich of a group of American female dancers and was particularly attracted to naked women performers, especially "Dorothy van Bruck," no detail of whose "blitz-tease escapes the penetrating gaze of Adolf Hitler, as he follows every movement of this completely undressed girl." Freidelind Wagner recalled that Hitler advocated that the female dancers should appear sans clothing in one of Wagner's operas performed at Bayreuth.[60]

Baroness Sigrid von Laffert, "extremely pretty with dark blond hair," arrived on the scene in 1934. According to Karl von Eberstein, at a dinner party Hitler "treated the Baroness with great distinction, and talked to her almost exclusively." She was among the honored guests at Nuremberg rallies, but then "she disappeared suddenly from Hitler's circle; it was rumored that she had connections with enemy intelligence."

A later entrant, circa 1938, was Marion Schönemann, the wife of a Munich contractor, who was Austrian, "blonde, with dark eyes and a lively disposition." Eberstein related that she was a frequent quest of Hitler's at his Munich apartment, at the Berghof and other places; moreover, "she was greatly feared because she said whatever came to mind." Eberstein believed that, spotting a rival, Eva Braun "eventually succeeded in having Frau Schönemann relegated to a rear position." On the other hand, Karl Brandt declared that Hitler's sometimes stormy relations with Marion "seemed not to be the cause of any jealousy on Eva's part." In fact, she was one of Eva's friends, who often was with Eva at the Berghof during the war years.[61]

Hitler took his responsibility as self-appointed national film censor seriously. A potentate in a neighboring territory also assumed the duties of chief cultural censor. When he was not involved in other activities, Comrade Stalin imposed ideological correctness in Russian literature, cinema and theatre. On the other hand, not having other artistic inclinations, he generally left music and painting alone. Since both of them had only slight direct experience in other countries, movies gave them a fictionalized and blinkered view of the outside world. But they both thought they already knew all they needed to know about lands beyond their own. An interesting film vignette took place between Stalin and Charles de Gaulle during World War II. After an unproductive Kremlin negotiating session followed by a prolonged banquet, Stalin treated his guest to a viewing of a popular film. Irritated by the deadlocked negotiations and tired, de Gaulle rose to leave at the end of the movie. When Marshal Stalin urged him to remain for another film, de Gaulle politely declined and departed, leaving the other quests, in his view, "paralyzed with astonishment." When his foreign minister did not also leave, le grand Charles sent word for him to do so. Stalin appreciated this bold action, which he saw as a ploy in the stalled parleying.[62]

The two great European dictators were alike in another respect. As Alan Bullock has pointed out, they both wanted monumental buildings to mark their achievements. Hitler planned to build the tallest domed structure in the world, while Stalin took great interest in what would be the largest building, topped with a hundred-foot-tall statue of Lenin. Hitler kept a wary eye on the Soviet plan, remarking when he launched the invasion of Russia, "Now this will be the end of the building for good and all." Neither structure was built.[63]

The presence of Hitler drew other Nazi leaders to the Obersalzberg. Bormann took over a nearby house that formerly had been a children's clinic. The three story structure was completely gutted and the interior rebuilt to luxurious standards. Göring had a residence at Obersalzberg during the summer beginning in the late 1920s. In 1933 he acquired a small house adjoining the Hitler property which two years later was expanded into a relatively modest two story chalet. Albert Speer was given a house there by Hitler in 1935 and two years later he built a studio, the Waltenberger Haus, that he had designed. He later said he made a "crucial error" by taking a vacation home near Hitler as he was at Hitler's beck and call. By the late '30s Hitler's two top military men were provided with houses on the Obersalzberg. Field Marshal Wilhelm Keitel got a large villa, while General Alfred Jodl had a smaller one. After the German takeover of Austria in 1938, Hitler gave Foreign Minister Joachim von Ribbentrop the use of Schloss Fuschl, a medieval tower house, across the way in Austria. At that time Heinrich Himmler, head of the SS, also acquired a retreat in the area—at Aigen, just outside Salzburg. This was an elegant castle surrounded by extensive parkland that once belonged to Prince Schwarzenberg, which Himmler modestly renamed "Bergwald." Wilhelm Wulff, Himmler's astrologer, noted that the castle, located at the foot of the Gaisberg mountain, had "magnificent views of the Salzburg Alps and the Untersberg."[64]

Joseph Goebbels, who disliked Hitler's Munich henchmen, did not have a residence on the Berg but frequently was a house guest or was accommodated in the Villa Bechstein, across the lower field to the Berghof, until 1936. At that time he began an extended affair with the Czech actress Lida Baarova. At length Magda Goebbels threatened divorce and began an affair with another man. This was at the same time when Field Marshal von Blomberg was forced to resign as head of the armed forces after his marriage to a prostitute. Hitler, who had a passionate regard for Magda, intervened to save the marriage, "for political reasons." To settle the matter, in January 1939 Hitler invited Goebbels to the Berghof, where he spent a dozen days. According to the house staff, after that Goebbels never spent another night there.[65]

Hitler never observed Christmas, almost always refusing invitations for that day and remained isolated. His mother had died shortly before Christmas. He refused to have a Christmas tree in his home. In the early 1920s he was said to have spent Christmas Eve alone at his old army barracks in Munich. In 1935 he told Leni Riefenstahl that on Christmas Eve he had his chauffeur drive aimlessly around the countryside; "I do that every Christmas Eve." The next year things were better. He told Emmy Göring that in September he had encountered a distraught young woman outside the Brown House in Munich who told him that her fiancé's Nazi activity had driven him out of Austria to a state of poverty. Hitler proceeded to rent a small apartment, which he furnished, and presented it to the couple on Christmas Eve. In this period he spent one Christmas day with the Bormann family. At another Christmastime, during the war, Eva Braun had pine boughs placed in the main rooms of the Berghof. In order to inject at least a bit of festivity of the season into Hitler, his Chancellery staff staged afternoon dinners on December 24 in a Munich beer hall, which Hitler always attended and greatly enjoyed.[66]

Although he otherwise abjured Yuletide activities, he always gave gifts, which he personally selected, to members of his staff, close associates and many artists. When he voiced his regret to Hans Baur, his principal pilot, that he could not visit stores for this purpose, instead of looking at catalogues, he rejected the suggestion that he should follow Göring's methods of touring these places after normal closing times. One Christmas during the war he presented everyone on his extensive list with a package of precious coffee, a shipload of which had been sent to him by a Middle Eastern monarch.[67]

Hitler made up for neglecting Christmas with an elegant New Year's Eve party at the Berghof, with piles of caviar, a favorite with the Leader. There were fireworks and a lead pouring ceremony conducted by Hitler. Molten lead was poured into a container of water and the solidified shape was examined for omens of the future. At midnight the Berchtesgaden Mountain Rangers in traditional garb arrived outside to fire antique weapons across the valley. This occasion was observed on the Obersalzberg until 1944.[68]

Bormann's most spectacular building project of the 1930s was on the summit of the Kehlstein (in English, "stone throat"), the mountain that loomed behind the Obersalzberg. Beginning in 1937, a winding five mile road was built from the Berghof to the foot of the peak where an elevator shaft 330 feet high was blasted out of bedrock. Beneath the brass-lined elevator cubicle was another deck, entered through a trap door, which accommodated extra but lesser passengers. The elevator opened in the middle of a large grey stone building consisting of an all-electric kitchen, dining room, a huge circular room surrounded by windows with a massive fireplace, a gift from Mussolini, and sunken adjacent lounge which jutted out from the mountain. Outside were a series of glass-encased terraces. The overhanging positioning of the structure, at least when looking up to it from the valley, "gave rise to the legend that Hitler's aerie was perched on a turntable and could be turned toward the sun."[69]

The road and tunnels to the summit were constructed by mostly German unskilled workers, but later Austrian, Czech and skilled Italian stonemasons were added. At the peak of construction 3500 men were employed on the project. Working a sixty-hour week in dangerous, demanding and isolated conditions, with only beer and films for entertainment and fights for diversion in the mountainside barracks and meeting hall, worker morale was a problem until Bormann agreed to build a brothel, code named the "P-Barrack," in a nearby secluded location. Twenty Czech, French and Italian women took up residence. Georg Mehr, an Obersalzberg employee, recalled, "It was a hell of a walk down and back up the mountain, but the laborers used to flock down there every chance they got. Nobody else could get in."[70]

The building at the top of the Kehlstein was originally called the Diplomatik-Haus, and commonly known as the D.-haus. After the war the occupying Americans gave it the name of the Eagle's Nest and, sometimes, Crow's Nest. It is inconceivable that Hitler, with his passion for architecture, did not have a dominant hand in designing the building. The project was finished in October 1938, long before Hitler's fiftieth birthday in April 1939. He enjoyed showing it off at first, but then seldom went there. He reportedly feared heights and worried that the elevator cables might break. When asked what would happen if the elevator stopped en route, Hitler was said to reply, "I suppose world history would stop for a couple of hours." Adolf did have a sense of humor. Altogether he used the building on fourteen occasions for official functions and three times for private purposes; his last visit was in 1940.[71]

There were a variety of press reports that the building was his residence or scholarly retreat. Writing in the London *Sunday Express*, Silkirk Panton declared that with a flood of supporters walking by, the Berghof "did not give the Führer the solitude he wanted." The result was "every chance he gets" he headed for the Kehlstein. "The eternal peace and his position high up in the air," Panton said, "suggest to him, perhaps, the German mythology and folklore which is so much in tune with his own mysticism." American journalist Frederick Öchsner believed that the building housed a secure archive of the most important Nazi documents, a "strong room" for Hitler's own sketches and paintings and several telescopes "for gazing at the stars." When the Americans occupied the site in 1945 a frequent comment among 101st Airborne guides was, "Perched up here, no wonder the s. o. b. thought he was God." This view was more eloquently expressed by Philip Hamburger of the *New Yorker* after he toured the building at that time: "Taking Nietzsche's words literally—Superman lives on the mountaintop—the master of Europe went into the clouds." To him the structure was a monstrosity: "From the outside the place could be a guardhouse of a state penitentiary. Inside, everything is out of proportion or off key—ceilings too low, windows too small, bronze doors here, wooden doors there, some rooms right out of an ad for Men of Distinction, others designed like a cheap bar and grill." It is most unlikely that the millions of other tourists since then shared his impression: the structure and its setting are unique, powerful and intimidating. After all, it was built as a mountain eyrie.[72]

The first foreign dignitary to be brought there, André François-Poncet, the French ambassador, was awed by the setting: "From afar the extracted place to which I was summoned looked like a sort of observatory or hermitage, perched at an altitude of over six thousand feet, atop the crest of a ridge of rocks. A hairpin road about ten miles long, cut boldly through the rocks, wound upwards." The building on top "gives the impression of being suspended in space, an almost overhanging wall of bare rock rises up abruptly. The whole, bathed in the twilight of the autumn evening, is grandiose, wild, almost hallucinating." He wondered about the purpose of the project: "Is it the work of a normal mind or of a person pursued by megalomania and who, obsessed by greed for power, seeks solitude; perhaps a victim of fear?" The American journalist Louis Lochner described it as "that weird eagle's aerie, the like of which no other living being can boast." Another personage given a personally conducted tour was the English journalist G. Ward Price, who had frequently interviewed Hitler and had written generally appreciatively about Hitler and his great plans for Germany.[73]

Pierre Huss, who was there once, described the building as a "fantastic engineer's feat of stone, steel and glass." He believed that its ultimate function was to serve as a mausoleum for Hitler. This "spectacular and ... grandiose idea" had an appropriate purpose: "Hitler the mighty, like Siegfried and the Teuton masters celebrated in the operas he loved so passionately, would come after death to his throne above the permanent snows and symbolically his spirit could go forth." According to Huss, after a visit to Napoleon's tomb in Paris in 1940, Hitler changed his mind on the matter: "The Führer felt that up at the Eagle's Nest he was far removed from the personal touch essential to the success of his plan; up at the Eagle's Nest there could be no crowds coming in future pilgrimage from the far corners of the earth to stare at him in silent awe and perhaps touch the crypt before them."[74]

The German press was forbidden to mention the extravagant structure and the outside world did not learn of it until March 1939. During World War II the U.S. Office of
Strategic Services estimated that Hitler originally saw the Kehlstein complex as his "eternal
mausoleum." In fact, he had a grander idea for his tomb. Walter Langer saw the structure
as a symbol of infantilism: "From a symbolic point of view one can easily imagine that this
is a materialization of a child's conception of the return to the womb. First there is a long
hard road, then a heavily guarded entrance, a trip through a long tunnel to an extremely
inaccessible place. There one can be alone, safe and undisturbed, and revel in the joys that
Mother Nature bestows."[75]

The showplace on the Kehlstein got very little use during the war, with Eva Braun occasionally taking some of her friends there to sun-bathe. The last event on the peak took place
in April 1944. Being denied the opportunity for such an event for herself, Eva arranged a
gala wedding reception there when her sister Margarete (Gretl) married SS General Otto
Fegelein, whom a year later Hitler had executed for attempting to abscond from the
Führerbunker in Berlin. Hitler hosted a luncheon for fifty at the Berghof, and then it was
off to the Kehlstein for an all-night bash. Apparently Hitler remained at his house. Some
of the guests extended the festivities for a week; Heinrich Hoffmann's photographs of the
fiesta appeared in newspapers after the war. According to Karl von Eberstein, the Munich
police chief, "The wedding caused great adverse criticism because of the protracted celebrations, the large number of guests, the colossal consumption of luxurious foods and the
donation of a large dowry, all taking place in the fifth year of the war." Several of the guests
were shortly killed in a bombing raid on Munich.[76]

Another large project followed the Kehlstein construction. In 1938 the Moritz
pension, close to the Berghof, was torn down and a large hotel, the Platterhof, was built
on the site. Dr. Goebbels' department announced that this was to be a national hotel for
the German people. It declared that any member of the *Volk* who came to see the Führer-
land could spend the night there for only one reichsmark. Martin Bormann had other plans.
Hitler, who loved to inspect works in progress, inquired about the location of the bar.
Bormann, knowing of the *Chef's* aversion to alcohol, had not provided for it. But he recovered quickly: it was to be in the basement, and into the basement it went, excavated out of
solid rock. When it was completed in 1941 it was hardly a *Volkshotel* and, said Josef Geiss,
it "became a hotel for Nazi wheels" until it was made into a military hospital two years
later.[77]

The same fate befell the nearby Hitler Youth Boarding House. Built about the same
time as the Platterhof, it was never used to give bed and board to youthful hikers. By the
time it was completed the *Jugend* were hiking elsewhere, in Russia, for example.[78]

Beginning in the mid–1930s Hitler at home greeted a variety of delegations of British
and French war veterans, whom he assured that, knowing at first hand of the horrors of
war, there would never be another one. He also was host to a menagerie of notable individ-
uals, including the weighty Aga Khan, the historian Arnold Toynbee and the American
newspaper tycoon William Randolph Hearst. There was also a steady stream of foreign political visitors. In fact, Hitler largely conducted his foreign affairs from there; in this, he could
be looked upon as a pioneer in the work-from-home movement. Meetings that took place
at the Berghof, rather than in Berlin, had the advantage that they could be held in a low-
key, informal manner without public notice. As Anthony Eden commented on one occasion, "A visit by a leading Cabinet minister to Berlin specifically to meet Herr Hitler would
arouse such publicity and speculation as would almost certainly defeat its purpose."[79]

The most important of his callers were prominent British figures. Invariably they were given a most cordial reception by their obliging and personable host. Young Anthony Eden's 1934 meeting was in Berlin, after which Eden told his wife, "Dare I confess it? I rather liked" the German ruler; but almost all the other ones were up on the Obersalzberg. Two years later the Führer greeted the aged David Lloyd George with the words, "Here is the man who won the war!" In return, the former British prime minister publicly declared that Hitler had achieved "a remarkable improvement in the working conditions of both men and women" and even a year later held to the view that Hitler was a great man. The "Goat in the Wilderness" privately was unrestrained in his praise of Hitler, comparing *Mein Kampf* with the Magna Carta and terming Hitler "the Resurrection and the Way" for Germany. Thomas Jones, the long-time cabinet secretary who accompanied Lloyd George, recorded his impression of the occasion in his diary: "The setting undoubtedly affected all of us— the lofty, spacious room, the mountain crags visible through the small group of eleven persons bunched together so as to miss no word of the dialogue of two men whose word had settled the fate of two nations and whose power for good and evil was not yet spent."[80]

The hapless Duke and Duchess of Windsor, while on an extended tour of Germany to study "housing and working conditions," were received there by Hitler in 1937. Driving through cities in an open car, the duke greeted the throngs with the Nazi salute. Before traveling to the Berghof, Edward had extravagant words of praise for the achievements of the German Labor Front in a speech at Leipzig. At a beer-hall gathering in Munich, and again speaking in German, the duke told the delighted crowd of his love for their city. After scattering words of praise about the new Germany during their tour, the Windsors had to be warned off from immediately embarking on a trip to the United States. An American correspondent commented to Thomas Jones about the activities of the ex-king: "The poor fellow must have very little discretion and must be very badly advised. His going to Germany and hobnobbing with Hitler and Ley [head of the German Labor Front] just before visiting America was enough to enrage every liberal organization in the country." Later, in 1940, Hitler contemplated restoring Edward as to the throne as part of a general settlement upon British capitulation.[81]

The visit of Edward Wood, now Lord Halifax, to the Berghof the same year began with a near-diplomatic disaster. Stepping from his car, the British cabinet minister, mistaking Hitler for a servant, was about to hand him his hat and coat when he was warned off by the German foreign minister. After that it was all smooth sailing for Hitler, as Halifax told him that Britain was prepared to support a negotiated revision of the Versailles treaty. Hitler was not impressed with Halifax, terming him "the English parson." General Sir Ian Hamilton, a strong advocate of friendly relations with the new Germany, was the Führer's house guest for a weekend in August 1938.[82]

The most important meeting with a British leader at the *Hitlerhaus* was, of course, that with Prime Minister Neville Chamberlain on September 15, 1938. Chamberlain's initial impression of Hitler were decidedly unfavorable. He viewed him as "the commonest little dog" he had ever seen, without one sign of distinction. At that time and place Chamberlain agreed "in principle" to the transfer of the Sudetenland from Czechoslovakia to Germany. Ernest Pope observed Chamberlain after his meeting with Hitler: "His collar was wilted, his mustache disheveled. He looked like a ruffled but unscathed Daniel emerging from the Lion's den." After this encounter Chamberlain told his sisters that, although he recognized Hitler's hardness and ruthlessness, "I got the impression that here was a man who could be relied upon when he had given his word."[83]

Others had a very different experience at the Berghof. While there in early 1938, Kurt von Schuschnigg, the Austrian prime minister, was beaten into submission by Hitler's temper and intimidation into effectively surrendering Austrian independence. Hitler's abuse was monumental: he snarled at Schuschnigg, "Listen, you don't really think that you can move a single stone in Austria without my hearing the most accurate details about it the very next day, do you?" And, after claiming he had a better right to call himself an Austrian than Kurt, he challenged Schuschnigg: "Why don't you try a plebiscite in Austria in which we two run against each other? You just try that." Austria had historically blocked the development of the German national idea, "indeed, all this sabotage was the chief activity of the Hapsburgs and the Catholic Church." Moreover, "The persecution of National Socialists in Austria must have an end or else I shall put an end to it." He continued with much more of the same. Reflecting Hitler's domination of European diplomatic activity of the period, historian Arnold Toynbee (who visited Hitler at the Berghof) voiced amazement at Hitler's "uncanny manipulation of the Austrian body politic from his wizard's cave at Berchtesgaden."[84]

Anticipating war, Hitler met there with a variety of likely impediments to his planned *Drang nach Osten*, including Col. Beck, the Polish foreign minister, and Carl Burckhardt, League of Nations commissioner in Danzig. He also welcomed a host of potential eastern European allies, including King Boris of Bulgaria, Admiral Horthy of Hungary, King Carol of Rumania, Count Ciano, the Italian foreign minister, and Prince Regent Paul of Yugoslavia. Hitler's war brought an end to the procession of most foreign dignitaries, although a declining Mussolini was brought there for rejuvenation on a couple of occasions. About forty-one diplomats and heads of government came to the Berghof during Hitler's years of power.[85]

With all the attention being given to his mountain home, Hitler wondered if the site would become a tourist trap after his death. He mused, "I can already see the guide from Berchtesgaden showing visitors over the various rooms of my house: 'This is where he had breakfast.'" He declared that he would prefer the building to be his funeral pyre. On another occasion he lamented that, the Berghof being too big, when he retired he would build a smaller house somewhere else. He once told Albert Speer that he planned to build the house along with two architects' studios, one of which most likely would be for Speer, "a few miles from Linz, on the Danube," and during the war years he looked for an appropriate site.[86]

According to Karl Billinger, from the perspective of early 1939 Hitler could view his achievements with a sense of considerable satisfaction: "As the Führer looks down from his 'eagle's nest' in the Bavarian Alps ... he can view his Reich with the proud feeling that he has increased his area by 63,000 square miles and the number of his subjects by 18,000,000. Such victories, accumulated within the short period of six years and won without any serious fight, are extraordinary indeed."[87]

On the eve of the beginning of another war, Hitler, as he had done in previous years, spent almost all of the summer of 1939 at the Berghof, but as usual traveling to nearby Bayreuth for ten days of Wagnernian bombast. He declared, "I shall stay at Obersalzberg as long as possible, in order to keep myself fresh for the difficult days to come." On 22 August, with agreement with the Soviet Union near at hand, he called a conference of his military leaders to inform them of his decision to attack Poland and of his future intentions, including the demolition of the Soviet Union. The war with Poland would be provoked by German agents in Polish uniforms attacking across the frontier. This was to be a war of extermination: "I have put my death-head formations in place with the command relentlessly and without compassion to send into death many women and children of Polish origins and language." Addressing the likely international response to such action, he declared, "Who after all is today speaking about the destruction of the Armenians?" Later he commented, "The world believes only in success." The fate of Russia was to be the same as that of Poland. He assumed Stalin was "a very sick man," and said that after his death "we will break the Soviet Union." This would be followed by "the dawn of German rule of the earth." His decision to attack Poland was final: "I have given the command and I shall shoot everyone who utters one word of criticism."[88]

When agreement with the Russians to jointly devour Poland was secured the next day, his entourage gathered with him late in the evening. Albert Speer describes the scene: standing on the terrace of the Berghof around 3 A.M. they "marveled at a rare natural spectacle. Northern lights of unusual intensity threw red light on the legend-haunted Untersberg across the valley, while the sky above shimmered in all the colors of the rainbow. The last act of *Götterdämmerung* could not have been more effectively staged. The same red light bathed our faces and our hands." A pensive mood descended on the group, with Hitler commenting to one of them, "Looks like a great deal of blood. This time we won't bring it off without violence."

Herbert Dohring has a much more dramatic recollection of the occasion: "Suddenly the sky above Berchtesgaden was in turmoil. It was blood red, green, sulphur grey, black as night, a jagged yellow. It was frightening." A Hungarian woman, one of Hitler's guests, approached him to say, "This augurs no good. This means blood, blood and more blood, destruction and terrible suffering." With that, recalled Dohring, Hitler became "completely crazed, his hair was wild, his gaze locked in the distance." At length Hitler responded, "Well, if it has to be, then let it be now," and shortly thereafter went to his room. The invasion of Poland began a week later.[89]

# CHAPTER THREE

# Festung

The beginning of a new European war did not deter Hitler's plans for continued massive building projects. Once victory had been achieved in France in 1940 he ordered that his vastly ambitious government center plan for Berlin should be implemented. Work at Obersalzberg also continued.

The director of the Berlin project, Albert Speer, was instructed to not get involved with military work. In April 1941, Hitler approved a plan to provide eighty-four thousand tons of iron annually for the Berlin extravaganza. Joseph Stalin took an interest in the monumental plans, but Hitler ordered that designs for the biggest buildings be kept secret so as "not to give Stalin any ideas." A large number of cities which were to have reconstructed centers were added to that list. Even after the invasion of Russia had begun in June 1941, Hitler insisted that the building projects continue.[1]

Largely because of the catastrophic winter of 1941–42 in Russia, Speer, when he became minister of armaments in March 1942, succeeded in getting Hitler to order the suspension of non-military building projects. Despite this, some party officials continued their own projects. Bormann convinced Hitler that the work at Obersalzberg served a military purpose. Speer responded by getting Hitler to order that this, too, be canceled. Construction did stop for a short period, but then Bormann managed to get work resumed. A large work crew, using a wealth of materials, continued at the Obersalzberg site until the end of the war. Two housing estates—Klaushohe and Buchenhohe—were built on the mountainside for construction workers and staff members.[2]

Bormann continued with another project begun in the late 1930s—the Agricultural Estate North. Located sixty-five miles south of Berlin in eastern Mecklenburg, its original purpose was to supply Hitler (and company) with a secure and controlled food supply. Bormann built up the area owned by the Obersalzberg administration to 25,000 acres. Despite rationing in almost every other part of the German economy, Bormann succeeded in securing a full supply of fertilizer, diesel fuel, machinery and other equipment.

The actual purpose of this facility was to prepare a retirement residence for an "Old Adolf." Although Hitler never visited the place, Bormann directed the renovation of Schloss Stolpe, a castle meant for the future use of the Führer, as well as the manor house of the Möllenbeck estate, which Bormann began using as his own retreat, while coveting the neighboring estate of Krumbeck. As always, Bormann was looking ahead. Several times he told his wife he anticipated a rich reward for serving as Hitler's ever-helpful chief assistant: "When it is all over, the Führer might possibly give me Krumbeck or another estate in Mecklenburg as a bonus and ancestral manor."[3]

Although Hitler had urged the German people to make sacrifices, with himself setting the example, he came up with some new projects. Rather than show visitors the ruins of Berlin, Klessheim castle, between Berchtesgaden and Salzburg, was renovated at great cost to serve as a conference center. An impressive neo–Renaissance structure surrounded by a large park, it offered sweeping views of the surrounding mountains from its many terraces. Aloof from the carnage of war, and apparently unknown to enemy intelligence until very late in the war, Klessheim was never disturbed by any nasty Allied bombers.[4]

As was the case in other resorts, Berchtesgadener Land area hotels, spas and other buildings were used to house wounded soldiers, officers on leave, and children evacuated from the cities. The Berghof guest house was converted into a military communications center.[5]

By mid–1943 the tide of war definitely had turned. The Allies had clearly achieved air superiority. Now was the time to start digging. Otto Dietrich said that at this time "the building of bunkers" became "Hitler's hobby." Hitler assumed that the Allies would seek out his headquarters and try to kill him. He personally supervised the massive reinforcement of his field headquarters in East Prussia. Speer described the result: "From the outside it looked like an ancient Egyptian tomb. It was actually nothing but a great windowless block of concrete, without direct ventilation, in cross section a building whose masses of concrete far exceeded the usable cubic feet of space. It seemed as if the concrete walls sixteen and a half feet thick that surrounded Hitler separated him from the outside world in a figurative as well as literal sense, and locked him up inside his delusions." A battalion of troops, equipped with tanks, artillery, and anti-aircraft guns protected the area while surrounding open spaces were mined. It seems strange that with Hitler's great concern for personal security, the workforce at the site was composed of eastern European forced laborers. Immediately after the assassination attempt of 20 July 1944, Hitler suspected the culprits were among these people.[6]

Hitler also took a keen interest in the construction of the Führerbunker beside the chancellery in Berlin. For instance, he had a well dug under the structure as an auxiliary water supply. As early as the summer of 1943 Allied bombing of Berlin had caused public concern about the departure of public offices from the city. Joseph Goebbels noted that "the Berliners therefore believe that in case more serious raids were to occur, the government would be the first to run away." That November Hans Lammers, chief of staff of the Chancellery, wanted to move his headquarters into the Führerbunker; homeless people would first have to be removed to other quarters. In September 1944, Albert Speer informed Hitler that 28,000 workers were involved in building bunkers in Rathensburg, Pullach, and Bad Charlottenbrunn. What Speer called an exaggerated concern for personal security on the part of *der Chef* inspired other Nazi leaders to build themselves underground bunkers all over the place. A better use of resources probably would have been to build more fighter planes or put into production an effective ground-to-air missile, available since 1942.[7]

A bomb shelter was also built under the building in Munich in which Hitler had his apartment. This supposedly was "one of the most modern and replete bombproof cellars in all Germany." After American troops found the shelter, a U.S. journalist declared, "The more one studies Hitler's various hideouts, the more one realizes how deceitfully official propaganda built him up as a simple man of the people, whose personal wants were the most modest and whose every hour was so concentrated upon Germany's welfare that he had no time for private life." But then, Hitler claimed to be the best actor in Germany. American GIs were disappointed to find that the safe in Hitler's apartment contained only "twelve copies of the first edition of *Mein Kampf*." At least most of them were autographed.[8]

Beginning in mid–July 1943, a huge underground network of shelters and tunnels, eventually extending to four miles, was built into the Obersalzberg. Göring already had built a shelter under his house. Under the persistent direction of Bormann, the work force, depleted by conscription but now augmented by Italians and Czechs, turned once again to blasting into rock. Hitler began to say that Bormann got his name because he liked boring; this was now truer than ever. Due to the dictatorial control Bormann exerted over the compound, he had also acquired other designations, one being *Schwarzer Schatten am Berg* ("Black Shadow on the Mountain"). Hans Linge recalled that in Berlin Bormann was known as "God Almighty from Obersalzberg."[9]

The first section was completed in time for Hitler's arrival on 24 December 1943. Individual shelters were connected by passageways. The system was equipped with heat, water, electricity, ventilation, communications, and kitchens. Within each of the twenty-nine entrances were anti-gas systems and machine-gun emplacements. The complex had seventy-nine rooms, but only the four under the Berghof were fully completed—suites for Adolf and Eva, a medical operating room and a dental clinic. Wiring for eight hundred telephones was installed and a direct underground trunk line to Berlin was laid. As well, an underground tunnel was built from the Berchtesgaden railroad station to the chancellery and military headquarters in Stengass, two miles away.

Emergency supplies were laid in, with some bunkers containing large quantities of such "necessities" as wine, liquor and chocolate. Bormann, for one, was ready for the long haul: he had so much food and clothing stashed in his shelter and elsewhere on the mountain (the beehouse had been converted into a storehouse) that his family could have subsisted off it for years. In February 1945 when Göring's *Hausmeister* asked for five kilos of honey, Bormann refused the request, arguing that "if the Führer's H.Q. should come to Obersalzberg we shall need a lot ourselves." He continued to build up a liquor supply in a secret storeroom under the "architectural" building. When additional supplies were dispatched to the site the bottles were called bricks.[10]

Bormann had ready access to food—from the two party farms in northern Germany. At the Berghof, however, strict rationing was observed. With Eva Braun in residence most of the time but without ration stamps, the head housekeeper had to struggle to secure enough food for the staff. Local farmers sometimes provided food outside of rationing.

Most of the tunnel system had been completed by the beginning of 1944, but work on it continued until April 24, 1945, the day before the buildings were subjected to a massive attack by British bombers. During the fall of 1944 a second tunnel system, located below the existing one, was begun but not completed. A planned elevator for Hitler's shelter was not installed. In the spring of 1944 Allied bombings of Munich became frequent, with the red glow of fires visible from the Obersalzberg on a clear day. Returning from the city to the Berghof one day in early 1944, Eva Braun told Hitler of the large-scale destruction she had seen. His response was that Britain soon would pay for this with rocket attacks; in January 1945 he asserted that Allied planes would be swept from the skies when the new jet aircraft became operational. When the housekeeper of his Munich apartment urged him to move its contents to safekeeping, he responded, "Frau Winter, we must set an example." Everyone in Munich would have learned of such a transfer. He did agree to have his collection of paintings shipped to the Obersalzberg tunnel system.[11]

It was not until August 1943 that a ring of anti-aircraft guns was installed around the Obersalzberg. A month later, Hans Schwaiger was replaced as commander of this unit. After the war, like a few other Nazis, Schwaiger got to South America. Upon his eventual return to Germany, he became a frequent quest at the rebuilt Zum Turken inn. Bernhard Frank was his replacement on the Obersalzberg. At that time, there a gap in the security ring— the Kehlstein. It was not until mid–1944 that Martin Bormann was convinced that flak guns needed to be installed there. Bormann obviously did not want to be disturbed while enjoying the fruits of his work—he was the most frequent user of the mountain building and enjoyed traversing the mountain trails in his four-wheel-drive vehicle. In October 1943, Frank's unit took control of the smoke screen machinery previously installed by the air force. Outlying radar units could track Allied planes approaching the mid–Alps area and then the Obersalzberg air-raid warning center would try to determine if the planes were heading there. Frank was in a difficult situation: he was instructed not to disturb Hitler's morning sleep unnecessarily; on the other hand he was also ordered not to set off the alarm too late. In mid–1944 his area of air defense responsibility was expanded from Berchtesgaden and Obersalzberg to include Bad Reichenhall and Salzburg. Frank also assumed control of the two hundred members of the Führer chauffeur column.[12]

By this time, Allied bombers repeatedly flew over the area on their way to Salzburg and beyond, but, strangely, there was only one air attack on Berchtesgaden—on a small scale, and "partially accidental" at that—until the very last days of the war. Alarm signals sounded almost daily and smoke machines covered the hillside in fog and anti-aircraft guns ringed the area. The flooding of the area in fog, sometimes several times a day, filled the air with chemical vapors, which affected Dr. Theo Morell's respiratory tract to such an extent that in May 1944 he secured Hitler's permission to move 1500 feet below to a hotel in Berchtesgaden. Hitler, when in residence, directed his staff down the sixty-five steps to the Berghof shelter during air raid alarms and stood at the top to assure that no one ascended until the all clear signal was given; only when the batteries began firing would he go down into the shelter.[13]

In the spring of 1944 the whole of the Obersalzberg complex was professionally camouflaged. The Berghof was painted dark green. Artificial trees and hedges crossed the area, and huge nets blended the buildings into the landscape. All the windows were covered in heavy drapes. Gloomy conditions within were countered by the constant use of artificial light. The Waffen-SS units guarding the compound were trained to respond to an attack in five minutes, complete with all equipment.[14]

With the American and British air forces conducting dozens of missions every day, why did they not bomb the Obersalzberg? Given the notoriety of the place, there was no question about its location. By early 1944 the British Special Operations Executive had a detailed knowledge of the Obersalzberg complex. Undoubtedly through Ultra intercepts, Allied Intelligence discovered that Hitler was directing the German resistance in Normandy from the Obersalzberg. Therefore R.A.F. developed a plan, called "Hellbound," to bombard the place. For four days beginning 16 June, American reconnaissance planes flew over the locality, filming it as the prelude to an aerial bombardment by the U.S. 15th Air Force from Italy, and a flight plan was prepared.

Within two weeks the U.S. Air Force leadership "sidetracked" the project on the grounds that it would prove too costly. Assuming that the area would be heavily defended, evaluators concluded that Hitler surely would survive the attack and that it would probably increase rather than diminish his support among the German people. As well, Allied officials probably would not have believed how often Hitler was there. Carl Spaatz, Air Force commander in Europe, referred the matter to Hap Arnold, the Air Force commanding general. Returning from a visit to Europe at this time, Arnold, in his characteristics breezy way, wrote in his diary on 20 June 1944, "The general impression among the higher officers in the Allied Air Forces is that," despite the many mistakes of the German air leaders, "[o]ur secret weapon is Hitler; hence do not bomb his castle. Do not let him get hurt, we want him to continue making mistakes." Noting the inept disposition of German ground troops, Arnold agreed with this assessment.[15]

The question of an attack on the Obersalzberg had obvious political implications, but it is not known if Arnold sought guidance from anyone with political authority in Washington. The impression is that he did not. Based on President Roosevelt's original position that military resources be used only for direct efforts to win the war, both the Air Force leadership and Eisenhower had previously had agreed that bombing should be restricted to legitimate military targets. This policy decision, however, was in opposition to the British program of area bombing of population centers, and did not concern itself with matters such as an attack on Hitler's residence. With a massive fleet of planes now available and a shift in Roosevelt's position in September 1944 concerning civilian targets, the U.S. Army Air Force began an unlimited and essentially indiscriminate assault on German cities, resulting in the death and mutilation of tens of thousands of non-combatants.[16]

In the immediate aftermath of the attempt by some German officers to kill Hitler on July 20, 1944, Allen Dulles, OSS chief in Bern, Switzerland, suggested that if the supporters of the coup managed to maintain themselves in any part of Germany that air raids be launched on the "Nazi stronghold in the region of Berchtesgaden." "Although the immediate military effectiveness of such action would be unimportant," he argued, "it is possible that the psychological reaction would be great. Naturally, any break in the communications channels between the region of Berchtesgaden and the rest of the country would be especially valuable."[17]

A "target information plan" for the site, dated 5 October 1944, was prepared, but no action was taken, although the First Allied Airborne Army considered a parachute drop on the Obersalzberg.[18]

In February 1945 the U.S. 15th Air Force put forward Operation Doldrum—a plan to bomb selected targets in the Berchtesgaden area. However, this was vetoed by the air force high command for a variety of reasons: the attack would require ideal conditions, the target area was small, and would require "one visual day" of clear weather (of which there were few), for the 15th Air Force. Further, since, Hitler's blundering leadership was an aid to the Allied war effort it was best to leave him be as he "can only be irrevocably discredited if he is at the helm when the final collapse comes."[19]

A third plan to bomb the Berchtesgaden-Salzburg area, Operation Dismount, emerged in the early spring of 1945. The attack was to be a combined assault by the 15th and 8th Air Forces with the objective being to isolate the area by destruction of both road and rail bridges. The plan was not acted upon.[20]

The idea of bombing the Obersalzberg continued to be considered, in an idle sort of way, by the American air force. On the very day that the area finally was attacked—April 25—by British bombers, the deputy intelligence officer of the 15th Air Force wrote an analysis report reviewing the pattern of inaction and recommended that six rail lines in the area should be bombed "upon [the] first opportunity." Although the report listed the Hitler complex as a possible target, it did not make it an objective in this plan. Avoiding the matter of attacking the Berghof was probably in line with the general military propensity to stay clear of matters having political implications. Moreover, there was a general assumption that the Obersalzberg area was heavily defended.[21]

When an armed reconnaissance flight encountered clouds at Congliano/Ljubljana on 20 February 1945 it proceeded to Berchtesgaden, where it made a brief attack on its rail facilities. Eight U.S. P-47 Thunderbolts of the 15th Air Force, based in Italy, made three passes over the town, encountering moderate flak on the second and third sorties. The lead officer in the formation reported that "the whole place looked like a peaceful summer resort. Rail and road traffic were heavy and seemingly moved without any fear of attack. Evidently Hitler's retreat is unaccustomed to war." The planes launched rockets at a train in the station loaded with troops. Another officer declared: "At the first shot they swarmed off and headed for the woods. Then we strafed the woods and set a fire going there." There was no opposing fire from the town, but from the Berghof area there was an "intense barrage of flak and machine-gun fire." Estimated impact of the raid: one locomotive and six rail cars damaged and two cars destroyed.[22]

The Berghof complex was not assaulted. According to *Life* magazine, "Allied air planners have long been aware that there is nothing above ground worth attacking." The article, which included a large photograph of the Obersalzberg buildings, claimed that Hitler "spends little time at the Berghof now. His favorite retreat, reached by an elevator shaft that is almost as high as the Empire State Building, is on the top of near-by Mt. Kehlstein." It also passed on the story from the Twelfth Air Force public relations office, based in Rome, that one American pilot dropped two empty gasoline tanks over the Berghof complex "as a gesture," but Major John I. Beck, who led the attack, denied that claim. Indeed, Beck said that "somehow or other he had never heard that the Führer lived in Berchtesgaden. He didn't believe the other pilots knew either." In the end, while the American air force temporized, it was the British who finally plastered Hitler's hideaway.[23]

In his study of Hitler's personal security, Peter Hoffmann has argued that "systematic and concentrated raids on Hitler's known abodes would have caused great disruption to the German military leadership" and would have forced Hitler to become, in effect, a fugitive. Indeed, "it would have been possible to kill Hitler with aerial bombs, given the will and the intention." A minor effort to achieve this took place on 4 November 1944 when four P-47s of the 12th Air Force bombed a hotel in Milan where Hitler was rumored to be staying.[24]

Beginning in mid–1944 the British Special Operations Executive, as an alternate to an air attack, proposed to take a different approach to eliminating Hitler—Operation Foxley. Justification for this action was based on the "abundant evidence" that Hitler "is regarded by a large section of the German population as something more than human; it is this mystical hold which he exercises over the German people that is largely responsible for keeping the country together at the present time." Its conclusion: "Remove Hitler and there is nothing left."[25]

The SOE already had pulled off a political murder operation—the assassination of Reinhard Heydrich, the deputy leader of the SS, in 1942. The retribution for this act was terrible—a village leveled, and scores of innocent Czechs executed. The planners of Operation Foxley proposed that the assassination of Hitler be made "to look as if the German army was responsible," which could precipitate civil war. Four methods of execution were proposed: killing Hitler along rail routes as well as three plans on the Obersalzberg—attacks by snipers along Hitler's route to the teahouse, followed up, if necessary, with a bazooka attack on the building; an ambush of Hitler's car as it left the Berghof compound; and a parachute assault by a battalion of the Special Air Service under the cover of an air bombardment of the area. In considering the bombardment idea, the SOE estimated that the entire security force on the Obersalzberg was a mere 260–280 soldiers, only a few of whom were stationed in the immediate area of the Berghof. The operation could be completed before German reinforcements could be brought from Bad Reichenhall and Salzburg. This plan, it concluded, "would be well worthwhile since it offers the best chance of eliminating the Führer as well as other leading Nazis in the Obersalzberg, Martin Bormann, for instance." Employment of any of these methods, however, could easily be traced back to the Allies.[26]

The planning for the operation indicates that the SOE had considerable knowledge of the Obersalzberg plus detailed information about security arrangements around the complex. A report of 31 October 1944 showed that security was being tightened there: new barrack construction, additional telephone lines, and increased air-raid protection, including two hundred smoke devices that could quickly blanket the area. At the same time, the full proposal listed Eva Braun as Hitler's secretary (at least she was not called his niece), estimated her age as twenty-four and stated that Martin Bormann rarely left the Obersalzberg, when, in fact, Bormann was invariably with Hitler at his various headquarters.[27]

The proposal was approved by the chiefs of staff on 21 June 1944 and was supported by Alfred Duff Cooper, chairman of the cabinet security committee, but when it reached government, or full cabinet level, debate raged about the utility of the plan's implementation. There was general agreement that Hitler was key to the entire Nazi structure; with him gone, the war very probably would end soon. On the other hand, it was argued that should the operation fail, there would be renewed German support for Hitler. Moreover, Hitler, making military blunders, was an asset to the Allies. Winston Churchill, for one, was unenthusiastic about the proposal; assassination is seen as a dirty game and Winston probably did not want to lose his prey until a total defeat of Germany had been achieved. The abortive assassination attempt by German army officers (using British explosives) on July 20, 1944, effectively put Foxley on hold. Hitler responded to this attempt with utmost brutality. Retribution could be expected following a British effort to destroy Hitler. The Germans had thousands of British prisoners.

All planning for the operation was focused solely on the Obersalzberg and rail and road approaches to that area. Ian Kershaw has pointed out that Hitler left the Berghof for good on July 14, so his departure overtook the plan. But Allied intelligence did not know where Hitler was until late April, when there was a press announcement that he intended to remain in Berlin. Lt. Alfred Dorner of the U.S. 9th Air Force recalled that sometime in late April he piloted a bomber towards the Berchtesgaden area. On board were eight British commandos whose task was to drop into the Obersalzberg, locate Hitler and mark the area for a bombing attack. En route the mission was abandoned when Dorner was informed that Hitler was in Berlin.[28]

When Operation Foxley apparently was being held in abeyance, the SOE in December 1944 proposed a "Little Foxley" operation—the killing of other Nazi leaders, particularly Joseph Goebbels, who, unlike Heinrich Himmler, "rarely leaves Berlin." This proposal met with a generally favorable response from the British government but, in the end, it was not put into operation. One SOE staffer noted that it was "unlikely to get sufficient up-to-date intelligence to plan a specific Foxley operation against Himmler or any other Party leader or prominent S.D. official."[29]

The SOE also considered action against third-level Nazis. One proposal was the targeting of "less prominent lights of the SS hierarchy" who were "potentially more dangerous on account of their comparative youth and the active part they might play in any Nazi underground movement." Elimination of some of these people "would probably have an immediate and marked effect on Party morale." Attention was given to Otto Skorzeny, rescuer of Mussolini and, after the Battle of the Bulge, *bête noir* of Allied intelligence. Skorzeny was described in one SOE report as "an inspiring personality to his admirers." According to a Wehrmacht officer, Skorzeny was a "typical evil Nazi" who had "fantastic notions and a predilection for dirty methods."[30]

As the Allies drove into Germany in April 1945 SOE planners turned to the possibility of capturing, rather than killing, Nazi leaders. SHAEF intelligence was reassured that the killing option "is not now under consideration." With the disintegration of the German war machine, "the balance of advantage would now lie in trying to capture R.S.H.A. officials of the Kaltenbrunner type alive." Moreover, SOE knew where their prey was likely to be found: "It seems reasonably possible that the majority of such people will eventually retire to the Berchtesgaden-Salzburg area."[31]

The junior partner of the SOE also had plans to dispatch Hitler. Although it was a new intelligence and special operations organization, the American Office of Strategic Services aggressively pushed into this twilight world. According to Stanley Lovell, who was there from the beginning of the "dirty tricks" department, the SOE came up with a variety of schemes to get to the Führer, none of which worked out. Informed by agents that Hitler and Mussolini would meet near the Brenner Pass in Italy, the SOE came up with a chemical compound which if placed in a water vase in the expected meeting room, would vaporize and permanently blind all its occupations. The Axis partners met at another place.

Based on the assumption that Hitler's sexual alignment teetered on the male/female line, the SOE came up with a plan to inject female sex hormones into the vegetables in his Berchtesgaden garden. Funds were disbursed to at least one German conspirator, but with no result. "Since he survived," Lovell ruefully recalled, "I can only assume the gardener took our money and threw the syringes and medications into the nearest thicket. Either that or Hitler had a big turnover in his 'tasters.'"

The quest went on. Lovell and company came up with the idea of hypnotizing a German prisoner, convincing him that Hitler needed to be killed and smuggling him back into Germany. Sadly, the OSS enthusiasts were informed by Karl and William Menninger that a person under hypnosis cannot be made to commit acts that are in conflict with his moral principles.[32]

In some ways Hitler proved to be an elusive target for those who tried to kill him. In March 1942 an Allied informant reported that all military officers at meetings with Hitler had to leave their weapons behind and "special police officers" attended all such meetings, "even with the highest army leaders." In the last two years of the war he seldom emerged from his bunker in East Prussia or was at the Obersalzberg. He frequently changed travel plans and departure times. To reveal information about these matters was an offense punishable by death. Hitler knew there was a group in the army who wanted to get him. Yet, Col. Claus von Stauffenberg, the leader of the assassination attempt, was twice—June 7 and July 11—in the Berghof with bombs in his briefcase. He did not make the attempt on these two prime occasions because the plotters believed that Göring and Himmler should be killed at the same time and place. The two did not attend the first meeting and Himmler was not there for the second. As time was to show, the Nazis without Hitler were like a circus without an elephant.[33]

As his end drew near, Hitler was somewhat perplexed that his adopted home area had not been bombed. In one of his final public statements—a proclamation on February 24, 1945—he expressed his regret that the Berghof had not been assaulted. With thousands of planes available, it does seem odd that the valley of the Berchtesgaden Land remained an oasis of safety in the midst of war. It appears that these same Allied generals came to the conclusion not to bomb Auschwitz because it was not a military target. For that matter, the Russian air force did not attack Hitler's headquarters in East Prussia, something that was of continuing concern to Hitler. He seemed puzzled that the Russians did not launch a paratroop assault on the place; he was perfectly prepared for the troop losses if he could have mounted such a coup: "What a catch it would be! If I could get my hands on the entire Russian High Command at one fell swoop, I would risk two paratroop divisions for it immediately!" Remembering his experiences in the first war, he also mused about the possibility of a gas attack. He was fitted for a gas mask in February 1945 and gas filters were installed in the Obersalzberg tunnel system. His concern increased as the Russians closed in on Berlin in April; his greatest fear was to be captured alive and put on display by the Soviets.[34]

Hitler had a continuing concern about his own protection. Considerable evidence exists that Hitler employed look-alikes (doppelgängers) to stand in for him on occasion. For purposes of deception and security, this was not an uncommon practice. Both Bernard Montgomery and Dwight Eisenhower employed doubles. Just before D-Day, Lt. Clifton James, a professional actor extracted from the British Army Pay Office in London, took on the guise of Monty and with appropriate ceremony flew from England to Gibraltar and then to Algiers. This was done in order to give the impression that the Allies were preparing to launch an invasion of southern France. During the Battle of the Bulge in December 1944, with rumors abounding that a Nazi murder squad was hunting Eisenhower, Lt. Col. Baldwin B. Smith assumed Ike's identity for a few days.[35]

As far as Hitler was concerned, some SS guards at the Reichchancellery said that doubles were used. The fictional Pauline Kohler declared that there were three of them, one each in Berlin, Munich, and Berchtesgaden. Contemplating an attack on Hitler in mid–1944, the SOE said that the marked changes in his appearance could tempt one "to credit the popular belief that he has one or more doubles," and could only conclude that evidence on this matter was "particularly conflicting."[36]

As the war's end drew near there was speculation in both American and British newspapers that the Führer would use such a double to elude capture or death. Hans Baur, Hitler's chief pilot, claimed that prior to Hitler's planned departure to the Obersalzberg at the end of the war, an Austrian who looked much like Hitler was brought to Berlin, where, in order to fool the Russians, he was to have been shot and partially burned. This doppelgänger was killed so that this plan would not be revealed. In those last days SS General Hermann Fegelein, one of the bunker staff, told several people that there were two Hitlers in Berlin. On the other hand, Hans Baur said that at least in the mid–1930s Hitler had contemptuously rejected the proposal to use a double for ceremonial occasions, declaring, "That's not my style. It's better for a flat-footed fellow like Stalin, who has to stand for hours on Lenin's tomb."[37]

But security concerns became much greater during wartime. Immediately after the war, Wilhelm Brueckner, one of Hitler's adjutants, said he doubted that Hitler employed doppelgängers: "The possibility is excluded because of Hitler's characteristic feeling of contempt for such measures." But Bruckner had ceased being an adjutant in 1940. Better evidence on this matter is provided by Johannes Hentschel, the chief electrician for the Chancellery and the last person to leave the Führerbunker, who declared he never saw a Hitler double. When the Russian SMERSH team arrived at the Führerbunker on May 2, there was a corpse that certainly looked like Hitler lying in a heap of bodies at the base of an attached water tower.

The team immediately believed they had found Hitler's body and excitedly photographed the corpse. Their elation was shattered when someone noticed that the corpse was wearing mended socks; that was not the Führer's style. After their capture, members of the chancellery declared they had never seen this man before. There has been speculation that Bormann, or possibly Brigadeführer Mohnke, chancellery commandant, produced the double to mislead the Russians about the location of Hitler's body.[38]

A few days after this photography incident the same members of the chancellery staff were required to give their judgment about Hitler's actual corpse. Three of them did not identify the remains as that of Hitler. One unidentified servant declared the body was that of a cook, whom he knew intimately, and stated that "the 'cook double' had been assassinated because of his startling likeness to Hitler while the latter had escaped from the ruins of Berlin." A Russian officer on the scene has declared that two doppelgängers were found—one in a nearby street and another inside the bunker. Yet Peter Hoffmann, the authority on Hitler's personal security, doubts that Hitler used doppelgängers, and David Irving, who spent many years studying Hitler, has found no evidence of this practice.[39]

Noting the large-scale exodus of German leaders from Berlin in late April 1945 and following Joseph Stalin's lead on the matter, Russian intelligence appeared convinced that Hitler had escaped capture by means of a double. For about a year after their capture, members of Hitler's inner staff were repeatedly questioned about the use of a doppelgänger. A few books of popular history kept the yarn going.

During the war, Hitler continued to spend long periods at the Berghof. He spent the summer of 1940 there, dithering over the question of launching Operation Sea Lion, the invasion of England. When Rudolf Hess made his apparently madcap "peace flight" to Scotland in May 1941, Hitler received the news at the Obersalzberg. He also was there when the Russians at Stalingrad began their counterattack in November 1942. In *Inside the Third Reich*, Albert Speer commented, "In the peaceful atmosphere of the Berghof he [Hitler] simply did not understand what was brewing." But Speer's Spandau recollections present a different and more atmospheric picture. He recalled that one day at that time Hitler selected him to walk with him to the teahouse. "It was one of those dismal Obersalzberg days, with west winds driving low-lying clouds from the plateau of Upper Bavaria down into the valley." Hitler took that opportunity to unburden himself: he had wanted to be an architect, but "the World War and the criminal November Revolution prevented that." The Jews were responsible for all Germany's misfortunes, but now there would be a reckoning: "This time not one will escape." Ten years later, Speer recalled the man who told him this: "An old man, a man who was really already defeated, stood there in the snow impotently squeezing out his stored-up bitterness, his toxic resentments."[40]

In April 1942, Hitler told Joseph Goebbels that due to his poor health he greatly needed to take three months' leave sometime, "but when, how and where can he go on vacation?" Agreeing that this was not then possible, Goebbels observed, "Thank God, at least he will now go to the Obersalzberg for a few days, even though it be for important talks with the Duce. The Obersalzberg always has a quieting effect on him." Two years to the month later, Hitler told Christa Schröder, one of his secretaries, "During all these years I have not even been able to take a holiday. When I was in the mountains my work went on just as in Berlin." While at the Berghof he continued to wear military style clothing. Someone like Churchill could adorn himself with silk blouses and cowboy hats, but the Führer had to dress with dignity, even in private. Moreover, "my knees are white as chalk anyway, and that looks awful in short trousers." British night bombing gave him a new rationale for staying up deep into the night—he would not go to bed as long as any enemy bombers remained over the Reich. During the war, Hitler gave much greater time to his work, as previously he had allowed himself abundant leisure.[41]

Although he had three other country residences, all more opulent than his house on the Obersalzberg, Hermann Göring retreated there on several stressful occasions. He seemed to have enjoyed an occasional stint of simple living (and hunting), but the mountain also allowed him to escape the fury of the Führer about the increasingly faltering performance of the *Luftwaffe*. Moreover, his wife and daughter had moved there for a time in 1943 and then returned in February 1945. After the failure of the *Luftwaffe* to adequately supply the German army surrounded at Stalingrad in the winter of 1942–43, the *Reichsmarschall* headed for *Landhaus Göring*.

A new direction for the war was obviously needed and in order to break the influence of Martin Bormann and the staff surrounding Hitler and commit the government to total war mobilization, Field Marshal Erhard Milch, Albert Speer, and Joseph Goebbels worked up a plan to revive the Reich Defense Committee, with Göring taking the lead. When Speer went to the Obersalzberg on 28 February 1943 to present this idea, he found Göring a rouged and lacquered lump of a man. When Goebbels joined them the next day it became obvious that Göring could not assert any leadership, though the scheme lingered for a while.

While Speer and Goebbels conferred with Göring, the RAF staged a massive bombardment of Berlin, and Hitler demanded Göring's return to the capital. Göring, however, skipped off to Italy, "to inspect the supply lines." After an unproductive meeting with Mussolini, he went on a major art acquisition sortie to Florence. Although Hitler moved to the Obersalzberg that March, the two leaders of Nazi Germany seldom conferred.

During the summer of 1943, when American bombers first attacked deep into Germany, Göring spent most of August in his mountain chalet. When American planes launched crushing assaults on German cities that October, Göring retreated from Hitler's wrath for the peace and serenity of the Obersalzberg. In March 1944, he joined Hitler on the mountain, though he attended few of the Berghof conferences. He remained there after Hitler moved back to his military headquarters in East Prussia. While the Nazi world was collapsing in the spring of 1945, Göring traveled at least twice to the Obersalzberg, his principal concerns being his wife and daughter and the transfer of his massive art collection. When Göring traveled there in March, "to inspect the flak," Joseph Goebbels voiced indignation in his diary: "He has now just gone off with two special trains to visit his wife in the Obersalzberg. It is horrifying to think that the man responsible for the German *Luftwaffe* can now find the time to attend to his personal affairs."[42]

After Stalingrad, Hitler withdrew from the public. In marked contrast to his almost hectic travel around Germany before the war, he became reclusive. He rarely visited front-line military headquarters. When he traveled by train it was usually at night; during the day the curtains were drawn when traveling through populated areas. He did not visit badly-bombed cities like Hamburg and Cologne to give heart to the people; in mounting defeat, he would not face them. His absence was noted. A rumor spread through the country in mid–1943 that the Führer had withdrawn, surely to the Obersalzberg, to write a new book— *Mein Irrtum* ("My Mistake").[43]

He did not make a public address, even to a hand-picked audience, after 1942, though he occasionally gave inspirational speeches to the Nazi gauleiters. He rarely gave radio addresses. His last broadcast was in January 1945. Observing that Hitler had developed an aversion to speaking on the radio, Joseph Goebbels wrote in his diary on March 30, "I cannot abandon my demand that he speak to the people as soon as possible. He must call off one or two conferences for a day or two." In his definitive biography, Joachim Fest noted that Hitler "was a person who continually needed artificial charging. Since he feared that he would not get this from the people, he turned to drugs."

Since the mid–1930s, Hitler's principal doctor had been Theo Morell, a specialist in venereal and skin diseases, who had cured Hitler's leg eczema. Beginning in 1942, Morell began injecting Hitler with a mish-mash of drugs; Göring termed the doctor the "Reich Injection Master." Morell's booster shots had a short-term positive effect. When Hitler spoke to a gathering of party leaders in January 1944 he appeared to be "radiant." When Dr. Richard Weber later in 1944 temporarily replaced Morell, he found Hitler looking fresh and healthy. Also, photographs of Hitler after the assassination attempt in July of that year show him in obvious good health.[44]

Despite this, his health was in steady and terminal decline. In December 1942 Felix Kersten, Heinrich Himmler's therapist, claimed he saw a medical file on Hitler which indicated that he was suffering from progressive paralysis, probably caused by a recurrence of syphilis. Gottlob Berger, Himmler's second in command, told Kersten that rumors were abroad about various causes of Hitler's deterioration. When Bernhard Frank saw Hitler at his birthday reception on April 20, 1944, Frank thought Hitler looked "surprisingly healthy." A few weeks later when, by chance, Frank encountered Hitler outside the Berghof, he was stunned by the difference in appearance: "His eyes were glassy, the face was puffed-up, deadly pale to grey, distorted tear sacs, his body bent forward like that of a very old man, one arm was shaking like the arm of a Parkinson patient." Frank attributed this transformation to the regimen of injections that Hitler was receiving. In late 1944, an informant told the OSS office that Hitler was prevented from public speaking because of a throat ailment. Moreover, "[h]is periods of depression and elation are so incalculable that his entourage cannot tell half an hour in advance how he will behave in a given situation." When Hitler gave his final address before a gathering of Nazi leaders on 24 February 1945 many were shocked by his appearance.[45]

A variety of people began to see Morell as an untidy quack who was slowly poisoning the Führer. Eva Braun refused to let him treat her. In late 1944 three of his consulting physicians, including Karl Brandt (hanged after the war for directing the euthanasia program), attempted to get Hitler to replace Morell, but this effort failed. Hitler continued to have complete confidence in Morell, who joined the inner circle at the Berghof and in East Prussia. He awarded Professor Morell with the highest civilian decoration and gave him one of the few electron microscopes in Germany for use in his clinic at Bad Reichenhall.[46]

Hitler was afflicted with frequent stomach pain and Morell was always on hand to give him a shot or other medication. Morell also attempted to improve Hitler's diet. He appointed Dr. Werner Zabel, the director of a Berchtesgaden nature clinic, to take charge of the matter. They soon had a food fight—for example, arguing whether or not salads should be briefly boiled. When Hitler met Anny Winter, his Munich apartment keeper in mid–1944, she saw before her an emaciated, weak, shaking man with only "scarecrow arms." He told her that the doctors would not let him eat anything he liked and appealed to her to show them how to cook something he would enjoy. As a result, Hitler got a new cook at the Berghof—Marlene von Exner, a cheerful Austrian of Nazi lineage, with whom Hitler enjoyed talking about their native country. Also, he very much enjoyed her cooking, especially rich soups, in which, unbeknownst to the vegetarian Hitler, she included bone marrow. This happy arrangement came to an end in late 1944 when Martin Bormann informed Hitler that investigation revealed that Frau Exner had Jewish blood on her mother's side. In parting with her services, Hitler not only provided her with a large gratuity, but also a certificate that stated she was a pure Aryan.[47]

While at the Berghof, Hitler received soldiers to decorate them for outstanding bravery. One army officer, Gerhard von Swerin, related his experience of May 1943: "The style of the Berghof pleased me, with its lack of glamour, ostentation and display of servants. The whole, including the buildings and the furniture of the Führerhaus, made a simple, respectable and dignified impression. The SS orderlies looked intelligent and thoroughly trained, and were well-groomed. The only thing I had to criticize was a somewhat cold and impersonal touch." The Führer came towards him "with slow and somewhat tired steps, a man bent by a heavy burden"; he had "dull, tired eyes of an unnatural faded blue." Yet Hitler talked to him "in a deep, sonorous voice, and with great warmth. What he said was simple, dignified and human, and raised within me a reciprocal sentiment of human feeling." Moreover, in an extended conversation, Hitler listened carefully as the officer told him of equipment shortages on the Russian front.[48]

Stuka ace Hans Ulrich Rudel had a similar experience in mid–1944: "I stand in the presence of the Führer in the magnificent Berghof.... I am impressed by his warmth and almost tender cordiality." During an hour or two of tea and conversation, Hitler told Rudel about the development of atomic weapons, "something quite different which will be so powerful that once we begin to use them they should end the war decisively. He tells me that their development is already well advanced and that their final completion may be expected very soon.... The impression left after every visit to the Führer is enduring."[49]

In March 1943, Goebbels noted the change of times: "The drive up to the Obersalzberg awakens a multitude of nostalgic memories. How often and in what different moods have I covered this stretch.... There isn't much left to indicate the grand-scale life of days gone by. The Führer's residence seems to be sleeping the sleep of Snow White." A month later he agreed with Hitler's desire to spend several more weeks at the Berghof: "If the Führer will use this opportunity to restore his health halfway, that will be advantageous for us all.... We all spent ourselves too much last winter."[50]

During 1943 Hitler was on the Obersalzberg from late March to June and again at the New Year, an occasion he always sought to observe there. He was there again from late February until the end of March 1944. These long sojourns there ostensibly were to allow the massive reinforcement of his headquarters in East Prussia. Speaking to a gathering of his western front generals at the Obersalzberg on March 18, he declared that "the whole outcome of the war depends on each man fighting in the west, and that means the fate of the Reich itself." At the end of March, Leni Riefenstahl and her new husband visited Hitler. She noted his "shrunken frame, the trembling of his hands, the flickering of his eyes; he had aged years since our last meeting." Despite his physical decline, "he still cast the same magical spell as before." Ignoring Leni's decorated soldier husband, Hitler launched into a monologue in which he talked about his plans for rebuilding Germany after the war, the failure of the Italian alliance, and his hatred of England for not coming to an accommodation with Germany. In a fit of anger, he declared, "As sure as I'm standing here no Englishman will ever set foot on German soil." It was their last meeting.[51]

In 1944, Hitler was at the Berghof in April and May as well. When the Allies landed at Normandy in June he got the news at the Berghof, after his usual late breakfast. He was so sure that the Normandy landing was a decoy designed to get the German military to commit its reserves there, that he carried on with his usual routine. He attended the scheduled meeting with the prime minister of Hungary at the nearby Klessheim Palace, where he appeared grandly confident about the unfolding events of the invasion. Never one to deviate from habit, Hitler had a late afternoon meal with Eva and a few visiting Nazis, the group adjourning to the tea house, followed by his usual hour nap and an 11 P.M. military conference. After spending a single day—June 17—at his advanced headquarters in France (called W2), he returned to the Obersalzberg. Shortly thereafter, at a lengthy conference with two hundred generals held in the Platterhof pavilion, "Hitler shouted so loudly that workmen in remote parts of the estate could hear his rasping voice as it pierced the clear mountain air." On June 29 he addressed a gathering of armaments manufacturers at the same venue. That day he clashed with Field Marshal Erwin Rommel, who declared that the effort to defeat the Anglo-Americans in Normandy had failed and urged Hitler to seek a political solution. Hitler responded by telling Rommel to stick to his military responsibilities and dismissing him from the conference; it was their last meeting. Claus von Stauffenberg, the colonel who would almost kill him on July 20, attended meetings at the Berghof on two occasions in June and early July, shortly before Hitler departed from the Berghof for the last time. At the June meeting Stauffenberg observed that Hitler appeared "in a daze," listlessly moving maps around with a trembling hand. Yet, in photographs of Hitler just after the assassination attempt, he appeared fit and healthy. Morell's shots seemed to have had the desired short-term effect.[52]

As has been seen, from mid–1943 Hitler no longer went to the front or to the industrial areas. According to Erwin Giesing, one of his physicians, Hitler "was not able to face the horrors and miseries that the exigencies of war produced at the front and among the civilian population." Heinrich Hoffmann declared that Martin Bormann "had gradually succeeded in transforming the idyllic Obersalzberg into a species of political closed shop." Although Bormann had a house nearby, "he spent all his time with Hitler at the Berghof and even took all his meals there."[53]

It was at the Obersalzberg and Klessheim Palace that Hitler met with his allies. Following the Stalingrad disaster, which was somewhat offset by the recapture of Kharkov in March 1943, Hitler had a busy interval in April shoring up their support. Commuting from the Berghof to Klessheim, he met in turn with Mussolini, King Boris of Bulgaria, Marshal Antonescu of Romania, Admiral Horthy of Hungary, Prime Minister Vidkun Quisling of Norway, President Tiso of Slovakia, Ante Pavelic of Croatia, and Prime Minister Pierre Laval of France. It is significant that he never held a conference with all of his allied leaders together at the same time.[54]

At the Berghof, there remained the same inner circle—Eva Braun, her sister and friends, his photographer Heinrich Hoffmann and wife, personal doctors, and secretaries. As the situation went from bad to worse in the war, the forced gaiety and "obviously feigned insouciance" that Hitler required became a burden to other guests. Otto Dietrich related that Hitler's adjutants "were kept busy trying to fill the gaps in the dinner company and the fireplace gatherings whenever the ranks began to thin." Albert Speer later declared that during the war "there was nothing more soul-destroying" than Hitler's entourage: "Always the same dreary faces, not susceptible to broader interests, completely uninterested in cultural matters...." During this time Hitler's two favorite subjects were the wonderful qualities of his dogs and his vast plans for reconstruction after the war. Heinrich Hoffmann often provided morbid humor with jokes about Dachau and Jews, which Adolf and Eva enjoyed.

On one notable occasion the light social chatter and the Führer's monologues were interrupted when a guest introduced a most difficult subject. In April 1943 Henriette von

Schirach, the daughter of Heinrich Hoffmann, and her husband Baldur, gauleiter of Vienna, were guests of the Führer. Baldur recalled that Hitler "would either remain completely silent during a meal or hold forth at great length, soliloquizing, and brooking no comment or opinion from his guests." Having known Hitler for almost twenty years, the outspoken Henriette took the liberty of telling him of her horror in witnessing the forced expulsion of Jewish women in Amsterdam. Her comments provoked a furious response from Hitler: "You are a sentimentalist! What business of yours is it! The Jewesses are none of your business!" Henriette later recalled her reaction: "The demons are devouring him." The von Schirachs promptly were ordered out of the Berghof. Although she knew she had gravely offended the national leader and would never return to the inner circle, Henriette "felt also somehow indescribably free." She told her husband that she "was certain Hitler was insane." A common refrain by many Germans concerning Nazi excesses was, "If the Führer only knew!" Obviously, Hitler knew what was happening.[55]

The same year Ada Schultze, a former party secretary dating back to 1926 and who used the "du" form of familiar voice with Hitler, wrote to warn that Bormann was "Germany's gravedigger." Hitler ignored the advice, declaring that Frau Schultze was a sick person. Her husband was removed from his position as leader of the Nazi college teachers organization.[56]

Whether at the Berghof or in East Prussia, Hitler liked to have all of his personal staff around him and usually had his main meal with his secretaries and aides. He was quick to notice any missing official or employee. Although he said that each staff member should have his own personal freedom, Christa Schröder declared that he expected everybody to attend his afternoon and evening teas and "was extremely displeased when anyone dared to remain away from these get-togethers." The married men on his staff had to spend so much time with Hitler that they saw very little of their families. To compensate for monopolizing their time, he sometimes would invite their wives "to a sort of family dinner."[57]

The American Office of Strategic Services believed some strange things might be transpiring on the mountain. Told by "a number of informants" that Hitler took delight "in witnessing striptease and nude dancing," the OSS said that "there is evidence that he often invites girls to Berchtesgaden for the purpose of exhibiting their bodies." Perhaps the informants were confused by the paintings of nudes in the great hall of the *Führerhaus*, though there is evidence that Hitler enjoyed watching provocative female dancing. Albert Speer recalled a time, probably in the 1930s, when Hitler was very excited about an almost naked American dancer in Munich. Goebbels and Hitler, reportedly incognito, attended a strip club in Paris; this would have been in 1940. But there is no evidence that performers of this sort were brought to the Obersalzberg. The proprieties were observed.[58]

The British Special Operations Executive spread a variety of stories about sex orgies, homosexual activity, an airborne brothel, and the like. Among the tales it disseminated was one that claimed an order had been issued giving top Nazi officials the exclusive right to evacuate their families to holiday resorts, including Berchtesgaden. It circulated a leaflet, *The Victims of Berchtesgaden*, which asserted that any victim of bombing who attempted to seek shelter in the Berchtesgaden district was "mercilessly shot." Among the stickers it distributed in Germany was one that read, "We want a leader of God's choosing, not a murderer from Berchtesgaden."

The SOE entertained a wide variety of proposals to undermine the German war effort. One of these, not adopted, suggested by its Spanish section in late 1944, was to create the belief that some German leaders were fleeing to Ireland or Argentina where they would attempt to form a free German government in exile. Lacking was the plausibility of a Spanish escape connection. At this stage of the war, General Franco would not have approved. General Gerald Templar, a fierce Ulster Unionist, tried to get the SOE to include neutral Eire as a possible refuge for Hitler, but was turned down for diplomatic reasons. As early as July 1944, however, Allen Dulles, head of American intelligence in Bern, Switzerland, forwarded a rumor that when it came time to flee Hitler "has chosen Ireland, as he is convinced that the Irish would not turn him over to the English." William "Wild Bill" Donovan, head of the OSS, drew President Roosevelt's attention to the report. The Irish prime minister had already rejected the request of the Allied governments not to give asylum to Axis leaders, declaring that his government would make its own determination on the matter. At the end of the war a British MP asked "if Premier Eamon DeValera of Eire was harboring Hitler"; Winston Churchill replied that he would have inquiries made. For years afterwards Hitler sightings flowed into the Federal Bureau of Investigation. One informant declared that the Führer was working as a fisherman on the Aran Islands off the west coast of Ireland. Obviously this was a case of mistaken identity as Hitler did not speak the Irish language.[59]

Soldatensender Calais, the British-operated radio station which presented itself as the voice of a dissident SS faction, broadcast a variety of reports of orgies on the Obersalzberg. According to Sefton Delmer, one of its operators, "We told of the adventures of the popsies brought in to amuse a tired Führer." Among the people who were included in such activity was blond Elizabeth Blanda, or "Blondie," wife of Hitler aide Walter Hewel, who "was one of the wealthy highsteppers among the mountain people." It reported that at a hilarious party at the Berchtesgadener Hof, Elizabeth shaved off the hair of SS General Hermann Fegelein. After the war, Kenneth Strong, SHAEF intelligence chief, recognized that Allied propaganda in claiming that the Nazi elite was preparing to protect itself while leaving ordinary soldiers to die at the front had the effect of developing a German popular belief that a mountain retreat was being planned.[60]

Throughout most of the war when Hitler was not there, Eva Braun was often at the Berghof with her sister Gretl and her friends Marion Schönemann and Herta Schneider and the latter's children. They joined her in long walks, mountain climbing, and skiing, although Hitler feared Eva might be injured while enjoying this sport, which he had banned on the Obersalzberg. In Dr. Karl Brandt's opinion, Eva's "extremely energetic" temperament and her love of physical activity indicated that she was somewhat masculine in nature. She was not allowed to be at her manfriend's military headquarters or to accompany him on his travels, but during the last two years of the war two rooms in the Chancellery in Berlin were reserved for her. As well, Adolf and Eva had nightly phone conversations.

Although Eva called herself the mistress of the Berghof and was sometimes referred to by staff members as *die Chefin*—the female chief—Hans Hasselbach, one of Hitler's physicians, later commented that "she claimed for herself only the rights of that position without attending to the duties connected with it.... With her personal wishes, and particularly with her complaints about failures to fulfill these wishes, she made life rather miserable for the adjutants." Herbert Dohring, the Berghof administrator through 1943, felt sorry for her. Albert Speer had a very positive opinion of her: she was "a man's woman, incredibly undemanding of herself, helpful to many people behind the scenes—nobody ever knew that— and infinitely thoughtful of Hitler. She was a restful sort of girl." This apparently was the answer to the question in the mind of Hans Linge, Hitler's long-time valet, who wondered why *der Chef* had remained attached for so long to "someone neither gifted nor particularly beautiful." The last time Henriette von Schirach saw Eva—late in the war—Eva was no longer the carefree girl of yesteryear. Now, she was drinking brandy, commenting to her friend, "That gives you courage and stops you thinking about things."[61]

Hitler obviously did not want the public to know about his mistress so he prevented her from mixing with anyone outside the Berghof circle. Although the Görings had had a chalet near the Hitlerhaus since the mid–1930s, Emmy Göring declared that she never met Eva. In 1941, Emmy decided to arrange a tea for the ladies of the Obersalzberg. Although she was willing to attend, when Hitler found out that Eva had been invited to the occasion, he summoned Emmy's husband to a 2 A.M. meeting to inform the *Reichsmarschall* that Eva would not attend, explaining that she was "so embarrassed and frightened" of Emmy. When Emmy had some dental work done in the Berghof dental clinic, Eva, sight unseen, carefully laid out towels, soap, etc. for Emmy's use. When Emmy requested that she be allowed to meet Eva to thank her for this thoughtfulness, Adolf said no.[62]

Britain's Special Operations Executive did know about Hitler and Eva. In a report compiled in late 1944, it provided a description of Hitler's "secretary": "Age about 24; brunette, attractive and unconventional in her costume, sometimes wearing Bavarian leather shorts.... Unapproachable, no make-up (Hitler, it appears, cannot tolerate the use of cosmetics)." The report observed that although Eva spent a great deal of time with the Führer at the Berghof, "relations with Hitler now appear to be of a platonic nature."[63]

Eva's younger sister, Gretl, was almost always with her, either at the Berghof or at Eva's house in Munich. According to Karl Brandt, Gretl served Eva "almost like her personal maid." He said Gretl was "generous and good-natured, but was far too easily influenced by others," probably referring to her reputation for sexual looseness. Hitler, who liked Gretl, "would often converse with her alone and enjoyed a certain 'mother-wit' which characterized her."[64]

Eva's friend Marion Schönemann provided, for a time, bracing conversation for the Führer. A lively and spirited Viennese actress, according to Brandt, "she never hesitated to criticize the shortcomings of any of the prominent Party leaders," particularly those in Vienna, which led to some "extremely heated" arguments with Hitler. After a while she stayed away from the Berghof when Hitler was there and he "did not ask for her presence."[65]

Ilse Braun, Eva's older sister, who rarely was in his company, was often critical of Hitler. As the war wore on, Ilse believed that Eva had become "arrogant, tyrannical and lacking in tact toward her family. Living with the great of this earth makes one selfish, even cruel." Ilse considered Eva to be imperious in her distribution of cast-offs from her huge wardrobe; moreover, she was stingy in providing Ilse with a handout of a mere ten marks a month. One change in Eva was that she had gone from being a non-political person to being outspoken in her support of Hitler's war. For her part, Eva informed Ilse that she would not ask Hitler for money for her family. As well, she forbade her sister to make caustic comments about Hitler's policies when she visited the Berghof, warning her, "If the Führer sends you to a concentration camp, I won't be the one to get you out." Had not Adolf allowed Ilse to move to the Berghof when she was driven out of her home in Breslau by the advancing Russians?[66]

Apparently after the assassination attempt, Getraud Weisker, one of Eva's cousins, joined her at the Berghof and remained there for the last six months of 1944. Security had been increased: "When we went out of the house, SS men walked behind us. We couldn't leave without them and we never knew whether they were listening in on our conversations." She found Eva to be compulsively trying to fill in empty time—changing her clothes five or six times a day, swimming, sports—"Things that don't matter."

Seeking outside information on the course of the war, Eva sent her cousin to the Eagle's Nest to listen to foreign radio broadcasts. The cousin was unaware that this was an act punishable by death. She claimed that the war news she relayed to Eva had a sobering effect on her. In early 1945 the cousins shifted to Eva's house in Munich, where they spent many hours in its basement shelter during air bombardments. On one of these occasions Eva gave her cousin some jewelry, commenting that she no longer had any need for it. "It was the moment," recalled the cousin, "when I knew she would go to Berlin and die with Hitler."[67]

Finding the Obersalzberg isolated and boring, Eva preferred to be in Munich, where in 1943, at the request of Hitler and in the name of war discipline, she nominally resumed her job in Heinrich Hoffman's photography studio. Her house there had a basement air raid shelter and an SS detachment next door. According to some girls in the neighborhood, "Eva was always taking something for some sort of pain." After every air raid on Munich, Hitler telephoned to inquire about her condition and he repeatedly requested that she permanently move to the Obersalzberg, but she liked the activity of the big city. Her life was an endless round of visits to friends, beauticians and dress-makers, spending a huge amount on clothing, theatres and restaurants. Anni Winter, Hitler's housekeeper in Munich, declared that during the long periods when she was on her own, Eva "threw one party after another. She invited all her young friends and she flirted terribly. She danced, she drank, she did all the things she was not permitted to do when Hitler was around." Frau Winter, herself, had a reputation for excessive drinking, and for excluding other residents from the Führer's air raid shelter in the basement.

As a war measure, all theatres were closed in late 1944, but a few months before the end of the war Eva "managed to reopen the Prinzregenten Theater in Munich so that she might be entertained," an act that "astounded not only the actors, but also the general public in the badly hit town." Despite this, Nerin Gun has estimated that in the nine-year period from 1936 to 1945 Eva spent two-thirds of her time on the Obersalzberg.[68]

Beginning around 1941, some people got the impression that Hitler would like to end the relationship with Eva. This was the view of Hebert Dohring. In 1943, with the tide of war turning against Germany, Hitler told Eva that, because he was worn down by care, "he could no longer satisfy her as a man." Not deterred, Eva urged Dr. Morell to give the Führer sexual booster shots. There is no record of his doing so. Frau Winter believed that if not for the war, "Hitler would have got rid of her somehow."[69]

When he was at the Berghof, Hitler observed his pledge not to see any general entertainment films while the war was on—with one exception. On a visit from Mussolini, a comedy was shown. Adolf recognized the need to cheer up Benito. Eva Braun regularly showed such movies in the basement skittle alley. She repeatedly tried to overcome Hitler's refusal to attend by arguing that he listened to music, and that film was also an art form. Moreover, no one would begrudge him the opportunity to watch a relaxing movie. Indeed, his presence at the showings would prevent staff members from taking official vehicles on nighttime sorties to the bars of Berchtesgaden.[70]

The security net on the Obersalzberg was tightened. Fences enclosing the area already had been installed in 1938. Two years later SS units were put on alert-readiness around the Berghof; yet, Hitler continued to walk at night along a lighted exposed walk-way beside the house. As well, local people continued to climb the fences to hunt deer. In May 1944, Bormann closed Berchtesgaden and the surrounding district from any further incursion by government and party agencies. In February 1945 this order was applied to "the families of leading Party and government dignitaries." An exercise to deal with a possible parachute assault was conducted in December 1944. In the period from January to April 1945 the U.S. 15th Air Force intelligence reported increased smoke defenses and flak weapons around Berchtesgaden.[71]

Hitler held his last military meeting on the Obersalzberg on 13 July 1944 where he delivered an address to about one hundred and sixty top SS officers selected to lead fifteen new divisions he proposed to create. In a loud oration audible to surrounding security employees, he exhorted this Nazi elite to renewed efforts. This was also his last major address. The effect of the assassination attempt a week later destroyed one of his greatest political assets— lengthy, emotional and emphatic public oration. At that time, he told General Jodl, "I would not trust myself to speak to ten thousand today. Nor would I trust myself to make a speech like that one I recently did on the Obersalzberg, because I might suddenly faint and collapse."[72]

On July 14, the day after his speech to the SS officers, Hitler was preparing to leave for his military headquarters in East Prussia. In the evening prior to leaving Hitler led two wives of staff members on a solemn tour of his collection of paintings and tapestries; when that was finished he bid the women not just good night but farewell. At this time Nicholaus von Below, his Luftwaffe adjutant, sensed that Hitler saw defeat looming ahead. Before leaving on the fourteenth, he told Eva Braun and the other two women that he had a premonition that shortly he would be in mortal danger. According to Christa Schröder, he gave Eva directions about what she should do if he died. When his convoy was about to leave, Hitler returned to the Berghof and stood alone looking out of the huge window in the great room. Just before driving off, he told one of the bystanders that he probably would not return. Bernhard Frank passes on this reported statement of Hitler: "Either I come back as the winner or I will not see the mountain again." Security was such that Frank did not know of Hitler's departure until the next day. While battle raged in Normandy, Göring was reported to have remained on the Obersalzberg, hunting in the hills, long after Hitler left.[73]

This was not the end of the presence of Nazi leaders on the Obersalzberg. Martin Bormann was there in December 1944 and March 1945. Göring was there in March 1945 and returned—with important consequences—that April.[74]

All during the war a group centered in the army plotted the overthrow of Hitler. Walter Schellenberg, a key member of the Reich security office, was approached in October 1942 by Karl Langbehn, a Berlin lawyer, and in March 1943 by Erna Hanfstängl, sister of Putzi Hanfstängl, former confidant of Hitler who had fled from Germany in 1934, with the same proposition. If the support of Heinrich Himmler and the leaders of the Wehrmacht could be secured, Hitler was to be evacuated by force to the Berghof to be relegated to the position of puppet head of state, while Himmler would direct the operations of government. Fräulein Hanfstängl's specific proposal was that Himmler would "forcibly abduct Hitler, with the aid of the Waffen SS to Obersalzberg, where the Führer was to be held secretly under SS detention though ostensibly and outwardly still in control of the reins of Government." Schellenberg later said he provided 500,000 marks to further the plan. Simultaneously with Hanfstängl's suggestion, Carl Gördeler attempted to gain the support of General Heinz Guderian for the plan to "intern" Hitler at his mountain retreat. Was the Obersalzberg Retirement Village an idea ahead of its time or a impractical fantasy? In fact, a proposal in May 1944 from the group that would attempt to kill Hitler two months later was received by the OSS, the American undercover organization, which included a massive airborne troop landing in Berlin and "the isolation in Obersalzberg of Hitler and high Nazi officials by trustworthy German units posted in the Munich region." At the end, in April

1945, Hitler suspected that certain of his inner military staff intended to do just that—drug him and cart him off to the Berg. Surrounded by totally loyal SS guards in the Führerbunker, known to some as the cement submarine, he declined to move to the better equipped and spacious shelters of the Wehrmacht and the *Luftwaffe* headquarters. Hitler had pledged that only death would force him to leave the seat of power, which to him specifically was the chancellery, and, as time was to show, he meant it.[75]

Hitler had nothing to fear from his immediate staff and security force: his attention to and consideration of their needs assured their complete loyalty. Even so, measures taken to protect Hitler proved to be inadequate. Claus von Stauffenberg, the leader of the army plot, twice—on 6 and 11 July 1944—carried concealed (British-made) explosives to conferences at the Berghof, but for various reasons he did not set them off. Following Stauffenberg's assassination attempt of July 20 in East Prussia, Hitler was urged to recuperate for a week or two on the Obersalzberg, but he refused. He sent part of his scorched uniform to Eva Braun at the Berghof, telling her, "I hope to come back soon and so be able to rest, putting myself in your hands. I greatly need tranquility." But he did not go back, even when he became seriously ill in the autumn.

Before these developments he was always eager to head for the mountains; now he felt, probably rightly, that if he were absent from the center of operations he would no longer be in control and new plots would emerge. The war situation continued to deteriorate. He argued that his presence in East Prussia reassured the people there and bolstered troop morale. Moreover, if he went to the Berghof his staff "would get their wives along," word of which would have had a "disastrous" effect on the German people. Indeed, if he went there, people would think he had given up his political and military leadership. However, given the total control of the media and tight security, very few people would have known that he was away from his East Prussia headquarters for a short period. Berlin was also out of the question, he said, because the Allies would soon learn of his presence there and this would result in increased bombing.[76]

Based on "usually reliable Vatican informants," in February 1945 there was a report that since the assassination attempt Hitler had been sequestered in a monastery outside Salzburg. Three Jesuit priests related that Hitler had "a large wound on the left side of his scalp" and was in a "dreamy and apathetic" state of mind. Moreover, he had refused to go to the Obersalzberg "because of morbid fear that the Allies would send agents to assassinate him despite great precautions taken to prevent any approach by unauthorized persons."[77]

## Alpenfestung

At the beginning of 1945, as Allied forces prepared to move into western Germany, their military leaders gave attention to several factors concerning continued German opposition. One was the purported Werwolf organization, designed to continue resistance behind enemy lines. There was also the German "super weapons" program, which had already produced the ballistic missile (V2 rocket) and jet plane. The German people were being told that other new weapons were on the way. Reports had been circulating since the fall of 1944 that Hitler and his Nazi war machine were preparing, if necessary, to retreat to the Alps and there to stage a final battle. Since the Allied powers would settle for nothing less than "unconditional surrender," Germany had to abandon any hope of a negotiated end to the conflict; from a Nazi perspective, there was no alternative but a fight to the finish. The myth of the "National Redoubt" was born. Until the very end of April 1945 debate continued about the truth of reports about an alpine bastion, in being or in formation.

The belief in this type of last-ditch fortress seems to have originated in the great underground complex that the Swiss, anticipating a German attack, had dug into the St. Gotthard massif just before the war and had extended to other areas in 1940–42. After the Italian defection in September 1943, German army engineers prepared a study of the possibility of fortifying the southern Alps. Heinrich Himmler, in May 1944, dispatched a team of geologists to survey the Alpine region for this purpose. This was linked to information that a huge underground network was being built into the Obersalzberg.[78]

These vague indications that the Nazis were considering creating an Alpine fortress began to be received by Allied intelligence as early as the fall of 1943. When a German journalist named von Knyphausen defected to the Allies in the summer of 1944, he carried stories that Hitler was planning a mountain stronghold that would support guerrilla warfare throughout Europe.[79]

With the defeat of the German armies in France after the Normandy invasion, top-level Allied speculation mounted about how the Nazi leadership would face defeat. A group of German émigrés within the Research and Analysis branch of the Office of Strategic Services came to the conclusion that the war would not end with a conventional capitulation, but, rather, would be sustained by some form of underground resistance. This judgment was based not on the scant evidence then available but on the belief that the tight control the Nazi regime had imposed on German institutions would make this possible and, based on Nazi ideology, would be the preferred Nazi response to conventional military defeat. Also, operating in an atmosphere of inadequate documentation, analysts within British intelligence came to a different conclusion. Noting the collapse of German cohesion at the end of the last European war, these British scholars believed the same thing would again happen.

The assumptions of the OSS study were accepted as the most likely scenario by the Joint Intelligence Committee of the U.S. Joint Chiefs of Staff in a report dated 9 August 1944. The probability that prolonged Nazi resistance would occur after conventional defeat was accepted by General William Donovan, the director of the OSS, in his report to the White House and the Joint Chiefs on September 2. On August 10 Richard Helms had distributed a report written by Emmy Rado speculating on Nazi post-war plans. It declared that, above all, "a legend will be built around" Hitler, who "lends himself so well to it—better even than Napoleon." As well, with a wealth of experience behind it, the "Nazi Secret Police," "adept at dealing with illegal warfare in all its phases," would be actively involved. It was likely that some lesser-known Nazis would be smuggled "into neutral countries where funds for continued Nazi operations have already been deposited." The report focused on what kind of people would take part in this operation. They included those who "have grown wealthy and powerful through the Nazi Party"; sincere, particularly young, Nazis; recently-promoted minor officeholders in party and state; feckless young officers; irredentists from lost German territories; Nazi women, who "are fanatically devoted to the cause"; physicists and scientists who were grateful for the opportunities provided by the Nazi state; and, finally, medical doctors, who "have been placed about strategically in hospitals and insane asylums," these facilities being "excellent hiding places for illegal workers."

Public speculation about the matter arose when J.F.C. Fuller, the well-known British military historian, in an article in *Newsweek* argued that the Nazi leadership intended to persevere whatever the outcome of the war. On 25 October 1944 Donovan sent President

Roosevelt a report "from our representative in Bern concerning the efforts of the Nazis to prepare their people for a fight to the finish."[80]

The likelihood of sustained but unconventional German resistance was proclaimed by George Axelsson in the *New York Times Magazine* shortly after the assassination attempt on Hitler in July 1944. Axelsson wrote, "It was not so long ago that the Nazis began teaching the peasants and other provincials partisan tactics." The over-all strategic plan, he asserted, was to sustain resistance "long after it has become impossible to maintain an unbroken front.... Ultimately this will lead to guerrilla warfare in the mountain forests of Germany."[81]

The specific source of origin of the concept of a "National Redoubt" in the Alps probably began with a report from an unnamed American diplomat in Switzerland who, in September 1944, reported to the State Department that its probability "was being discussed very energetically" by Swiss and U.S. representatives. He declared that if such a fortress were constructed, it would prolong the war by six to eight months and cause greater U.S. casualties than all losses up to that point. Moreover, the redoubt would act as a rallying point for Nazi adherents, with the result being that "all Germany will be subjected to an endless and self-propagated stream of sabotage and other forms of resistance on the part of some activists, while others will find ways and means to get through to their comrades in the 'Alpen-Reduit,' and thus reinforce it day by day."

This is the version of Franz Hofer, gauleiter of the Tyrol, who was given a copy of the intercepted report by Hans Gontard, the SD officer in charge at the border town of Bregenz. The report was part of rumors about a redoubt "which started abroad," Hofer recalled, "before any German government or military official had even thought of such a thing." Thus began what he called the "Redoubt psychosis."[82]

Once German military intelligence discovered Allied, particularly OSS, interest in the story of a final mountain stronghold, it began feeding reports to agents, and double-agents, about ambitious plans for a Wagnerian show-down. This is the same approach it took concerning the Werwolf story. Both yarns were designed to force Western Allied leaders to contemplate extended German resistance. This, hopefully, would have the effect of modifying the Allied demand for unconditional surrender. Until the very end, when some effort was made to make the National Redoubt a reality, German propaganda agencies carried on a deception process, which substantially deceived its opponents.[83]

The probability of a final stand became a staple of American journalism from November 1944 into the new year. Concern about this was undoubtedly stimulated by the unexpected German offensive in the Ardennes that December—perhaps Hitler had further surprises in store. The apogee of this newspaper story was reached in Harry Vosser's article "Hitler's Hideaway," which appeared in the *New York Times* magazine section of 12 November 1944. Vosser claimed that the entire area around Berchtesgaden was mined and could be ignited from a central location in the Berghof bunker. But there was more, much more. Supposedly, a massive fortress had been blasted into the Untersberg, a couple of miles from the Berghof across the Austrian line. Underground facilities were fully equipped. "Nothing has been spared to make the area impregnable."

Journalistic interest in the matter continued until the end of the war. On 11 February 1945, also in the *Times* magazine, Victor Schiff speculated that Alpine-based resistance could extend the war for another year. Following defeat and surrender of German forces elsewhere, "SS formations are likely to retreat swiftly southward to a region already selected as the last theatre of operations in Europe." As war criminals with nothing to lose, "practically all the upper stratum of the Nazi leadership is likely to follow Hitler and Himmler into the mountains." Although he noted the difficulties of supplying the area, "It would be comparatively easy to defend this 'fortress' for a very long time with some twenty divisions, perhaps much less, behind the formidable barrier of the gigantic chain of the central and eastern Alps."

The April 2 issue of *Newsweek* declared that "week by week it has become more likely that the Nazis will be able to carry out their plan for making a last-ditch stand in the south." It cited reports that fully-equipped SS divisions were "being withdrawn from the fighting lines and presumably transferred to the southern fastness." With strong fortifications in place and masses of food, arms and supplies being sent to the area, there was "plenty of evidence" about the Nazi project: "The conversion of the very center of Europe into a sort of vast inner core, where large armies can be deployed, fed and supplied."[84]

The London *Times* remained deeply concerned about the possible Alpenfestung until the end of April. On April 24 it reported that it was difficult to know what preparations had been made there, but "considerable movement" into it "has been observed for some time ... presumably of none but idolatrous Nazis and as a military objective the national redoubt has now far greater implications than the ashes of Berlin." Thus, "The 'Götterdämmerung' phase has begun." Two days later its military correspondent declared that there was "no doubt of the German intention to resist in the mountains; the only question is the ability." The position was not clear: "If it was a vast, entrenched camp, under which aspect it is often contemplated, then it is an improbability, though it might suit the allies better than its reality."

The U.S. Army newspaper *Stars and Stripes* also assumed the Alpine redoubt was a reality. On April 4 it printed a United Press report with the alarming opening, "Adolf Hitler has almost completed his 'laboratory test tube' in which he hopes the germ of national socialism can be preserved after the end of the war, emerging in the future as strong as ever to conquer the world." Based on articles in Swiss newspapers, it reported, "Virtually impassible mountains have been turned into a system of pillboxes and anti-aircraft positions, connected with caverns and salt mine shafts which have been enlarged to supply depots." This and similar accounts came from informants in Switzerland and Sweden. There was no need for alarm: the Allies with their thousands of underemployed mountain troops and their new eleven-ton bomb could deal with the threat. On April 27, the *Stars and Stripes* declared that "the battle for Germany has now become the battle for the Redoubt."

In the spring of 1945 an Allied intelligence report declared that there were twice as many German divisions in the south as in the north. Air intelligence reported considerable military activity in the mountains, including construction of bunkers and increased anti-aircraft protection, but there did not seem to be a uniform plan behind the effort; rather, there were separate defenses for various parts of the region.[85]

The armchair warriors in Washington felt that the threat of an Alpenfestung was not being considered seriously by those conducting the Allied war effort. On February 15 the War Department issued an assessment: "Not enough weight is given the many reports of the probable Nazi last stand in the Bavarian Alps.... The Nazi myth, which is important when you are dealing with men like Hitler, requires a *Götterdämmerung*. It may be significant that Berchtesgaden itself, which would be the headquarters, is on the site of the tomb of Barbarossa who, in German mythology, is supposed to return from the dead."[86]

After the 20 February 1945 minor air attack on Berchtesgaden, a report in the *New York Times* two days later declared, "The town itself would be of real importance as an air target only if it were being used by the Nazis in building up the inner Bavarian citadel for prolonging the war. It has been among the spots mentioned in foreign reports as a possible last-ditch refuge for top-flight Nazis after Berlin falls." Editorially, it saw the broader air operation as having great significance: American planes had "penetrated through what is perhaps the most formidable anti-aircraft defense in the world." Its message was clear: "Berchtesgaden is Hitler's last hide-out, where he is likely to make his last stand, and the attack on it is a demonstration that even this last sanctuary is no longer safe for him."

Much of the evidence about the possibility of a mountain fortress was episodic and vague. On March 3 the OSS supplied the Joint Chiefs with a report from its Bern representative that at a meeting on 20 February Hitler opposed the evacuation of Berlin and that he had developed a plan "to create a Stalingrad in reverse against the Soviets when they reach the northern suburbs." Although Hitler expected that "this counterblow will meet with great success," his military staff advised him that "there are insufficient German troops to keep the Soviets out of Berlin once the Oder Line has been breached." In addition, they warned that they expected the Russians to by-pass the city and drive southwards towards the industrial areas of Saxony.

Just eight days later SHAEF intelligence reported a major development: "The main trend of German defense policy does seem directed primarily to the safeguarding of the Alpine Zone. This area is, by the very nature of the terrain, practically impenetrable.... The evidence indicates that considerable numbers of SS and specially chosen units are being systematically withdrawn to Austria." Moreover, "Some of the most important ministries and personalities of the Nazi regime are already established in the Redoubt area." It emphasized the full magnitude of the matter: "Here, defended by nature and by the most efficient secret weapons yet invented, the powers that have hitherto guided Germany will survive to reorganize her resurrection; here armaments will be manufactured in bomb-proof factories, food and equipment will be stored in vast underground caverns and a specially selected corps of young men will be trained in guerrilla warfare, so that a whole underground army can be fitted and directed to liberate Germany from occupying forces."

This alarming estimate was followed by that of the intelligence chief of the Seventh Army on March 25, who saw the possibility of a redoubt of "an elite force, predominantly SS and mountain troops, of between 200,000 and 300,000 men. This veteran force ... would be well-equipped, trained for mountain warfare and thoroughly imbued with the Nazi spirit." Supplies were pouring into the area, with "three to five very long trains ... each week." New weapons were being produced from underground factories, and more. It concluded: "The Nazi elements which control Germany have the will and imperative need to continue to resist." In addition, "The German army and people, incapable of disobedience, will follow Nazi orders."[87]

The OSS, primarily an intelligence organization, provided further evidence. At the end of March it reported that "the entire SS-Führer Division was transferred to the Obersalzberg area at the beginning of March 1945. It is believed that eventually the Redoubt will hold 15–25 divisions composed chiefly of SS Storm Troop detachments, Hitlerjugend and the special OKW Führer Reserve created for service in the Redoubt."[88]

Allen Dulles, the much-heralded OSS head agent in Bern, Switzerland, having failed to anticipate the German offensive in December 1944, sent a series of reports to Washington on the likelihood of an Alpine stronghold. Although he remained cautious about the matter, the information he transmitted indicated that the redoubt was taking shape and an effort at final resistance would occur. On 18 January 1945 he declared, "This idea of a defense in a mountain fortress is in line with the Wagnerian complex of the whole National Socialist movement and the fanaticism of the Nazi youth. Hitler and his small band of brigands, who started in the beer-halls of Munich, may find their end not far away in the Bavarian Alps, after having laid most of Europe in ruins." Four days later he reported, "The information we get here locally seems to tend more and more to the theory of a final Nazi withdrawal into the Austrian and Bavarian Alps.... This seems more likely than a dramatic attempt on the part of Hitler and the present Nazi leaders to escape by submarine or other modes of flight."

By mid–March he saw particular significance in the fact that German forces were concentrated in western Hungary and around Vienna, which he believed was evidence of a Nazi attempt to maintain an underground organization after the military collapse and that such an organization would be based in the Alps. To the end, with only a bit of wavering, Dulles persisted in his belief that all would culminate in the Alpine fortress.[89]

The OSS operation kept busy. On 16 February 1945 it transmitted to Washington an alarming assessment of the situation culled from the views of neutral military attaches in Berlin: "The Nazis are undoubtedly preparing for a bitter fight from the mountain redoubt.... Strongpoints are connected by underground railroads" and "several months' output of the best munitions have been reserved and almost all of Germany's poison gas supplies. Everybody who participated in the construction of the secret installations will be killed off."[90]

Charles de Gaulle, provisional president of France, also saw the possibility and danger of sustained Nazi resistance in the Alps. The restoration of French political legitimacy and economic recovery required a speedy end to the war. In his memoirs, General de Gaulle recalled the situation. He, too, had been receiving accounts that the Nazis were assembling huge amounts of material in the Alps. There were reports that "they were concentrating the mass of prisoners, deported men and forced labor in the interior of this fortress." De Gaulle mused that "it was not inconceivable that the Führer would attempt here a supreme strategic and political maneuver." Sustained resistance would mean that the Allied powers would no longer be separated but would be "side by side on the same terrain, to inflict upon each other all the friction inherent in such a contiguity." Soviet domination in eastern Europe, British actions in the Middle East and American intervention in Asian countries, together with the resulting delay of reconstruction in western Europe, could drive the continent into political and social revolution. "Universal chaos," De Gaulle believed, "would therefore be Hitler's last chance or at least his supreme vengeance." The stakes were as high as they could be.[91]

Winston Churchill was also concerned about this possibility. In mid–March 1945, noting Hitler's "strange resistance" at Budapest, an abortive offensive at Lake Balaton, also in Hungary, plus the appointment of Field Marshal Kesselring, master of defensive warfare in Italy, as head of German forces in the south after the Allies had split Germany in half, he speculated that Hitler might be planning to center remaining German strength in the southern mountains. On 17 March Churchill requested an assessment of the situation from the intelligence committee of his chiefs of staff. He was told that a prolonged German campaign in the Alps "was unlikely on any serious scale." Nevertheless, on 21 March he cabled Joseph Stalin, saying, "It looks to me as if Hitler will try to prolong the war ... by a death struggle in southern Germany and Austria." Alarmed by Soviet actions, Churchill was now adamant that the western Allies drive as deep into central Europe as they could; he particularly wanted them to get to Prague.[92]

In a report on 10 April the SHAEF Joint Intelligence Committee sized up the situation. It declared that "there is no evidence to show that the strategy of the German High

Command is being conducted with a view to occupying eventually the so-called National Redoubt." With the probability that the Allies soon would split the German army in two parts, however, "[t]here would be a natural trend in enemy operations to withdraw part of their forces southwards" to the Alps; these would be joined by "selected remnants" of German forces from the west, east and south. Lack of natural resources would prevent extended resistance.

On the other hand, it noted that "there is evidence that preparations have been made within the Redoubt area to house German ministries." It was aware of "numerous reports" of preparation of a fortified area in the Alps and speculated on what would be the objects of the redoubt if it did come into being. These including dragging the war through another winter campaign, fostering disruption of Allied occupation of Germany, creating the myth of "a legend that Nazism, the symbol of Germany, never surrendered," and, finally, playing for time, in the hope that the Allies would come into conflict (this last being a firm belief of the Führer). If Hitler did initiate such a plan, "The garrison must consist of the war criminals, Gestapo and SS under 30 years of age; in fact, the cream of the remaining manpower." A relatively small force of 150,000 elite men would be "capable of putting up an energetic defense in extremely difficult terrain. This would permit the flying in of leaders and others to the area." The committee recommended that strenuous efforts be taken to prevent this from happening.

Another indication that the Nazi government intended to continue even after the fall of Berlin was revealed when Hitler ordered all but a skeleton representation of foreign diplomats to be evacuated on 13 February. At that time Foreign Minister Ribbentrop told the Japanese ambassador that "it was planned to transfer the German High Command and government to the south after they had watched developments a little longer." The destination of the displaced diplomats was Bad Gastein, a mountain resort forty road miles east of Berchtesgaden in Austria. Intercepting the ambassador's report to Tokyo, having long before broke the Japanese diplomatic code through the Magic system, U.S. intelligence evaluators commented, "it seems unlikely that Bad Gastein would have been picked for the diplomatic corps if the Government were not planning to settle in the same general area."[93]

Bernhard Frank, SS commander for the Obersalzberg area, has stressed that the compound never was a fortress. The only weapons installed on the Obersalzberg were flak guns, which could not be positioned to resist ground attacks. He argued that to prepare strong points, trenches and the other means of ground resistance would have been looked upon as "defeatism." Furthermore, if it was made into a fortress, then obviously everything else already would have been lost. By the end of 1944, most able soldiers had been transferred to combat units from there, with fifteen- and sixteen-year-old boys manning the flak guns, while girls from the Nazi women's organization took over operation of the smoke machines.[94]

Having advocated the development of an Alpine fortress since mid–1944, Franz Hofer, gauleiter of the Tyrol, noted the attention given to the threat from Allied forces advancing from the south—through Italy. In a report to Hitler on 6 November 1944, he proposed the creation of a full-fledged Alpine fortress, including construction of defenses on the northern side of the mountains. All non-combat personnel, including those in official bureaus as well as various categories of fugitives, would be excluded from the area, but 30,000 Allied prisoners would be brought in, obviously as hostages. Conquest of the mountain stronghold would be enormously costly in Allied casualties and might extend German resistance for as much as two years. At the time of Hofer's proposal, however, Hitler was fully occupied with plans for attack, not defense.[95]

Even without Hitler's command to do so, there were indications that such a battlement was in the works. In the first two months of 1945 a large number of refugees of eastern European governments that were allied with Germany were housed in the Alps, at Altaussee, Austria, about sixty road miles east of Berchtesgaden. They were joined by a variety of German civil servants and Nazi Party officials. Soon the SS would establish its final headquarters at nearby Fischhorn, where it already had a horse farm. August Eigruber, the gauleiter of Upper Austria or Oberdonau, sought to make the Altaussee area the center of the proposed Alpine bastion. Through at least mid–April Eigruber made a series of fiery radio addresses in which he claimed that his area "will stand to the last man"; one listener observed, "In his rhetorics he copies Adolf." Eigruber remained at his *Gau* until the very end—May 8—in the expectation that Hitler's private papers would arrive at Altaussee, where he intended to secret them in a local salt mine. What the mine did contain was a large collection of confiscated works of art. The anticipation that this locality would play an important role in the final stand in the mountains by the Nazis may explain the presence in the area of Ernst Kaltenbrunner, second only to Himmler in the SS, in the last few weeks of the Third Reich.[96]

Hofer's repeated requests for a response to his proposal to create an Alpine fortress were ignored by Martin Bormann until March 1945, by which time the military situation had changed drastically. By then, the Wehrmacht (and, apparently, the RSHA, the Reich security and intelligence organization) sent Hitler a similar report, whereupon Bormann gave Hitler the Hofer proposal. As a result Hofer spent two days—April 11 and 12—meeting with Hitler and other leaders. On April 20—with the Third Reich practically on its death bed—Hitler agreed to the creation of an Alpine fortress and a directive was issued to that effect four days later. The directive, which would create "a last bastion of fanatical resistance," ordered the closure of the area to civilians, provision for accommodation of American, French and British hostage POWs, stockpiling of supplies and construction of emergency munitions factories, and employing disbanded soldiers for the work. Hofer was appointed Reich Defense Commissar for the Alpine front, while General Winter, in military command of the area, began an effort to throw together a defense organization with the appointment of General Jaschko to direct the northern approaches.[97]

Field Marshal Albert Kesselring promptly reviewed the situation in the Alps when he took command of all German forces in the south at the end of April. The southern rim, facing Italy, had been fortified, but "in the north and facing northeast there were no fortifications, nor by April 20 had any been begun. Nor were there any troops permanently stationed there." What was happening was that military staff and sundered troop detachments "from all four points of the compass" were flooding into the redoubt area, creating food and accommodation shortages. A Bavarian petrol-station attendant observed the influx: "I never knew there were so many staffs and so few fighting troops. No troops have come through, but staffs! Talk about staffs!" He observed an officer enter a telephone booth to change from his uniform, after which the officer enquired about where he could get his license plate repainted from its army designation. Moreover, the attendant declared that "fancy" army and SS uniforms could be seen hanging from trees all along the road. A source of puzzlement to him was that many of the parade of vehicles contained pretty young women but no children. When a German captain was asked in Siegsdorf why troops were not manning anti-tank obstacles, he replied, "Staffs, but no troops. Plenty of staffs and not a single fighting man." What Bavarians satirically called the "northern invasion" continued apace.[98]

Even if there was not a prepared position, the German military might yet have thrown one together, thus prolonging the war. Caution required that this, at least, be prevented. British Major General Kenneth Strong, the SHAEF intelligence chief, stated this case: "The redoubt may not be there, but we have to take steps to prevent it being there"—the German surprise offensive at the Ardennes was fresh in his mind. He noted that reports of intensive defensive preparations "were confused and unconvincing." Moreover, air reconnaissance did not reveal extensive activity. Indeed, Strong declared, Allied propaganda helped to stimulate belief in the fortress, inasmuch as the message it projected to the German people was that the Nazi elite was preparing a safe hideout for itself while ordinary troops were being left to die at the front.

No high-ranking German officer captured at this time confirmed the existence of such a fortress; all of them said they had never heard of it before late April. SS General Friedrich von Eberstein declared that the first he had heard of preparations for such a stronghold was in mid–April. "Prior to that nothing had been said about the Alpine Redoubt, not even officially," he asserted. "No one believed in the Redoubt any longer as Hitler remained in Berlin." Ludwig Muhe, a police official in southern Bavaria, recalled that before mid–April, "I received no official information as to the planned establishment of a 'national mountain-position.'" He did make inquiries: "It was only from private sources that I repeatedly heard the word 'Alpine fortification' mentioned; however, I was not able to obtain any explanation as to its meaning." The commander of a mountain troop division surely would have had prompt orders about the planned *Festung*, but one of these, August Marcinkiewicz, heard nothing about it. In his opinion, the matter of the fortress was all propaganda designed "to bolster up once more the rapidly sinking fighting will of the nation and its armed forces." He concluded that "no real attempt was, in fact, ever made actually to realize the conception of the 'Alpenfestung.'"

Another German general said that the people of the area, rather than supporting further resistance, would be concerned with spring planting "to prevent starvation in the coming winter." According to a security police report in February, for most people in Berchtesgaden the fiery Hitler proclamation in observance of the twenty-fifth anniversary of the formulation of the Nazi Party program "whistled by like the wind in the empty boughs."[99]

Given the torrent of claims by Goebbels and other German propagandists concerning a fight to the death, Allied intelligence logically assumed that Nazi diehards would organize a last ditch stand somewhere, and where better than in the mountain range encompassing southern Bavaria, western Austria and northern Italy—an area of 20,000 square miles. Had not Hitler made the Obersalzberg his home? Surely he had some final dramatic gesture in mind. He saw himself and his movement as being of world historical importance. With Wagner as his favorite composer, why not a *Götterdämmerung* in the Alps? Allied intelligence knew of the underground bunkers that had been built there. As well, large underground factories to produce the super weapons had been constructed in the southern mountains. In February and March 1945 aerial observation revealed seventy places where underground construction was underway. In March, Ultra, the British intelligence organization, decoded a report that the German military headquarters would withdraw to the Alps.

By early April a stream of German military and political leaders was heading south. Among others in the mountains were the leaders of the German rocket program, collaborators such as King Leopold of Belgium and Marshal Pétain of France, and important political hostages. At that time a former League of Nations official reported that "hundreds of thousands of foreign prisoners are on a forced trek towards Bavaria, to be used by Hitler as a human bulwark against Allied guns and bombs in a showdown fight." The mass transfer of a quarter million American and British servicemen (almost 94,000 Americans) had been underway since late 1944 as the Russians drove in from the east. There was mounting concern in the Allied high command that as total defeat confronted Hitler and his cohort a massacre of p.o.w.s would take place, which was joined to another fear that many of them would become hostages within the national redoubt; that was the general belief of the ragged and hungry prisoners who plodded their way south. The Moosburg camp near Munich was overflowing with 80,000 prisoners.[100]

A spasm of fear undoubtedly went down the backbone of some Allied leaders when a report circulated that commando extraordinaire Otto Skorzeny would direct the resistance in the reputed Alpine fortress. Skorzeny had earlier driven Eisenhower into seclusion and forced him to use a double during the Ardennes offensive. In reaction, thousands of wanted posters were distributed in the quest for Skorzeny's capture. There was no mistaking his importance: "This man is extremely clever and very dangerous. He may be in American or British uniform or civilian clothes." As shall be seen, Skorzeny did not lead the Alpine resistance, but he certainly worked to make it a reality.[101]

The OSS belatedly had organized parties of agents to be dropped into Germany, but terrible weather in the winter of 1944–45 delayed most operations. Only a dozen three- and four-man teams had been dispatched by March 1945, with thirty more waiting for better weather. There was also a large formation in waiting—the "Iron Cross" mountain infantry company, originally composed of 175 German anti–Nazis led by Capt. Aaron Blank, which, posing as a Wehrmacht unit, would parachute into an area between Kufstein and Innsbruck, along the main supply route to Italy and about a hundred miles by road from Berchtesgaden. Their mission was to conduct sabotage, induce defections and capture leading Nazis moving into the area. By mid–April, with the growing story of the redoubt in mind, emphasis was shifted to capturing Nazi leaders, including, if possible, Hitler. The unit was trained in storming buildings and extracting persons from armed vehicles. "Wild Bill" Donovan, the head of the OSS, told the unit commander to "get Hitler" alive. Then, at the end of April the operation was canceled. The reason for this was the war was just about over and almost all of the members of the unit were Communists or Communist sympathizers, many of them veterans of the Spanish civil war. Problems could arise if a hundred men of this political persuasion were let loose in an area about to be occupied by U.S. forces.[102]

Looking back on the situation forty years later, William Casey, who was appointed head of OSS Operations in 1944, said of the redoubt myth, "We were unable to explode it and we should have, easily." He noted that his organization had a dozen teams in the area, none of which reported "anything justifying belief that enough military strength could be generated in that pastoral, underdeveloped country to resist five million Allied troops for more than a few weeks." Most of the agents Casey refers to were parachuted into the Austrian Alps around Innsbruck about a month before the end of the war; their principal activity was to elude the pursuing German security forces. None of these was dropped in the area around Berchtesgaden, but this undoubtedly was due to the assumption that that area would have maximum security. Furthermore, few of the members of the thirty-eight "successful missions" in 1945 had any means to communicate to OSS headquarters elsewhere. In his definitive study of the OSS, Christof Muauch has declared "much of the reported success of these operations is a myth."

In September 1944, the OSS Research and Analysis Branch had issued a report on the various resources available to the Nazis in southern Germany; the report demonstrated that there could be no sustained Alpine resistance, but this did not register with unit intelligence officers who were preoccupied with ongoing operations. The problem, Casey concluded, was that the U.S. Army had failed to develop a central organization to coordinate and evaluate all kinds of intelligence. The situation was that "we had the resources to marshal facts into coherent analysis but we found no one who would listen." Research and Analysis also conducted an exhaustive study of the possibility of a Alpine last stand, concluding on 20 March 1945 that this did not exist. No one bothered with that report either. R & A had developed a reputation as being a coterie of distinguished professors who viewed the task of basic research as being beneath their professional eminence.[103]

The British Special Operations Executive also had little success in dropping agents in Austria at the end of the war. In October 1944 an attempt was made to establish a safe route to and "encourage resistance" in Salzburg. This was Operation Seafront, which went astray when its agents were dropped in Germany by mistake. Salzburg also was the objective of Operation Duval in February 1945, with the goals of contacting an underground organization and assisting in sabotage, but the party was captured. In Operation Greenleaves, one group managed to parachute into the Klagenfurt area of southern Austria on 2 April 1945, but when its documents and photographs were captured, it was withdrawn to Bari in Italy. Operation Hamster, staged in the same area and initiated on 21 April 1945, claimed to have armed small resistance groups and stimulated attacks on road and rail transport. These operations of the OSS and SOE stayed far away from Berchtesgaden Land and would appear to have had little more than nuisance value.[104]

If Hitler and the German high command were serious about building up a strong Alpine fortress, surely the much-vaunted Ultra decoding organization would have picked up indications of such intentions. There have been various claims that Ultra provided Allied leaders with all kinds of important information about German preparations and actions, but this operation did not produce any clear evidence that a "National Redoubt" was being prepared. What Ultra did provide were fragmentary indications that the head offices of many German government departments and military organizations were leaving Berlin in April, with many of them heading to the southern mountains, hardly top-secret activity, which would have been known to many people in Berlin.[105]

The takeover of the Abwehr intelligence organization by the Nazi-controlled RSHA in February 1944 greatly reduced the volume of communications that Ultra could decipher. The code machine used by the RSHA could not be penetrated by Ultra analysts. Thus, Allied intelligence lost a major source of information and made the matter of continued German resistance all the more difficult to determine.[106]

Omar Bradley later said that both the rapidity of the Russian advance on Berlin, and Ultra indications that the German organizations were heading south, were the determining factors in Eisenhower's decision to direct a central thrust into Germany rather than to drive towards Berlin. Bradley was perhaps the most persistent believer that the Nazis would stage a "heroic" finale in the Alps. Honest man that he was, he recorded in his memoirs, "Both Ike and I were early converts to the 'redoubt' myth"; moreover, he said, "Concern over the Alpine redoubt had a decisive impact on my thinking and planning." Based on this belief, he was determined to direct his forces into the center of Germany to link up with the Russians and prevent "a further migration of German military and civilian agencies to the southern Alpine areas." As late as April 29 he remained convinced that the redoubt was a reality and, as a result, "we may be fighting one month from now and it may even be a year."

This kind of speculation was not reserved to the high command. Sherman Pratt, a lieutenant in the 3rd Infantry Division, recalled that as early as March among many soldiers there was "disquieting talk that Hitler might withdraw his remaining forces into the Bavarian Alps to a mountainous retreat and delay for many months the end of the war." He noted that in April *The Stars and Stripes* printed a map of the area labeled "Supposed Mountain Redoubt." Already German soldiers had demonstrated an excellent capacity for mountain warfare in Italy. In the Alps they would be fighting on home ground, a much more physically intimidating environment to their enemies.[107]

Bradley admitted "chagrin" when he learned that the fortress idea was a fraud. Looking back on the Alpine caper, he commented, "It grew into so exaggerated a scheme that I am astonished we could have believed it as innocently as we did. But while it persisted, this legend of the Redoubt was too ominous a threat to be ignored and in consequence it shaped our tactical thinking during the closing weeks of the war." He misjudged German intentions in the Ardennes and the reality of the redoubt, but, despite these failures, he successfully directed his army group to victorious results.[108]

By late March, Eisenhower and his staff had come to the conclusion that whatever was Hitler's final destination, the rest of the German government and military would operate out of Berchtesgadener Land: "The evidence was clear that the Nazis intended to make the attempt" to create a mountain stronghold in the Alps. One of his principal objectives, he said, was to prevent "the consolidation of German resistance in [a] Redoubt in southern Germany." In his war memoir, he modified his belief in the redoubt: "The strong possibility still existed that fanatical Nazis would attempt to establish themselves in the National Redoubt, and the early overrunning of that area remained important to us."[109]

Without conferring with his British counterparts, Eisenhower sent a message to Joseph Stalin that the western Allied armies would not head for Berlin, but rather drive into central and southern Germany. The message was delivered to the Soviet leader by the U.S. and British ambassadors on March 31. Obviously relieved that Berlin would be left to his forces, Stalin warmly endorsed Eisenhower's plan, declaring that it would achieve the important objective of dividing Germany in half; moreover, "He felt that the Germans' last stand would probably be in the mountains of western Czechoslovakia and Bavaria." While directing the bulk of Russian military might toward the German capital, in his reply to Eisenhower on April 1 Stalin declared that Berlin had "lost its former strategic importance" and that his forces would be concentrated in the south. Probably through an intelligence intercept, Hitler believed that was what the Russians would do. There was a vital need to retain control of Germany's last source of oil. Confident that the bulwark on the Oder river, forty miles east of Berlin, would hold, he sent half his remaining armored forces (the Sixth Panzer Army) to the south to deal with the continuing Russian advances, not to shield any Alpine redoubt.[110]

A further conclusion Eisenhower reached at this time was that an extensive Nazi underground network was probably in existence and, with the same certainty, was linked to the southern mountain fastness. This determination clearly was stimulated by an OSS report of 23 March 1945 that Bill Donovan believed demonstrated the emergence of such an organization. George Marshall cabled Eisenhower with a request for a public statement about this likelihood. Eisenhower responded with a letter to President Roosevelt (printed in *Stars and Stripes*, among other places) on April 5, in which he declared it probable that "there never will be a clearcut military surrender of enemy forces." If this proved to be the case, "it would mean that eventually all areas in which fragments of the German army, particularly paratroop, panzer and SS elements, may be located will have to be taken by application of or threat of force." This situation in turn "would lead into a form of guerrilla warfare which would require for its suppression a large number of troops."[111]

Three days later, Ike told Harry Butcher, his navy (and public relations) aide, that the need to drive south was based on the fear that "if Hitler and his small group of Nazi leaders could hole up in [and] around Berchtesgaden" they could use radio to urge the remaining pockets of German military, in the Netherlands and Norway, to fight on, thus delaying the end of the war. This view was shared by Walter Bedell Smith, Eisenhower's chief of staff, who, speaking off the record to a group of journalists on April 21, declared, "As long as Hitler or any of his representatives are standing on a rock around Salzburg, proclaiming they are free Germans and broadcasting to all isolated fortress areas holding out that everything is going to come out all right, they are going to hold out." Smith concluded, "We may find that when we have cut off the head from the snake the tail won't wiggle very long." Indeed, the Nazi government had dispatched equipment for two radio stations to the Alpine area.[112]

On April 14, Eisenhower informed the Combined Chiefs of Staff that if the Allied forces continued their rapid advance into the center of Germany, there was the danger of exposed flanks: "The two main areas where the enemy could offer prolonged resistance are in Norway and in the National Redoubt in the south. In the National Redoubt winter operations would be most laborious—in Norway they would be almost impracticable." The drive to join forces with the Russians in the Danube Valley would greatly reduce German resistance in the south, "but even then the National Redoubt could remain in being and it must be our aim to break into it rapidly before the enemy has an opportunity to man it and fully organize its defenses." Therefore he would "stop on the Elbe and clean up my flanks." Movement towards Berlin "must take a low priority in point of time unless operations to clear our flanks proceed with unexpected rapidity."[113]

The War Department in Washington saw the situation somewhat differently. As early as the end of March, it had concluded that there was no National Redoubt to worry about. On April 2 Army Chief of Staff George C. Marshall delivered a report to President Roosevelt which concluded that the many accounts about such a possibility "lack substance." Indeed, "No reliable information has reached the War Department of unduly large storage of supplies in the 'redoubt area' and there are no indications that any fortifications are being constructed in Bavaria or Austria to prevent Allied ingress into the 'redoubt area' from the north." The report also speculated on the fate of the Führer: "If Hitler is true to the character he has shown in past crises, he will make his exit bravely and dramatically and thus remain a psychological force for his enemies to reckon with for decades." Surely, the position of the War Department on the redoubt was communicated to Eisenhower and the other Allied leaders.[114]

SHAEF issued its final, but muted, assessment of the matter on April 16; it declared: "Although real information does not establish in a certain fashion the intention to organize a final resistance in the Alpine redoubt, it is sufficiently important to give a certain credence to this idea." Bedell Smith also told reporters he did not know where Hitler was, but as a wild guess he thought Hitler was at Berchtesgaden organizing the defense. When asked about the possibility of an airborne assault on the area, he declared, "We are keeping Airborne divisions available. We will have all sorts of airborne operations." There were no further airborne operations. A SHAEF Planning Staff memorandum, "Operations against the German National Redoubt," dated 16 April, did not appear urgent as it did not arrive at 7th Army headquarters until April 28.[115]

British intelligence, with far greater experience in the field, did not put much credence in the rumors of a great Nazi stronghold in the Alps. British General Kenneth Strong,

**Members of Seventh Infantry Regiment on German railroad gun, Bavaria, April 1945. (National Archives, Signal Corps photograph)**

SHAEF chief of intelligence, was of that view, but, then, in August 1944, Strong believed the war would be over in three months. MI4, one of the British intelligence agencies, was all along dubious about the idea of a Alpine fortress. It observed that ground reports, many of which denied preparations for such, were often unreliable and that Ultra traffic, until almost the very end, was not showing any indications of this development. In a report on 15 April 1945 it declared, "Whatever German plans may be—and evidence tends to show that no large-scale development of defense lines have taken place—the ultimate boundaries of the redoubt area must be defined by the speed and direction of the Allied advance." It conceded that there could be an Alpine bastion thrown together at the very end, but if a speedy advance took place it "will force the German desperadoes back into the hard core of the mountains, from which they may be difficult to dislodge."[116]

Many British military leaders, including Alan Brooke, chief of the Imperial General Staff, believed that the American preoccupation with the redoubt would reduce the resources committed to the original Allied plan to conquer Germany—a British-led (Field Marshal Montgomery, commanding) northern sweep to the Baltic and beyond. In effect, Eisenhower's chasing after a mythical National Redoubt prevented the western Allies from capturing the German capital. By the end of the war, it was clear that many Germans, fearing vengeance, would stoutly resist the Russian invaders, but would, at best, offer greatly reduced opposition to the Americans. Intelligence reports indicated that many Germans welcomed the prospect of a U.S. occupation, certainly as opposed to that of the Russians. The road to Berlin was open but it was not taken.[117]

There was considerable speculation about the fate of the Nazi leaders—would it be death or flight? As early as July 1944, Allen Dulles had received a report that it would be flight: "They will go to various countries: the Argentine, Japan, Ireland." He wondered if the "astounding inactivity of the German submarines" might be a prelude to "a massive delivery of submarines to Japan." His speculation continued: "Japan will probably not be anxious to receive the Nazis, unless they got good value with them, but if Germany could deliver with a few Nazis a hundred submarines, plus crew and technicians, the Japs might take the high Nazis thrown into the bargain." In March 1945, Dulles was informed that a four-engine JU 290—part of the *"Fliegerstaffel Adolf Hitler"*—was being equipped with armored plate, bullet proof glass, guns fore and aft, etc.," at the air field in lower Bavaria near Braunau. The plane was supposed to have been delivered to Berchtesgaden by the end of February, and Hitler was "greatly disturbed over the delay." Was the Führer going somewhere? Otto Dietrich later noted that "during the last years of the war there was much talk that Hitler was preparing to escape by plane to Japan or Spain," but Hitler never contemplated such action.[118]

Inasmuch as the occupation zones in Germany had been set at the Yalta Conference in February 1945, Eisenhower on March 28 decided to stop at the Elbe River—sixty miles west of Berlin. His troops halted there on April 14. Why not go on to the capital? The bloody battle for that city, which was in the proposed Russian zone, was left to the Soviet troops. The Soviets had a score to settle with the Nazis for the carnage they had inflicted on Russia. Moreover, there was the need for a planned, orderly meeting-up with advancing Russian forces: a large river would suit. On the other hand, there was clear evidence that only weak German opposition would face a western thrust to Berlin and that most Germans would welcome an American occupation rather than one by the Russians, whom they had good reason to fear. The bulk of German defensive arrangements faced east. William Simpson declared that his U.S. Ninth Army could get to the outskirts of Berlin in twenty-four hours. In any case, the Russian April 16 breaking of the Oder River defenses, immediately to the east of Berlin, effectively ended the question of an American assault on the capital.[119]

Given the possibility that there was a national redoubt, on April 22 Ike directed a large part of his forces in that direction. Their most important objectives were the destruction of the fighting capacity of German forces in the Danube valley and the speedy capture of the Alpine area. In his widely-read study, *The Struggle for Europe*, Chester Wilmot declared that the result was nothing more than a "wild goose chase." However, the seizure of this territory was no trivial or compensatory activity. Running on parallel lines, George Patton's Third Army and Alexander Patch's Seventh Army headed south, with the Third Army reaching the western part of Czech territory while Patch's army ended its march in the Alpine passes, where it joined elements of the U.S. Fifth Army advancing from Italy.[120]

Joseph Goebbels decided to exploit Allied fears of a Nazi mountain bastion. He organized a special propaganda section that in January 1945 began feeding material to foreign journalists and others about a massive defensive complex, complete with blueprints and construction reports. He also trumpeted the formation of "Werwolf" formations, organized by the SS, to carry on sabotage behind enemy lines. These units, led by Otto Prützmann, began training in September 1944, while Otto Skorzeny began forming his own sabotage cadres the following November. Radio Werwolf began broadcasting on March 30, declaring the werewolves would "daily and joyfully" conduct a campaign of terror without regard for "childish rules of so-called decent bourgeois warfare." Within a week Goebbels believed that the phantom force was having the desired effect: "Our Werwolf activity is now being taken extraordinarily seriously in Anglo-American circles, so seriously that Eisenhower is said to be toying with the idea of using gas against Werwolf detachments." The dual threats of guerrilla warfare and mountain-based resistance sent shivers down the spines of many Allied soldiers and commentators.[121]

Walter Schellenberg, now head of German intelligence, took a very dim view of the Werwolf effort. He considered Prützmann to be merely a Nazi "desperado" of weak mentality. The force that Prützmann was attempting to build up was disorganized, with both Skorzeny and Ernst Kaltenbrunner, head of internal security, working to undermine the effort. Schellenberg recalled that he remained aloof from the affair, "for the disorder within the so-called 'retreat organization' had become uncontrollable" in the last months. At the end, he declared, "everything was compressed as in an accordion: Party, Hitler Youth, D.A.F., N.S.V., Stapo, SD, Klein Kampf Verbaende of the Wehrmacht Werewolf, SS Jagdverbaende—everything upside down and everybody responsible for everything." Kenneth Strong, SHAEF intelligence chief, later declared that the rapid capture of Werwolf headquarters precluded "the creation of a widespread network of Resistance posts which might well have interfered with our operations." The reality of the National Redoubt was yet to be ascertained.[122]

There was a very large group involved in the war who were directly concerned with the likelihood of a Alpine stronghold. These were the 270,000 British and American prisoners of war in Germany, 93,000 of whom were Americans. In late 1944 and early 1945 as Russians forces drove in from the east and western Allies advanced at the other end, there was a massive transfer, usually by forced marches, of POWs into the German interior. Rumor began to spread among the prisoners that many of them would be sent to the Alps as hostages within the supposed redoubt, a proposal, unknown to them, made by Franz Hofer in November 1944. In March 1945 there was a huge transfer of American POWs from Stalag XIIID, the major camp outside Nuremberg, to Stalag VIIA at Mooseburg, thirty miles north of Munich. Not only among POWS but also some Allied leaders there loomed the possibility that the prisoners could become unwilling participants in a bitter mountain struggle which could prolong the war for months.[123]

There was no doubt that one group of POWs had been directed to the Bavarian Alps. On 13 April, twenty-one prisoners at the maximum security prison at Colditz were herded into two trucks and driven into the heart of the alleged redoubt, arriving in Berchtesgaden in early May. This group of British prisoners were known as the *Prominente*, persons related to important British figures.[124]

The anxieties of the Allied prisoners massed together at Moosburg quickly dissipated due to the terms of a unique agreement. This was an arrangement, agreed to by the Allied high command on April 22, that there would be no further movement of Allied POWs. When, four days later, the German camp commandant at Moosburg ordered air force POWS to be prepared to march to the Alps, the agreement was brought to his attention and the march was cancelled. This development surely was an indication that there was not going to be a fight to the finish in the mountains.[125]

## Approaching Germany

The Allied drive south into Bavaria and Austria was a Franco-American affair. The Sixth Army Group, composed of the U.S. 7th Army and the French First Army, was given the

General Jacob Devers, commander of the U.S. Sixth Army Group with his fourth star on helmet, March 1945. (U.S. Army Military History Institute)

task of capturing the redoubt area—from Salzburg west to the Swiss border and south from Munich into the Alps, with the ultimate objective being the seizure of the Alpine passes to Italy. The group was commanded by Jacob Devers, a fifty-seven-year-old 1909 West Point graduate of Irish and German extraction, providing him with useful qualities of temper and determination. Describing him as a "Pennsylvania Dutchman with Irish charm," journalist Hanson Baldwin, in 1944, declared that Devers "has the confidence and support of his men, who know him as a slasher of red tape and a dynamic, pushing man with a wide grin."

George Marshall had selected Devers from among 475 colonels for appointment to the rank of brigadier general in 1940. Five months later Devers was promoted to major general, the youngest in the army. As Commander of Armored Forces beginning in August 1941, Devers was responsible for reshaping the composition of an armored division. The result was a triangular unit, with equal balance of tanks, infantry and self-propelled artillery. It was fully motorized, with half-tracked vehicles for off-road movement, and with spotter planes for artillery observation. This became the model for all armored divisions, and not just those that were American.

The newly appointed head of the European Theatre of Operations, General Frank Andrews, and his staff were killed when their plane crashed into a mountain in Iceland in May 1943. Devers was quickly appointed to the position. He declared, "I was sent to London just out of the clear sky." However, Eisenhower was appointed in December 1943 to command Overlord, the proposed invasion of the Continent.

Devers was not informed about the Eisenhower appointment, learning about it from a British general, nor did he get the opportunity to meet with Eisenhower at the time. Lacking combat command experience, Devers said much later that he knew he would not be given the position. George Marshall had a different impression, recalling, "Devers got in there temporarily and he thought right away he was the coming commander." After conferring with Ira Eaker, his air force commander who also was being replaced, Devers wrote in his diary, "We both feel a little deflated."[126]

In putting together his staff, Eisenhower found no room for Devers. To General Marshall it appeared that the Eisenhower group was determined to ship out all of the cadre of leading officers who were there before them. Bradley later commented on the Devers situation: "It was a comedown for Devers, and thereafter his relations with Ike were frosty." George Patton wrote to his wife at the time, "Jake feels like hell as he went up hill with quite a drop. Well, anyway he got further than he was ever intended to." Marshall then appointed Devers commander of the U.S. forces in the Mediterranean, where he later organized the Sixth Army Group and directed the invasion of southern France in August 1944. Later, Marshall was critical of Devers: "Did good work in Europe at first. Got the personal ambition thing in too much.... It changed my view of him. He got into the ambition class."[127]

Determined not to be tied to his headquarters desk, Devers spent a great deal of his time out with the troops. According to Charles MacDonald, Devers "left planning mainly to his army commanders, while he himself, using a little liaison plane in all but the most abominable weather, became a familiar figure at subordinate levels." Devers put great store in such contact; he later described his approach to problems or conflict: "My system was to handle them directly and personally—not by written order or command or through the staff." As well, he let his staff prowl the battlefield and make changes in operations, only requiring that he immediately be informed of alterations.[128]

A man used to high command, Devers held strong views. As the Allied effort in Italy bogged down in near-stalemate, Mark Clark told him that "he did not think the British would fight" and that the American units "would have to drag them along." Devers noted a strong anti–British current running through the U.S. military there. "As a good team player," he recorded, "I fully realize that Anglo-American relations should be fostered and have done everything possible to this end, but it takes two to play this game, and the British are not playing." He found that in American ranks there was "a definite feeling that the British will not fight hard enough to make a go of it." As a result, Devers strongly recommended that all American forces "be withdrawn from Italy as soon as possible. It is a waste of time, effort and manpower."[129]

The British military and its self-appointed advisor, Winston Churchill, opposed the invasion of southern France, preferring an Allied attack in the Adriatic. But Operation Dragoon (formerly "Anvil") went ahead. Devers noted, "It was a personal fight on my part from this end to get that operation mounted." Shortly after the invasion began, Churchill, arriving in Italy, greeted Devers with, "You know I was against you. However, I wish to congratulate you on the fine battle you are carrying on in southern France. You are advancing right up the old Napoleon road." Although the Normandy invasion had begun ten weeks before, Churchill requested that Devers immediately give up his landing craft for some unspecified purpose; Devers recalled, "I personally have fought for landing craft from June 1943 up to the present." Churchill also talked with him about tanks; Devers noted, "He is way off on that subject also."[130]

After the war, Devers did not understate what he saw as the significance of the invasion of southern France: "No operation in our history had, up to then, produced more decisive, dramatic, swift and far-reaching results at so little cost. The operation on the southern coast of France will probably go down as a classic for surprise, exploitation and results." His army group's rapid movement northwards was greatly facilitated by Hitler's orders, two days after the invasion began, to withdraw most of the German military from southern France. As a result, the Sixth Army Group developed its own secure supply lines through the southern ports and, thus, avoided the logistical nightmares of the Allied armies in the north who, until November 1944, were still dependent on bringing supplies from the beaches of Normandy.[131]

Eisenhower did not like Devers (Patton wrote in his diary that Ike hated him) and doubted his ability. He told both Patton and Bradley that Devers was .22 caliber, meaning a small-time operator or a person of narrow outlook, not a man of broad vision like themselves. Yet Eisenhower assured Marshall that he thought Devers "was doing a fine job," denied that he was opposed to him, and said he had nothing against him. Eisenhower's doubts about Devers, he explained, had been "based completely upon impressions and, to some extent, upon vague references in this theater ... [which] never had any basis in positive information."[132]

Nevertheless, in his rating of general officers in February 1945, probably drawn up with input from Bradley and Bedell Smith, Eisenhower ranked Bradley tied at first with Carl Spaatz, while he listed Devers as 24th of 36. In brief notations on his list of generals, the only one on whom he made critical comments was Devers. Though he cited Devers's enthusiasm, loyalty and energy, he also declared that Devers was "often inaccurate in statements and evaluations." Moreover, alone among those he evaluated, Eisenhower added a commentary, by asterisk: "The proper position of this officer is not yet fully determined in my mind. The over-all results he and his organization produce are generally good, sometimes outstanding. But he has not, so far, produced among the seniors of the American organization here that feeling of trust and confidence that is so necessary to continued success."

It seems strange that of all the generals listed, he could not make up his mind only about Devers. Could it be that by leaving the matter open, Eisenhower could make his final determination based on what way the political wind was blowing in Washington or elsewhere? Smiling Ike was a very calculating man who was often accused of putting off difficult decisions as well as shifting his position depending on the prevailing situation and the company he was in. As well, who were the seniors—himself, Bradley, Bedell Smith, possibly Patton? What were the examples of inaccurate statements and evaluations attributed to others? Probably the instance that Eisenhower had in mind was Devers's claim, in late 1944, that he would quickly eliminate the Colmar pocket west of the Rhine and his failure to then do so. (The ill-equipped and undermanned First French Army got bogged down in the attempt and, reinforced by a couple of U.S. divisions, collapsed the pocket in February 1945.) Though Eisenhower offered to send the list to Marshall, apparently Marshall did not request it. When he left Germany after the war, Eisenhower was anxious to get hold of his wartime office diary, which contained negative remarks about Devers and others.[133]

Although Devers was fully able to vigorously fight for his position in contentious matters and did openly question some of Eisenhower's decisions at meetings within his group, he later denied that there was personal animus in his differences with Eisenhower and declared that Eisenhower was the best man to be supreme commander. When Eisenhower became army chief of staff shortly after the war, he appointed Devers head of the army's ground forces.[134]

While the war was on, however, the two generals crossed swords on a variety of matters almost from the beginning of their relationship. Given that they were the chief commanders in two different regions—originally Devers in London and Eisenhower in the Mediterranean—and then switched positions, there was bound to be at least some friction. When Eisenhower asked for additional bombers for North Africa, Sicily and southern Italy, Devers declined to send them. When Ike requested that several officers be transferred to the European theatre, Devers denied that request. In both cases, Marshall backed Devers's position. On the other hand, Devers promptly responded to other of Eisenhower's requests.

Then came a matter of grand strategy. After a bitter campaign in the Vosges mountains, Devers's armies were the first to get to the Rhine, with the French First Army arriving on November 18 and XV Corps of the 7th Army five days later. Anticipating such a development, Devers's staffs vigorously developed bridging plans and Patch promptly sent patrols across the river, which found the area largely undefended. Devers proposed a prompt, powerful thrust across the river before German forces could regroup, to be followed by a drive north to the Saar industrial area.[135]

The surprising success of the Sixth Army Group and its proposal to lead the way into Germany north of Strasbourg was a challenge to Eisenhower's set plan. Here was an opportunity to employ a different avenue of approach—an opportunistic maneuver that would catch the Germans by surprise—all within SHAEF's overall plan, of course, but Ike was having none of it. With Bradley as back-up, Eisenhower had an all-night encounter with Devers on November 25, with Eisenhower emerging "mad as hell" and Devers wondering if he "was a member of the same team." The role of Devers's 7th Army was to head north to help good buddy George Patton get his 3rd Army, now mired in mud, moving towards the Rhine.[136]

In his diary on November 26, Devers declared, "The decision not to cross the Rhine was a blow to both Patch and myself for we were really poised and keyed up to the effort and I believe it would have been successful. The Germans are certainly disorganized." It was a lost opportunity.[137]

There were several reasons why Eisenhower turned down Devers's proposal. One argument against the proposal was that the area across from the Sixth Group in its southern end was the Black Forest, with its primitive road network, but Devers proposed to cross north of that. Another objection was that the British would have taken grave exception to a Franco-American leap across the Rhine; it was to be an Allied action—in fact, to be led by Montgomery. The joint crossing was planned by Eisenhower to be further the north—into the major industrial area of the Ruhr. The bad relationship between Devers and Eisenhower surely played a part in this matter.

Later, George Patton said that the Seventh Army should have plunged across the Rhine, a view shared by Martin Blumenson, the editor of Patton's papers, who concluded the Sixth Army Group could have easily crossed the Rhine at this point and could thereby have shortened the war. Blumenson believed that Eisenhower refused permission for Devers's plan because Eisenhower was determined to pursue a broad front strategy to allow American and British forces to win the war together. In *Riviera to the Rhine* (part of the army's sponsored series of its involvement in the war), Jeffrey Clarke and Robert Smith are obliquely critical of Eisenhower's vetoing the Seventh Army's plan to jump the river; the chapter dealing with this is titled "Lost Opportunities." Devers's basic criticism of Eisenhower's strategy was that it was based on seizing territory instead of destroying enemy forces. Eisenhower's broad front approach almost came to grief three weeks later when Adolf Hitler, observing the overstretched Allied lines, punched a hole in them through the Ardennes.[138]

**Seventh Infantry Regiment crossing the Rhine, Frankenthal area, 26 March 1945.
(National Archives, Signal Corps photograph)**

Eisenhower's decision to prevent Devers from crossing the Rhine was followed by a row about army boundaries and transfer of divisions. Eisenhower directed that Patton's army spearhead the destruction of German forces west of the Rhine. To facilitate this action he wanted two of Devers's divisions transferred to Patton's force and Patton's front to be shortened at the expense of the 6th Army Group. Devers "protested vigorously," but Eisenhower shortened Patton's front only by half. Devers clearly had his own view of who should take the lead in the campaign: "Since I had the supply establishments and the units, I probably could regroup more quickly, and that I felt that my army commanders had demonstrated that they were well out in front in carrying out successful operations." Moreover, "Patton's army should come to the Sixth Army Group. Why they do not do this, I do not know. Far be it from me to ask for more command."[139]

## Nordwind

The Germans, in the wake of their stalled Ardennes offensive, launched Operation Nordwind on New Year's Eve against the strung-out Seventh Army. Anticipating the offensive, Eisenhower ordered the Sixth Army Group to immediately retreat to the Vosges mountains, which would have led to German reoccupation of Strasbourg, a city of great significance to French nationalism. After the humiliation of having thousands of U.S. troops surrender in the Ardennes, Eisenhower at all costs did not want a repetition. On December 26, Devers was informed that "I would not get any replacements—in fact they were taking replacements away from me—and I would get no more ammunition and no more help." Devers responded that he was not interested in territory, but that Strasbourg and Mulhouse should be held if at all possible. Devers was concerned about "the integrity of my troops and the protection of the people we have liberated." He said he would "pull back slowly; it cannot be done rapidly unless I am forced to do so, because of the terrific rearrangement we have gone through in the past few days to get out reserves for Patton."

The retreat order was seen by the Sixth Army Group leaders as another example of Eisenhower's favoritism toward Omar Bradley's 12th Army Group. In addition, they observed that as yet there was no German breakthrough and that a flight from Strasbourg would be a "political disaster" for the French government. Alexander Patch, commander of the 7th Army, objected to retreating without a fight from ground won at the cost of high casualties. Devers noted, that like himself, Patch "hates to retreat."

Devers tried to get Eisenhower to change this order, which would result in giving up "the whole Alsatian plain." He noted that he was giving up positions that were "much stronger than the ones to which I go." Obviously dragging his feet, Devers said that the withdrawal would take place "just as fast as sound tactics will permit," and he expected the move to be completed by January 5. This was not good enough for Eisenhower, who on New Year's Day charged Devers with not properly carrying out orders for an immediate retreat, an accusation Devers rejected.

An explosion from the French government soon came. Provisional President Charles de Gaulle ordered the French First Army to remain in Strasbourg, which would be treated, if necessary, as another Stalingrad. Devers informed de Gaulle's liaison officers that this action would "just mean the destruction of the city and of a lot of lives" and the French forces barricaded in the city "would have to be rescued by American forces." But to drag matters out, Devers requested "a clear directive from General Eisenhower as I wanted no confusion in my withdrawal to the Vosges."[140]

The crisis was resolved when Eisenhower met with de Gaulle in Paris on January 3, with Winston Churchill flying in to act as mediator. Eisenhower relented: Strasbourg was not to be abandoned. The 42nd Infantry Division would be replaced by elements of de Lattre's First French Army. The reversal came on the very day when Devers had issued a directive that the evacuation would take place as ordered. The episode did not improve Eisenhower's appreciation of Devers. Smiling Ike could be a sore loser. By this time, his attitude towards Devers became consistently negative, hectoring and critical, but that did not prevent Devers from leading his forces to success in every operation. Direct contact between the two men was kept to a civil minimum.[141]

When one has a clash with someone's boss, his loyal assistants will join in on the boss' side. This is clearly the case with Walter Bedell Smith, Eisenhower's chief of staff. Remembering the various tussles of 1943–44, Smith, armchair warrior, took ample opportunity in 1945 to belittle Devers, this commanding general of a group of successful armies. According to Carlo D'Este, Devers was mistaken in believing that Smith was understanding and supportive in the problems Devers faced.[142]

When the mercurial George Patton needed Devers's approval early in the war, he was fulsome in his expressed sentiments, effusively thanking Devers for a favorable performance report and telling Devers that he was "one of my dearest friends." However, when they became rivals for resources and in strategy, Patton shifted to bitter hostility towards Devers, in his diary calling him a liar, charging Devers with attempting to steal units from Patton's army ("May God rot his guts") and "messing things up and at the same time running counter to Destiny," his name for Eisenhower. To be sure, Patton in his diary had hard words for just about everybody, including Eisenhower, whom he called "yellow." Bradley, he termed "timid," and he lavished various epithets on the great Field Marshal Montgomery. Devers recorded a brief meeting with Patton on September 21: "He seemed subdued and not too friendly. For this I am sorry." In December 1944, however, Patton almost had a change of heart about Devers: "I am not sure that, as the lesser of two evils, it might not be better to be in his army group; he interferes less and is not as timid as Bradley."[143]

Bradley, a man of few words, had taken a strong dislike to Devers when, as a cadet at West Point, he observed that Devers as an instructor talked excessively but said nothing. His much later judgment was that Devers was "overly garrulous, egotistical, shallow, intolerant, not very smart, and much too inclined to rush off half-cocked." Bradley aide Chester Hansen, undoubtedly reflecting the general opinion of the people around Bradley, wrote in his diary on 24 April 1945, "Devers has been remarkably unimpressive and his record within the service is not regarded as a particularly good one. His stature does not even approach that of General Bradley.... Despite these professional limitations, however, he is a charming fellow though inclined to overrate his abilities and certainly his achievements." Recalling events of three years before, Hansen said that Devers "was most offensive on this score during our earlier days in England." What is lacking in these negative assessments of Devers is almost any specifics as to failings in organization, planning and execution of operations.[144]

Between Bradley and Devers there were marked differences in styles of command. Surrounded by a staff of 1200, Bradley largely remained in his headquarters, studying maps (he didn't know about the bocage in Normandy) and preparing detailed orders for everything (he was surprised and confused by the German offensive in the Ardennes). With a staff half that size, Devers, like Eisenhower, spent a great deal of his time visiting his units. Modest, aloof, even taciturn, Bradley became known as the "GI General." Upon the suggestion of Eisenhower that he "discover" Bradley, Ernie Pyle, the so-called soldiers' journalist, interviewed Bradley during the campaign in Sicily. Noting Bradley's modesty, courtesy and determination to spend half of each day traveling to his division headquarters, Pyle was overwhelmed: "I don't believe I have ever known a person to be so unanimously loved and respected by the men around and under him." A legend was born, which Bradley took care to maintain. There are those who believe that Bradley did not deserve this accolade, which easily could have been given to Devers.[145]

There seem to have been a great deal of disguised animosity among almost all of the American high command. Bradley is said to have grown to despise Patton for his flamboyance and unpredictability; he supported the proposal to remove Patton from command after Patton's assaults on shell-shocked soldiers. After the war, Bradley had very little to do with Eisenhower and even later was extremely critical of Eisenhower's generalship. In his diaries, Patton poured out his intense dislike of all of his colleagues. Eisenhower did all he could, in the circumstances, to put down Devers. Although Devers sometimes criticized Eisenhower's plans at meetings within his army group, as far as recorded evidence goes, the only one who did not express deeply-rooted animosity towards the others was Devers. In any case, the grudges and disgruntlements were kept beneath the surface and as far as is known did not have a noticeable effect on operations.[146]

Devers's subordinate in the Sixth Army Group, Jean de Lattre de Tassigny, commander of the French First Army, had a completely different assessment of Jake Devers. Uniformly generous in his memoirs, de Lattre declared that Devers "showed me the most friendly confidence from our first meeting." In support of his army, de Lattre acknowledged that he was involved in "semi-permanent interventions" with Devers, who almost always was able to accommodate de Lattre's wishes. Devers had several French-speaking liaison officers to maintain good relations and effective communication with French commanders.[147]

The major component of the Sixth Army Group was the U.S. Seventh Army, and its commander was the modest and taciturn Alexander Patch, who did not live long enough to write memoirs. While Devers heaped praise on Patch, there is no direct statement from Patch about his assessment of Devers. Yet all references to Devers in Patch's correspondence with Patch's wife are cordial and affectionate. As well, there is no instance of disagreement between the two generals, on matters great or small.[148]

One of his divisional commanders, John S. "Tiger Jack" Wood of the 4th Armored Division, held Devers in the highest esteem: "Jake Devers, in my opinion, is probably the greatest of our leaders, except MacArthur, in this war." Wood declared that Devers was "primarily responsible for the formation and equipment of the sixteen armored divisions that finally comprised" the tank units. Moreover, Devers possessed the rare qualities of "warmth, understanding, sympathy, whatever you want to call it, the intangible essence of human comprehension that emanated from Lee and from Washington."[149]

There were others who also had a high regard for the ability and character of Devers. During an inspection tour in the summer of 1943, General Alfred Wedemeyer said that the appointment of Devers as commanding general of the European theatre was "a happy selection. He is rapidly winning the respect and confidence of the British, and all the Americans are uniformly pleased with the manner in which they receive decisions and sound directions." He added the comment, "Perhaps a better field man than a negotiator." Ira Eaker, head of the air force during Devers's tenure both in London and the Med, while head of the Eighth Air Force in England was lavish in his appreciation of Devers: "I never have had, and never expect to have, better relations with my Commander than now prevail with General Devers and his staff.... He is as strong a supporter of true air force operations as I have ever seen."

There were those in less exalted positions who also admired Jake Devers. Karl Bendetson, an officer in the Allied command in London at that time, later declared, "I developed much esteem and affection for General Devers before he left London. He was exceptionally helpful and considerate. Our relationship has endured." Major General William Hoge, commander of the 45th Armored Division, remembered Devers as "a great friend" and "a great man.... He really was the father of the Armored Force."[150]

After fighting its way through the West Wall, the Seventh Army began crossing the Rhine on March 16 and then turned south. The French First Army soon followed and raced ahead to capture Stuttgart. Since the capital of Württemberg was out of the French zone, Devers ordered the army to withdraw, which it refused to do. Charles de Gaulle, determined to establish a French zone of occupation in Germany, ordered de Lattre to hold onto the city and establish a military government, adding, "To the eventual observations [of the Americans] you will reply that the orders of your government are to hold and administer the territories conquered by our troops until the French zone of occupation has been settled between the interested governments, which so far as you know has not yet been done." Informing Devers of de Gaulle's position, de Lattre assured him that there would be free passage through the city for all elements of the Sixth Army Group. On April 26, the commander of the 100th Infantry Division informed Patch that the situation in the city was "the worse imaginable," that "rape, pillage and plunder have been rampant." He urged the immediate removal of French forces "before conditions have gone beyond repair." Devers concluded that the situation in Stuttgart was "chaotic" and that French troops there "were no longer kept in hand." De Lattre quickly rejected these charges and an investigation by the 6th Army Group inspector general determined that the claims were exaggerated and disorder had been largely caused by released foreign laborers and the "native criminal element." Even then, Devers told the chief of staff of the French division that its command needed to "take immediate steps to correct these conditions" and that "the impression made upon the American troops had been so disastrous that the French people themselves would suffer."[151]

The matter of who should occupy Stuttgart generated some government-level heated exchanges, and, as a result, Eisenhower was forced to compromise. Although he declared that the French action violated agreements regarding the rearmament of French forces, he could do nothing but accept the situation. On April 28 the 7th Army ordered all U.S. troops out of the city. France later got its own zone in Germany.[152]

This episode was followed by another unauthorized expedition by de Lattre's army. One of its elements moved into the town of Ulm, scene of a famous victory by Napoleon in 1805. De Lattre knew very well that his forces should not have been there, but he wanted to celebrate a renewed French presence in that place. In ordering out the French unit, Devers did it vigorously; de Lattre's chief of staff reported, "Devers—that good and upright Devers—was angrier than I had ever seen him." French units ranging over the area south of Stuttgart became a matter of serious concern to the American high command.[153]

Before the capture of Strasbourg in November 1944 the Sixth Army Group was given the top-secret assignment of facilitating the operations of a unit of the Alsos group, whose purpose was the capture of German nuclear scientists, their facilities and records. The unit was led by Colonel Boris Pash, a refugee from the Russian revolution, with this group's chief scientist being Samuel Goudsmit, a Dutch Jew whose parents were gassed by the Nazis. Pash later said of Devers, "He was the top military commander who was to give Alsos its greatest support and whom all Alsos men—scientists and military alike—learned to admire and respect." For his part, Devers referred to the Alsos team as "Pash and his gang of cutthroats," a description that Pash obviously enjoyed. The capture of several German nuclear scientists and the seizure of their laboratories in Strasbourg produced considerable evidence that Germany was not even close to producing an atomic bomb, Hitler's claim to the contrary, so there was an urgent top-level demand to confirm this.

In late April, intelligence reports indicated that the principal cadre of German nuclear scientists, including Otto Hahn, the discoverer of nuclear fission, had gathered in the villages of Hechingen and Tailfingen in the Swabian Alps, fifty miles south of Stuttgart. A major difficulty was that this area was in the zone of the French First Army's advance. Vigorously urged on by Henry Stimson and George Marshall, Eisenhower issued orders that French forces would not be allowed to take control of the German scientists and their research. Among steps proposed to head off this possibility was the dispatch of a U.S. Army corps across the French zone. But, supported by a combat task force, Pash executed a less elaborate operation. Acting quickly and covertly, the Alsos team managed to elude and divert French units, and, on April 22 and April 24, captured the bulk of the German scientists, their equipment and records. Although it found a uranium pile laboratory, it was relieved to discover that German scientists would not be able to produce nuclear weapons. When informed of this coup on April 27 Eisenhower sent an "eyes only" message to Marshall: the Alsos team "have hit the jackpot."

Nevertheless, there were missing pieces to the picture. A few days before the arrival of the Alsos team, SS personnel had removed Kurt Diebner, a leading physicist, his equipment and key staff to a location in the Bavarian Alps. Two other top physicists, Werner Heisenberg and Walther Gerlach, already had left the area, reportedly also moving to the Alpine retreat. They were pursued and captured by Pash and his men in early May.[154]

In the final offensive, Devers's army group was to provide only southern flank protection for Bradley's force as well as to "be prepared later when the situation permits to advance to join hands with the Russians in the Danube Valley." This assignment seemed to be a source of satisfaction to Chester Hansen: "Jakie Devers effort to the south remains a subordinate one with limited objective advance on his front." Devers's command was given twice as wide a front as Bradley's. Despite this, the involvement of the Sixth Army Group was to be much more than merely giving flank protection, but Eisenhower's orders were typical of his treatment of Devers: all favorable attention was focused on Ike's good friends Bradley and Patton, while Devers was relegated to the sidelines. In his comprehensive history of the American army in the European war, Charles MacDonald put this situation in perspective: "One top American failed through no fault of his own to make the close-knit team. This was the other army group commander, Jakie Devers, who needed all the charm of a winning smile, protruding ears, and boyish features to hold his own in a company when he lacked the full confidence of the chief." MacDonald added, "[C]ountry cousins coming without patriarchal blessing seldom work their way fully into the family fold."

With the end of the war rapidly approaching and only the reputed National Redoubt to be dealt with, Eisenhower found himself with a large mass of unused units—SHAEF's reserve divisions as well as the First Allied Air Army and the newly arrived 13th Airborne Division. These he offered to the Sixth Army Group, which, for the first time, would be at maximum strength. They were no longer needed. Although Devers lived to the age of ninety-two, unfortunately he alone of the World War II four-star generals did not write his memoirs and has no full biography.[155]

The Sixth Army Group now confronted the German forces in the south. Despite repeated defeats on all fronts, the German military in this area contained many of the best remaining units—armored, SS, mountain troops and jet aircraft groups. The battered and worn German army units involved—the First and Nineteenth Armies—were in the process of being revived and rearmed. Pressure on this concentration of nearly a million troops was coming from three directions—from the east with the Russian drive through Vienna, from the south—in Italy—as German forces were being pushed into the Alps, and from the north by the U.S. and French forces. The best intelligence indications were that the German formations were attempting to hold their lines and not withdrawing into the mountains.[156]

What the Sixth Group command did not want to do is to drive the remaining German divisions into the redoubt area. In his study of this campaign, General Reuben Jenkins, head of group intelligence, later noted, "If only a comparatively few of these Germans reached the Redoubt Center, and the Redoubt Center contained only a small fraction of the reported supplies, the Allies would be faced with an arduous and costly campaign in the Alps." The objective of the Sixth Army Group was to divert and thrust aside these still formidable German divisions while it drove to Munich and then to the Alps. This would require effective coordination and speed, but first there was the need to give the two German armies a "breathing spell" to induce them to remain in their present positions. A factor in favor of this desired outcome was the well-established propensity of German forces not to initiate any retreat.[157]

The disposition of the German Nineteenth Army ranged from the Black Forest north of the Swiss border across northern Bavaria where it joined with the German First Army, whose area extended to the east above Nuremberg. The Allied plan was that the French First Army would bottle up the German Nineteenth below the Black Forest along the Swiss border down to Lake Constance, while the U.S. 7th Army would hold at least most of the

German First Army to the north and east of Nuremberg, thus leaving the road to Munich and the Alps open. The plan worked.[158]

While the French First Army held the battered German Nineteenth in the west, the U.S. Seventh contained the remains of the German First in the east and then unleashed a fully motorized assault to split the two German forces. By April 30, the U.S. Seventh spearhead was forty miles south of the main flank of the German First, which could only withdraw on foot. The leading force of the Seventh Army then swung around to the west of Munich, cutting off German Nineteenth elements that had escaped from the French encirclement.

In an operation of eighteen days, the French First captured 200,000 soldiers of the German Nineteenth, while the U.S. Seventh captured 400,000 soldiers of both the German First and Nineteenth armies. This 600,000 total was almost as great as that of the strength of the two armies in the U.S. Sixth Army Group. As a result of this effective strategy, no large German combat unit retreated intact into the redoubt. On April 28 General Winter, head of the German operations staff in the south, told Hitler that the Americans were approaching Munich and that a fighting retreat to the Alps would result in the loss of soldiers needed for the front line of the fortress.[159]

The experiences of two German generals probably are representative of the condition of the German forces facing the Sixth Army Group. Helmut Kleikamp, commander of the 36th Volksgrenadier Division, found that by May 3, "With enemy forces pursuing in our rear, and others cutting off our line of march, the annihilation of the division was completed before it could carry out its last mission: the occupation of the position between the Waginer and Chiem lakes." Otto Hoffmann, a Waffen-SS general, attributed the failure to defend the National Redoubt position to "the sweeping thrust, particularly of the Seventh American Army, [which] made it impossible for the German troops, retiring from the North to the alpine fortress, to occupy the positions envisaged or ordered." He added, "I do not know whether these defense positions were planned or dug in advance. To me, at least, they seemed to be improvisations."[160]

The U.S. 7th Army was composed of eight divisions—the U.S. 3rd, 36th, 44th, 45th, 79th, 100th and 103rd infantries, as well as the French 2nd Armored Division. The army's commander was Alexander M. "Sandy" Patch, a fifty-four-year-old, tall, erect, scholarly man (who collected first editions of Kipling) who was born into a military family in Arizona. Graduating from West Point in 1913, Patch took part in the Pershing expedition into Mexico and commanded an infantry battalion in France during the first war. After a successful command at Guadalcanal and a bout with malaria, he assumed leadership of the 7th Army in March 1944. Together with Devers, he planned and fought for the oft-threatened plan to invade southern France.[161]

Anxious to avoid the logistical problems that had arisen in the Normandy invasion, Patch readily accepted the advice of General Charles Corlett, experienced in amphibious operations in the Pacific, in preparing for the successful assault on southern France in August 1944. According to Corlett, Eisenhower, Bedell Smith, Bradley and company disregarded Corlett's proposals: what went on in the Pacific theater was "strictly bush league stuff" compared to what the leaders who had "sand in their boots" were doing in Europe. The failure to act on Corlett's advice resulted in a supply logjam, including an acute shortage of artillery shells.[162]

Despite the many achievements of his army, Patch gained little public attention and made no effort to compete with George Patton, epitome of the colorful warrior, whose army was running roughly parallel to his. He was given cover-story treatment in *Time* magazine for leading the invasion of southern France, which gave him attention he shunned. He wrote his wife at that time that "this temporary notoriety will soon die out.... All will change with reverses—which will come."

Chester Hansen described Patch as "tall, tanned, wearing the sun glasses that normally obscure his face and make you feel as though you were talking to something from a Guy Fawkes bonfire, erect in pink breeches, looking the part of a cavalryman." General Lucian Truscott remembered him as "thin and wiry, simple in dress and forthright in manner—obviously keenly intelligent with a dry Scottish humor." In addition, Patch's "quick and almost jerky speech and movement gave me the impression he was nervous and found some difficulty in expressing himself."

Boris Pash had an interesting, probably characteristic, encounter with Patch. At the 7th Army headquarters seeking support for his Alsos mission, Pash was encountered by "a tall, lean general with sharp but friendly features.... 'Who is Pash?' he snapped. 'I am, sir.' 'Start talking.'" After Pash gave a brief statement, Patch asked if he had anything else to say. When told no, Patch "stood up and walked out without a word. I was astonished." The puzzled Pash was quickly informed that this meant that Patch had no objections to Pash's request.

Patch's colleague in the Sixth Army Group, Jean de Lattre, commander of the French First Army, was most impressed with him: "Quiet, somewhat taciturn, his ascetic features above a violet scarf, General Patch impressed one with the clearness of his affecting, bright blue eyes." He also found Patch to be "a resolute commander, of high and clear intellect, and exceptional steadfastness." Denis Johnston, Irish playwright and British war correspondent, having attended a press briefing in the spring of 1945, which included Patch, noted that Patch was "a very good general, but a little nettled by the free-and-easy habits of his left-hand neighbor, George Patton, who has a way of boasting openly about the strength of the forces under his command, which discloses to the enemy the fact that the Seventh Army had been denuded. He was also harassed by the standard of living that the public at home expects for the boys in the field." In an assessment made twenty years later, William Quinn, his intelligence chief, declared of Patch, "His reputation was that he was a finalist, not flashy but the bottom line was that he always won."[163]

To Jake Devers, "Sandy proved to be a great army commander, if not the best." He was "an excellent administrator, and he was also a good field commander because he knew tactics and strategy." Noting Patch's propensity to pneumonia, Devers assigned a medical officer to him with the instruction, "You stay with Patch and don't let him do these things and keep him going."[164]

Unusual for a man of his rank, Patch was pleasant and cheerful with his troops. On Guadalcanal he was often observed talking with soldiers "while he rolled a cigarette from a sack of Bull Durham." During the seizure of Munich he came upon some of his soldiers attempting to blast their way into a bank. "Doing a little reconnoitering, boys?" he inquired. When told that was what they were doing, he replied, "Carry on," and went on his way. War cartoonist Bill Mauldin recounted a story going around about Patch. Driving along in his command car in southern France, Patch gave a ride to a hitchhiking paratrooper who told him he was heading to Cannes, which was "off limits." Despite this, Patch gave the trooper a hand-written pass. Mauldin commented, "It doesn't matter whether the story is true or not. If Patch had been a martinet, nobody would have bothered to repeat the yarn." Above all, Patch was noted for conducting operations that "never needlessly expended a GI's life." He was to die from pneumonia at the end of 1945.[165]

Lieutenant General Alexander Patch, commander of the U.S. Seventh Army, at right, with Field Marshal Karl von Rundstedt and son, Augsburg, Germany, May 1945. (U.S. Army Military History Institute)

His only son, a company commander in the 315th Infantry Regiment, was killed in the Vosges in October 1944. Patch's characteristic reserve is seen in a comment he made about the death of his son: "Well, he is not cold, and wet, and hungry." The following January, Patch confirmed two death sentences; he told his wife that the sentences were for "two of our white soldiers who committed foul rape of a young 17-yr-old French girl. Dreadful case— revolting. If only they could have been shot by the enemy in place of some of our fine noble young men." He must have had his son in mind. Omar Bradley observed that the "psychological effect on Patch" of his son's death "had been so devastating as to impair his effectiveness as army commander." It was partly for this reason that Bradley refused to assign Eisenhower's only son, newly graduated from West Point, to an infantry company; he was given liaison duty within Bradley's group. According to an estimate, at that time the life expectancy of a second lieutenant as a rifle platoon commander was about three weeks.[166]

The French First Army was created in north Africa after the Allied occupation of that region. It was composed of five divisions—the French First Armored, French First Motorized, Moroccan Second Infantry, Colonial Ninth Infantry and Algerian Third Infantry. Completely equipped with American weapons, vehicles and at least some uniforms, the force was led by Jean-Marie de Lattre, a fifty-five-year-old career officer. The British military theorist

B.H. Liddell Hart observed that de Lattre "had dynamism and creative imagination" along with a "sense of drama in history and love of the dramatic touch" which, contrary to his critics, were not evidence of theatricality and vanity. This was seen in the fact that "he seemed to enjoy insubordinately inclined subordinates." Yet he drove his force with mighty energy. One of his staff members paid him what is probably the ultimate compliment for a man in his position: "General de Lattre is a terrible man to serve—but I wouldn't care to serve anyone else."[167]

The French First took part in the invasion of southern France in August 1944 and, a month later, became part of the Sixth Army Group. This army grew to about 400,000 soldiers in eleven divisions, as compared to the U.S. Seventh Army with 345,000 men in twelve divisions. On the last day of 1944, Devers described the condition of the French army as being "short approximately 8000 infantry replacements, ... composed largely of colonial troops who are presenting a serious morale problem due to a shortage of officers with experience in handling colonial troops, and ... badly in need of complete re-training and refitting."

De Lattre took a cavalier attitude toward orders from Devers and frequently ignored them, safe in the belief that if push came to shove, Charles de Gaulle would support him in the name of French honor, prestige, and all the rest. While Eisenhower had to deal with Bernard Montgomery (with Winston Churchill as Monty's back-up), Devers had to handle Jean-Marie de Lattre de Tassigny.

Coalition warfare has its trials. But Devers claimed that he had an effective working relationship with de Gaulle: "Whatever they said about him politically wasn't bothering me, because he knew his stuff in the military sense and he was very cooperative." When Devers conferred with him about his plans, de Gaulle "always improved what we were trying to do, because we didn't know everything, either." For his part, de Gaulle termed Devers "a good ally and a good comrade," which certainly was high praise from le grand Charles.[168]

Devers also claimed that, despite everything, he got along well with de Lattre. Though he confessed that he never learned to properly pronounce de Lattre's full name, Devers took a generally permissive attitude towards almost all of de Lattre's unordered initiatives. On one occasion he claimed that, because of translation problems, he did not know what de Lattre was doing, although he had fluent French-speakers on his staff. In his biography of de Lattre, Guy Salisbury-Jones observed, "For Devers there was often much provocation, but nature had endowed him with a store of patience that seemed inexhaustible." At a French victory celebration in May 1945, Devers said of de Lattre, "For many months we have fought together—often on the same side!," but paid tribute to the French general as a great fighting military leader.

In the midst of war, the relationship was often rocky. The two had a fiery encounter on November 7, 1944, with the issue being the transfer of some French troops to Paris. Devers recorded in his diary, "When I showed him the list of troops that were to be relieved from his army ... he went into a tirade, which I had to curb very firmly.... He is a very difficult man to handle, hears only the things he wants to hear and retains only those items which he believes in." The row did not end in a breach: "We were back on an even keel before he left but only after a very stormy conference, in which I had to take a very strong and determined stand."

A completely different picture emerges from Devers's entry on November 25: "Had a great day with the French. General de Lattre was at his best.... Feel sure the French are going to bag the five German divisions which were on their front. They have been very smart, and while they have been counterattacked on four different occasions, each time they have been able to cut off the penetration and destroy some of the enemy." Later, in April 1945, Devers's patience was put to the ultimate test as the Franco-American Army Group moved through Germany. Although it was not in his zone, de Lattre decided to capture Ulm because of its association with his hero Napoleon. Devers furiously ordered the First French Army to immediately withdraw. In the end, de Lattre became involved in a race for the Alpine passes with Alexander Patch's Seventh Army, which he lost.[169]

Although Devers assured de Lattre that both armies in his group were treated equally, the French army was badly clothed and shod, and totally dependant on American rations that often were half that of an equivalent U.S. unit (a sore point being the American cigarette ration). De Lattre (and his wife) attempted to prevent the distribution of American Red Cross packages to wounded soldiers in Leclerc's division. He brought his catalogue of grievances to the attention of the visiting George Marshall, who responded that he was tired of hearing his complaints. Marshall had more to say to de Lattre after the war. Having witnessed a de Lattre eruption about the apportionment of supplies, Marshall told him, "You celebrated all the way up the road. You were late on every damn thing and there weren't any [supplies] to divide and you were critical of [General Truscott], who is a fighter and not a talker," and more. But at the time help was on the way. Lt. Colonel (and ex–U.S. Senator) Henry Cabot Lodge Jr., a fluent French speaker and army group liaison officer to de Lattre, took it upon himself to extract from army group supplies "considerable quantities of clothing and especially several thousand pairs of trousers of which our F.F.I. [French Forces of the Interior] had the most urgent need," noted de Lattre. With winter weather setting in, at least the north African troops could now get out of their robes and look like other Allied soldiers.[170]

Lodge proved an effective link with the French. Devers noted that Lodge "understood the military as well as the political situation and he had selected good men to help him." At some conferences with the French general, recalled Devers, de Lattre would "get mad, mad as hell. But Lodge always was able to handle it in a way that kept it from boiling over." De Lattre found Lodge to possess not only exceptional intelligence but also great uprightness of character.[171]

The last serious and sustained opposition to the march of the Sixth Army Group took place in Franconia in northern Bavaria, ending in mid–April. As the army group moved south through the wedge it had created, it met varying degrees of resistance. At Hambach on April 11 the 3rd Infantry Division captured a German anti-aircraft searchlight battalion "composed of 50 percent Yugoslavs who had previously been German" prisoners of war. The unit commander "was not very enthusiastic that he had command of female personnel and states that they are much harder to discipline than men." At the same time the division captured a similar unit composed of men who had only been in the army fourteen days and were without weapons. Their officers had advised them "to break up and try to get to their homes or to areas not yet occupied by the Allied forces," but the "majority of their men are unable to go very far since most of them had foot troubles already on account of long marches." Six days later at Forchheim the division encountered the *Volkssturm*, the "People's Storm," a hastily-assembled militia composed of over-aged men. The colonel in charge of a *Volkssturm* unit there declared in surrendering that the Nazi Party district leader, after urging him to appeal to his men to fight on, "took off 'to secure weapons' but was never heard of again." The only evidence of the people's militia that Lt. Russ Cloer of the Third Infantry Division found was "a few arm bands we found in some of the houses."[172]

There remained strong pockets of German resistance along the way. On April 17 the division command declared, "Enemy infantry again utilized every village in the Division zone as minor strongpoints, withdrawing and surrendering only when the pressure of the attack became too great. Enemy AA artillery, employed on ground targets, was very active during the period. Enemy planes were active during the night, bombing and strafing in the Division zone." The division also encountered innovative weapons—radio-controlled Goliath tanks and observation planes firing *Panzerfausts*.

But there were also signs of enemy disintegration. When a company of the Third entered Heroldsberg on April 17, it ran into both SS troops and members of the Volkssturm. It reported that "the SS troops offered strong resistance but the Volkssturm were in an intoxicated condition and surrendered readily." The same day at Erlangen the division encountered four companies "made up of newly inducted men, 17–18 years of age, or men who were discharged and drafted again. A large number of these were equipped just a few days before commitment and some had only half of their army clothing."[173]

From there it was on to the walled city of Nuremberg, site of the famous Nazi Party rallies, where determined German opposition was anticipated. On April 19, on the eve of Hitler's birthday, the Seventh Army issued a warning that "defiant demonstrations of violence may occur." The 45th Division reported "severe fighting and heavy shelling" as it approached the city. In a three-day fight, during which veteran soldiers had "never experienced more accurate enemy sniper fire," the division battled against "Luftwaffe troops, crack SS panzer grenadiers and Volksturmers." It was the experience of the 7th Regiment of the Third Infantry Division that a majority of enemy forces were *Luftwaffe* personnel converted into infantrymen. Lt. David Daub "watched our tanks batter down walls." Another young lieutenant in the Third, John Toole, recorded his experience at Nuremberg: "With the towering flames, the shooting, the looting and the sobbing, I had the sickening, miserable feeling that I was watching a great nation deliberately committing suicide."

After an adamant resistance, the city fell to the Americans on April 20. Among the materials secured was the so-called "Spear of Destiny," alleged to have been the instrument that pierced the side of Jesus on the cross and which had been a treasured relic of the Hapsburgs for a thousand years. Hitler claimed that when he was a young man in Vienna he had a mystical experience when viewing the spear. After the incorporation of Austria in 1938 he had the instrument moved to Nuremberg. In capturing the city, the army also seized a document which set out the Nazi program for observing the birthday of the Führer. The proceedings "should be held in a big hall in a dignified manner" and, after songs, quotations from Hitler and speeches, each unit commander was to conclude his remarks "with the following words: 'We pledge faith to Adolf Hitler until death and salute him as the greatest son of our nation with the old battle cry: Adolf Hitler, Sieg Heil, Sieg Heil, Sieg Heil!'"

A report of the 3rd Infantry Division commented, "So far as is known, the only speech made in Nuremberg on 20 April 1945 was one delivered by Maj. Gen. John W. O'Daniel to officers and men of the 3rd Inf. Div." O'Daniel ordered the blowing up of the huge concrete swastika at the Zeppelin Stadium. An order from General George Patton that this emblem be protected for later shipment home came an hour too late. On April 22, five members of the division received medals of honor. The division's official history proudly recorded, "Never before had five men of one division been awarded the Medal of Honor at a single ceremony." Before the war ended, thirty-six members of the division received this highest decoration, including Audie Murphy, the most decorated soldier of World War II.[174]

The day of Hitler's birthday also figured in an intelligence report of April 15, stating that there had been "persistent civilian reports that there will be an uprising of the 'Werewolf'" on that anniversary. The report continued: "The object of this uprising is said to be for each member of the Werewolf to kill an Allied soldier even at the cost of his life.... Because of the severe military defeats ... this would be similar to the rise of the 'Phoenix from the Embers of the Fire,' a more or less supreme sacrifice for the Führer." Despite this rhetorical report, there was no noticeable increase in German partisan activity on this date. A rumor among the German population was that "all children would be taken from their parents and shipped to the United States as slave labor." As a result, some families hid their children until they found out that the yarn was untrue.[175]

One intelligence report was confirmed—that south of Nuremberg the *Luftwaffe* had secreted a thousand planes. The Third Division came upon the cache hidden in wooded areas along the autobahn. Lt. Russ Cloer recalled the scene: "The center-dividing island of the Autobahn, which was grass elsewhere, had been leveled, paved and painted green so that it would look normal from the air." The planes were in good condition, with plenty of ammunition, but no fuel.[176]

Along the route of march a variety of intelligence reports warned troops to beware of anticipated Werwolf attacks. On the other hand, XXI Corps intelligence reported on April 15 that a German prisoner had declared that this type of underground activity stood "little chance of success" due to tardy organization, lack of secret depots and an inability to provide a continuous flow of food, ammunition and weapons. This made conditions for carrying on partisan warfare basically different from those that existed in Russia and France. Moreover, the excellence of the German road network would allow U.S. military vehicles "to penetrate any sector, even in the dense forests of Bavaria (Bayerischer Wald) or the Central German mountains (Harz, Thüringer Wald)." Even climatic conditions would not be a problem as these "are in favor of operations throughout the year, while several months of Russian winter precluded such activity in hunting the fastnesses of the Partisan command."[177]

This is not the way 7th Army intelligence saw the situation. In a report dated May 2, it declared that "the Werewolf organization is not a myth. Nearly a third of the members of the central directorate of the Gestapo have been assigned to this service and have been working furiously since last September at establishing agents in all important communities in Germany." Intelligence noted that in Bavaria there was "much concern as to Nazi reactions after Allied occupation, for numerous assaults, assassinations and acts of sabotage are expected, for which the whole population will suffer." There also were reports of innovative weapons to be used by underground opposition—a People's Hand Grenade (extremely unstable) made of concrete, belt buckle pistols, and delayed-impact poison to be slipped into soldiers' drinks. Concern was heightened when Radio Werwolf began broadcasting at the end of March. But the Werwolves, like the *Volkssturm*, turned out to be an ineffective force in the defense of Germany.[178]

Radio Werwolf soon left the air. A 7th Army Counter-Intelligence report for April noted, "Results of the German resistance planning ... showed up on a small scale, as did a few hastily organized and frenetic 'Save the Fatherland' groups." When, in mid–April ten Hitlerjugend were arrested in Bensheim, they were found "supersaturated with Nazi fervor and each ... sworn to kill an American soldier." They had been ordered to "await secret orders concerning sabotage and assassination, to remain always good Nazis and to suppress attempts at democratic re-education." An attempt to form a Werwolf unit in Munich came to nothing: "A half-hearted meeting of Nazi and police officials was held, the headquarters was evacuated from Munich and nothing was accomplished." Counter-Intelligence concluded, "With the entire nation sliding hell-bent, very few people wanted to play follow-the-leader." An army intelligence officer observed that Germans in occupied areas were "behaving more like sheep than werewolves."[179]

Harold Zink later noted that Patch made effective use of military government units in his march down Germany, this in contrast to George Patton, who failed to provide "reasonable support" to similar units in the Third Army. The result was that "the detachments were so interfered with by the tactical units and so lacking in authority that they found it extremely difficult to handle their jobs effectively." The outcome was stark: "The detachments in the Seventh Army area naturally achieved very much better results than their counterparts in the Third Army area."[180]

The leadership of the Seventh Army was looking ahead. On April 25 a meeting of company commanders within the Third Division was told that the army had a final objective: to be first to Berchtesgaden. Lt. Colonel Lloyd Ramsey informed the assembled leaders, "With seven armies racing to be the first into the Bavarian redoubt area" they should banish the thought that "this army commander is going to forgo the opportunity to be in on the kill." General Patch was determined "to see that the 7th Army beats all others to this last plum of the war," and the Third Division was to be the spearhead in this effort. A plan to accomplish this was laid out to the commanders.[181]

Meanwhile, the division plowed ahead. The next city encountered was Augsburg, where, on April 28, its troops rapidly seized control. As the division prepared to attack, General O'Daniel ordered his artillery to hold fire: "I don't want you to fire into Augsburg at all unless it is actually observed firing [from the German side].... Keep your eyes open for white flags or other indications of surrender as we have many indications" that probably would occur. Peter Furst, a German-born reporter for the *Stars and Stripes* arranged by telephone with the city mayor that the American occupation would not be opposed. The German military commander had obviously agreed to this position, since members of his staff claimed that they assumed that the American soldiers who suddenly appeared were POWs. The U.S. Army newspaper declared that an anti–Nazi group "handed the city" to the division. The same day at Siegelbach the German commander surrendered his company, composed of "previously wounded soldiers" who had already been disarmed by SS troops, because "the type of men he commanded would only throw the weapons away."[182]

Beyond Augsburg the division advanced swiftly, meeting "only light resistance in the form of road blocks and scattered small arms fire." No definite enemy front line now existed. Munich lay straight ahead. A captured German officer estimated that the city "will be the scene of fanatical resistance because of Hitler's sentimental attachment to Munich as the 'Capital of the Movement.'" U.S. troops should anticipate that "we will have to contend with sabotage and terror" instigated by Nazi zealots. Yet, on the eve of the American occupation, now that it was safe to do so, some Bavarian nationalists staged a rebellion against Nazi authority.

Just northwest of the city was Dachau, the first of many Nazi concentration camps established by Hitler, which was seized by the 45th Infantry Division on April 29. Its inmates were liberated and many remaining SS guards were executed. The machine gunning of the guards was a clear violation of the Geneva Convention and General Patch ordered the Seventh Army Inspector General to investigate the incident. However, in the summer of 1945 when the report got to George Patton, then military governor of Bavaria, he took no action.

Closing in on Munich, the 7th Regiment captured Pullach, fifty miles west of Munich, where they discovered another of Martin Bormann's establishments, a luxurious estate complete with an underground communication center and elaborate bomb shelter. Among the items confiscated were a fourteen passenger sedan and 1200 bottles of champagne.

GIs met varying receptions in Munich—acclaim and showers of flowers in some parts, and bitter resistance in others. Colonel John A. Heintges of the 7th Regiment recalled that in the districts of opposition it was "more like a game of cops and robbers" dealing with Hitlerjugend teen-agers. The city was secured on April 30.[183]

Reports about a National Redoubt in the Alps continued to come in. Like the threat of an effective Werwolf organization, it was a sometime thing. In a major assessment of the possibility of an Alpen *Festung*, a 7th Army intelligence report at the end of March declared, "Enemy plans for eventually defending the redoubt Center are indicated in numerous reports from what are considered reliable sources." The report noted that "the terrain which comprises the REDOUBT Center presents the most compact, mountainous, inaccessible area available to the enemy.... Its extreme relief (to 12,000 feet), narrow, abrupt valleys and sheer winding roads" were "admirable for determined defense by a minimum force well-armed with modern equipment." What it saw as "probably more significant than the reports themselves is the present disposition of the enemy's forces." In northern Germany where Russian forces were smashing in from the east and Allied armies attacking from the west, "the enemy's continued occupation in strength of Northern Italy and the Balkan area is hard to justify if the Redoubt theory is disregarded." Equally inexplicable was the location in the south "of one of his most significant forces, the Sixth SS Panzer Army, in the Vienna area." It concluded that "if allowed time to withdraw on his own time schedule the enemy can create an elite force, predominantly SS and Mountain troops, of between 200,000 and 300,000 men." The National Redoubt idea was back in business.[184]

On April 15 the XXI Corps intelligence arm passed on an alarming report "from a very good source" that the German military had produced super missiles. "These will enter action," it reported, "when the siege of the redoubt begins. The air arms will have a greater caliber and radius of action than the V-1 and V-2, and from their firing points in the alpine redoubt should be able to hit the large cities of Central and Western Europe." At the same time, another informant denigrated the danger of a "last stand in the mountains." This source declared that "German Military Experts have convinced Himmler that an Alpine Redoubt could not hold out for more than 4 to 5 months." This conclusion would force Hitler and the other Nazi leaders to forego a last minute shift to the Alpine area. Rather, "the leaders would leave for Japan while SS Officers continued resistance in the Alps." The report also observed that "since the Autumn of 1944, reports have continued to be received from normally reliable sources of the movement of supplies and stores of all kinds into the Redoubt area." This flow was continuing despite the fact that this material was desperately needed by German armed forces elsewhere. It noted, however, that "the tonnage of supplies required to maintain guerrilla-type warfare in mountainous country for a considerable period in no way approximates to that required for normal operations."[185]

Three days later, 12th Army Group Intelligence issued a report based on information from a captured German soldier that a new mountain division was being formed. This, concluded its G-2, "is the first of many special formations, which sources have identified in the Redoubt area, whose existence can be accepted without the usual load of salt." Information gathered from other captured German soldiers continued to swing from one extreme to the other on the matter. This can be seen in a 7th Army assessment of April 25. A German captain declared that "the entire region of the high Alps will be defended fiercely and fanatically as possible by Waffen SS and other troops which the Germans will be able to put in that area." Yet he believed that the Redoubt "would not hold up the Americans longer than a week or two," largely because its defenses "had not been completed as planned, and because communications and supply routes have been completely disrupted throughout that area."[186]

It was in this state of uncertainty that the American forces advanced on the Alps. After the stunning surprise of Hitler's Ardennes offensive the previous December, almost anything seemed possible.

## Adolf Bunker

Meanwhile, in Berlin, the final days of Nazidom were rapidly approaching. The military high command assumed that when the situation in the capital became desperate Hitler would move to the Alps. Towards the end of March when the Berlin commandant told Hitler that, due to the horde of people that poured into his bunker during constant air raids, he could not properly conduct operations from there, Hitler told him, "You may use my bunker for your headquarters, because when the fight for Berlin is on, I shall not be there." As the Russians closed in on the city in April, Hitler had to decide whether to stay put or flee south. For several weeks he discussed his options, particularly with Martin Bormann.

By that time the German military had done little to prepare the Alpine region for continued resistance. As has been seen, Franz Hofer was probably the earliest advocate of the project. Through Swiss sources, he garnered information on American concerns about a mountain stronghold. In September 1944, he proposed that the Alps be used for this purpose. Two months later he sent his proposal to Bormann for Hitler. At that time, Hitler was focusing all of his attention on the Ardennes offensive. After the failure of that effort, any talk of a last stand in the Alps would have been viewed by Hitler as an example of defeatism, but he did agree that Hofer should fortify the area. In mid–March 1945 SS General Ernst Kaltenbrunner, deputy to Heinrich Himmler and commander of Army Group Center, recognized that little work had been done on the fortifications. He went to see Hitler about it on March 23, but was diverted by Hitler's talk about a miraculous reversal of German fortune.[187]

Martin Bormann was the most persistent advocate of a shift to the Alps. As has been seen, he made careful preparations for a move to the Obersalzberg. He worried about the condition of his wife and ten children, but he had to be very careful in planning their departure from the area. Hitler wanted family members of his inner staff to retreat to nowhere but the Obersalzberg area. When Hitler discovered that Dr. Karl Brandt, one of his physicians, had relocated his family to Thuringia, an area soon to be occupied by the Americans, he set up a court-martial and demanded the death penalty. Himmler secretly had the doctor moved out of harm's way to north Germany. Albert Speer was worried that Hitler would find out that on April 6 he had moved his family from the Obersalzberg to Holstein, in the far north. When around that time Eva Braun inquired about the Speer family whereabouts, which he rightly suspected Hitler had put her up to, he told her that they were staying in a lakeside cottage between Berlin and the Elbe. Speer said that Hitler "wanted me to promise" that Speer's family "would go to the Obersalzberg when he retreated there." This showed that Hitler, at this time, intended to withdraw to there in the final phase of the war.[188]

Beginning in late 1943 Bormann shifted his family to northern Germany—to the Agricultural Estate North, a part of the party's agricultural research facilities connected to the Obersalzberg. Then he shifted them to the Schluchsee in the Black Forest, and from there to his house in Pullach, about fifty miles west of Munich, which had an elaborate bomb shelter. They were back on the Obersalzberg for Hitler's long sojourn there in the first half of 1944. After Hitler left in July, Bormann again moved his family to the Black Forest, but early in 1945 they returned to the Obersalzberg. Bormann opposed any development that would attract air attack. He stopped any transfer of government departments and businesses to the area, forbade the establishment of aircraft manufacturing near Salzburg and, in February 1945, banned the migration of families of party and government officials to the Berchtesgaden district.[189]

The Führer's chief assistant was obviously thinking ahead. There already existed a German intelligence network in South America. According to one report, in response to Bormann's orders, several planeloads of gold and other wealth were flown to Argentina in 1944. There were also reports in 1944–45 of huge transfers of funds into accounts opened for the benefit of Nazi leaders, and tales of submarines carrying money and precious metals to that country. "A trusted OSS informant in Switzerland" passed on the report that, having paved the way with money transfers and other arrangements, Hermann Göring and Robert Ley were planning to flee the crumbling Germany for Argentina in November 1944. The U.S. State Department believed that a large amount of Nazi money was transferred from Swiss banks to those in Argentina in the last months of the war.

A story going had been around since 1941 that Hitler had bought a large parcel of land in Argentina. As well, there were two unconfirmed reports that the Führer himself was transported by U-boat to the Argentine after the collapse of the Third Reich. There was contact between German-occupied Europe and South America during the war. A German converted lobster boat made a round trip to Argentina in mid–1944 and two submarines arrived there in the summer of 1945. But stories about the flight of Nazi leaders and transport of gold were essentially part of a hoax concocted by British propaganda agencies to undermine the morale of German soldiers. The FBI could find no evidence of substantial Nazi activity in Argentina. U.S. intelligence did not make the unpleasant discovery that this was part of British disinformation until April 1945. In his study of the matter, Roland Newton terms the affair "the Great Nazi Bug-Out Hoax." On the other hand, an escape route through Austria and Italy did develop after the war, and a variety of nasty Nazis, including Adolf Eichmann, Erich Priebke and Josef Mengele, did find their way to Argentina.[190]

For a long time Joseph Goebbels was the sole advocate of Hitler remaining at the seat of government. To him, this would be a fitting, Wagnerian finale to a great experiment in political and cultural transformation. According to Otto Günsche, around this time Goebbels reminded the Führer of the oath they had taken together when they came to power: "We shall never abandon this building voluntarily. No power in this world can ever drive us out." Hitler told him on March 27 that "at present" he was "determined to remain in Berlin even if the position becomes critical." An opposite view of the situation was expressed by Captain Helmut Beermann: "We were all silently hoping that Der Chef would take off. Better to face death in the sunlight, and in the Alps, than to perish like miserable rats in a musty cement tomb in Berlin." Near the end, General Alfred Jodl told Hitler, "I will not stay in this mouse hole. Here one cannot work, fight or operate." He stayed.[191]

Hitler managed to get Eva Braun to leave Berlin on February 9, telling her that she needed to take charge of things at the Berghof, where she would be safe. Further, he stated, "I shall be leaving for the front any moment" and she was only in the way. Although he forbade her to return to Berlin, he promised that at Easter "we'll be together again." Eva agreed to leave at this time because she wished to take her dogs to Munich, look after her flat, visit friends and family, and have a delayed celebration of her birthday.[192]

Eva did not go to the Obersalzberg, but got her Mercedes out of storage, secured a driver and made the extremely hazardous drive to Berlin, arriving on February 23. Although Hitler tried to be angry about her reappearance, he was pleased: "Who else would have come back when they had the opportunity to go to the Berghof!" With Eva's return, Gerda Christian, one of his secretaries, concluded that Hitler would not leave: "Berchtesgaden, in the person of Eva Braun, had come to Berlin." One of the SS guards saw her as "*der Todesengel*," the angel of death. Rudolph Semmler, one of Goebbels's aides, noted in his diary of March 27, "Now all the preparations are being made for a real 'Twilight of the Gods' scene."[193]

## South to the Mountains

### The Flight of the Golden Pheasants

During the last year of the war about a million people left Berlin, refugees from almost incessant bombing. Various government agencies began leaving in March 1945. On March 29 Goebbels took note of the absence of most members of the Berlin State Opera, who "have largely vanished from Berlin and are leading a drone-like, parasitical existence in Upper Bavaria or the Tyrol, drawing their high salaries through the post."[194]

Hitler was well aware of the closing net. He was asked on March 23 if the smoke screen on the Obersalzberg could be discontinued when he wasn't there; the chemical-smoke supply was dwindling. At first he agreed, commenting, "But if that goes, everything goes. We've got to realize that. It's one of the last hideouts we have. Nothing will happen to the bunker but the whole site will be gone. If someday Zossen [military headquarters in Berlin] is smashed up, where would we go?" So the request was denied.

When on April 16 Soviet forces began a massive assault on the Oder-Neisse defense complex fifty miles east of Berlin, Christa Schröder, one of Hitler's secretaries, asked him if they would now be leaving Berlin. He denied the situation was that serious, but clearly understood the desperate situation: "Time! We've just got to gain time!" But time had run out.[195]

As the Russian vise closed around Berlin, a decision to a shift at least part of the Chancellery staff to the south finally came on April 20, Hitler's birthday; he had ten days to live. The decision was based on one that had been made on April 10—that if the Allies cut unoccupied Germany in two, then separate north and south commands would be established. This division was about to take place. April 20 also was the day Hitler ordered the formation of a fortress in the Alps. Bormann had continued his effort to get Hitler to go to Berchtesgaden. On April 10 he dispatched some servants to the Obersalzberg to prepare the Berghof for Hitler's arrival, where furniture and paintings had been stored in the shelter. Many members of the headquarters staff left for the Alps on April 14, joining various members of other military and civilian departments already there. Bormann informed the staff secretaries that the Führer's birthday would be the date of the inner group's departure. Erich Kempka, the head of the motor pool, had prepared a list of vehicles and passengers for the motorcade.[196]

Hans Baur, head of Hitler's personal aircraft unit, had three new super long-distance six-engine Junkers 390 planes standing by for Hitler's use. He informed Hitler that they could be flown anywhere in the world. Baur had maps and flight plans for Greenland, North Africa, Madagascar, Tibet and Manchuria. Hitler dismissed the idea of intercontinental escape: "Once out of Berlin, I would be like a Tibetan lama without his prayer wheel." Baur later asserted, "Right up to the last day, I could have flown the Führer anywhere in the world."[197]

Even before Hitler died, Russian press reports declared that he had fled Berlin, probably leaving a double to perish "heroically" in his place. When Hamburg Radio announced his death, Moscow radio responded by declaring the report as "a new fascist trick" designed to "prepare for Hitler the possibility of disappearing from the scene and going underground." The parents of Hermann Fegelein were told by a courier that both Hitler and their son had flown to Argentina, where they were "safe and well." After the war, CIC officers accused Hanna Reitsch, famous German test pilot, of planning to fly Hitler out of Berlin to the Argentine.

On Hitler's last birthday in Berlin there was a final gathering of the Nazi leadership in an undamaged chancellery building. Göring, who had come down from Carinhall, his estate north of Berlin, with truck loads of treasure, attended in a new outfit—olive-drab in color with simple cloth epaulets; "Looks like an American general," someone remarked to Albert Speer. Hitler told the gathering, "I shall leave it to fate whether I die in the capital or fly to Obersalzberg at the last minute."[198]

Göring, for one, wanted to get out of there. He told Hitler he had unnamed "urgent tasks awaiting him in South Germany" and, with permission, would leave Berlin that night. Only a single north-south route was still open to Bavaria. Hitler indifferently agreed and Göring headed for the Obersalzberg. Since he made no attempt to maintain his *Luftwaffe* responsibilities, was he merely trying to get away from it all? Hans Baur has stated that Göring and Hitler had a two-hour meeting the next day, just before Göring departed, and that they separated on the best of terms. Hitler was said to have been relieved that Göring had arrived safely at the Obersalzberg the night of April 21. This was the day that Hitler told his military conference that the war was lost, that he could do no more, and that any negotiations should be left to Göring. According to Hanna Reitsch, "It was the talk later at the Doenitz war council and elsewhere that Göring's departure was governed solely by his realization" that the defense line at the Oder, approaching Berlin, "would be crossed and by his unfulfilled hope that the partially completed 'Redoubt' area would hold." But at the time that Göring left Berlin Albert Speer referred to the Reichsmarschall as "that dodger Göring."[199]

The *Reichsmarschall*'s wife and daughter had been at their house on the Obersalzberg since the beginning of February. While the Reich was falling to pieces, Göring gave his attention to his huge art collection. At the beginning of that month he ordered that it be shipped from his two northern residences at Carinhall and Kurfürst to the Alps. The works were sent by train in three large shipments—in February, March and April. Since the Obersalzberg shelter for the collection had not yet been completed, the first two shipments went to a castle in Veldenstein and then were transferred to Berchtesgaden when the third shipment arrived on April 16. Most of the giant collection was stored in a *Luftwaffe* shelter at Unterstein, midway to the Königssee. The remainder was left on a train in the Berchtesgaden train tunnel. On April 19 Göring transferred a half million marks to his bank in Berchtesgaden.[200]

Heinrich Himmler and other SS leaders contemplated fleeing to the Alps. Himmler had a palatial residence about seventy miles west of Berchtesgaden and the SS Field Headquarters were established at nearby Fischhorn at Altaussee. On April 18, Himmler put his astrologer Wilhelm Wulff to work probing the outlook on a proposed "Obersalzberg Plan"; Wulff reported the signs were dire. At length, Himmler decided to attend Hitler's final birthday gathering on April 20, but three days later, after extended negotiations, he submitted a proposal via the Swedish diplomat Folke Bernadotte calling for unconditional surrender to the Western Allies but not to Russia.

Himmler had some kind of plan in mind for leading an SS effort in the Alps, but on April 25 Gottlob Berger, his newly-appointed deputy in Bavaria, told Himmler's chief of staff at the field headquarters that there was strong hostility in the area to Himmler. On April 28 Himmler's surrender proposal was revealed. Although Himmler denied the report, an enraged Hitler ordered the arrest of "loyal Heinrich." Despite this, Himmler the same day sent a message to Berger urging him to gather together all SS forces in the south. This was followed by another message, probably on April 29, pleading with Berger "to collect the SS units militarily under your command and head them yourself. Defend the entrance to the Alps for me." As late as May 1 Ernst Kaltenbrunner still had hopes of an effective mountain-based resistance. At that time, he declared to Himmler that the Tyrol would provide the appropriate site: "There various interests of Allies or neutrals come into conflict. Conflicts could be made more acute by skillful political games and military energy in Tito manner and German resistance preserved." In the event, however, Himmler went north to Flensburg. Himmler had the misguided expectation that Admiral Dönitz would require his services in the last German government before the general surrender.[201]

During the last days in the Führerbunker most Nazi leaders continued their efforts to get Hitler to shift from Berlin to the Obersalzberg. Obviously, they wanted to get out of a doomed Berlin and end the war in the fresh air and sunshine of the Alps, but they could not leave until Hitler did. In a long telephone conversation, Himmler urged Hitler to leave, arguing that it was senseless to remain in Berlin when in the south there was still the defensible Alpine redoubt. Foreign Minister von Ribbentrop tried to enlist Eva Braun in urging Hitler to leave for the mountains. Field Marshal Wilhelm Keitel, who had a home there, was insistent that Hitler leave for the south. Hitler turned the table by ordering Keitel, together with General Alfred Jodl, to shift to the Obersalzberg to take command of that sector. Albert Speer now joined Goebbels in urging Hitler to stay in Berlin, arguing that if Berlin fell, the war was lost. Goebbels declared that it was only proper and dignified that the end should come at (or below) the chancellery, rather than at Hitler's vacation house. That night, Hitler decided this was what he would do. He had made his final great decision. He would not be "a dishonored runaway." Indeed, "I would consider it to be a thousand times more cowardly to commit suicide on the Obersalzberg than to stand here and fall. No one shall be able to say, 'You, as the Führer....'" Thus, "I will fight and win the battle of Berlin or perish." Moreover, "I am the Führer as long as I can really lead. I cannot lead by sitting down somewhere on a mountain.... I did not come into the world solely in order to defend my Berghof."

On the evening of April 26, Hanna Reitsch, the famous aviator, flew into the battered chancellery area with Ritter von Griem, Göring's successor as *Luftwaffe* commander. She was told that Hitler's decision to remain in Berlin was made on April 22 when he found that little had been done to fortify the "Alpenfestung," that "preparations to make the 'Redoubt' resistance a success would never be completed in time." This realization, she declared, "was the major cause of Hitler's breakdown." As well, Karl-Otto Saur, the *de facto* armaments minister, having inspected the area told Hitler on April 19 that there was not enough time to establish substantial arms production in the Alps.[202]

Hitler also believed that by his staying, "all the troops of the land would take courage through my act, and come to the rescue of the city." He stated the case another way: "It makes no sense at all to sit in the south because I would have no influence, no armies. I would be there alone with my staff. Therefore, the only possibility I see to recover the situation is to gain a victory at some point. And I can only gain a success here." According to Theodor Morell, his principal doctor, Hitler refused a further injection at this time because he "knew that the Generals wanted to put him to sleep in order to cart him off to Berchtesgaden." He rightly suspected that once he left the seat of his remaining control, the state machinery would quickly dissipate. He began to think that the failure to mount a rescue effort by General Steiner was a ploy to force him out of Berlin. He told his assembled generals, "If you gentlemen imagine I'll leave Berlin now, then you have another think coming. I'd sooner put a bullet in my brain." At the same time, he was convinced that the Russians knew where he was and he feared that they might use new gas shells which could incapacitate a person for twenty-four hours. Despite this concern, he did not kill himself until Russian troops were almost within a stone's throw of the Führerbunker.[203]

The Führer ordered the evacuation of almost all of his staff, with only a core group remaining with him. Among those shifting to the south was Dr. Hans Heinrich Lammers, head of the chancellery staff; this indicated that those going to the Obersalzberg would resume their work from there. Hitler told two of his secretaries that he would follow as soon as possible. Christa Schröder recalled that Hitler told her he was starting a resistance movement in Bavaria and said, "I shall be coming down there myself in a few days."

All of the long-term staff members liked to call themselves "*die von Berg*," the mountain people, as over the years they had spent so much time on the Obersalzberg; others named them "the golden pheasants" due to their privileged position in the Hitler inner circle, with gold trim on their uniforms. In early April, Hitler had asked Heinrich Hoffmann to convince Eva Braun to leave Berlin. Now he urged both Eva Braun and Magda Goebbels to go to Bavaria; both replied they would stay with him to the end. On April 21 he contemptuously dismissed his doctor, Theodor Morell, already a sick man who was to die three years later. Morell found a place on the convoy of planes that left just past midnight on April 22 and went to his home in Bad Reichenhall, next to Berchtesgaden. Hitler obviously was getting all but a bare staff among the inner group out of the doomed city. One of those who left at this time told Leni Riefenstahl that Hitler had misled the evacuees: "The Führer lied to us. He said he would follow us using the next plane, and now the radio says that he's staying on in Berlin."[204]

Despite frantic efforts of Bormann to get others to urge Hitler to fly south, their chief had determined to stay. On the night of April 21 Operation Seraglio, probably prepared in the first week of April, was put into operation, followed by further departures on the next two nights. Hitler spent most of April 21 talking with the departing bunker group. Once they had left, and upon Hitler's invitation the Goebbels family moved into the Führerbunker, which would ring with children's voices for the next eight days. Ten planes of the first Führerflight, with forty members of Hitler's staff and footlockers of files and recordings of Hitler's speeches and evening monologues, departed from the last safe airfields around Berlin. Departure time was 2 A.M. so the trip could be made in darkness. Nine of the planes arrived safely; the tenth, departing late, crashed. This happening upset Hitler, as that plane contained his office files and words of wisdom: "In that plane were all my private archives, that I had intended as a testament to posterity. It is a catastrophe." According to Hugh Trevor-Roper, in the crash there were four hundred paintings and drawings by Hitler, including many sketches of Eva Braun, some in the nude. Several reasons have been given for the delay in that plane's departure—engine trouble, tardiness of some passengers and the action of the ground crew, who are said to have thrown the baggage off the plane when they realized that the Hitler staff was fleeing the besieged city.[205]

Years later, in 1983, the German magazine *Der Stern* announced that some Hitler diaries had been found, having survived the plane crash, and that it would begin publishing excerpts. Serial rights were sold to publications in many countries, including *Newsweek* and the *London Sunday Times*. Hugh Trevor-Roper, for a time, believed the diaries were genuine. It soon turned out, however, that they were forgeries. Eva's sister, Gretl Fegelein, could have saved everyone a lot of bother. She told CIC interrogators at the end of the war, "Hitler didn't keep any diaries."[206]

Early on, Eva Braun believed Hitler would shift to the Obersalzberg. In late April she wrote to her sister Gretl at the Berghof, "It's now about time for us to move out; we are already under fire." But then Hitler decided not to leave Berlin. On April 22 she wrote to her friend Herta Schneider at the Berghof, "Please leave the mountain. It is too dangerous a place for you to be when all this comes to an end." The next day she wrote to her sister urging her to pack her correspondence with Hitler in a watertight container and bury it. She also implored Gretl to destroy evidence of her extravagant clothing expenditures: "Under no circumstances are bills from Heise to be found." She ordered the division of her jewelry and provided tobacco for "Pappa" and chocolate for "Mutti." As for other possessions, "destroy everything only at the last moment." Her letter was delivered on April 27 by Julius Schaub who, on Hitler's orders, had flown down from Berlin two days before.[207]

Did Allied intelligence not have a single agent at the airport, or anywhere else, who could have reported a major departure of the *Führerstaffel*? If so, did it assume that this indicated that Hitler either had or intended to go to his Alpine retreat? In his book *The Bunker*, James O'Donnell speculates about these possibilities. There was a security leak at the Reich Chancellery, a matter that was of constant concern to Hitler. Hermann Fegelein probably told his woman friend, who was assumed to be British, about such plans; she disappeared at the time of his arrest. If SHAEF intelligence knew about this movement, would this not have given increased credence to the Alpine fortress story? But there is no evidence that SHAEF knew about it. The OSS had only begun to try dropping its own people into Bavaria, and German informants fed it largely a mélange of speculation and rumor. Possibly the British SOE (Special Operations Executive) might have had better information; that file was closed for a hundred years. "Marta O'Hara," reportedly an Irishwoman married to a Hungarian diplomat, was a British agent. O'Donnell also says that he had found no evidence that either Western or Russian intelligence knew where Hitler was in the last hundred days or of the existence of the Führerbunker.[208]

By the second week of April the ULTRA system for de-coding German military communications indicated that there was a flow of troops and supplies to the south as well as the transfer of government agencies and military headquarters from Thuringia to the Salzburg area. These decrypts revealed nothing about a mountain bastion in the making until the very end of April, when some German radio traffic began to refer to "the Alpine Fortress." The paucity of German communications about the matter caused some ULTRA analysts, remembering how Hitler had used radio silence in his build-up to the Ardennes offensive, to believe that the same ploy was being used to disguise the scope of this effort. In fact, almost all of the vehicles heading south were transporting a mass of non-combatant personnel as well as huge amounts of paintings, precious metals and other valuables to Alpine salt mines.[209]

On the night of April 21, on Bormann's instructions, a caravan of vehicles containing the heads of government agencies and the military staff of Army Group B departed for the south. By that time most government agencies had already left, with most transferring to southern Bavaria. Some personnel went south even later. On the night of April 22, Gerhardt Herrgeselle, one of Hitler's stenographers, flew south with the transcript of that day's conference. He found Gatow airport, the only one around Berlin still in German control, already abandoned, "but a full crew was there with a big Condor transport plane." The next night Paul Schmidt, head of the Foreign Office press section, flew to Salzburg, in the belief that "the redoubt area of Germany would be held for some time. Plans were to make the small town of Bad Garstein the focal point of the redoubt defense."[210]

As has been seen, the families of several top officials already were at the Obersalzberg. These included those of Bormann, Göring, Speer and Keitel. Himmler's mistress and her children were down the road at Königssee. Bormann had sent his wife several sealed courier pouches, which supposedly included notes from Hitler's final late-night conversations, some of Hitler's water-color paintings and Bormann's correspondence. Bormann saw that the time to move his family had come. He had arranged with Franz Hofer, gauleiter of the Tyrol, for accommodations near Bolzano for both the party chancellery files and the Bormann family. Together with her nine children and with a half-dozen children taken from the Obersalzberg facility and probably some from that at Garmisch, Frau Bormann could pose as a director of an evacuated children's group. On April 28 Bormann told his wife to immediately leave for the Tyrol. She managed to move the group to the south Tyrol site, which was located by the Counterintelligence Corps in October; she contracted a fatal disease and soon died.[211]

## Geld

More than just people were heading for the Alps. On the night on April 8–9 Walter Funk, president of the Reichsbank, secured the reluctant assent of Hitler, as a purely precautionary measure, mind you, to transfer most of the gold and monetary holdings of the national bank to the mountains. The Nazis had accumulated a huge hoard of gold and currencies, including large portions of the national reserves of Belgium, France, Hungary, Italy and Czechoslovakia, then valued at a half billion dollars. Branches of the state bank were instructed to send their gold holdings to Berlin, a process which was largely completed by April 13. A treasure of 750 gold bars (weighing nine tons) and heaps of gold coins were assembled. That day, the currency holdings and bank officials departed on two trains, which, due to bomb damage, had to take a roundabout route and arrived in Munich two weeks later—on the eve of the American occupation of the city. On April 14, the gold bars were shipped out by road, using a half dozen Berlin police trucks, and arrived in Munich in just five days.

The same day, the 19th, bank officials concluded that Munich was no longer safe, so the convoy, with no clear destination in mind, headed into the Alps. Two days later it arrived at Mittelwald, ninety miles south of Munich, perched on the Austrian border. Here was the headquarters of the Mountain Infantry Training School. After some discussion, it was decided to store the holdings at a building called the Forest House in the remote village of Einsiedl. About April 24 the first shipment arrived—eleven very heavy boxes, lined at their tops with bottles of wine, from Berchtesgaden. The truck driver who delivered the shipment said it was dispatched on orders from Dr. Funk, although Funk later denied he had done so. Apparently, this shipment was not part of the Reichsbank consignment and it soon disappeared. Where did it come from, whose was it, and how did it get to Berchtesgaden?

The currency that arrived in Munich by train seems to have been widely distributed

en route and afterwards. A bit of the hoard was brought to Berchtesgaden at the very beginning of May in the back of a Volkswagen by Dr. Funk—two gold bars and three bags of currency. He sent a message to Otto Skorzeny requesting that the commando leader, who was
in and out of Berchtesgaden at this time, provide security for accumulated bank wealth and
himself; Skorzeny later claimed that he had not responded to this request. Funk then gave
his cache to Karl Theodor Jacob, the *Landrat* (governor) of the district, who deposited it in
the Berchtesgaden Savings Bank. There has been the allegation that Jacob kept back $67,000
in currency. Helmut von Hummel, Bormann's economic affairs advisor, is said to have been
given a hoard of 2200 gold coins at Berchtesgaden (intended for the planned Führermuseum in Linz) and had them buried in a secret location in the Austrian mountains. Thus
began many stories of the missing Nazi gold.[212]

Even before the state bank began transporting its wealth south, the *Schutzstaffel* was
sending its enormous haul of confiscated wealth to the mountains. Otto Skorzeny reportedly was involved in shipping and securing specific shipments to the south. On April 22 a
force of SS men robbed the Reichsbank headquarters of its remaining gold and other wealth.
It was shipped out on one of the last planes from Berlin and, in Salzburg, it was loaded
onto a truck. Some of the treasure was buried in a nearby hill, while the rest was distributed among SS officers, including Skorzeny. Much of this loot was eventually found by U.S.
military personnel, but not, apparently, the Skorzeny cache. After three years of imprisonment, he escaped and, after various travels, lived in Spain at a most comfortable level until
his death in 1975. Other SS loot arrived at Altaussee in the Tyrol, home base of Ernst
Kaltenbrunner. Reports that large amounts of gold, jewels and other valuables were dumped
in area lakes persisted long after the war. Over a half century later, in 2000, an American-
Israeli group organized a mini-submarine search of the Toplitzsee, a lake in Upper Austria.
There was no report of recovered treasure.[213]

Various other state organizations, on a much more modest scale, also stashed bullion,
jewels, currency and more in the Alps. Among these bodies were the Foreign Office, Military Intelligence and the Wehrmacht. In February entire collections of art work, along with
Reichsbank gold and all kinds of foreign money, were stored in mines in Merkers, a town
in Thuringia, two hundred miles southwest of Berlin. This incredible cache was discovered
by U.S. troops on April 7.[214]

There was also a mass of Hungarian people and wealth moving west into the supposed
Alpine Redoubt. As Russian forces approached Budapest in November 1944, the Hungarian civil administration shifted to the western fringe of the country and then into Austria.
Later, the U.S. Army counted 89,000 Hungarians in its occupation zone in Austria. In
December 1944, just before the Russians surrounded Budapest, two huge train convoys
departed the capital, one transporting the money and gold reserves of the National Bank
of Hungary, while the other, the so-called Gold Train, carried away gold and other valuables confiscated from Hungarian Jews, as well as a large number of government officials.
After numerous delays due to damaged rail lines, the Gold Train arrived at Hallein, Austria, in early April, then moved through southern Bavaria past Berchtesgaden to Hopfgarten.
With no Alpenfestung in which to shelter this load and as the war drew to a close, it mean-
dered south to Bockstein, then north to Werfen, where, after a month's delay, U.S. forces
finally took control of it on May 29, with senior U.S. Army personnel freely helping themselves to its contents. Sixty years later the U.S. government finally agreed to acknowledge
the guilt of its agents and provide twenty-five million dollars for the victims of the Hungarian Holocaust.[215]

Reinhard Gehlen got the jump on the migration to the south. The head of the eastern front intelligence organization, Gehlen investigated places in the Alps to store his files as early as December 1944. In early March 1945 key files were microfilmed in triplicate. Outraged by what he saw as Gehlen's faulty intelligence estimates, Hitler removed him as head of the unit on April 9, but this did not prevent Gehlen's organization from shipping fifty-two containers of microfilm to Bad Reichenhall, near Berchtesgaden. From there they were secreted at three places—at a village south of Chiemsee in Bavaria, near Kufstein in the Tyrol, and in the mountains above Valepp, also in the Tyrol. The process was completed by April 28. Remaining in hiding until then, Gehlen and his colleagues surrendered to a unit of the U.S. Army on May 22. The embryo American intelligence service quickly recognized the importance of Gehlen's data and personnel. His organization was employed first as branch of the Central Intelligence Agency and then, in 1956, as the West German intelligence service, with Gehlen as its head.[216]

When, on April 21, Hitler finally stated that the war was lost, he ordered the burning of his personal papers in the bunker and instructed Julius Schaub, his veteran *aide de camp*, to fly to Munich and then to Berchtesgaden to destroy his personal files; Eva's sister Gretl, who was still there, met Schaub drunk and on the arm of his mistress in the Berghof on April 27. Obviously determined to prevent any of his personal papers from falling into the hands of his enemies, Hitler had already dispatched Karl-Jesko von Puttkamer, his naval adjutant, to deal with this matter on the Obersalzberg, and, further, sent Johannes Göhler, another aide, on the same task. Göhler, who flew to Munich on the night of April 22, sent SS officer Franz Konrad to Berchtesgaden to destroy Hitler's papers.

Over the next few days, a collection of Eva's correspondence with Hitler, photographs and movie film was among the material moved to Fischhorn Castle at Altaussee in Austria, the last headquarters of the SS. Hitler's library of 2000 books was transferred to a nearby salt mine. At this time, Gretl Fegelein and her friend Herta Schnieder left for Garmisch. The books were discovered by U.S. troops and the bulk of them were eventually transported to the Library of Congress. The Counter Intelligence Corps tracked down most of the Eva Braun material in August and October 1945, but some of it had been taken by Franz Konrad and other SS members as well as by CIC personnel.[217]

The situation in Berchtesgaden was chaotic. There were no further accommodations in the town. The Alpenfestung was little more than a refugee camp for a defeated elite. To prepare for what seemed like inevitable occupation by the American army, Bernhard Frank, the Obersalzberg commander, created a mountain retreat for those who wanted to absent themselves from this event. There was a much larger influx into Garmisch-Partenkirchen, a major resort area and the site of the 1936 Winter Olympics. This area already had 10,000 wounded soldiers.[218]

Bormann was still hoping that Hitler would depart for the south. He pleaded with Goebbels, his long-time adversary, to urge *der Chef* to do this. When Speer paid Hitler a final, and dangerous, visit on April 23, Hitler asked him, "Should I stay here in Berlin or fly to Berchtesgaden? General Jodl has told me I now have, at the most, twenty-four hours to make my final decision." Speer repeated his advice to stay, to which Hitler replied, "I, too, have resolved to stay here in Berlin."[219]

In fact, Speer wanted to get the war over with and Hitler's staying in Berlin would serve that purpose. Already, Speer had frustrated Hitler's Nero order to destroy all public facilities as the Allies drove into Germany. As well, he had secretly supported General Heinrici's decision not to defend Berlin. When Hermann Göring, viewing events from the Obersalzberg, proposed flying to meet with Eisenhower about peace terms, Speer responded by urging the jet-fighter commander in Bavaria "to do everything to prevent an airplane flight by Göring." It would appear that Speer was accumulating evidence of good deeds that would prove invaluable at his looming war-criminal trial and he did not want Göring to get into the act. Speer, apparently the only "normal" person in the Nazi hierarchy, was to escape the gallows.[220]

The same day, now that the country had been cut in half, Hitler created separate military commands for the north and south of what was left of Nazi Germany. Field Marshal Albert Kesselring, commander of forces in northern Italy, was given the added responsibility of those forces in Bavaria and Austria. Göring was merely "the Führer's personal representative" in the zone.[221]

Despite the claims of Joseph Goebbels and the *Sicherheitsdienst* (SD), the Nazi security agency, nothing had been done about Franz Hofer's proposal of November 1944 to fortify the northern approaches to the Alps. As has been pointed out, Hofer's persistent requests for a response were blocked by Bormann. Now, in the dying days of the regime, Hofer at last got to see Hitler—on April 11. Nine days later Hitler decided that the area should be fortified "as a last bulwark of fanatical resistance" and declared that the area be closed to civilians, provision made for American, British and French POWs, stockpiling of supplies and creation of emergency factories for munitions production. In a directive issued on April 24, he appointed General August Winter to take command of the operation. When Winter arrived in Berchtesgaden, he quickly recognized that time did not permit an effective creation of a mountain fortress. Nevertheless, he joined forces with Reich Defense Commissar Hofer and issued orders to block northern entrances to the Alps.[222]

Then there was General Georg Ritter von Hengl, who was not only a mountain infantryman but also chief of the National Socialist Guidance Staff of the army. When appointed on April 20 to take command of the northern Alps, he found that almost nothing had been done to defend the area—no supplies, fortifications or plan of defense. Only some tank obstacles and a few isolated field positions had been built. Nor was there an army combat division to be found, but there was a small number of detached military units, including two SS battalions. On the other hand, there were swarms of civilian officials and army officers milling around, "in particular, high ranking staffs without troops, but above all, air corps ground personnel" who flooded the area "contrary to the specific order that 'no extra chow-hounds are to be permitted in the Alpine fortress.'" The most von Hengl could pull together from depleted training and replacement depots were 3000 soldiers. He knew nothing about SS units reportedly in the mountains, probably numbering around 7000 personnel. He estimated that ninety percent of the military people in the area were noncombatants. Battered remnants of the forces which had opposed the Americans were expected shortly. Only a small number of ragged remnants of the First and Nineteenth Armies made it to the Alps. However, after the May 8 surrender whole, well-equipped SS units came marching down from the mountains. An extraordinary total of about 300,000 German military surrendered in the Berchtesgaden area.[223]

To stem the tide of civilians moving into the area, Kesselring on May 1 ordered German officials to remain at their offices and stay out of the Alps. The next day, checkpoints were established in the northern foothills to turn back both military and civilian refugees. In addition, the local population clearly did not support the idea of a bloody finale on their Alpine ground. If the Führer should withdraw to the Obersalzberg, they recognized that the area could easily be plastered every day by hundreds of Allied bombers with nothing else to do.[224]

There also was the problem of the onrush of Soviet forces. On April 25, Hitler gave Field Marshal Ferdinand Schorner a new responsibility. While continuing to fight in Bohemia, he was to take command of the Alpenfestung for the purpose of stopping western penetration by the Russians, not the Americans. This focus was a change in policy and in keeping with Hitler's final hope—that there would be conflict between the Allied powers. Goebbels told Schorner that there also was a "North Project" being built up by Admiral Dönitz; the two masses of disciplined troops could be used for bargaining with the Western Allies. Kesselring's thinking was generally along the same lines—that resistance in the Alps should be used to allow as many German troops as possible to move west ahead of the Russians. But Schorner, having first directed his troops in Bohemia to head west, did not arrive in the Alpine area until May 8.[225]

In March 1944, a group of leading Austrian Nazis speculated that the threat of an Alpine fortress, centered around the Tyrol, could be used for the sake of Austria. After 1938, Hitler had obliterated Austria as an entity, dividing the country into several districts. As defeat loomed, Austrian nationalism revived. An SS group led by Wilhelm Höttl, Wilhelm Waneck and Werner Gottsch hoped to use this state of mind to secure an Anglo-American occupation of Austria. They sought to enlist the support of Ernst Kaltenbrunner, an Austrian and deputy leader of the SS, to scout out possibilities. Kaltenbrunner dispatched an agent to talk with a representative of Allen Dulles. Kaltenbrunner was informed that Dulles was understanding about the Austrian desire to dissociate itself from the Nazi connection. What Dulles undoubtedly was doing was trying to delay preparations in the redoubt.[226]

Then there was an Italian angle. Karl Wolff, SS chief and the Wehrmacht's leading general in Italy, was in the process of negotiating the capitulation of German forces there. When he learned of this, Kaltenbrunner immediately sought to stop it, as it would mean German forces in northern Italy could not withdraw to the Alps and, thus, the whole southern flank of the purported redoubt would be exposed. From his headquarters in Salzburg, Kaltenbrunner oversaw the distribution of food, equipment, money and gold to various Nazi elements determined to carry on the fight. A representative of Otto Skorzeny collected 50,000 French francs in gold coin, 10,000 Swedish crowns, 5000 U.S. dollars and 5000 Swiss francs as well as five million reichsmarks. On May 1, Kaltenbrunner left Salzburg for Altaussee where his mistress was waiting; from there, on May 7, he fled into the Austrian Alps and on May 11 was captured by a U.S. Army unit.[227]

In the last days of the war, even after the death of Hitler, some German generals continued to foster the belief that conflict between Americans and Russians was inevitable and that this would provide an opportunity for some sort of an arrangement with the Americans. Rumors spread among Germans troops coming in from east that if they held on in the Alps they soon would be joining forces with the Americans. This belief was reinforced by a mighty Russian offensive through Austria and Czechoslovakia. The Russians obviously were attempting to preclude American occupation of the area. What was required was strong opposition to the Russian advance until the Americans arrived.[228]

Hermann Göring arrived at Obersalzberg on the evening of April 21. In the midst of the final crisis of the Third Reich he was preoccupied with his huge art collection, which had departed by rail for Berchtesgaden from his Cairenhall estate on March 13. A week later he got Hitler's permission to go there to "inspect the flak." Hitler was not deceived about Göring's intention: "He's just gone down to the Obersalzberg again with two trains, to see his wife." Göring was again on the mountain on April 10, when he met with Adolf Galland, head of the *Luftwaffe* fighter arm, ostensibly on air force business. Galland concluded that the meeting was an attempt by Göring to cover the real reason for Göring being there—to supervise the securing of his art treasures.[229]

On Göring's final journey south, his convoy refueled at Sudetengau, where he was greeted by cheers and requests for autographs; it also went through Pilsen, to where the Air Ministry had been evacuated, but stopped only to get more fuel. Six freight cars loaded with his art treasures were waiting for him in Berchtesgaden. The next day, Hitler, in a rage, declared that the war was lost, that he was giving up his authority, and that Göring could see to the ending of the war. Gerhardt Herrgesell, one of Hitler's stenographers, told American interrogators that he heard a "slightly hazy" and distracted Hitler tell Bormann, Keitel and Jodl, "Go to southern Germany. Göring should form a new government. In any case arising, Göring should form a new government." Alfred Jodl, chief of Hitler's inner war staff, just after midnight on April 22–23 told Karl Koller, Göring's chief of staff, "The Führer has surrendered his command and has resolved to remain in Berlin, directing the defense and shoot himself as a last resort." Jodl reported Hitler as saying, "There is not much more to fight for, and when it comes to making peace, the Reichsmarschall can do that better than I." But Hitler never explained whether he meant Göring should act immediately or should wait until after Hitler was dead. This matter was of importance, at least to Göring. Indeed, the next day, upon the urging of various Nazi leaders, Hitler decided, after all, not to give up the struggle.[230]

The *Reichsmarschall* had already considered how he might end the conflict. Apparently Göring was informed about what Hitler said even before Koller came to the Obersalzberg on April 23. When told of these statements by Koller, Göring questioned Hans Lammers, who had possession of the relevant documents pertaining to Göring's right of succession. Later that day, the *Reichsmarschall* sent a radio message stating that if he did not shortly hear from Hitler he would assume that Hitler had lost his freedom of action and he would take over the leadership; he concluded his message to Hitler with, "May God protect you, and speed you quickly here in spite of all." Göring told those who were with him that he would seek an immediate end to the war. He claimed that this objective was to have been deleted from the message that he sent to Hitler, but later concluded it must have been transmitted. Believing that he was about to become head of state, Göring remarked to his wife, "Now that the whole of Germany is being put in my hands, everything is destroyed and it's too late! The Führer should have given me full powers in December! I begged for them passionately at the time!" He proposed that the next day he would fly to Eisenhower's headquarters and, in a man-to man meeting, end hostilities. His confidence was such that he sent messages to key cabinet ministers telling them of his assumption of power should there be no response from Hitler or when the succession decree went into effect.[231]

He then called in Bernhard Frank, military commander of the Obersalzberg area. When Frank encountered Göring, whom he had not met before, he saw before him a man "in a silky white uniform; much gold, bemedaled," with cosmetics on his face and an "unnatural shine in his eyes," which reminded him of Hitler's radiant appearance at the Führer's 1944 birthday reception. Göring told Frank of his message to Hitler and of Göring's desire to end the war by negotiations with the Western Allies. Göring then "asked me whether I would be ready to help him with all of my powers, whether I would risk my life if necessary"; Frank answered yes.

Hitler responded by informing Göring that "my freedom of action is undisputed" and forbade him from assuming the leadership. Göring responded by telegram canceling any such action. According to Albert Speer, who was with Hitler at the time, Hitler repeated his statement that Göring could "negotiate the surrender. If the war is lost anyhow, it doesn't matter who does it." Apparently acting on his own, however, Bormann sent a message to the Obersalzberg radio center ordering the arrest of Göring. The order was addressed both to Bernhard Frank as well as to SS leader Bredow, Bormann's chauffeur, who, according to Frank, "had no military function on the Obersalzberg." Frank spotted Bormann's hand in the order. He decided to show Göring the message without comment and let Göring respond.

Before doing so, Frank decided, in the light of these developments, to order the sealing off of the "extended Führer zone" and put everyone there under preliminary detention "with honor." He also cut off all news connections. These actions met with a flurry of inquiry on the Berg. Frank then returned to Göring's house, where the *Reichsmarschall*, though he found the order hard to believe, agreed to being arrested. Frank saw to it that this confinement was little more than the house arrest that applied to everyone else on the Obersalzberg.[232]

Learning of Göring's arrest, Heinrich Himmler ordered Ernst Kaltenbrunner to go to the Obersalzberg to determine what was happening there. Whether Kaltenbrunner actually went there is doubtful, but he reported to Himmler on the evening of April 25 that he did not know what to do with Göring and that he feared an Allied air drop might be attempted to capture Göring.[233]

Frank, who makes no mention of Kalterbrunner's presence, at this point decided that, since the Americans were expected shortly, Göring was in great danger and, with the support of his SS superior in Salzburg secured on April 24, he decided to accede to Göring's request to be moved to his mansion at Schloss Mauterndorf, forty miles beyond Salzburg. Before Frank could execute this transfer, he was confronted with more instructions from Berlin. Göring was to be stripped of all of his offices. If Göring took charge, that would be the end of Bormann's power and probably the end of Bormann. Albert Speer suspected that this was Bormann's final ploy for getting Hitler to go to the Obersalzberg—would not the Führer go there to deal with this attempt at usurpation? For the last week of his life, Hitler denounced Göring, declaring among other things, "The fat pig! He doesn't have enough courage to die with us." From the Obersalzberg Koller radioed detailed arguments that Göring had done nothing wrong; his plea was ignored, and, for his pains, he was ordered to fly to Berlin. Koller got as far as Rechlin, the airport nearest Berlin which was still in German control. When his radioed pleas to Hitler had no effect, he returned to Berchtesgaden.[234]

Then, the next day, April 25, came the only air attack on the Obersalzberg complex, but it was devastating. Coming at the tail end of the war, the attack seemed to be only an afterthought, but it did serve the purpose of effectively precluding Hitler's withdrawal to the place. The U.S. Air Force had prepared a detailed target information sheet, dated 5 October 1944, for the bombardment of the Obersalzberg, and subsequently considered two attacks on area transportation networks in early 1945, but these did not result in action until almost every other likely target in Germany had been pulverized.

The assault was made by the Royal Air Force in its last major attack of the war. The obvious purpose of this belated attack was to discourage if not prevent to Hitler using the place as headquarters for a last-ditch stand in the mountains. It probably also acted as a final reminder to the Germans of RAF power. Because almost all of the outlying radar warning posts had been captured by the Allies, the Obersalzberg radar had only five minutes' warning that the bomber fleet was heading its way. It took at least thirty minutes for the fog to cover the area, so the fog machines were ineffective. With trained crewmen transferred to other more urgent posts, the anti-aircraft guns were manned by young, inexperienced operatives who did not have time, nor, probably, the desire, to immediately man their guns.

Arriving in two waves, an hour and a half apart (9 A.M. and 10:30 A.M.), a fleet of 375 British planes—359 Lancaster and 16 Mosquito bombers, escorted by 88 P-51 Mustang fighters of the U.S. Eighth Air Force—dropped 1232 tons of bombs (including four 12,000-pound "Tallboy" bombs) on the Nazi complex. Only two of the bombers were lost. The massive tonnage of bombs was based on an Allied intelligence assumption that the site contained huge underground fortifications.

The *New York Times* reported that the Berghof, "painted white, appeared to be covered with snow to some pilots but it stood plainly out from other buildings surrounding it.... Heavy anti-aircraft fire [was] put up by the Germans after they recovered from the first shock." Continuing, the *Times* declared that "there was 'one terrific flash' from a six-ton missile falling square on the chalet and two heavy bombs struck either side of the building, 'as near as makes no difference,' an RAF rear gunner said." The newspaper reported that first reconnaissance photographs of the attack showed a "large number of bombings bursting on the chalet and on the SS [Elite Guard] barracks." The RAF after-action report declared that "the bombing appeared to be accurate and effective."

In fact, the giant bombs landed beyond the Berghof, which was on a lower slope and the first building in the line of attack, leaving a huge crater about a hundred fifty feet past it, just before the kindergarten and architectural buildings. In his history of the regiment, Nathan White commented, "The 7th Infantry discovered on 4 May '45 when it captured Berchtesgaden that the hideaway was never hit by a bomb though many had struck nearby." That the Berghof did not sustain damage was confirmed by four Allied witnesses who arrived on the scene nine days later. This was also the case for the adjoining Platterhof hotel, Speer's studio, the *Luftwaffe* staff building below Göring's house, the outlying buildings of Bormann's "experimental farm" and the two clusters of staff housing. Many other structures, particularly the SS barracks complex higher up on the mountain, were severely damaged, but accumulated snow prevented the spread of fires. The inaccurate bombing was due to the inability of the Mosquitoes to employ markers to best advantage. According to the RAF post-action report, "Mountains intervened between one of the ground stations transmitting the *Oboe* [target location] signals and the Mosquitoes could not operate even though they were flying at 39,000 feet! There was some mist and the presence of snow on the ground also made it difficult to identify targets."[235]

About 3500 persons sheltered in the tunnel system; only thirty-one persons were killed—nine children, seven women, one soldier and seven SS members. Both Goebbels and Eva Braun derived satisfaction from Göring's being caught in the bombardment. Hermann survived in his bomb shelter, although his house was wrecked along with Bormann's house. The building on the Kehlstein was not hit, nor was Berchtesgaden. At the same time 278 B-24 Liberators of the U.S. Eighth Air Force struck at the four rail lines ringing Berchtesgaden—bombing the lines at Traunstein, twenty-five miles northwest, Salzburg, fifteen miles north, Hallein, ten miles northwest, and Bad Reichenhall, fifteen miles northwest.[236]

Even at this point Hitler sought to maintain some sense of his authority. He ordered Albert Bormann, brother of Martin and one of Hitler's adjutants, to establish a new southern Führer headquarters at the Gasthof Alpenhof at the nearby Lake Hintersee. About forty people (of about eighty) transferred there, including all of the Berghof house staff and a few party officials and SS officers. Among Hitler's possessions which were moved was his five-ton armored Mercedes Benz. The headquarters staff of Army Group B, which had moved to Berchtesgaden on April 20, shifted from the nearby Strub Kaserne to the Hotel Schiffmeister on Lake Königssee.[237]

With the breakdown of teletype communications with Berlin, a top-secret radio system went into operation. In February 1945 Bormann had secured at least two special radio trucks from Admiral Dönitz with the latest Enigma ciphering equipment. Two of these trucks were transferred south with the headquarters of Army Group B. Florian Beierl, a Berchtesgaden native who has spent years researching the subject, was told by an informant that on the day after the bombardment of the Obersalzberg, on April 25, one of the radio trucks positioned itself at various points on the Kehlstein and began transmitting to Berlin and elsewhere. The other truck soon joined this activity. Guarded by forty SS men, the vehicles operated out of a secret bunker, which Beierl later explored. The mobile radios continued to communicate with a variety of places until May 1. Most of the messages appear to have been sent to two German agents in South America. The next day the trucks left the Kehlstein and went to army headquarters on Lake Königssee. According to Ronald Lewin, British codebreakers at Bletchley Park were determined to get hold of these vehicles because their Enigma machines had codes the British had been unable to break since February 1945. Probably on May 3, a British commando group, led by Oskar Öser and guided by the broadcast coordinates, arrived at Köngissee (by air drop?) and, without resistance, confiscated the machines. Also, they reportedly went to Bischofswiesen and secured the radio equipment on Field Marshal Kesselring's train.[238]

Immediately after the bombing of the Obersalzberg site, workers began to clear exit roads, and a thousand persons were evacuated by April 29. Three days after the air assault, upon Frank's instruction, Göring left with his SS guards for Mauterdorf, where he remained in luxurious confinement for ten days.[239]

It was the retrospective view of the authors of the U.S. Military Government report for the first year of American occupation that the April 25 bombing destroyed "the intention of the Nazi war lords to stand at bay for their last struggle on the Obersalzberg." The report stated the belief that before the attack "in month-long day and night work, thousands of workers had built fortifications, considered impregnable, trainloads of ammunition, weapons and food had been streaming in a continuous flow into the Berchtesgaden marshalling-yards and crack SS-divisions and other picked troops had been stationed in the Landkreis." With the Obersalzberg complex destroyed, it declared, the assembled Nazi leaders quickly "retired to the interior of the Tyrol," not before taking "everything worth looting" and obtaining false identity papers from the Landrat's office, "partly by force." This is the inaccurate and false story it assembled in the wake of the war.[240]

In the Führerbunker the end was rapidly approaching. When Hanna Reitsch arrived there on April 26 she found its denizens in a state of mounting hysteria. Goebbels was strutting about making his final histrionic statements, while his wife Magda was full of tears about her decision to kill her children but was adamantly determined to remain at the side of her beloved Führer to the end. Martin Bormann was preoccupied with recording every event in the shelter, convinced that his narrative would be a proud document in German history. Although she found Eva Braun to be a "very beautiful woman," Hanna thought that there was "an adolescent tinge" to everything Eva said, indicative of a "rather shallow mentality."

Both Reitsch and Griem were provided with poison capsules and attended a suicide preparatory meeting on the night of April 27, where there was agreement that when the Russians reached the chancellery "the mass suicide would begin." Concerning Göring, Hitler told Hanna that "against my orders he has gone to save himself at Berchtesgaden." She told

Hitler, "When the news was released that you would remain in Berlin to the last, the people were amazed with horror." She urged him to live by taking flight. His reply: "No Hanna, if I die it is for the honor of our country, it is because as a soldier I must obey my own command that I would defend Berlin to the last."[241]

Hitler retained his grip on many Germans to the end. Hans Baur, his chief pilot, recalled that "it seems astonishing that there were people even then who still wanted to see Hitler." Less than a day before his suicide, Hitler responded to wishes of the nurses in the underground hospital adjacent to the Führerbunker that he come to them. With the Goebbels offspring leading children in song as he entered the room, Hitler, with his hands purposefully in his coat pockets, merely nodded to the nurses and left.[242]

April 28 was Adolf Hitler's wedding day. The idea for the last minute nuptials probably came to Hitler from the desire of at least two couples to get married in the dramatic setting of the Chancellery under siege. They were married on April 26 in the shattered main hall of the building with Hitler and Eva offering congratulations. Even at this stage marriage would be pleasing to both Eva and her parents. The Hitler nuptials were in the bunker. In any case, the Adolf-Eva marriage was short-lived. The next night there was a final gathering of the remaining members of the inner circle. In the midst of almost constant bombardment and massive casualties, Dr. Ernst-Günther Schenck came upon the group drinking away around a table, Eva Hitler included, but not her husband. Schenck observed that "they kept talking on and on about life in Berchtesgaden, of how they had lived up there, enthroned like Wagnerian gods, above the clouds that encircled the foothills and cut them off utterly from other Germans, all other lesser mortals."

A day and a half later—April 30—Hitler's bride joined him in death. Before his suicide, Hitler bade farewell to the assortment of people still in the Führerbunker. One of those present, nurse Erna Flegal, provided a histrionic account of these events. "At the end we were like a big family," she told her CIC interrogators. "We were Germany, and we were going through the end of the Third Reich." Those who shook hands with Hitler included "secretaries, the cleaning women and a few strangers who had taken refuge in the shelter." To Flegal this was a significant occasion: "I had a feeling that for Hitler we were the forum of the German people to which he was presenting himself once more since he had no more extensive one." One of his final instructions was that the Führerbunker was not to be destroyed because "I want the Russians to realize that I stayed here to the very last moment." But the next day—May 1—two staff officers set the bunker conference room on fire, although the blaze did not spread to the other parts of the shelter.[243]

The fate of Martin Bormann has been a subject of speculation for many years. 200,000 wanted posters seeking his capture were put up around the American zone. In the early days of the American occupation of Berchtesgden, soldiers searched the countryside for him. As has been seen, Bormann had taken good care to see that his family got away to the Tyrol so it was likely that, if possible, he would have headed south from Berlin. He undoubtedly was involved in transferring money and precious metals to South America. Several historians have argued that he was the force behind the creation of the Odessa network, an escape route for Nazi officials who passed through the Mittelwald to the Tyrol and on to Italy. Ladislas Farago has claimed that Bormann himself escaped this way and made it to South America, where he lived within a Nazi coterie for many years.

On the other hand, Bormann was also reportedly killed on May 1, 1945, while fleeing Berlin. On April 29, Hitler ordered Hans Baur to transport Bormann, who was to deliver the original copy of his political testament and several instructions, to Admiral Dönitz at

Flensburg, using one of Baur's planes at Rechlin. On May 1, the two departed from the bunker together. Baur was shot and disabled, later losing a leg. It was then that Bormann must have realized that he was not going to escape and taken poison. In 1972 human remains with fragments of plastic vials locked in the jaws were found at the site where he reportedly died, and these remains were identified as those of Bormann. A Munich court in 1998 came to the same conclusion. Martin Bormann did not live to laugh at the world from a South American hideout.[244]

In Berchtesgadener Land Nazi officials, bewildered refugees and disorganized soldiers piled up on top of each other. The flotsam of a dying empire was milling about. There was Norman Baillie-Stewart, an ex–British Army officer who in 1932 had been convicted of passing military data to the Germans and during the war was an assistant to the radio propagandist William Joyce, "Lord Haw Haw." Walther Funk arrived by car with two gold bars and bags of currency. Robert Ley, head of the German Labor Front, had a small group of followers prepared to carry on the fight in the mountains. Paul Giesler, the gauleiter of Upper Bavaria, having urged the people of Munich to resist the invaders to the bitter end, fled to Berchtesgaden on April 29 and a few days later killed himself. The army was so short of vehicles it was forced to commandeer civilian cars that were hauling possessions into the area; one of these was transporting some of Göring's carpets. On May 1, Dr. Helmut von Hummel, special assistant to Bormann, demanded and received a case of confiscated gold coins and promptly disappeared.[245]

The group of twenty-one prominent Allied prisoners, transported from Colditz, also appeared on the scene. Under apparent orders by Hitler to be executed, the two truckloads of them passed through Berchtesgaden in the first days of May. With the town's Nazi reputation, the prisoners surmised that this "must be the journey's end." Michael Alexander recalled the place: "The little town of Berchtesgaden still had the air of a holiday resort in spite of the large amount of military transport parked in the streets. With its hotels, cafes and shops selling carved wood objects, it invited the tourist to stop. But we hurried on— out the other side and into the mountains in what seemed a more westerly direction."

Arriving at a makeshift encampment at Markt Pongau, this group was informed by SS General Gottlob Berger that, contrary to orders from above, he was releasing them. The escorted convoy soon met American troops advancing from Innsbruck. Alexander described the sensation of arriving in the midst of a random unit of the U.S. Army: "Tanks were parked in the village square, their crews, slung with every conceivable weapon, were standing around smoking and chewing gum.... Most surprising of all, even to us, were the negro soldiers, who seemed to have come from another planet." Alexander was told by some of the soldiers that because they found that some of their comrades had been murdered, they shot all captured SS troops. The relevant members of the Nazi elite obviously got the message: the Americans came upon "piles of dead German soldiers with their uniform jackets missing and SS tunics lying round about." When brought to trial at Nuremberg, Berger cited his release of the prisoners as evidence of his assistance to POWs; it saved his neck.[246]

As has been seen, Heinrich Himmler remained interested in the possibilities of the Alpine retreat, where his wife, mistress and children were located. After his contacts with Swedish intermediaries about an end to the war were disclosed on April 28, Hitler had ordered his arrest. The same day Himmler, out of reach of the avenging arm of the Führer, instructed Gottlob Berger, his newly-appointed deputy in Bavaria, to assemble all SS forces in the south. Also the same day, Ernst Kaltenbrunner sent Himmler a radiogram in which he extolled the suitability of the Alps for sustained resistance while awaiting the anticipated conflict between the western Allies and the Soviet Union. Himmler obviously decided not to go there himself, because by May 2 he had proceeded north in a failed attempt to gain a position in Admiral Karl Dönitz's twilight government.[247]

By this time, things began to become unhinged on the Obersalzberg. SS troops continued to guard the Berghof until May 4, and, until April 28, Göring's house. Meanwhile, security for the other buildings and the tunnel system lasted until the end of April. Commander Bernhard Frank gave permission first to the compound workers and then to area residents to take food and other provisions from the Obersalzberg. Once the guards left, there was chaos. Local people swarmed up the hillside. According to Josef Geiss, "People came, some of them even with horse carriages, to loot.... Huge amounts of food, linen, clothes, shoes, china, soap and others lay before wondering eyes, and found new owners. Works of art were burnt or taken away. In Bormann's supply tunnel people stood knee-deep in butter, sugar, flour and other food." Another attraction was the huge wine collection in the Göring bunker. According to historian Percy Knauth, the people were stunned to discover the extravagant lifestyle of the Hitler entourage while for years they had been experiencing severe rationing. "Berchtesgaden had many bitter comments," he noted, "on Hitler's oft-professed concern for the people's welfare...." Local people also looted the shelter under the *Luftwaffe* headquarters at Unterstein on the road to Königssee. Soon attention was directed to the freight cars containing Göring's art hoard at the Berchtesgaden railroad station. These too were plundered.[248]

## The Last Prize

By the end of April, with the virtual collapse of German opposition, there was not much more territory to be occupied by the Western Allies; Berchtesgaden was the last prize. On May 2, units of General Patch's Seventh Army began its advance from the north, while mountain troops of the French First Army went in from the west. Kesselring had ordered that these Allied forces should be opposed with all available means. Nazi Berchtesgaden leader Stredele urged a fight to the finish and printed a flyer which proclaimed "Women and children to the shelters; men to arms!" In a defiant gesture the last unit of the Nazi Party to be organized in Germany was formed on the Obersalzberg on April 20. In the theatre hall before a large audience of compound employees, obliged to attend, Stredele gave a fiery speech which concluded, "There will be a miracle soon; Hitler himself will be this miracle!"

Anticipating the imminent arrival of the Americans, SS troops at the Berghof removed the personal belongings of Hitler and Eva from storage bunkers on May 1. All of the belongings were burned, with the exception of a trunk of Hitler-Eva correspondence and other material that Eva had asked her sister, Gretl, who was on the scene, to safeguard. Major Johannes Göhler arranged to have the trunk shipped to Fischhorn, the SS field headquarters near Zell am See. When Göhler went to Fischhorn on May 8 he was told that the contents of the trunk had been burned, but SS Captain Franz Konrad kept some of Eva's material—a final brief diary, photo albums and short films she had made.[249]

With the war drawing to a close and Germany in total defeat, the people of Berchtesgadener Land were not interested in heroics. The area was packed with refugees and wounded soldiers. In one of the last public opinion surveys done (in March), a resident of Berchtesgaden declared, "If we'd have imagined in 1933 how things would turn out, we'd never have voted for Hitler." The same month, at a meeting to honor war dead at nearby Markt Schellenberg, when an officer called for a "Sieg Heil" for the Führer, there was no response from the gathering of soldiers, *Volkssturm* and civilians. SS General Friederich von Eberstein found that the *Volkssturm* he had with his division "had no will to fight" and that "the population in Upper Bavaria and Swabia could not be won over for partisan activities and furthermore were tired of war." Otto Hoffmann, another SS general, recalled two occasions in Austria when his troops were fired on by *Standschützen*, members of the Tyrolean organization who had been mobilized to resist the invaders, which "indicated that certain elements of the population were not reliable." It was clear to him that "the intention of defending and keeping the Alpine fortress was secretly or openly strongly opposed by the population." In the days leading up to the arrival of the U.S. Army, the *Berchtesgadener Anzeiger* merely noted the clear probability of this event and urged that order be maintained.[250]

Serious opposition to Allied troops would have meant the destruction of Berchtesgaden by air assault. Garmisch, which capitulated on April 29, had barely escaped this fate. General Hengl was confronted with groups of local people who "constantly called on me and the various subordinate commanders asking for the battle to be stopped or that their localities should not be occupied." At this point Karl Theodor Jacob, the *Landrat* or administrator of the area, took charge. Described as "a big, bluff extremely personable Bavarian," he had joined the Nazi Party in 1930 and had served as *Landrat* for several years; he was to continue to play a most constructive role after the war.[251]

Jacob had already reached an agreement with Bernhard Frank that there would be no military resistance, provided that the bombed-out people on the Obersalzberg were given assistance. With the support of town leaders, his argument for surrender prevailed. On May 3 *Kreisleiter* Stredele handed over his authority to Jacob and "escaped into the mountains," to be followed by the *Ortsgruppenleiter*. On the morning of May 4, just after the Americans occupied Bad Reichenhall, Jacob dissolved the local *Volkssturm* and prevented the distribution of the fiery SS poster, handing out his own sheet, which stated that there was to be no opposition.[252]

On May 4, Stredele and some remaining SS troops set fire to the Berghof, and Stredele, at least, fled on the day American troops entered Berchtesgaden. Field Marshal Albert Kesselring and his staff also hurriedly left town that day. According to one report, General Gustof Kastner, a Hitler adjutant and Göring friend, remained at the compound, telling Göring's caretaker that he would kill himself when the Allies entered the area. When this occurred, he proceeded to shoot himself at the *Luftwaffe* officers' club on the road to Königssee. The American journalist Curt Reiss reported, "In the ensuing confusion of occupation, nobody cared about the dead general. On Tuesday, May 8, a few Berchtesgaden peasants buried the man who once belonged among the most important leaders of the Third Reich."[253]

The competition for the taking of Hitler's town was intense. By this time the competition was limited to three units of the Seventh Army in the race—the Third Infantry Division, the 506th Parachute Infantry Regiment of the 101st Airborne Division and the French Second Armored Division.

The Third Infantry Division had fought across North Africa, had taken part in the invasion of Sicily, and then had broken out of the infamous Anzio beachhead. In August 1944 it swept into France from the Mediterranean, fought in the battle of the Colmar pocket, pushed across the Rhine and then headed to southern Germany. During its thirty months of combat, the division sustained 34,000 casualties—"more than any [other] of the 60 divisions in the European Theatre—in its 3200-mile trail from Casablanca to Salzburg."

When General Lucian Truscott became commander of the Anzio enclave in February 1944, he was succeeded as leader of the Third by John W. O'Daniel, a short, peppery soldier of fifty-one years who had risen from the ranks of the Delaware National Guard and was given the nickname of "Iron Mike" for his hard and demanding appearance and behavior. A combat veteran of the first European war, O'Daniel was a person who invited colorful description. Jean de Lattre saw him as "this warrior, with features that might have been carved out with an axe, all of them betraying his uncommon personality, will and energy, who had turned his division into a tool of exceptional quality." To Marguerite Higgins he was "a rough-talking, rough-looking soldier of the old school." Truscott described him as "a rugged, gruff-voiced Irishman, who thoroughly enjoyed fighting, and had no equal in bulldog tenacity or as a fighting infantry division commander." His only son, a member of the 101st Airborne, was killed in October 1944 during Operation Marketgarden in Holland. Eisenhower, noting that O'Daniel and another general had just lost their only sons in the war, wrote to George Marshall, "This shock and stress, coupled with the abnormal strains always borne by an active Division Commander, are really more than any one man should be called upon to bear."[254]

"If there was anyone who gave the Third Division its pride, its sense of identity, its personality," recalled John Toole, one of his junior officers, "it was this short man with the

Major General John O'Daniel, commander of U.S. Third Infantry Division, and unidentified soldiers in Rome, April 1944. (U.S. Army Military History Institute)

huge scar on his cheek. He looked ferocious and could be ferocious, yet every man in the Division was proud of him." His first view of the general was when he saw him striding up a hill, a little man with helmet too big for his head. O'Daniel was certainly aggressive: when the division was preparing for the invasion of southern France in August 1944 he told his troops, "You can take it from me, boys—hate the Germans! Hate the bastards! Cut your initials on their goddamned faces!," a statement which met with a roar of approval. Hugh Scott recalled that at one point in the division's drive into southern Germany, O'Daniel "flew over our most advanced units in a liaison plane with a loudspeaker attached, commanding the troops below to 'Keep moving! Keep moving! Keep the pressure on!'" He was the inventor of the battle sled, a steel rounded sheet for a single infantryman, several of which could be towed by a tank up to enemy lines. No other division adopted what John Toole called "this nightmarish device."[255]

The 506th Regiment of the 101st Airborne had an equally adventuresome war. It dropped behind enemy lines in the darkness of D-Day in Normandy, took part in Operation Marketgarden, the confused Allied attempt to sweep through the Netherlands in September 1944, and was in the center of the Battle of the Bulge in its defense of Bastogne. In April 1945 in Germany it joined with the rest of its division as part of the 6th Army Group in its drive to the south of Germany. Its commanding officer was Colonel Robert F. Sink, a 1927 graduate of West Point who had a "sensible, realistic, humorous approach to combat."[256]

The French Second Armored Division originated with Free French troops in the French colony of Chad in central Africa in November 1942. It was led by Philippe Leclerc, a forty-two-year-old grizzled soldier of unusual daring, determination and vivacity. Leclerc was not without a volatile temperament. When his division was approaching Paris in August 1944 he told George Patton, in a "very much excited" way, that if he was not allowed to advance

General Philippe Leclerc (right), commander of the French Second Armored Division with unidentified staff on the Obersalzberg, May 1945. (Mémorial de Maréchal Leclerc de Hauteelocque et de la Libération de Paris et Musée Jean Moulin, Musées de la Ville de Paris)

on the capital he would resign. Patton: "I told him in my best French that he was a baby, and I would not have division commanders tell me where they would fight, and that anyway I had left him in the most dangerous place. We parted friends."

Leclerc's force, not yet a full division, initially was attached to the British Eighth Army and took part in the Tunisian campaign. It was then organized into an armored division, using American clothing, equipment, weapons and vehicles. As part of the U.S. Third Army, it participated in the Normandy campaign and, for purposes of national honor and prestige, led the way in the liberation of Paris in August 1944 and Strasbourg the following November. For its involvement in battles along the German frontier—at the Colmar pocket—in November 1944, the division was awarded the Presidential Unit citation, the first non–U.S. unit to receive it. The citation declared that in "this magnificent operation" the division "destroyed the combat effectiveness of four enemy divisions, opened the gateway to the Alsatian Plain, liberated the capital of Alsace and contributed greatly to the success of Allied arms." In a reciprocal gesture, the French Government awarded the 3rd Infantry Division the *Croix de Guerre*.

Though briefly part of the First French Army upon its formation in the summer of 1944, Leclerc later succeeded in detaching his division from General de Lattre's army in February 1945—he wanted to be with the Americans because of their weapons, equipment and supplies. In addition, he wanted nothing to do with de Lattre and the other leaders of the French First Army: "I will not serve with any commanders who previously obeyed Vichy and whom I considered to be turncoats."

On the drive into southern Germany the French division was attached to the XV Corps of the 7th U.S. Army, whose commander was General Frank Milburn, who succeeded Wade Haislip, a career officer who had spent two years at the *Ecole Superieure de Guerre* in the 1920s and spoke French fluently. Haislip had an unusual relationship with his subordinate: "I never issued orders to Leclerc. Whenever I wanted him to do something, I would say: 'Leclerc, this is what I am planning to do. It looks to me as though you could do this and that and so forth.... I want you to go away and study it and tell me what you think.'" Milburn had only the usual problems with the French force.[257]

Leclerc's division ran a loosely parallel course with American divisions on the drive to Munich. One American soldier recalled that the French force was seen sometimes and at other times disappeared. He also recalled that when the French tankers had accumulated sufficient loot, a loaded lorry was dispatched to France. PFC David Webster recalled a brutal action: a French tank man casually and deliberately blew the brains out of three teenage German soldiers cowering on the ground. The division, as well as other French units, however, had been subjected to a high degree of attack from Werwolfs and by-passed German soldiers, in part because their combat units, in their desire to occupy as much territory as possible, raced well ahead of their support forces. This extension was based on the desire to establish a claim to a French zone of occupation.[258]

After the seizure of Munich, and with snow covering the ground from a late-season storm and a cold wind blowing from the mountains, the Seventh Army drove south with mounting excitement—the Alps were ahead. One factor had changed—there would be no Hitler to lead the defense of the area. His suicide on April 30 was announced on German radio on May 1. But even the death of the Führer did not preclude the possibility of a fight to the death by extreme Nazi elements in the mountains. But the end of the war was drawing near. After the capture of Munich, the Third Division announced that leave passes for Brussels were available. "There were no takers," William Kunz recalled; "Everybody wanted in on the finish." Kunz was soon hospitalized with a malaria attack, but managed to get back to his unit by May 8—"the end of our war! I wasn't going to miss that if I had to crawl back."[259]

The Seventh Army plan was that tanks of the French Second Armored Division would be allowed the honor of leading the 506th Regiment of the 101st Airborne into Hitler's town of Berchtesgaden. Some members of the 506th believed that their unit, based on its extreme exertions at Bastogne, had been selected by Eisenhower to arrive first. When the tanks of Patton's Third Army had pushed far ahead of its infantry support, there was alarm in Eisenhower's headquarters that many German troops retreating from the east would take the opportunity to pass through the Salzburg Gap into the Alps. As a result, the Salzburg area was transferred to the Sixth Army Group and the Third Infantry Division was ordered to take the city of Mozart, one hundred miles ahead.[260]

Taking advantage of the Munich to Salzburg autobahn, the Seventh Infantry Regiment launched a high speed dash forward on the night of May 2, designed to surprise German defenders along the way. For this to happen, several bridges had to be seized and, under orders to ignore enemy fire and surrendering soldiers, this action was successfully carried out by L Company of a task force of the third battalion led by Capt. Robert Horton. The *Luftwaffe* had been using the autobahn as a landing strip and had hidden aircraft in adjacent wooded areas. Lt. Sherman Pratt, commander of L Company, recalled the amazement of the men in his unit when they saw the dispersed planes: "The aircraft we were seeing ... were unlike anything we had even seen before. They had no propellers. Instead, there was simply a round hole at the front of the fuselage where a prop would ordinarily be mounted." These were, of course, the new jet planes. Driving through unseasonably cold weather and light snow, L Company captured the first two bridges, but found the last one already blown; other units of the task force proceeded by using side roads.[261]

As other elements of the 7th regiment followed, their principal activity was dealing with a mass of POWs, among whom there were "[o]ne admiral, a navy captain, and six generals, and an estimated 13,000 other officers and enlisted men." There was the mistaken belief that Otto Skorzeny had been captured at this time. An unusual message was handed to one of its truck drivers: "Take care of one sister Pia, one of Hitler's female friends, in Diesenhofer, who is said to try to organize some mischief in the back of the American Army."[262]

There were episodes of determined resistance. Some elements of the 7th Regiment headed directly into the Alps. One of these was the artillery unit in which William Kuntz served; he recalled that this was "our last artillery action of the war!" After a serious fire fight, he discovered that the opposition was composed of Hitler Youth: "All children, wearing back packs, many of them young girls. Fanatical, they fought us right down to the end with only rifles and panzerfausts! Innocent looking when in captivity, the casualties they inflicted on us were far too real!"[263]

After a bout of opposition at its airport, Salzburg was secured by noon on May 4. The Sixth Army Group later was to make the claim that the transfer of the Salzburg objective to its Seventh Army and its rapid capture by the Third Infantry Division "probably brought about the collapse of [German] forces in South Germany." Up to the time of its seizure, however, there had been no marked movement of German units through the area to the Alps. It was while General O'Daniel was negotiating the surrender of Salzburg on the night of May 3, that Field Marshal Kesselring sent an emissary to begin the process of capitulation of the three armies he commanded.[264]

The Third had made such rapid progress to Salzburg that on that night General Patch, commander of the 7th Army, "found immediate capture of Berchtesgaden as feasible as it was desirable and gave the go-ahead to the 3rd Division." According to Sherman Pratt, 7th Army leaders as early as April 25 had been hoping and planning to win the race to Hitler's town, with the 3rd Infantry Division leading the way. According to Christian Girard of the French division, O'Daniel "was charging along like a brute."

Now, with that opportunity presenting itself, "Iron Mike" wasted no time. Two battalions of his 7th Regiment "were organized as Task Forces to move SE to seize Berchtesgaden." The regiment was called the "Cotton Bailers," a name dating back to the battle of New Orleans in 1815. It was led by Colonel John A. Heintges, a strapping thirty-three year old native of Germany, who commanded a regiment in combat as long as anybody in the U.S. Army during the war. He had dreamed about capturing Berchtesgaden, had prepared a strategy—"Plan Orange"—for doing so and now he had his chance.[265]

His strategy was a two-pronged advance on the town. L Company of the Third Battalion drove directly south-west from Salzburg through a twenty-five mile long valley, while C Company of the 1st Battalion came in from the north-western side.

Exploring the mountainous northwest area on the night of May 3, a reconnaissance patrol led by Lt. Col. Lloyd Ramsey, the regimental executive officer, found there was still a small footbridge as well as a railroad bridge across the barrier of the Salzach River. The problem with the railroad bridge was there were four railroad cars on it, with blown brakeshoes, which dropped the cars onto the rails. Working through the night, and under occasional machine gun fire from across the river, the 10th Engineer Battalion used bulldozers to tip the cars into the river, rip up the rail lines and lay down a wooden surface that would support tanks, a task that was completed by ten o'clock in the morning.

The road from the bridge went to Bad Reichenhall. Turning towards Berchtesgaden, Heintges's First Battalion convoy encountered a defile with high cliffs on either side, with the road blocked with SS troops entrenched in defensive bunkers. To deal with this obstacle, Heintges recalled, "We just backed off, and fired the artillery and all kinds of things. And, all of a sudden, by God, no more reaction."[266]

Meanwhile, the 506th Regiment of the 101st Airborne Division was proceeding on its assigned mission of capturing the town. One of its soldiers later recalled, "As we approached our last high ground, the Bavarian Alps, the mood changed and a certain tenseness set in, for we had all heard a little too much about the so-called National Redoubt.... As we rode the Munich-Salzburg *Autobahn* and looked up at the huge, dark, sharks' teeth mountains on our right, we wondered if they held the last fanatics." David Webster, a soldier in the 101st, recalled his impression of the mountains: "They were dark and ominous, immense, towering over all wars and all humanity. Everything about them was cold and hostile: the grey rocks, the thick grass and heavy moss that ran from tree level to the rocks, and the blue-green pine forests that cloaked their massive bases." Then there was the weather: "A bitter wind blew down at us from the blinding white snow on the fangs that were their summits." Jack Agnew, also of the 506th, recalls that there was no particular apprehension among the soldiers he was with as they approached the Alps: "After what we had been through—Normandy, Marketgarden, Bastogne, and in all kinds of weather and terrain—this was just one more battle to come."

On that day, "high in the Alps," one of the 506th's two battalions ran into SS opposition—a "last tragic ambush"—which resulted in the death of several U.S. soldiers. The other battalion moved back to a nearby village, "where we shook down the stray supermen sauntering in from the foothills for liquor, watches, cameras and pistols—in that order—and spent the night frying eggs and drinking new milk and old brandy."[267]

The advance resumed the next day, but on May 4 the regiment was halted by the Third Infantry Division, which claimed that the paratroopers were encroaching on its territory. Iron Mike O'Daniel, the Third Division commander, was determined that the prize would go to his division. Earlier, he had been unsuccessful in having the town included as an objective for his unit. What O'Daniel was doing was most irregular, but, as one of his officers said, "If Iron Mike gets his ass in a sling with the Army commander or others, he will have to sort it out." O'Daniel meant business: he put a heavy guard on the only bridge along that route into the town.[268]

According to David Webster, a soldier in the 101st, Maxwell Taylor, his division commander, "gave a direct order to the 3rd Division's one-star general to let the 506th Regiment through to Berchtesgaden. We went." The bridge was not opened to the 101st or any other division, however, until O'Daniel had been notified that his own 7th Infantry Regiment had entered the town.[269]

French troops were, of course, also taking part in the race and were several hours ahead of the 101st. Units of the French Second Armored Division pursued three routes to the objective. One of them, moving south of Tegernsee on May 3, encountered an SS battalion firing mortars, automatic rifles and two 88 anti-aircraft guns. In the ensuing shoot-out, the French unit claimed forty dead Germans and the capture of 700. Another unit, coming from Bad Reichenhall, met with masses of surrendering soldiers along the road. Emil Fray, a French soldier and one of the participants in the race, recalled, "We pushed on very fast in competition with the Americans. We were operating in groups again, and ours had a pretty straight run through, with only odd spots of opposition."[270]

The main French force also ran up against the barrier of the Salzach. During the night of May 3 General Leclerc asked Colonel Heintges if his division could use that single bridge. Heintges sent him to O'Daniel, who "really threw a fit and he went up in the air. He said, 'Absolutely not.'" The next day, Leclerc made strenuous efforts to get across the bridge. On two occasions when Leclerc was confronted with American soldiers, his driver recalled that Leclerc ordered him "to drive right through them and make them jump. I did—and they did." Leclerc's jeep almost ran down a column of German prisoners of war. On the bridge, William Rosson, a twenty-five-year-old lieutenant colonel, saw Leclerc "standing upright in his vehicle, assuming the role of a commander with authority and great assertiveness." According to Rosson, to thwart Leclerc's demand a column of French vehicles was diverted to a road which eventually went to Berchtesgaden, but unknown to the French this road was blocked by a mass of fallen trees that "would require major engineering effort to clear."[271]

The officer in charge of the bridge was Lloyd Ramsey, the regimental executive officer. When Leclerc told Ramsey that O'Daniel had authorized him to cross the bridge, Ramsey replied that O'Daniel had told him that any crossing by other than Seventh Infantry soldiers had to be based on direct orders from O'Daniel to Ramsey. This delaying tactic held back the French unit long enough for the Seventh Regiment to gallop ahead to the town.[272]

O'Daniel called Wade Haislip, commander of XV Corps, to complain that "the French had appeared and were getting in the way" Haislip noted, "Everybody and his brother are trying to get into that town." He told O'Daniel, "Just you block the roads and that will stop them." When Leclerc registered his outrage, Haislip told him, "You aren't supposed to be there at all. You've had Paris and you've had Strasbourg; you can't expect Berchtesgaden as well." When, four hours after they had crossed by bridge, O'Daniel learned that his troops had arrived in Berchtesgaden, O'Daniel opened the bridge to the French unit.[273]

Heading for the town along the open valley from Salzburg, Sherman Pratt, commander of L Company, noted that the German forces seemed to have disappeared, which made the going "both weird and scary." However, the quiet atmosphere was shattered at the village of Schellenberg when one of the company's tanks blasted a lone German scout car. An opportunity to get in a last shot? Pratt feared the blast would alert every German soldier that the Americans were coming. When several German soldiers were spotted in a corn field beside the burning scout car, Pratt left behind a squad to try to coax them into surrendering. On to Berchtesgaden.[274]

On that day shortly after 2 P.M., with the support of Bernhard Frank and accompanied by Ingenieur Grethlein, a community leader, Karl Jacob, the regional governor, went to Hallthurm. There he anticipated he would meet the main body of the American soldiers advancing on Berchtesgaden from Bad Reichenhall. When the encounter did take place, Jacob informed them that there would be no resistance. Mayor Sandrock of Berchtesgaden formally handed over his authority two days later.[275]

Without further incident, three elements of the 7th Regiment arrived in the town a few minutes before 4 P.M. on May 4. The Yanks did not go marching into the town of Berlin, but they did so in the "other capital" of Germany. As a result of O'Daniel's obstruction, French soldiers did not arrive in the town until around 8 P.M. Coming in on the Bad Reichenhall road and suffering two killed and one wounded, elements of the 506th began trailing in the early hours of May 5.

In the town square, Col. Heintges was greeted by another colonel—Fritz Göring, nephew of the *Reichsmarschall*, who told him "he had been left behind to turn over" Hermann Göring's headquarters and records to the Americans. The two German natives repaired to the upper floor of a *Gasthaus* overlooking the square, where, over a couple of bottles of Moselle, they discussed the situation. One of first orders issued by Heintges was the imposition of a curfew until the following noon.[276]

When Sherman Pratt's L Company drove into the town, he was amazed by what he saw: "Berchtesgaden looked like a village from a story book and a fairy tale. Its houses were of Alpine architecture and design. Some had gingerbread decorations such as I had seen in *Hansel and Gretel*." What impressed William Rosson about the place was that "the streets were lined with German officers, and a few noncommissioned officers, and other ranks as well. The officers were in their grey longcoats, with sidearms and baggage, awaiting orders." John Heintges recalled that the American soldiers discovered large wheels of cheese which they began rolling around the place. The only casualties during the town's capture occurred when two soldiers were injured by the explosion of a time bomb in the local Nazi Party office. Over two thousand German soldiers surrendered.[277]

There was another race on May 4—to the passes which led through the Alps to Italy. With the end of the war clearly in sight, a patrol of the 7th Army's 103rd Division, followed by elements of the 85th Division, after arriving in Innsbruck late on May 3, conducted an all-night dash. With headlights blazing, the column roared by bemused German troops through the mountain pass and arrived in Brennero to be greeted by soldiers from the Fifth Army, which had rapidly advanced up to the Italian frontier.[278]

De Lattre's First French Army also rushed for the Italian border. Jake Devers was highly critical of de Lattre's methodology: "General DeLattre has been tactically unsound in that he let his armor run loose with pockets everywhere with no infantry to back it up." Another problem was that "it is the old French custom of celebrations in every town they capture." Despite this, "They have accomplished much more than I expected for they cleaned up the Black Forest, closed the Swiss border and finally entered Austria." Devers had assigned Patch's army to take the main route south to Landeck, but advised that if there were any serious delay in this advance, de Lattre's army should be prepared to advance on that town. Without waiting, de Lattre simply launched his force forward. Devers had had enough of de Lattre's unilateral actions. He moved the boundary between the American and French forces so that the French were pushed over to an area which offered no road connection to Italy. With admirable élan, de Lattre responded by organizing a ski patrol over the mighty Arlberg massif, but the patrol found that the Americans had already arrived in Landeck. Thus, the French military did not get to the Italian border.[279]

As the 7th Regiment swept towards Berchtegaden its communications units raced ahead setting up radio and wire locations. Very early on May 4—about 6:30 A.M.—Lt. David Daub and Sgt. Jack Brettel of the 3rd Division drove their jeep up a lane above Bechtesgaden and, unexpectedly, came upon a completely intact Berghof—the first Allied witnesses to the fact that the building had suffered no damage from the April 25 bombing. The front door was unlocked and no one was found in the building.

After briefly enjoying the panoramic view from the famous picture window, noting the decorations in the great room, and removing a photograph of Hitler from that room's wall, they proceeded to the lower level where they discovered the liquor supply. After grabbing a couple of ceremonial daggers and a box of what they thought to be cigarette lighters (which actually were Minox cameras) and loading their jeep and its trailer with bottles of brandy, they received a radio message advising that things were moving so fast in the direction of Salzburg that there was no need to continue reconnoitering in that location, and were instructed to rejoin their company. First to the Berghof—but without fanfare or recognition![280]

Meanwhile, back in Berchtesgaden, some of the "Cottonbailers" did not merely enter the town. In addition, as recorded in the 7th Regiment's daily report for May Noon 4–Noon 5, a few soldiers of its 1st Battalion went up to Hitler's compound on the Obersalzberg on the afternoon of May 4 where they "seized the mountain hideout and tore down the Nazi flags by Hitler's old hangout, Der Berghof Obersalzberg, as it still smoked, the result of recent bombings." This patrol included Capt. Fred Rachicle, a battalion surgeon. Sherman Pratt has related that when his company entered the town they were informed by a German civilian of Hitler's compound on the Obersalzberg. Pratt quickly assembled a platoon and proceeded up the mountain. They saw the damage, supposedly caused by the bombardment of April 25, and spotted a few other soldiers, these from C company, and only a couple of fleeing German military. They entered the underground tunnel network where they found rooms filled with paintings, silverware and a wide range of household goods.[281]

Isadore Valenti, a medic in K Company, also has written an account of going to the Obersalzberg in the late afternoon of May 4. He said that together with two officers, Capt. Frank Syladek and 1st Lieut. Douglas Dickey, he found the main part of the Berghof was little damaged, and that they encountered two remaining staff members—a woman in her forties who was a household servant and a man in his fifties who was a groundskeeper. They were told that all the other staff members had left shortly before. When the American trio heard a clamor outside they discovered that French troops had arrived, so Valenti and company quickly departed. On the way down they were subjected to verbal abuse from French tankers who were on their way up. As darkness descended, all of the American soldiers on the Obersalzberg had returned to Berchtesgaden.[282]

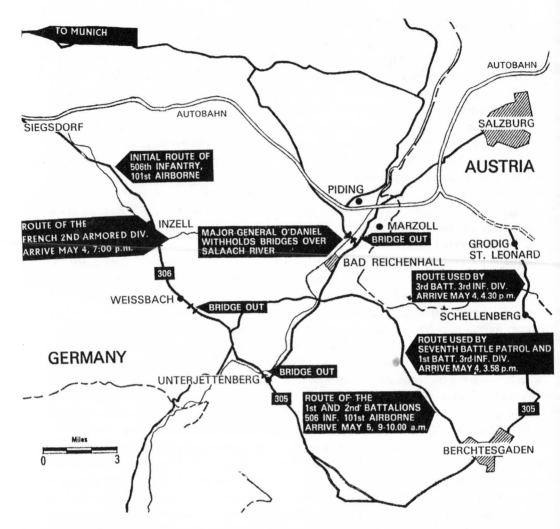

Map of Berchtesgaden area with approaching Allied forces, May 1945. (Courtesy Andrew Thomas)

As has been seen, the 506th closed in on the town in the evening of May 5. David Webster saw before him an Alpine gem: "A bright, clean resort village of about eight thousand inhabitants, Berchtesgaden rested, for the most part, on the south slope of a hill surrounded by glittering mountains of breathtaking beauty." He assumed that the people there, due to the impact of German security agencies, were fanatical Nazis; however, there is no evidence that Berchtesgadeners gave greater support to Hitler and his party than did other German citizens. Webster also had heard that this was a resort town, but by May 1945 it was jammed with wounded soldiers and refugees.[283]

Meanwhile Heintges had to deal with the French tankers, who continued to arrive. Around two A.M. on the night of May 4–5 a French colonel came to him to say that he had written orders to assist in the occupation of the area, something that Heintges claimed to know nothing about. Drawing a line along the railroad track into the town, Heintges assigned the French force to one side of it, which included the Obersalzberg. According to Heintges, the fact that his unit had captured the area was "a terrific psychological thing for the

French. So, I gave it to them because I knew that that would be a good thing for international politics, really." He also thought he was getting rid of the responsibility for a place that already had caused him problems. The French unit arrived in Berchtesgaden about a half hour after the lead units of the Seventh Regiment.[284]

Although in his war memoir he acknowledged that the Third got there ahead of his unit, years later Maxwell Taylor made the claim that his division occupied the town without mentioning the prior arrival of the Third Infantry or the French division. This erroneous perspective on what the 101st did was reinforced by Stephan Ambrose's *Band of Brothers*, which was reflected in the 2001 television series of the same name. This distortion of the record has generated heated objections from several veterans of the 3rd Infantry Division.[285]

According to some German observers, in the French force were wild Moroccans, whom German soldiers feared. Supposedly, the Moroccans came in shooting, looting and raping. This is the recollection of many people in Berchtesgaden. Some women smeared themselves with cow manure to fend off the attention of these soldiers. Georg Mehr remembered the soldiers in the French division as being "Moroccans and Arabs and so on—pretty much like the Foreign Legion, and just as tough." Maxwell Taylor recalled that the French soldiers "celebrated their entry into this holy city of the Nazis by emptying their guns into the buildings with the abandon of Hollywood bandits raiding Dodge City." Lieutenant Russ Cloer of the 7th Infantry observed the French troops in the town: "They immediately began looting it, with a precision that smacked of long practice. They parked a half track crossways at the end of each block to prevent escape and then went through the houses and stores one by one, throwing their loot out the windows into the street. What they deigned to keep, they loaded aboard the half tracks and the rest was left behind." Soldiers in the French division had a reputation for looting among some American troops. On this occasion Heintges attempted to restrain the French troops and Cloer has said, "We were careful to disassociate ourselves from the whole operation." According to David Irving, the wife and daughter of Reich minister Hans Lammers committed suicide after being raped by French soldiers in the town. On the other hand, there were several suicides among the families of leading Nazis at this time. There is no doubt that French troops pounced on Göring's train full of art works, sometimes firing randomly into the collection. One French soldier recalled he stepped on what he thought was a brick, but what turned out to be a priceless XVth century book looted from the Rothschild family in France and eventually returned to them.[286]

The French version of their brief presence in the town is quite different. Raymond Dronne recalled, "The little town was bristling with white flags. The populace didn't give us a bad reception." One of the division's command posts was established in a pension for daughters of Nazi officials. Dronne declared, "All went well. There wasn't the slightest abuse; everyone, officers and men, conducted themselves with dignity. They owed it to the boarders ... to give a good impression of the French army." But there was fear abroad as well. One woman threw her arms around a French officer imploring him for aid and protection. Due to their red caps, she had mistaken the Spahis, the French colonial soldiers, for Russians! Fearing rape and worse, she refused to leave the French headquarters.[287]

Veterans of the French division reject most claims of abuse caused by their soldiers. They point out that their commanding general, Philippe Leclerc, highly regarded by his soldiers, was a strict disciplinarian and would not have tolerated such actions. They dismiss the statements reportedly made in a booklet produced in Berchtesgaden about violent French actions.[288]

It is difficult to characterize the conduct of the French troops. The majority of those in this unit were French and Spanish, with some Algerians. French formations, in general, from the Black Forest to Lake Constance, were the targets of many guerrilla-type assaults by a variety of rear-guard Germans. When a French Algerian division occupied Stuttgart in late April, the commander of the U.S. 100th Infantry Division told General Patch, "Situation in Stuttgart worst imaginable. Urgently recommend Fr. forces including their Mil Govt. be removed immediately before conditions have gone beyond repair. Rape, pillage and plunder have been rampant." As they later did in Berchtesgaden, French officers rejected the charges, and, upon investigation, U.S. liaison officials declared the claims were overblown. Christabel Bielenberg recalled that in the part of the Black Forest where she was living, French colonial troops—Spahis from Morocco and Goums from the Sarhara—"raped up and down our valley"; the victims included "every female between 12 and 80." For those from France, there was a very strong feeling that it was payback time for a range of German actions which occurred in their country during four years of occupation.[289]

French veterans claim that in Berchtesgaden Americans also looted. This is borne out by one U.S. soldier who recalled "seeing men looting various things. He saw one man with a large chandelier on his back. Another man had unscrewed a toilet seat and was carrying it home. He was making jokes about how Hitler's ass probably had set right there." For himself, he took "several small paper booklets he looted from a tourist shop nearby, with pictures of Hitler, and a postcard with Hitler's picture." French Lt. Paul Gloaguen observed American soldiers cutting out canvases from picture frames and folding them under their field jackets. There were also reports of raping by U.S. soldiers.[290]

While the soldiers of the American division were enjoying themselves in the town, some of the French soldiers, more knowledgeable about the area, proceeded up to the Obersalzberg. One French officer told another, "Leave the Americans, count your prisoners and slip off discreetly." Captain Laurent Touyeras, who had earlier passed through that area as a P.O.W., later commented, "The Americans believed that once in the village that the finish line would be reached; they stopped there. That done, they forgot that the true goal was still beyond, that the Führer's house and his out-buildings, the Berghof, the sanctuary, was not found in Berchtesgaden itself." Around 4:30 P.M. Touyeras sought permission to go up to Hitler's retreat. Although his commanding officer, Lt. Col. de Guillebon, doubted he could get up there—"There is surely a U.S. combat command up there. I believe you will have trouble"—Touyeras was given permission to try.

With Touyeras at the wheel of a jeep and with his driver, Francois Borg, manning a machine gun mounted on the hood, they drove up the Obersalzberg. They soon encountered a group of about thirty Hitlerjugend marching down, who, threatened by Borg with his machine gun, promptly surrendered. They tossed their rifles, pistols and daggers into the adjoining gully. Touyeras ordered them to proceed towards Berchtesgaden, "where you are awaited," while he continued to the Berghof, arriving about five P.M. When Borg and Touyeras got to a guardhouse, they were met by forty-five soldiers wearing *Notshilfe* ("emergency rescue") armbands, who offered no resistance. Through their tatooed blood types, they were later identified as SS soldiers. With the arrival of the Allied troops, Bernhard Frank had dissolved his military authority, with a final command: "March off back home at your own risk." At least some SS members obviously headed for the hills. Frank, himself, did not get very far. He was caught in a massive traffic jam near Lake Chiemsee and, after rough treatment, put in a prisoner of war camp.

Touyeras ordered a German sergeant to assemble his troops in formation. He then drove with the sergeant to the Berghof, which, still intact, "suddenly blew up literally and burned like a box of matches." The charges set by the SS troops had ignited. At this point, Touy-eras returned for help. His superior, Lt. Colonel de Guillebon, dispatched about forty-five soldiers of the 12th company of the 3rd Battalion of the Infantry Regiment of Chad. The force was led by Lt. Albert Messiah, a Parisian Jew. When this group arrived an hour and a half later they found that the upper part of the Berghof was wrecked and on fire, but that the basement was largely intact. This contained a "dining room, bedrooms, office, library, kitchen, metal cupboards furnished with files and presents." One of the French soldiers found a Dutch flag there; as there was no French flag available and the Dutch flag had the same colors, it was spread along a wall and a notable photograph was taken of Lt. Messiah with the flag in front of the Berghof. Raymond Dronne declared that "I was delighted that the unit who camped in the holy of the holies of Hitlerism was commanded by a Jew.... The presence of Messiah at that place had a symbolic value of punishment."[291]

As has been seen, this unit was assigned to take control of the Obersalzberg area. To secure the place, and, incidentally, keep the Americans out, Sherman tanks blocked the road to the Obersalzberg. French soldiers were authorized to open fire on American troops if they trespassed. A confrontation soon took place between French Sergeant Sarcelet and two jeep loads of American officers, led by a captain. According to a French account, when the American officers were denied passage, "the adversary is at first incredulous, then the tone escalates very fast to screams. The English schooling of Sarcelet is quickly submerged by the linguistic storm peppered with attributes concerning the French." Sarcelet was informed that everything the French troops had was American. Sarcelet understood that "All their equipment is American, from the cartridges to the socks," yet "flesh and blood also counts." The encounter got nasty: "threats, insults, fist blows ... finally all except a shot, which would make things worse." The Americans said they would soon be back.

When Touyeras returned to Berchtesgaden that night he had a tommy gun pushed into his stomach and a Colt .45 pressed against his head by American tankers. According to Christian Girard, Touyeras "nearly had to chop through the Americans who had mounted an attack with tanks." The next morning when General Leclerc received the good news, "he beamed. They were the French, and the ones from Tchad, and they were there, in the heart of the end" of it all. He proceeded up to the Obersalzberg and a ceremony of celebration was held. At the same time French troops, ordered by Leclerc and led by a Capt. de Castellane, proceeded to the Eagle's Nest on the Kehlstein. (On their own, two enlisted men got to the mountain top before the official party.) Riding on half-tracks and a jeep, fearing an ambush, the soldiers struggled for four hours through fallen trees and snow. Along the way they captured three German soldiers in mountain gear whom they enlisted as guides. When they arrived at the elevator area below the summit, they found two elderly maintenance workers in attendance, but the elevator was out of commission. After a final icy climb, they raised a French flag above the "diplomat house" at 5 P.M.[292]

Thus, French soldiers believed that not only did they get to the Berghof first, but also to the Eagle's Nest before the Americans. Indeed, the French—as an assigned, organized unit—were first to both places. Although the race to occupy these areas had no military or political significance, this matter was an important game at the fag end of the war. General Leclerc inscribed a book "To Capt. Touyeras, who won the course." During their single day of exclusive occupation of the Obersalzberg, the French soldiers searched the basement remains of the Berghof. Although most of its contents were buried in rubble, some things survived—a tiled heating stove, a refrigerator with dishes of food, a barber's chair tipped over, scattered papers ("some documents signed Hitler, Bormann, Goebbels, Göring or Himmler").[293]

With little time, they managed to make only a cursory examination of the underground rooms, "gathering up forks and some spoons marked "A.H." ... The champagne and the cognac hardly attracted their attention because of the overabundance." Probably in the area under the Platterhof hotel, some of them found a cache of military reports, which they turned over to their intelligence people. They also smashed furniture and carried off what they wanted from the hotel. The head of the construction company on the site, Georg Gethlein, and his driver were shot to death outside the Platterhof by a drunken French soldier. Among things taken by French troops were gifts to Hitler, including "many magnificent watches bearing inscriptions that were gifts to the Führer from his loving people." They riddled the equipment in the underground operating room with bullets.[294]

The morning of May 5, Colonel Heintges led elements of the 7th Regiment up to the Obersalzberg for a flag-raising ceremony. They were accompanied by a swarm of about a hundred journalists. Problems soon developed. Stopped by a road block, with French troops looking down from their American tanks, Heintges, who spoke French as well as German, had a "lively discussion" with various French officers, who finally received permission to let the Amis come up. To placate anticipated Gallic sensibilities, Heintges proposed a joint flag-raising event. "They thought it was fine that since we had captured the place," Heintges recalled, "that our troops would be there." His executive officer Lloyd Ramsey, who was present, has noted that the French "strongly objected, since they were supposed to have taken Berchtesgaden." At this point there was a French effort to secure an appropriately sized French flag, but none could be located. In any event, some French troops did participate in what followed. To avoid the possibility that no ceremony, however brief, would take place, Heintges proceeded to a "rehearsal" of the event, which satisfied the press photographers. In his account, Lloyd Ramsey said that only the American flag was raised and, due to a French restriction, only a short distance up the makeshift mast for a short time. "Colonel Heintges did not like this arrangement," Ramsey has said, "but he thought that it was better than no ceremony at all." After the brief ceremony, the Americans left and were back in Berchtesgaden before noon.[295]

The veterans of the Third Infantry Division apparently blocked out the French involvement in the capture of Berchtesgaden and Obersalzberg. The official history of the division mentioned neither the French nor the 101st. Rather, it provided a muted account of the arrival of its soldiers in Berchtesgaden and gave much more attention to the division's involvement with the surrender of the forces left to Field Marshal Albert Kesselring. However, Sherman Pratt had a lot to add. In his memoir, he asserted that his company and others in the division were the first on the Obersalzberg on May 4, without any reference to French troops. In his description of the flag-raising ceremony the next day, he mentions that French troops were there, but says nothing about why they should have been involved. The photograph of this ceremony in the division's official history does not include a photograph of the French flag. Nor is there one in the Archiv Leclerc in Paris or possessed by the veterans' association of the French division. But Florian Beierl recently has secured a broad range photograph which shows a few French soldiers standing at either end of the formation.[296]

It was at 4:30 P.M. on May 5 that General O'Daniel issued a long-awaited order: "Effective immediately there will be no more fighting unless fired upon or attacked." This was followed at 10:45 that night by another message: "An armistice has been agreed upon with Army Group G. Terms to be effective 061200B May 1945." Thus two years and six months after it landed in Morocco the war came to an end for the Third Infantry Division.

According to one keen participant, the ceasefire announcement was met by the soldiers of the Third Division by an eerie lack of emotion—"Everyone was quiet. There wasn't a sound."—a response that puzzled John Heintges. "I expected the same kind of reaction that you'd get at the end of a football game." After talking about this with other commanders, "We finally came to the conclusion that, possibly, the division had been through so much and had so many victories and successes, that the end of the war really didn't mean much to them because it was just another step in this war of ours." Heintges also came to another, slightly different conclusion: "The troops were disappointed, really, that this was the end."[297]

David Daub, another member of the division, had a distinctly different recollection of the response to the order to cease offensive action. His unit having moved to near Salzburg, he recalled, "The moment we got the news that hostilities were finito, it seemed that each and every GI was emptying his weapon into the air, for there was a rain of 30 and 45 calibers coming back down like a hailstorm. I thought I might get wounded again from 'friendly fire' before going home. Thank goodness for that 'pot' on my head."[298]

A military government detachment quickly arrived on the scene. On the morning of May 5 it moved into the local office of the Nazi Party and took over civil administration. The initial relationship with county and town officials was difficult and wary, "as a mine had exploded in one of the bureaus shortly before—probably placed there by the Kreisleiter—injuring two members of the staff of Military Government." The detachment specifically trained to administer the Land, led by Captain Michael DiPietro, arrived a week later.[299]

On May 6 military police of the 101st Airborne took charge of security duties. While rummaging around Hitler's book collection in the tunnel area under the Berghof, Capt. Alain de Boissieu found a copy of Charles de Gaulle's insightful study from the 1930s, *Wars of the Future*, with annotations which he believed to be in Hitler's handwriting (one such being, "Guderian will explain this to me"). This was not surprising inasmuch as Hitler had said he had read and re-read de Gaulle's book. When de Boissieu attempted to leave with the book, an American guard took it from him and tossed it into a flaming barrel. A French truck dispatched to get another load from the Berghof liquor cellar was turned back by American MPs. That party was over.[300]

Another unit of the French division occupied the area around the Berchtesgaden *Bahnhof* the night of May 4–5. In examining Göring's "treasure train" the next day, they not only found a vast collection of art and precious metals, but also documents about the German "miracle weapons"—V2 rockets and jet planes. These documents they turned over to their intelligence service. Nearby stood a military barracks. A French tank forced open the barrack's huge double doors to reveal the presence of about 2000 German soldiers, who claimed they had been demobilized that day.[301]

There was also a third French group in the area—one that had collaborated with the Germans. A dozen members of two SS units—the Charlemagne Division and the Frankreich Brigade—were captured by an American unit at Bad Reichenhall on May 5. Turned over to the French division the next day, they were briefly interviewed by General Leclerc, who asked each of them why they had joined the Nazi military organization. One of them asserted he had done so to oppose Communism, and thus uphold the military honor of France. Leclerc responded, "One does not talk about honor when you serve in the Boche uniform," to which he was told, "What about you? You are serving in an American uniform." The dozen young men were executed by firing squad a few hours later.[302]

After the strained relations between American and French soldiers on the Obersalzberg, the French were told to stay out of the center of Berchtesgsden, an order that obviously was a prudent measure. Almost certain barroom brawls, or worse, were not images the Allies cared to project at the time of the final German surrender. After the prompt transfer of the French unit and the 3rd Inf. from Berchtesgaden, however, a series of nasty incidents took place between members of the two proud organizations.[303]

As has been seen, elements of the 101st trickled into the town on May 5, with the Third Battalion of the 506th Regiment arrived that evening. The 502nd Regiment and the 327th Glider Regiment followed. The night was apparently a wild one in town and country. Members of the 101st joined with men from the 3rd and the French soldiers on the Obersalzberg.[304]

## Wild Day on the Berg

David Webster of the 506th has provided a vivid description of the events of the day. When his squad arrived in the town they were delighted to be assigned housing at "a settlement of long, white two-story chalets on a highway about a mile and a half north of Berchstesgaden." The buildings had been used by families of the Obersalzberg security guards and, after the residents had been expelled, the 101st soldiers looked with deep appreciation at the fully equipped facilities. Then came the revelation that the Obersalzberg contained a massive supply of alcoholic beverages. Roaring through the town in a confiscated *Schwimmwagen* (like a miniature DUKW), at the base of the Obersalzberg they encountered a 3rd Division soldier staggering down the middle of the road swigging champagne and firing a pistol in the air.

Other military personnel had the same objective. Close to the Berghof and its wine cellar the road was jammed with vehicles—"Recon cars, command cars, jeeps, DUKWs, halftracks, Volkswagens, Schimmwagens." Before Webster stood the wreck of Hitler's house with its front yard "a hideous mass of bomb craters, blackened timbers, broken glass and jagged chunks of brick and mortar." Milling about were "scores of paratroopers, Frenchmen and 3rd Division soldiers." Webster's group was greeted by "a couple of French tankers in GI overcoats and dark-blue berets with bright-red pompons." When the French soldiers learned a cease-fire had gone into effect, an uproar of pistol shots, dancing, shouts and toasts spread amongst all the troops on the spot.

Russ Cloer of the 7th Regiment joined a platoon who consumed their liquor supply in the seclusion of a "chateau." "We were smart enough to stay inside the chateau," he recalled, "because the odds of getting killed accidentally rose sharply with all the drunken soldiers wandering about firing weapons in celebration of the War's end." Although Allied intelligence believed the Obersalzberg area would be heavily fortified, this did not turn out to be the case. "It looks to me," commented one American officer, "like they were expecting to defend the place with wine bottles."[305]

American photographer Lee Miller arrived in Berchtesgaden on May 5. On the Obersalzberg, she photographed the burning Berghof that night. "In the morning," she noted, "the fire was nearly out and so were the looters—in force—legally, because this was Wehrmacht property." Allied soldiers hauled away the contents of cases of A.H.-monogrammed silver and linen. "It was like a very wild party with champagne corks whizzing over the flagpole and the house falling down over our ears," she recalled. "Every once in a while a great cascade of masonry would slide off the roof, and from the bowels of the house an explosion (the French CIC trying to blow Hitler's safe) would shake the hillside and spout smoke and bricks out of the passages." She doubted if any archives were still there, "but if there were

**American soldier views the burning Berghof, May 1945. (National Archives, N.A., RG-111-SC-204344S)**

when the French took over, there aren't now. There isn't even a piece left for a museum on the great war criminal."[306]

Another American journalist, Marguerite Higgins, was also on the scene, where she observed stores of china, glassware, linen and silver in the cupboards and storerooms in the Obersalzberg tunnels. Soldiers and journalists alike seized whatever they could stuff into their knapsacks. One soldier made off with 4–5000 negatives of Hitler photographs, many of a personal nature, including several of Eva Braun pretending to breast-feed a baby.[307]

For the next three days, at least, Webster's unit conducted drinking bouts, confiscated vehicles of their choice, traveled up to the Eagle's Nest and undertook cursory treasure hunts in the surrounding hills. Col. Sink, the 506th's commander, cruised about in a massive black Mercedes, while General Taylor had Hitler's armored convertible. Webster's platoon sergeant roared through the town in a fire engine, bells and sirens going full blast. A soldier in the platoon summed up the situation: "Isn't this the life? Everything on the house. Want a car? Take your pick. Need gas? Help yourself. Deutschland kaput."[308]

Journalist Percy Knauth had a frightening experience when his car got stuck in mud outside Berchtesgaden. As he tried to roll the vehicle out of the quagmire, he heard "a confused noise of shouting and singing, and the unmistakable roar of truck engines." Bearing down on him was an Army convoy, which included a 6×6 truck filled with enlisted men. "The soldiers in it not only looked as drunk as forty monkeys," he recalled, "they *were* as

Berghof in ruins, May 1945. (U.S. Army Military History Institute)

drunk as forty monkeys." Obviously in a generous mood, one of the soldiers yelled at him, "Have some of Hitler's goddam wine. We got it right out of his goddam house and we're having a helluva time."[309]

When Helen Kirkpatrick of the *Chicago Daily News* and *Time* magazine illustrator Bill Walton got there a few days after the first troops, they found that the Berghof had been stripped almost bare. Walton managed to retrieve only an ice cube container, while Kirkpatrick found a frying pan, which came in handy for their lunch of powdered eggs and bacon.[310]

It was not all mad drinking and looting on the Obersalzberg. Soldiers of the 327th Glider Regiment found some files in the basement of the Platterhof on German military preparations before the war, including Case Green, dated 22 April 1938, for the occupation of Czechoslovakia. The material was turned over to army intelligence. As has been seen, French soldiers had also located military records in the hotel, which they gave to their intelligence unit.[311]

On May 6, the French division was ordered to leave Berchtesgaden for Diessen the next day, without taking any civilian vehicles. Leclerc managed to delay the move until May 8. The delay resulted in an eruption by the chief of staff of the XXI Corps, who, according to a French staff officer, "became enraged about the pillage and the devastation around the place in our parade zone, invoking rules, etc." This French officer recalled that German soldiers in France had burned down his house and had killed his brother. On May 8, General Frank Milburn, the XXI Corps commander, met with the leaders of the French division at nearby Bad Reichenhall to confirm the movement. After listening to a round of American accusations, General Leclerc counterattacked: his division had not been treated courteously by their allies, the Germans had carried on looting in France on a massive scale and, moreover, he knew of an American unit in a nearby town that had broken into a church during Mass, carried off all the portable religious objects and subjected those in attendance to body searches. The French and American forces separated in bad humor, with a French soldier in a Nazi Mercedes convertible managing to elude an American military police unit surrounding Bad Reichenhall. Franco-American relations continued to remain raw after the two divisions withdrew from the area. A series of nasty incidents occurred until mid–May, that is, as long as the two units were close together, with the leadership of the French division claiming that the encounters had been sparked by American soldiers. Some of them were ignited by German charges of rape by French soldiers, ill-treatment by Americans MPs, raising a French flag in an American-controlled area and French fraternization with German women (who turned out to be Polish, Russian and Yugoslavian). A French military report declared, "The French-U.S. climate is becoming unbearable."[312]

Relations between troops of different American units were also strained. In his candid and revealing diary, John Toole recorded being with another lieutenant of the Third Division when they encountered two soldiers of the 101st Airborne lying in the grass drinking beer. When the soldiers failed to observe proper military courtesy and worse, Toole's companion pulled them to their feet and delivered a succinct lecture on the relative merits of the two divisions: the 101st "only fought three battles in the whole goddamn war and he's speaking for 35,000 dead and wounded men in the Third Division against their 5000." Then he knocked them both down. Although Toole claimed to be horrified to see an officer physically assault enlisted men, he secretly was "tickled": "I don't like those arrogant 101st bastards." According to Toole, this was not an isolated incident. There were nightly bar brawls between soldiers of the two units.[313]

Since the capture of Munich and the clear prospect that the war was drawing to a close, there had been a buildup of politicians and other civilian VIPs anxious to be in on the end of it all. The numbers grew to such proportions that Arthur White, 7th Army chief of staff, noted in his diary, "Should furnish guide books to Alps. Germans least of our troubles. They never give us a moment's worry." As the capture of Berchtesgaden neared, the 7th Army set up a Special Accommodations Section to assist the civilian gawkers, going so far as to provide a suitable array of souvenirs, including German army ceremonial daggers. These could be useful in Washington. Pale, grinning politicians in wide hats and broad-shouldered suits soon were seen popping up in the Alps like the flowers of May. Some visitors acquired other mementos. Several U.S. senators were observed carrying out a few books from Hitler's collection, which had been stored in the tunnel system. Portly Colonel James B. Kraft, none the worse for K-rations, was given the honor of escorting distinguished guests and other bigshots to the famous locations.[314]

Military tourists immediately poured into the town. On May 5, Berchtesgaden was overwhelmed with "Allied people of every background, rank and specialty"; vehicles jammed the roads. A group of intelligence officers from Eisenhower's headquarters was due to arrive very soon. O'Daniel told Heintges, "If there's any looting going on, I'll have your skin, and you're going to lose your regiment." The town was already swarming with "about 100 to 150 souvenir hunters—correspondents and every Tom, Dick and Harry that didn't have a part in the fight." To control the situation, Heintges assigned guards for all of the principal buildings in the town.[315]

In time, nearly every high-ranking army officer made the trek to the Obersalzberg. Ike came at least twice, the first time with Mark Clark and Kay Summersby in early September. When he saw a sign that restricted the elevator to the Kehlstein Teehaus reading "For Field Grade Officers Only," he ordered it removed. How long it remained removed after he left is not known. He later returned with his wife. In his memoirs, General Lucius Clay described his visit to Hitlerland as if it was a state visit. The flood of visitors, military or otherwise, was so great that thirteen members of the 327 Glider Infantry of the 101st Division were assigned as guides. Until this came to the attention of the "brass," they commuted from their billet in one of the *Führerkorp* limousines. For the *Stars and Stripes*, Berchtesgaden and vicinity quickly became "like a zoo without animals."[316]

South of Berchtesgaden at Lend, in Austria, the disarming of German soldiers by members of the 506th resulted in the accumulation of heaps of weapons and equipment. Fred Bahlau saw a pyramid of German helmets thirty feet high. Donald Burgett recalled that "soon convoys of jeeps hauling noncombat rear-echelon officers made daily pilgrimages from Munich" to pick through the weapons, some of them carrying away bags of pistols, which he suspected they sold in Munich.[317]

The Third Division's enjoyment of winning the race to Hitler's town was to be short-lived. After providing him with an expansive luncheon on May 5, Col. John Sink told Heintges that his unit, the 506th regiment of the 101st Airborne, was taking over the area the next day. Heintges had expected his regiment to remain for five or six days. Now he had to tell Sherman Pratt, one of his officers, "We have to get our butts out of here as rapidly as we can. Aren't even supposed to be here, as you know." On May 6, his unit departed, "very reluctantly," with a vast haul of choice liquors, two of Göring's grand limousines and a massive, fully-equipped mobile home, a gift for General O'Daniel.

Still, Heintges felt hard done by. Standing with Lloyd Ramsey, his executive officer, as the regiment departed, they concluded, "Boy, this is a hell of a note. Here we captured the last prize of the war, and we haven't got a damn thing to show for it." They decided to investigate Göring's administrative headquarters. Bluffing their way past 506th guards, inside they discovered two dead generals—one of them being Gustof Kastner—twenty-five suitcases of Emmy Göring's belongings, cartridges of film and a huge supply of miniature Minox cameras, used in aerial observation. They managed to pack about 400 cameras, a heap of film cartridges, including some of Göring's pornographic movies, into their two jeeps, roared through the gates and, upon arrival in Salzburg, achieved great popularity through their liberal distribution of the booty within the regiment and beyond.[318]

General O'Daniel had already moved into Ribbentrop's nearby chalet and on the night of May 8, V-E Day, hosted an appropriately expansive celebration. O'Daniel had ordered all the big guns of his division to open fire at just past midnight. Marguerite Higgins recalled the occasion: "For nearly half an hour red and blue flares, tracer bullets, anti-aircraft guns, and even tank guns fired into the midnight sky. Below us the Salzburg valley and in the distance the heights of Berchtesgaden roared and shook with the noise."[319]

Nearby, on that occasion, Philippe Leclerc issued a brief victory statement to his troops: "*Officiers, Sous-Officiers et Soldats de la 2e Division Blindée. L'ennemi a capitulé. De Tchad à Berchtesgaden, partout vous l'avez battu. Au nom de la France, je vous remercie et je vous demande de montrer au service de pays, la même energie demain dans la paix qu'hier dans la guerre. Vive le Général De Gaulle, Vive la France!*"[320]

When German General Förtsch surrendered his Army Group B on May 4, he estimated that his command in the Alpine area contained from 250,000 to 350,000 German military. According to Reuben Jenkins, who was present, "This number astounded his listeners.... The fact that the greatly advertised 'Redoubt Center,' now holding over 250,000 men, was surrendering so soon was almost unbelievable." General Förtsch explained: there were only about six days' worth of provisions for this mass of men. Although Förtsch did not say so, by this time everybody knew the Americans had vast quantities of food and other supplies.[321]

Berchtesgadener Land was now in the exclusive hands of the 101st Airborne. Soldiers of the division proceeded to conduct a search for loot, but found the town had been well picked-over by their predecessors. Even before the 506th got to the town, the regiment's commander, Colonel Robert Sink, ordered the second battalion commander, Major Richard Winters, to secure the famous Berchtesgaden Hof as regimental headquarters. When E Company of the battalion arrived on the morning of May 5, Winters proceeded to his assignment and, with another officer, confiscated a supply of the hotel's silverware and, to complete his task, posted a double guard around the place "to stop further looting."[322]

The famous salt mines attracted the military's attention but they discovered nothing but salt in the upper tunnels, while exploration of the lower tunnels was impossible due to German destruction of the air pumps. When the division's engineers later got the pumps working, they found a horde of art works, gold and currency. Donald Burgett and other soldiers investigated a freight train parked on the outskirts of the town which they found contained carloads of gold bars and bags of American currency. Their reverie about the division and distribution of the treasure was disrupted by the arrival of General Taylor, Colonel Sink, the burgermeister and jeep loads of MPs who proceeded to take charge of the horde. The division's area of control extended into the Zell am See, a large lake in Austria. At the nearby town of Bruck, Donald Burgett, while on guard duty, observed the strange sight of a German division coming down from a nearby mountain at night carrying torches and singing in a mighty chorus.[323]

Lt. Fred Bahlau of the 506th had a more mundane experience at Berchtesgaden compared with his previous encounters in the war, which included jumping into Normandy on

D-Day, fighting in Operation Marketgarden and being decorated for bravery by General Anthony "Nuts!" McAuliffe at Bastogne following the Battle of the Bulge. Bahlau's company came into Berchtesgaden via Bruck by Zell am See in Austria, where it briefly occupied another of Hermann Göring's residences. Bahlau took the opportunity to spend a night in Emma Göring's bed. A drive in one of Göring's Mercedes convertibles and the confiscation of a case of Lueger pistols completed the visit.

Arriving in Berchtesgaden around May 7, Lt. Bahlau's supply platoon took over a small hotel, where the proprietor, anxious to avoid damage caused by looting, led Bahlau down to a basement cache of flour, from which he extracted two pistols and a set of field glasses. During the four days spent in the area, Bahlau's platoon guarded the remaining art work in the tunnel system on the Obersalzberg. By this time, there was no French presence, but he recalled that on his platoon's first trip up the mountain a German military vehicle blocked the road. He also recalled the distraught reaction of Italian art recovery personnel when they discovered that the nose had been broken off of a marble statue, obviously of Italian origin, which had been dragged out of one of the tunnels. He was involved in two other but related activities: breaking open the doors of storage areas in the lower basements of the Platterhof hotel, which revealed choice liquor supplies, and a social and coordination meeting in Berchtesgaden in which Russian liaison officers participated.[324]

The idyll of the 101st was finished by the end of July when the 42nd Infantry Division took over.

Surveying the scene from the Kehlstein on May 7, *New York Times* journalist Richard Johnston wrote, "Standing on this spot and looking down on the small town of Berchtesgaden below today, it was hard to realize what this place once meant to all Europe and the world." All changed now: "Like the regime whose leader it housed, it is gone in a hideous scramble of broken trees, huge bomb craters and shattered buildings." An unnamed reporter for the London *Times* was impressed by the scope of the Hitler compound. In a report published on May 9, he declared that the area "is one huge air raid shelter and fortress which looked like it could have resisted siege for years."[325]

After hearing from some American soldiers about the *Teehaus* on the Kehlstein, Victor Bernstein of the New York newspaper *PM*, with obvious sarcasm, suggested: "Perhaps all approaches should be permanently blocked and the house be left to the mercy of the Winter winds that blow through the Alpine peaks, so that the simple Germans of the valleys can foster the legend that the soul of Hitler still broods over the mountain top and that the night winds are his voice whispering the old refrain: *Deutschland, erwache!*."[326]

Another observer of the scene recorded his impressions in his journal later that summer. Navy Lt. John F. Kennedy, having been discharged from active duty in early 1945 because of war injuries, was traveling in Europe as a journalist, "to present the GI's point of view," and joined the party of Secretary of the Navy James Forrestal in Germany. On August 1, having flown from Frankfurt to Salzburg, the group drove to Berchtesgaden. Kennedy noted that "It is a beautiful town in the mountains" with "no bomb damage, and there is plenty of wood to take the place of coal." That evening the army provided its usual private repast for delegations of visiting politicians—a six-course dinner, with Rhine wine, champagne and some of Hermann Göring's cigars—at the former headquarters of Field Marshal Keitel at Stangass. For home-town consumption visiting politicians were usually photographed with Eisenhower or other top brass seated at wooden benches eating out of mess kits. The next day the group went to the gutted Berghof and then up to the Eagle's Nest, where Kennedy declared that "the view was beautiful—the living room being round and facing out on every side on the valley below."

Sketch of Obersalzberg by Jacques DeLauriston, *Moteurs en Route* [*Start Engines*]. (Courtesy Berger-Levrault Editions, Paris, 1946)

"After visiting these two places," Kennedy wrote in his journal, "you can easily understand how, within a few years, Hitler will emerge from the hatred that surrounds him now as one of the most significant figures who ever lived." Although Hitler, with his boundless ambition, was "a menace to the peace of the world," Kennedy observed, "he had a mystery about him in the way that he lived and in the manner of his death that will live and grow after him. He had in him the stuff of which legends are made."[327]

# CHAPTER FOUR

# Occupation and After, 1945–2005

### *Taking Over*

The arrival of U.S. Army soldiers in May 1945 marked the beginning of a half-century of American military presence in Berchtesgadener Land. In the immediate post-war period this presence was extensive and intrusive. All the hotels were taken over by the U.S. Army, and military police patrolled the countryside. Swarms of soldiers paid visits to the Land, the Obersalzberg and the Kehlstein. Because the area was made into a recreation area and not a military base, however, the American presence gradually was reduced until by the mid–1990s, with the withdrawal of the bulk of the U.S. Army in Germany, it disappeared altogether.

Unidentified French soldiers attempt to mount flag for joint flag-raising on Obersalzberg, 5 May 1945. Two American officers (at left) view the proceedings: Col. John Heintges, commander of the Seventh Infantry, and Lt. Col. Lloyd Ramsey, chief of staff of the regiment. (Photograph by Sherman Pratt)

The condition of things in early May 1945 was very much a war-time situation. A military government was established and the Counter Intelligence Corps began to comb the hills for Nazi refugees and Nazi gold. As late as May 21 the Allied high command was concerned that some Nazi elements were still trying to get into the mountain area, and road blocks and check points were maintained until that time. There were a wide variety of German military units in the surrounding area. Following the cease-fire announcement on May 5, long lines of German soldiers began to come down from the hills. The initial destination for the first of them was a prisoner of war camp about a mile and a half outside Berchtesgaden on the main road to Munich. Until a few days before it held about 3000–4000 American and British prisoners.[1]

David Webster observed the mile-long procession of German soldiers slowly passing by his new quarters. All kinds of formations were included: division headquarters units, *Volkssturm* companies, antiaircraft platoons, quartermaster supply battalions, all of whom were "left with no supplies and no one to give them to if they had them, for almost the whole army had disintegrated in the broken terrain and the wild scattering of the last days of the war." In that terrain, what if they had been mobilized to fight? What surprised Webster's colleagues was the large number of women trooping by—"German WACs, Luftwaffe Mädchen, young refugees from bombed cities who had attached themselves to soldiers for bed and board."[2]

The presence of "unattached" young women among surrendering German troops was widely noted by other members of the 101st. Indeed, "a walk through the barns and little shacks thrown up by the camped German troops almost always revealed German privates and noncoms apparently happily set up at housekeeping with a field *Frau*." GI discovery of cartons of V-packets (prophylactics) at the sites of antiaircraft batteries ringing the Obersalzberg also indicated a female presence.[3]

**Joint American-German check point. Lend, Austria, 10 May 1945. (Photograph by Donald Straith)**

At the camp all German vehicles were confiscated and GIs made their selections. Guards from the 101st had rewarding duty at the site, stripping prisoners of watches, cameras, binoculars, pistols and anything else of interest. Camp followers were invited to share American accommodation in town and elsewhere. After being checked against a master list of war criminals, almost all of the German soldiers were released after a few days. They were directed to Munich, some by train, others in a menagerie of motorized vehicles using everything from charcoal to wood for fuel and a great mass of them in horse-drawn wagons. Marguerite Higgins wrote a report about the spectacle of a half-million German soldiers making their own way back to Munich.[4]

For the first few days German units continued to appear. In the Alpine area around Berchtesgaden over 300,000 military surrendered. Instead of just a small number of ill-trained troops available in the Redoubt area as claimed by some German generals, there was a huge body of veteran soldiers in the surrounding mountains. Almost all of them had fled into the area only shortly ahead of the Russians, but what if they had been organized into a cohesive fighting force? South of Berchtesgaden on May 8, Major Edward French and Sergeant Louis Dorsky of the 101st Cavalry Group had an unnerving experience. While scouting out a location for a headquarters and being separated from French's vehicle, Dorsky decided to take a walk from his half-track and, around a bend, was confronted by a mass of German soldiers sprawled along the road. Before he could retreat, he was met by a high German officer in full dress uniform with sword who told him that Field Marshal Albert Kesselring wished to surrender his command. Dorsky, dressed in rumpled fatigues, replied that his officer was not with him and that the German officer should return with Kesselring. Shortly thereafter Major French came flying along in his jeep and led Dorsky in a rapid withdrawal from the area.[5]

Three 101st soldiers on a confiscated fire engine also had a unique surrender experience. Locating the vehicle several miles south of Berchtesgaden on May 6, they headed back but were stopped by a blown bridge at the village of Hirschbichl just over the border in Austria. Captured by SS troops, the sergeant and two privates were brought before Lt. General Theodor Tolsdorf, commander of the LXXXII Corps. Pvt. McFarlan Barnson, who could speak some German, conducted an all-night negotiating session with Tolsdorf, while S/Sgt. William H. Bowen and Pvt. Harry A. Barker swapped war stories with SS soldiers. The next morning the two privates were dispatched to Berchtesgaden, sans the fire engine which would not start, while the sergeant was held as hostage. The division sent out a mere captain to negotiate with General Tolsdorf, but shortly thereafter another mass of German troops were on their way to confinement, while Tolsdorf and his staff descended in thirty-one vehicles "loaded with personal baggage, liquor, cigars and cigarettes." To facilitate the gathering of all German personnel, equipment and arms, local surrender terms allowed armed German soldiers to supervise the process, with German MPs directing traffic, which was mildly dismaying to some American soldiers.[6]

The surrender of the German 82nd Corps presented quite a spectacle to 101st troopers. According to a press report, "A German general in an army vehicle led the parade. Behind him were 30 other vehicles, each packed with staff officers and personnel.... The Germans also brought out truckloads of liquor, cigars and cigarettes, and arrogantly posted guards over their treasures." Other scenes followed: "A German first lieutenant in charge of an SS military police outfit was unloading baggage. Out spilled a brand new swastika flag." As a GI reached for it, the German officer responded, "You Americans! After the war you'll need a ship apiece to take souvenirs home!" He was met with the reply, "Well, we've got the ships for it."[7]

Mixed in with the German military in the Berchtesgaden area were units of the Hitler Youth, one member of which was fifteen-year-old Helmut Kohl, later Federal Chancellor. Kohl's unit had been ordered from Ludwigshafen in the Palatine to Berchtesgaden at the beginning of April to train as anti-aircraft gunners. At the local soccer field they were given a fiery speech by Arthur Axmann, *Reichsjugendführer*. With the approach of American troops, Kohl joined the other teenagers in his unit in a long trek home that was the common experience of multitudes of German soldiers. Assaulted by newly-released Polish forced laborers, assigned to farm work by a unit of the U.S. Army and interrogated by military police, this boys' brigade returned to their ruined city after a march of several weeks.[8]

Ernst von Solomon had an unpleasant experience at the hands of the U.S. Army. A member of the *Freikorps* in the early 1920s but not a Nazi, as a forced member of the *Volkssturm* he was swept up in the chaos of retreating Germans in Alpine Bavaria. When unnamed elements of the Seventh Army occupied the Siegsdorf area, he reported a half a dozen rapes the first night, with the military police being the worst, and the homicide of the seventy-year-old women who refused to hand over her watch to a GI. Solomon was arrested as a "security risk," was incarcerated with a range of Nazi officials and, after an extended period of beatings and humiliations, was finally interrogated and released. The procedure took a whole year.[9]

The experiences of the people of Siegsdorf and Solomon were certainly not typical. Moreover, the CIC had a massive job dealing with thousands of German military and civilians, many of whom had taken vigorous measures to conceal their Nazi affiliations. A story current in immediate post-war Germany recounts that the body of Hitler was found in a street in Berlin; in its grasped hand was a note which declared, "I was never a Nazi."

## Die-hards

The Werwolf threat quickly faded away, but in the first few days after the end of the war in Germany there remained a mass of armed German soldiers, some of whom chose, for a time, to remain free. A member of the 101st Airborne was killed by a sniper in Berchtesgaden. Two soldiers of the Third Division were fatally wounded while sunning themselves of a beachfront roof at Lake Königssee. Although the area had a huge number of German soldiers waiting to surrender, the 506th Regiment met with no opposition as it moved into occupation of the Bruck and Zell am See districts in Austria. At the end of May the London *Times* had an alarming report that in the mountains leading to the Resia pass there was "a regular fortress, where every cliff conceals prepared gun positions, and subterranean galleries stocked with ever sort of munitions." It also claimed that scores of arms dumps had been found in the area, with "many more likely," and that "young werewolves" might initiate partisan warfare. Lt. John Toole recorded an encounter with German soldiers in the Austrian mountains, near Niedernfritz, forty-five days after the surrender. When a wounded young boy was brought to his battalion command post, an investigating patrol was fired on by about fifteen German soldiers. Toole led a platoon to the high country which encountered the German soldiers. No exchange of fire took place, but Toole's platoon did spot a woman running out of a house who in her flight dropped a suitcase containing a Schmeisser machine pistol. Toole claimed this was the first time he had heard of Werwolves. There was no aftermath to the incident. As well, there were only very occasional acts of sabotage in the area in the immediate post-war period.[10]

## *Roundup*

The most famous Nazi leader to be captured in the southern mountains at the end of the war was Reich Marshal Hermann Göring. As has been seen, largely for his own safe-keeping, he had been shifted from the Obersalzberg to his family castle at Mauterdorf on April 28. Two days later a final message was radioed to the Berghof compound from Berlin: "Shoot the traitors of April 23 if we should die." The order obviously was generated by Martin Bormann. Berhard Frank, who had frequent contact with Göring, decided to ignore the message, and he was supported in his judgment by Field Marshal Kesselring, the regional commander.[11]

After a bit of maneuvering, the *Reichsmarschall* surrendered to a unit of the 7th Army on May 7. On that day Göring's senior aide-de-camp, Colonel von Brauschitz, passed through the lines of the 36th Division at Kufstein in the Tyrol with a letter from Göring to Eisenhower. With Brauschitz's directions, Brigadier General Robert Stack, the assistant division commander, drove across German lines, meeting up with hundreds of unguarded Allied prisoners of war. His quest for Göring ended when he encountered Göring's convoy in the early evening. Having decided for safety's sake to remain behind German lines that night, Stack, as a guest at Göring's castle, had the opportunity to ask about preparations for the alleged National Redoubt, to which Göring replied, "There had been some talk of such a plan a year before but nothing at all had been done to implement the plan." The next day Stack delivered Göring and company to his division headquarters at Kitzbühel. The following day Göring was flown, with difficulty, by Piper Cub to the headquarters of the Seventh Army in Munich.[12]

Meeting with Alexander Patch, Göring gave him his five pound *Reichsmarschall's* baton, which was decorated with an incredible 640 diamonds, 20 gold eagles and 20 platinum iron crosses. Eisenhower sent Patch a message inquiring if Göring still had "his famous collection of emeralds." In June Patch presented President Truman with the baton at a White House ceremony. The baton was used in war bond activity until the end of the Pacific war and, after Patch's death in November 1945, given to his widow, who, in turn, donated it to the museum at West Point.[13]

The matter of the confinement of Göring soon erupted into controversy. Göring had proceeded to ingratiate himself with U.S. Army officers. Dressed in full uniform, he was photographed shaking hands with an American general and talked extensively with Allied journalists. He attended at least one army drinking bout where he obligingly played the accordion. Jovial Hermann was doing his thing. At Augsburg on May 11 he met with the press in the pleasant setting of a garden. Göring told the reporters that, along with many other German leaders, he knew so little of the concentration camps that "we thought all the atrocity stories were just propaganda." The biggest surprise of the war and the most fateful events for him was the employment of the American long-range fighter plane. He declared that during the last year Hitler had been often sick and he had heard that there was something "wrong with Hitler's brain."

Following press reports about the gentle, apparently hospitable treatment of Göring, there was a storm of protest in America and Britain about the wildly inappropriate behavior of American officers towards a man who was already being branded a war criminal. General Marshall quickly told Eisenhower to put a halt to the celebrity treatment of enemy leaders. Responding to what he claimed were allegations about such behavior, Ike issued a stern order, noting that "if such instances have occurred, they have been against my express orders." The public relations aspect was important: "I am not going to have the whole public effect ruined in America by such ill advised actions on the part of any officers." He ordered each high-ranking commander to "call before him the offending officers and express my intense displeasure that my orders on non-fraternization have been so flagrantly disobeyed." Apparently the American military had not thought to develop a policy of how to treat captured Nazi leaders. Affable Hermann easily manipulated the U.S. generals he first encountered.

The Göring caper ended on May 12 when he was transferred to the 7th Army interrogation center at Wiesbaden. Nuremberg followed where he continued to successfully ingratiate himself with similarly pliant American officers.[14]

Field Marshal Albert Kesselring was the commander of all of the forces in southern Germany at the end of the war. In his memoirs he noted that although almost nothing had been done to build up defenses of the area facing the onrushing Americans, he fought to the end in order to hold a base towards which the German forces in the south-east could withdraw to elude the Russians. After attempts to gain concessions through negotiations on May 4 at Salzburg, Kesselring's force surrendered two days later, his claim being, "My headquarters staff was the only group in the Alps which had not yet surrendered." While the Third Infantry and 101st Airborne hassled for four days over who was to make the capture, Kesselring moved the remaining members of his staff to Heinrich Himmler's special train at Saalfelden.[15]

There were problems in achieving the surrender of Kesselring's Army Group G. At 8 P.M. on May 4 a delegation of ten German officers, led by General Förtsch, commander of the German First Army, came to the headquarters of the Third Infantry Division in Salzburg. After negotiating surrender terms, the German delegation on May 6 "encountered SS troops who, at first, refused to give it a safe conduct through their zone. Later other SS troops blew a crater in the road in front of the delegation and established two roadblocks behind it." Only Förtsch managed to get through while the other German officers returned to the Third's command post. The next day the officers were able to travel to Kesselring's headquarters.[16]

A mere American major arrived to accept the capitulation of the staff and to escort Kesselring to Berchtesgaden. The field marshal, who was allowed to keep his personal weapons, medals and marshal's baton, made several stops along the way to urge German soldiers to cease resistance. Members of his staff followed. His full entourage—ninety-one staff officers, twenty-six orderlies and thirteen chauffeurs—were provided accommodation at the Berchtesgadener Hof, the best hotel in town. American guards were required to come to attention when approached by German officers, who retained their side arms. Together with Maxwell Taylor, Kesselring met with available journalists to whom he declared that he expected Hitler at the end would travel south to the Alps and he was "most surprised at the decision of Der Fuehrer at the last moment to fight with his soldiers in Berlin." A photograph of the press conference gave the impression that the two military leaders had conducted a friendly, alcoholic, almost jovial, session. The photograph appeared in American and British newspapers, with the caption in the latter press usually reading something like, "Another back-slapping party with the Nazis."

Following in the wake of the Göring reception, this report caused rumblings in the U.S. high command. Maxwell Taylor recalled, "Almost at once inspectors from Army Headquarters descended upon Higgins [another general] and me, and I nearly lost my job before I could tell the full story." But Percy Knauth, who was at the news conference, noted the relaxed, cordial mood of the event: "The Field Marshal sat in a deep armchair, cigar in hand, Major General Taylor sat beside him, and adjutants of both armies hovered respectfully in the background. There were cognac and vermouth on a low table for those who wanted them."[17]

At that time many enlisted men were being court-martialed for violating the no-fraternization order for doing such outrageous things as walking around with German girls. Conviction resulted in demotion, heavy fines and even imprisonment. At the same time, ten generals were investigated on the same charges. Their treatment was very different. In one case a general ordered the expulsion in the middle of the night during a rain storm of U.S. soldiers staying in a Munich hotel in order to provide suitable accommodation for a party of German generals. He said he was unaware that the hotel was full and that took care of that. Two generals who showed Göring a good time were found only to have "engaged in social contact." Three other generals were found to have similar contact with Field Marshal Gerd von Rundstedt. No court-martials, demotions, fines or imprisonment followed.

In the case of Albert Kesselring, despite the fact that he had the full and free run of the place around Berchtesgaden for several days, investigators concluded that General Taylor, Brig. Gen. Gerald J. Higgins and Brig. Gen. William N. Gilmore had only "engaged in contact with" Kesselring, which did not constitute fraternization. The investigators recommended that "no further action be taken."[18]

In order to facilitate the demobilization of scattered German units, for several days "Smiling Al" Kesselring was allowed to travel freely in the area, escorted by a single U.S. lieutenant, in the course of which he had many interviews with Allied journalists. All of this changed when on May 15 when he was taken to a camp at Mondorf, stripped of his paraphernalia and made a prisoner. He later claimed that his staff members were greatly surprised by this turn of events. He remained in confinement until 1947 when he was sentenced to death by a British military court in Venice for his role in the massacre of Italians in Rome in 1944. His sentence was reduced to life imprisonment and he was released on the grounds of ill health in 1952. His memoirs were published the next year and he died in 1960.[19]

The man who was the principal proponent of the idea of a National Redoubt was quickly located by Third Infantry Division intelligence. Gauleiter Franz Hofer informed his captors that there was only a remnant left of German opposition in the area from Salzburg to the Brenner. Of his original fifty-six *Volks* battalions, only three remained in formation and he was out of contact with them. Although he denied having them, a search of his house revealed several weapons and a short-wave radio. After a final Nazi salute and "Heil Hitler," he joined the herd of other leaders of the Third Reich in prison.[20]

Otto Skorzeny, noted SS commando leader, claimed that during the last months of the war he had been busy transporting the accumulated wealth of Nazi leaders, including that of Martin Bormann and Ernst Kaltenbrunner, to secret locations in the Alps. In order to disguise this activity, Skorzeny said that much of the loot was transported in military ambulances. He also said that he stashed a complete set of Reinhard Gehlen's intelligence files deep in the mountains. Moreover, he was active in trying to organize the Werwolfs and, finally, in the Alpine region, he struggled to get army leaders to join with the SS in defending the redoubt region. In the last days he was in Berchtesgaden, where Walther Funk asked him to take charge of his gold supply and provide personal protection, but Skorzeny had other things to do. He reportedly was the beneficiary of a great loot dispersement at Wald on May 7.

A few days later, he related, he went to Annaberg where he tried to surrender his formation of 300 men, but was met with indifference by an American officer. After a conference at Salzburg on May 16, he finally effected his capitulation. Like Kesselring and other German military leaders in the area, he met with Allied journalists and regaled them with tales of his adventures. He was acquitted of war crimes by an Allied tribunal and escaped from a German internment camp in 1948. Having dyed his hair, he reportedly spend several months in the Berchtesgaden area. Given his demonstrated ability to do the unconventional, this is not implausible. He eventually went to Spain, where he conducted extensive business activities, wrote a guarded memoir and lived extremely well. In 1959 he purchased a 170 acre farm in County Kildare, Ireland, where he bred horses and spent the summer months. There was a general but unsubstantiated belief that, at least in part, his source of funding for these activities was the gold he extracted in Austria in the final days.[21]

By the time German resistance came to an end, Ernst Kaltenbrunner was already in the Alps. The head of the Reich Main Security Office (RSHA) and second man in the SS had brought a large amount of gold, American dollars, Swiss francs and diamonds with him, some of it, at least, taken from the Berlin *Reichsbank* on April 22. To the end, he remained an enthusiastic supporter of the idea of an Alpenfestung. He abandoned his headquarters at Salzburg on May 1, but, four days later, was responsible for preventing the blowing up of the salt mines near the mountain resort of Altaussee which contained a massive collection of art works. After that he retreated with his mistress to a hideout in the Tyrol.

On May 4 Robert Matteson and his translator Sydney Bruskin, of the 80th Division's CIC detachment, began a ten-day trek that resulted not only in the capture of Kaltenbrunner but the seizure of a variety of second-rank Nazis in the Austrian Alps. With the assistance of members of the anti–Nazi Austrian Freedom Movement and a British agent dropped into the area on April 20, the duo discovered that Altaussee, high in the Totes Gebrige range, was not only a refuge for prominent actors and musicians, but was the communications center for Nazi resistance in the Alps. The plan for such an undertaking had been formulated by Kaltenbrunner, Otto Skorzeny, Wilhelm Höttl, head of intelligence for south-eastern Europe, and other Nazi officials at a meeting in Strobl on May 3. Heading south, Adolf Eichmann and some of his staff passed through the resort on May 6 or 7. After shutting down a Nazi transmitter and arranging the incarceration of the Nazi coterie there, Matteson finally caught up with Kaltenbrunner in a mountain-top cabin on May 15. Following conviction of war crimes Kaltenbrunner was hanged in 1946. Wilhelm Höttl, having revealed to American intelligence the existence of a network of underground agents left behind in south-eastern Europe and where other SS transmitters were operating in the Alps, was employed by two U.S. spy agencies until he was eventually dismissed as unreliable and no longer useful.[22]

Sepp Dietrich was for long Hitler's favorite SS general. After Dietrich's Sixth Panzer Army failed to prevent the Russian advance in Hungary in March 1945, however, Hitler ordered that the soldiers in its SS divisions be stripped of their armbands. After shattering defeats at Vienna and elsewhere, Dietrich's army disintegrated. With that, he proceeded, in early May, to Zell am See, south of Berchtesgaden, which was the SS southern headquarters. When he arrived on May 8 he found that Kesselring and company had already departed under guard for Berchtesgaden. He decided to follow, probably to surrender, but he made a wide detour to pick up his wife at Sonthofen and on May 9 was captured at Kufstein, both in the southern Tyrol. On May 15 Dietrich joined other German leaders at the U.S. Army interrogation center at Augsburg.[23]

Several other important German military leaders also were captured in the Land, among them being General Gottlob Berger, chief of the SS Main Office and Himmler's deputy in Bavaria; Karl Oberg, SS commander and chief of German police in France; the noted panzer general Heinz Guderian; and Eric Kempke, Hitler's long-time chauffeur who managed to make his way out of the caldron of Berlin all the way to the Alps.[24]

At the end of the war almost all German leaders fled from Berlin, which, as has been seen, was Hitler's intention. Some, such as Himmler, Rosenberg, Speer and Ribbentrop, went north, towards the headquarters of the new German government assembled at Flensburg by Admiral Dönitz, Hitler's designated successor. Others headed for the mountains—south to the Alps.

In the north, Himmler's offer to serve under Dönitz was rejected on May 2. Three days later Himmler told the final gathering of his entourage that he was going to go into hiding for a time in the clear expectation that a new role for him would develop with the anticipated division between the Western Allies and the Soviet Union. Where else to hide but in the Alps, where other remnants of the SS were gathering to organize Werwolf resistance. On May 10 he joined with a few of his staff, all disguised as ordinary soldiers, in the trek south. Preceded by intelligence reports that he was heading for Bavaria, he did not get far, as he was captured by British soldiers south of Hamburg on May 21 and, when identified, promptly killed himself with poison.[25]

A variety of Nazi luminaries who initially had taken refuge in Berchtesgaden, rather than pursue Wagnerian resistance in the *Festung*, decided to squirrel themselves into the flood of displaced persons in the area.

Robert Ley, head of the German Labor Front, having been selected to lead the Adolf Hitler Free Corps, promised his Führer that the members of this unit would "fight like lions, like heroes—just like the Russian partisans. They will ride silently through the woods on bicycles and mercilessly attack the enemy." In the event, he brought a small group of followers down to the Alps and took to the hills, then thought better of the heroic deed. On May 15 he was reported as being in the village of Scheching, forty-five miles south of Berchtesgaden. A detachment from the 101st arrested a suspect with a stubble beard and a morose, haggard appearance. Upon interrogation, he declared that he was Dr. Distelmeyer, a chemist researching dehydrated food (in fact, he had a doctorate in chemistry) who had worked his way through Russian lines around Vienna and was on his way home to Düsseldorf. When his true identity was established, he breathed defiance: "Life doesn't mean a damned thing to me; you can torture me or beat me or impale me, but I will never doubt Hitler's acts." He committed suicide in his cell before he was put on trial as a war criminal at Nuremberg.[26]

Julius Streicher had developed a fairly elaborate disguise. Veteran Nazi, champion Jew baiter and ex-gauleiter of Nuremberg, he also ran for the Bavarian hills at the end. An informer directed members of the 101st to a farmhouse near Waldring where they found Streicher posing as a person named Joseph Sailor, an artist without political interests. One account has Streicher's apprehension as a matter of sheer luck. American Jewish Major Henry Blitt, driving near Berchtesgaden, stopped to ask a man his view of the Nazis. The man declared, "I am an artist and have never bothered about politics," to which Blitt replied, "But you look like Julius Streicher." The man blurted out, "How could you recognize me." Streicher too was corralled for the Nazi war trials and went to the gallows shouting obscenities.[27]

Walther Funk had arrived in Berchtesgaden as part of the entourage that escorted the

Reich gold reserve south. As has been seen, he personally participated in the shipment of the bullion, arriving with two gold bars and a bag of gold coins in the back seat of his car. Rather than wait for the Americans to arrive, he attempted to leave with retreating soldiers when he was captured on May 6. The U.S. military was particularly interested in using him to track down the locations of the gold hoard.[28]

*Reichsleiter* Philip Bouhler, chief of Hitler's chancery (or party staff) and director of the euthanasia program, came to Berchtesgaden with Hermann Göring on April 21. When they heard of Hitler's collapse, Bouhler urged Göring to act. Arrested by the SS with Göring, he was released by Kesselring when the field marshal learned of the suicide of Hitler. Joining a rank of Nazis who headed there, Bouhler went to his apartment in Fischhorn Castle near Zell am See. Ranked number 12 on the CIC wanted list, he remained there, apparently awaiting capture, until mid–May (10th or 19th). As American soldiers approached, his wife and he committed suicide. The 101st's CIC believed it had captured Bouhler. A press release declared that it had arrested him on May 21. The statement declared, "Expecting to be treated as a prisoner of state, he had packed a huge trunk with luxurious garments." Quickly disabused of his illusions about his position, Bouhler was led away carrying a small suit case. Shocked at the loss of his status, "his wife threatened to kill herself unless he was released immediately."[29]

An important activity of American troops in the area was to try to capture Martin Bormann. Complete with roadblocks, an extensive but fruitless search was undertaken. 200,000 wanted posters were distributed. In all probability, despite his efforts, Bormann never made it out of Berlin.[30]

Among the second-rank Nazis taken at the time were Hans Lammer, Reich administration minister, who was on the Obersalzberg, he said, for "a short vacation," and Franz Xavier Schwarz, the long-time treasurer of the Nazi Party. Hitler's doctor Theodor Morell was located at nearby Bad Reichenhall on May 21, where his capturers marveled at the twelve-ton electronic microscope, a gift from the Führer. In a state of terminal decline, he died the next year. Among others captured by the Seventh Army were Wilhelm Frick, long-time minister of the interior, who was found at his mountain estate "dressed as a Bavarian country squire," and Max Amann, who had been Hitler's sergeant in the first war, publisher of the Nazi newspaper *Völkische Beobachter* and financial angel to the Führer.[31]

Arthur Kannenberg, Hitler's major-domo and court jester, took refuge in a "secret valley near Berchtesgaden." American journalist Marguerite Higgins and her English colleague George Millar managed to locate him. Higgins got the clear impression that Kannenberg believed that if he provided them with sufficient accordion playing and song he would not be affected by the outcome of the war. Kannenberg was shortly arrested, interrogated and released. Through the agency of a local Catholic priest, Fritz Sauckel, who had been in charge of "labor mobilization" in eastern Europe, surrendered at Berchtesgaden on May 8 or 9.[32]

Several members of Hitler's staff, including stenographers, secretaries, cooks, a barber and other household workers were arrested. There also a round-up of Nazi relatives—Himmler's wife and daughter, his mistress and her two children as well as the family of Albert Speer. For some reason this did not happen to the wife of General Alfred Jodl. About 2000 political and military people in Berchtsgaden were put into confinement.[33]

No sooner had the 506th Regiment of the 101st Division set up office in the Nazi district headquarters on May 5 when some members of Hitler's stenographic staff offered their services. They had arrived in Berchtesgaden on April 20 and 23 in anticipation that Hitler would soon follow them there. Already, in mid–April, a transcript of the Führer's supreme command conferences from September 1942 to that time had been dispatched there. With the approach of American troops into the area SS soldiers had burned and buried the records at the village of Hintersee, about five miles from Berchtesgaden. With the assistance of the stenographers, George Allen of the CIC detachment unearthed the remains and stenographers partially reconstructed the transcripts.[34]

The Counter Intelligence Corps also went to work in the Berchtesgaden area interrogating a wide variety of persons, including Paula Hitler, Adolf's only full sibling, who had been brought to Berchtesgaden from Vienna by SS members in mid–April and was living in the Dietrich Eckart house when the Americans arrived. A quiet, unmarried office-worker, she had played no role in the government of her brother or in the Nazi movement, but the CIC could hardly have ignored her presence. After a brief interview on about May 16, she was placed under house arrest but was shortly released; a further interview took place that July and another in June 1946. In all of them, her comments were unremarkable: she told her CIC interrogators of her life during the war and of her recollections of her brother. Until her death in 1960 she continued to live mainly in the area and is buried in a cemetery on the outskirts of Berchtesgaden.[35]

At some point the CIC also got to Hitler's half-sister Angela Hitler Raubal Hammitzsch, who had survived the massive bombardment of Dresden in February 1945 and was staying, together with her half-sister Paula Hitler, in the Berchtesgadener Hof when the Americans arrived. Like Paula, she was not a party member, and the interrogation was without political significance. Her second husband having killed himself shortly after the war, Angela was a widow once again. She continued to live quietly in Dresden until her death on October 30, 1949.[36]

The CIC apparently never caught up with Hitler's half-brother Alois, who, of course, knew even less about Adolf's activities. During the war Alois ran his cafe in Berlin, all the while avoiding irritating Adolf, and, afterwards for a while resumed his business and, for a fee, signed A. Hitler on postcards. He seems to have drifted around in the post-war years, emerging briefly in the early 1950s to make a couple of fiery super-nationalist speeches. As far as is known, he had no contact with American-based wife number one Bridget Dowling or his son William Patrick. In his last years he lived with his second family in Hamburg, where he was joined by his cousin Hans Hitler (who collected material about Adolf). Alois died on May 20, 1956.[37]

There were assorted evacuated diplomatic delegations sheltering in the surrounding mountains. Following a report of a reconnaissance unit, A Company of the 506th on May 11 rushed from its base in the Austrian village of Lend to the resort town of Bad Gastein, where the entire Japanese diplomatic group had taken refuge in a hotel. When the order for the Japanese to vacate the premises met with studied delay, General Maxwell Taylor arrived on the scene and in fluent Japanese told them to get out immediately. The pleasure derived from this action was ended four days later when the Third Infantry Division, recalling its abrupt departure from Berchtesgaden, discovered that the proud airborne troops of the 101st were in its zone. An article in *Stars and Stripes* credited the 3rd Infantry with the seizure of the delegation.[38]

The codebreaking organization at Bletchley Park in England also had its eyes on the Alpine region at this time. Knowing that a substantial portion of the German military command had been shifted to southern Bavaria, it formed a team, the Technical Intelligence Committee (TICOM), to capture as much German communications equipment as it could.

Immediately upon the end of hostilities it sent members to Pfunds, along the Swiss and Italian border, where it seized several Enigma machines as well as a Lorenz device, which was used to encode teleprinter messages between Field Marshal Kesselring and Berlin. They then proceeded to Berchtesgaden where they found more communication equipment. Some team members pushed on to Rosenheim, where they located a group of German decoders who had developed the ability to decipher top secret Russian communications. Although the group hoped to remain free in exchange for continuing these intercepts, they and their equipment were promptly transported to the environs of Bletchley.[39]

## Objet d'art

One of the first tasks of the 101st was to secure the massive art collection that Hermann Göring had transported to Berchtesgaden. Located on a siding just outside of the town was a train of eight box cars which had been partially looted, with considerable damage having been effected by French troops firing into the cars. Then there was another collection from a second train which had been concealed in a vault under the *Luftwaffe* headquarters at Unterstein, on the road to Königssee. There was also Göring's ten-car personal train, which Marguerite Higgins reported "contained huge tile bathrooms with separate dressing rooms with giant double beds.... There were drawers full of Göring's medals, which were set with the finest jewels, rubies, emeralds, diamonds and other precious stones. Wine goblets were of solid gold, and one of the ten cars was filled with cases of champagne, scotch and other liquor." Major Harry V. Anderson, the division's Fine Arts and Monuments officer, directed the assembling of the art collection in a *Luftwaffe* barracks. Göring's purchasing agent and curator Walther Hofer was on hand and was put to work cataloging it all. Due to Anderson's understandable concern about fire, *Landrat* firemen and equipment were required to keep a twenty-four-hour watch outside the building. The transfer of the Göring art work continued, with more than a thousand paintings and sculptures being gathered in six buildings.[40]

Then there was the massive art collection which Hitler planned to install in his projected Führer museum in Linz. At the beginning of 1944 Hitler ordered that the collection be moved from the *Führerbau*, the Nazi headquarters in Munich, to an island monastery in the middle of Lake Chiemsee, and from other places in southern Bavaria to the more isolated and secure location in a salt mine above the village of Altaussee in Austria. When American troops captured the area in early May 1945, they found that the collection contained an incredible hoard: 6755 old master paintings, 230 drawings, 1039 prints, 95 tapestries, 68 sculptures and 43 cases of *objet d'art* as well as 119 cases of books from Hitler's library in Berlin and 237 cases of books for the library of the Führer museum.[41]

Supported by soldiers from the 506th, the 7th Army CIC promptly made a sortie to Fischhorn Castle at Bruck, the last headquarters of the SS. There they found a trunk filled with looted paintings. Outside the castle they discovered two rows of newly-constructed storage buildings, one of which was filled with motorcycles while another contained a mass of Nazi and army insignia. The garage-like buildings quickly became meccas for American soldiers of all ranks.[42]

One of the great treasures looted from Russia was the Amber Room, eighteen-hundred square feet of paneling inlaid with thousands of pieces of amber and highlighted with jewels, which was taken from the Czarist Summer Palace outside Leningrad in December 1941. The artwork was lost and apparently destroyed in Königsberg at the end of the war. In the early 1990s speculation arose that it might have been stashed, along with other treasure, in a mountain cave in Berchtesgadener Land, but this apparently this turned out to be just another wild rumor.[43]

As part of a large-scale effort to recover stolen art works, Robert Roirmer of the Monuments and Fine Arts Agency, after examining treasure troves at other locations in Bavaria, arrived in Berchtesgaden around May 15. Supplied with information by Göring's housekeeper, Roirmer located valuable paintings under *Haus Göring* and urged the intelligence officer present to secure them. When Roimer returned there a few days later he found the paintings smashed on the ground. Roimer also examined Göring's treasure train, while his colleague Calvin Hathaway set to work to organize the art records, which were strewn about. Their request that the records be taken to MFAA headquarters for analysis was refused by the 101st leadership. Lynn Nicholas has commented, "In the National Archives today, the muddy footprints of World War II boots still adorn these documents of greed." It would appear that a major interest of combat units concerning art hoards was to erect signs at the hideouts noting their role in their capture: "The Hermann Göring Art Collection—Through Courtesy of the 101st Airborne Division." The exhibition attracted considerable attention and, in the name of security, was shortly terminated.

Having found out that Emmy Göring possessed some of the most valuable paintings, Anderson went to Zell am See, where she was living in the Göring castle. Although she tearfully told the major that the paintings were her personal property, Anderson confiscated the lot.[44]

Given the confusion of the time, some of the art work disappeared, including a tiny painting of Madame de Pompadour, which an American officer took from Berchtesgaden and presented to his girl friend who was working for an American agency in Paris. Long after, when it was discovered that the painting had been taken from a branch of the French Rothschilds and the insurance paid out, the painting remained in this woman's possession. Another of Göring's field marshal batons was recovered after a GI attempted to mail it home. Also in Berchtesgaden, an army colonel confiscated silverware belonging to Hitler and Göring, and crystal goblets that Göring acquired from the property of Napoleon, shipping them home to Austin, Texas, where some of the items were later sold for as much as $25,000 each.[45]

The residents of Berchtesgadener Land had been requested, and then ordered, to turn in all "found objects" of value, but the response was minimal. But the search went on. In all 2000 cashes of stashed art work and other valuables were discovered by the agency. In 1947 one of its officers, the German-born Edgar Breitenbach, "roamed the villages around Berchtesgaden dressed in lederhosen, attempting to recover objects from the Göring collections from the reluctant locals." The Berchtesgaden police chief was puzzled by reports of a man "who was running around the country in lederhosen, speaking with a Hamburg accent through a pipe and claiming to be an American officer and a doctor of arts." Bernard Taper, Breitenbach's partner, declared that they "retrieved a fair number of interesting art items along with a quantity of kitsch." But some of the loot remained in the hands of residents of this Alpine area.[46]

Maxwell Taylor recalled that he never had enough men to provide security against theft in his fifty-mile-square area, and since the collection was of enormous value he "never slept easily until it was evacuated to Munich for disposition by the Allied authorities there." However, he spent most of this time on leave in the U.S.A. participating in victory celebrations and visiting his family. When his division left the area at the end of July there was still much that was missing. It turned up at all kinds of places. Six paintings adorning the office of Lucius Clay, military governor of the American zone, were found to have been originally looted from the Netherlands. Speculation that there were hidden art works around Berchtesgaden continued. Almost fifty years after the war ended, in 1994, a Czech *Schatzsucher* ("treasure seeker") launched a search for the "amber room" treasure, looted by German forces from the Catherine palace outside Leningrad, which he believed was secreted in a cave in the surrounding hills. Sixty years later there were reports of looted art works being identified in Europe.[47]

## Gold in the Hills

As well as a vast hoard of art works that were secreted by the German government and its Nazi officials in the Alps, there was also a massive amount of precious metals, jewels and currency in the mountains. Most of this treasure was located on the other side of Munich around Garmisch and Mittelwald, but Berchtesgaden and environs also had a lot. Around the grounds at Kaltenbrunner's place at Altaussee U.S. soldiers unearthed 75 kilos of gold coins and several gold bars. At Berchtesgaden on May 23 Gottlob Berger relinquished four million dollars in currency of twenty-six countries, which, upon Heinrich Himmler's instructions, he had buried in mailbags under the floor of a barn near St. Johann. A huge amount of reichmarks were dug up at Ruhpolding-Zell a week later. Walther Funk was separated from the gold bars he had brought to town.[48]

The saga of the Salzburg Coin Collection began on May 15 when a military police unit in Salzburg was alerted that the Austrian national coin collection, along with many other valuable objects, were secreted in a salt mine in Hallein. The MPs arrived at the mine to find soldiers of the Third Division busy looting gold-plated Walther pistols, ceremonial shotguns and liquor. The trans-shipment of the mine contents resulted in extensive theft, but eventually almost all of the coin collection was restored to the Salzburg Museum.[49]

A spectacular discovery occurred on May 16 when the 15th Regiment of the Third Division came upon a massive trainload of gold, jewels and a vast assortment of other wealth in a railroad tunnel at Tauern, sixty miles south of Salzburg. This was the "Hungarian gold train," containing the Hungarian bullion reserves that had been slowly moving across Austria ahead of the Russian army, with Switzerland being its objective. Guarded by soldiers of the 101st Division and the Hungarian army, the train was brought to Salzburg in July.[50]

There were stories that just before the Americans arrived in Berchtesgaden Mercedes sedans were secreted in deep underground bunkers, never to be found. But American soldiers did find many such cars in barns in the surrounding hills. Of greater interest, were the accounts that retreating SS officers buried treasure in tunnels of the nearby Hohe Brett mountains, but a rigorous search by Florian Beierl and others had no results. Still, things do turn up: in 1975 a large but empty bunker was found on the Obersalzberg.[51]

The large scale securing of hidden Nazi gold soon ended, although some of it occasionally was located here and there. In September 1945 the gold recovery unit of SHAEF asserted that it had recovered 98.6 percent of the $255 million that had been removed from German banks. Still missing were ninety-two gold bars and 147 bags of gold coins; sizable thefts usually involved various European currencies. For some believers, however, there remained a conviction that some Nazis had gotten away with a huge haul of precious metals. There were accounts of ex–Nazis Skorzeny, Josef Mengele and others of their ilk living off the proceeds of wealth stripped from Europe during the war. The recent Swiss banking

Surveying the Obersalzberg tunnel system, July 2002. From left, Florian Beierl, Obersalzberg Institute, Josef Siren, Art O'Misteal. (Photograph by Arthur H. Mitchell)

scandal concerning gold and currency deposits of German, not to say Nazi, origins has once again stimulated interest in possibility of discovering heaps of gold bars, jewels, etc. that had been hurriedly buried or transported by the Nazis in defeat.

More recent results of the treasure hunt have been skimpy. Speculation has centered on Lake Toplitz, sixty miles on the other side of Salzburg, which was included in the touted National Redoubt area. Near the end of the war this was the location of experiments in firing V-2 missiles from submerged submarines. In the very last days of the conflict there were reports that, upon orders of Ernst Kaltenbrunner, truck-loads of large wooden chests were dumped in the lake. In 1959 the German magazine *Stern* sponsored an exploration of the lake which turned up only forged British banknotes that had been manufactured at the Sachsenhausen concentration camp near Berlin in early 1945. A 1984 dive found nothing. Advanced technology could be the answer. In the summer of 2000 a venture with a budget of $600,000, financed by the Columbia Broadcasting System and the World Jewish Congress, employed Oceaneering Technology, which had found the *Titanic*. Using a miniature submarine, the expedition found only more forged British paper currency; no gold bars.[52]

## Moving In

The U.S. Army made full use of all appropriate Berchtesgaden facilities. All of the hotels were taken over, with the Berchtesgadener Hof becoming the residence for officers, the headquarters of the local Nazi Party the Bellevue Hotel, the *Luftwaffe* headquarters the Alpine Inn, Albert Speer's studio the Evergreen Lodge, the Dietrich Eckart house the Winterbrand Lodge, and the Hotel Deutsches Haus, a Wehrmacht facility, the recreation area's reception center. For a shorter time the American military also commandeered the Watz-mann, Wittelsbach, Post and Geiger hotels in the town, as well as the Königssee and Schiffmeister hotels on Lake Königssee.

In order to avoid the carnage and destruction that took place on the Obersalzberg, the 101st, immediately upon its arrival on the scene, occupied the chancellery building at Stan-gass, just outside of Berchtesgaden. A mass of reports and maps were confiscated and a huge underground communications center was secured. With the removal of a Nazi eagle sym-bol on its facade, the facility became the 101st's headquarters. On the Obersalzberg, Hitler's private farm was transformed into the Skytop Sports Center. The Platterhof Hotel was rebuilt in 1955 and given the name of the "General Walker" after Walton Walker, the com-mander of the Eighth Army killed in the Korean War.[53]

The immediate need of the 506th Parachute Infantry Regiment was to secure surren-der terms from the outlying areas and to handle the large numbers of German soldiers com-ing in from the hills. On 10 May the 506th began moving into the Lend-Bruck area in Austria, which included the Zell am See resort, about thirty miles south of Berchtesgaden. The 502nd proceeded to Mittersill, Austria, another resort area about the same distance away. The 501st, which had just arrived, remained in Berchtesgadener Land and became the transfer center for "high point" soldiers in the division already being discharged. Some of the 501st soldiers had the pleasure of breaking into a sealed SS barracks on the Obersalzberg where they found a wealth of military regalia and racks of Mauser rifles.

The 327th Glider Infantry Regiment was assigned responsibility for occupation of the town and absorbed the remainder of the 501st when that regiment was inactivated on June 25.[54]

When the first battalion of the 506th entered the Austrian natural wonderland it com-prised about 600 men and was faced with elemental processing of about 25,000 armed Ger-mans. It did this without difficulty; furthermore, it encountered no Werwolves. Over the next month 43,000 German soldiers were evacuated from the regimental area. It arrested thirty-one suspected war criminals, including SS *Obergruppenführers* Philip Bouhler and Her-mann Senkowsky. Apparently Adolf Eichmann, transport meister of the Holocaust, in the uniform of a *Luftwaffe* corporal, was among the departing German soldiers but was not apprehended. The most important military technology discoveries were that of a jet-pro-pelled helicopter and an infra-red torpedo steering mechanism.

The regiment soon settled down to days of minimal duty, continuous recreation, beer and rest. "VD films were shown" and young troopers were "instructed that the taking of a prophylactic will in no way be construed or implied as a violation of anti-fraternization." (This position was undoubtedly in the spirit of the stance attributed to George Patton: "Copulation without conversation is not fraternization.") The division commander, Gen-eral Maxwell Tayor, was the guest of honor at one of several parties at Zell am See hosted by the regimental commander, Col. Robert Sink, at the end of which a few young officers (yes, officers!) drained most of the fuel from Maxwell's Mercedes, which duly ground to a halt late at night when the general was being driven back to Berchtesgaden. There were semi-serious repercussions the next day. However, this did not prevent the colonel from staging a spectacular Fourth of July observance at Zell, which, due to rain delays, took place on 6 July. In attendance was a large contingent of local Fräuleins wearing DP armbands. After a day of vehicle and horse races, athletic competitions and parachute landings in the lake, the evening featured raucous parties for officers and enlisted men.[55]

Put in charge of the principal motor launch on Zell am See, PFC Jack Agnew had the interesting experience of encountering one of his former opponents. He was approached by a one-legged German soldier from the 6th Parachute Regiment, which had fought the 101st in Normandy, Holland and Bastogne. Agnew secured the man a job maintaining the motor boats, in exchange for which the man presented him with his gold wings from the 6th Para. A somewhat similar episode took place at the Königssee. Having been a prisoner of war in Texas, among other states, Hans-Georg Zabel applied for the position of boatsman. The soldier in charge, a Texan, chose Zabel over other applicants, remarking, "We Texans have to stick together."[56]

To get away from the madding crowd, the 101st shifted its headquarters to Bad Gastein, well to the south of Berchtesgaden, in the Tyrol in the middle of July. In the resort town it found not only many wounded German soldiers occupying the hotels, but also a variety of diplomats who had fled Berlin as well as a collection of foreign supporters of the Nazi regime. There was a Palestinian group led by the Grand Mufti of Jerusalem as well as a delegation from Afghanistan. The soldiers were removed and the others assembled and arrested.[57]

As in the other parts of the American zone, there were a raft of road accidents and fatalities. To amuse themselves some officers rounded up horses and formed a polo club. Enlisted men organized motorized posses to shoot and dismember cattle. Confiscated German planes were flown until an officer was killed in a crash. Until their vehicle was confiscated for officer use, a group of soldiers in Richard Elliott's platoon of the 101st commuted from the SS barracks to the Kehlstein in one of Hitler's convertibles. Some soldiers in the Third Infantry Division stationed near the Salzburg autobahn assembled a variety of German luxury cars, which they called the "Enlisted Men's Motor Pool." Nightly races were conducted on the superhighway. William Kuntz remembers the end of the caper: "When word came down from HQ that possession of said vehicles would result in post-war delay or cancellation of returns home, all the vehicles were driven off a cliff! It made quite a bonfire!" When a similar order came to some of the soldiers in the 506th they responded by testing the bullet-proof capacity of the Nazi limos they had accumulated, the result being that when the vehicles were transferred to the "brass" they were found to be unfit for use.[58]

Other soldiers engaged in more pacific recreation. A few members of the 506th discovered what they were informed was Hitler's private fish pond near Zell am See. With the fish almost jumping out of the water and using surgical needles in place of hooks, they caught over sixty golden trout in an hour. As well as dipping into Göring's wine hoard, they skied on the upper slopes and swam in the lake. Although they encountered no Werwolves, they had the disconcerting experience while walking the trails of encountering a few fully-armed German soldiers seeking to surrender. When they requested a keg of beer from the local brewery, the owners were surprised and pleased that these American soldiers paid for it.[59]

The idyll of "Screaming Eagles" came to an end on August 1, when they departed for France for transshipment to the U.S. on the way to the war in the Pacific. They were succeeded by the 42nd Infantry Division, which, together with the Third Infantry Division, had fought its way south.[60]

## Amerika Comes to Deutschland

The American occupation of southern Germany was both a great success and an unacknowledged fiasco. Despite grim warnings, absurd formal restrictions and administrative ineptitude, the German people were not subjected to the heavy hand of foreign domination.

Indeed, American military government gradually was reduced to irrelevance. Moreover, after nearly three years of severe conditions, the west German economy made a remarkable recovery and the institutions of self-government were quickly built from the bottom up. The U.S. government and, for that matter, its military government in Southern Germany, deserves a large measure of credit for these achievements.[61]

There was also another side of the story—GI murder and mayhem, gross corruption, callous exploitation of a poor, defeated people and brazen opportunism, particularly in the officer ranks, by American military personnel. Having observed such activities during the first year of the occupation, Marshall Knappen noted, "an occupation army is an army at its worst." The outside world knew little of the situation as complete military censorship was maintained for two years after the war. Yet almost all the really bad things happened in the immediate wake of the occupation.[62]

In those first two years of the U.S. occupation there was a barrage of criticism and more in American newspapers, magazines and books. This situation caused J. Lawton "Lightning Joe" Collins, the army's chief public relations officer, to travel to Germany in the summer of 1946 to urge American journalists to lessen their exposés and show some of the positive aspects of the occupation. He asked them to give attention to "the real picture of Germany," rather than "the superficial picture of the pregnant Fräulein, venereal disease and scandal."[63]

The condition of the U.S. Army in Germany was reduced to near chaos by rapid demobilization. The demand of many soldiers for their prompt return to the United States and domestic agitation "to bring the boys home" created this situation. Army divisions became little more than replacement centers. Lucian Truscott, who succeeded George Patton as commander of the Third Army and governor of Bavaria in September 1945, was appalled by what followed. In his memoirs, he declared, "There has probably never been in all history a comparable destruction of a fighting force by the people to whom the force belonged." As a result of this "hysterical demand," he asserted, "[w]hat had been a magnificent fighting force became little more than a rabble—an undisciplined mob." He faulted the army leadership (read "Eisenhower") for not presenting a strong case about the dangers of the feckless dissolution of the American military presence in Europe. Truscott's charges were echoed by Brig. General George Eyster, who was in charge of redeployment from the European Theatre. According to Russell Hill, "The main concern of the men, and not only of men, but of officers, was to watch their points, try to figure out when they would get home, and in the meantime concentrate their efforts on securing Fräuleins, liquor and loot." Worse was to come with replacement troops—young men who had not been in the war but were now being shipped to Germany.[64]

The underlying difficulty with the U.S. occupation in Germany was that after a brief interval there was to be governance and administration by American civilians. This did not happen, and as a result the U.S. Army, ill-equipped for this task, took charge of the American zone. Almost every study of the occupation agrees with this judgment. One of the earliest assessments of the matter was provided by James Warburg, who in a book published in 1947 declared of those employed in military government, "With very few exceptions they knew literally nothing about Germany. They neither spoke the language, which forced them to rely upon unreliable interpreters, nor had they been given any idea of German history, politics or economic problems."

In his 1977 study of the occupation, Edward Peterson declared, "Yet because no other agency was able or willing, the army remained holding the bag three years longer than it planned or wished." With an urgent need for administrators, the American military government became a haven for hordes of colonels, generals and the like who rushed to take advantage of the privileged life offered by the occupation, rather than being turned out on the street at war's end. According to Russell Hill, "The man who did volunteer to stay on ... was generally among the least competent; he was the man who feared he could not get as good a job at home, or the man who wanted to stay because he could live cheaply and make money on the black market." Some of the things, not isolated incidents, that happened in the very early period of occupation seem extraordinary, bizarre and almost incomprehensible.[65]

The 7th Army established its interrogation center at Seckenheim. Major Kenneth Hechler, an army historian, went to the camp to interrogate some leading German generals. He recalled the camp commander, "Major K.," as being "one of the rottenest characters I have ever met in or out of the Army." "Major K." not only stripped incoming high-ranking prisoners of anything of value, "[h]e even went so far as to allow certain prisoners to go home and get valuable belongings they had hidden, and then rob these prisoners on their return."

The camp commandant did, to be sure, take an active interest in interrogating a certain category of detainee. Seckenheim had the distinction of containing many of the mistresses of high-ranking Nazis, and Major K. took it upon himself to examine them closely. For his own purposes, his technique was most effective: he would summon *liebe Fräulein* individually to his office, dismiss his staff for several hours and lock his door.

Hechler observed that a casual spirit permeated the camp. Enlisted men would fight to get night guard duty around female housing. While Hechler was being taken across the camp by a soldier, they encountered a "young girl prisoner, apparently clad only in a bathrobe," who called out to them, "Hey boys, one long look for three cigarettes." The GI price for cigarettes was five cents a pack! This mad-cap regime did not last long. In October or November 1945 "Major K." was court-martialed and dismissed from the service.[66]

Even before the U.S. Army had secured its area of Germany there were criticisms of American military government. Having garbed himself in the uniform of an enlisted man in order to get an inside view, Congressman Albert Gore (Democrat from Tennessee) in late March 1945 declared that some "misfits" had gotten into the organization: "There is evidence that some personnel was transferred to this branch of service," he asserted, "because they were surplus or misfits in other branches." Moreover, he condemned the non-fraternization policy because "it will be [as] impossible to make the American soldier uncivil and unresponsive to human wants and acts of personal friendship as it is to suddenly make disciples of the Golden Rule out of the Nazi SS trooper."[67]

In Bavaria some of the American officers appointed as town commanders demonstrated a degree of arrogance and irresponsibility that was breathtaking. In Augsburg the occupation began with wholesale looting, mindless destruction of property and the killing of local policemen. When the 7th Army shifted its headquarters from Augsburg to Heidelberg a new round of stripping ensued. During the summer of 1945 the city was under the authority of a Major Cofran, who hung a sign behind his desk reading, "I hate all Germans," and had a large card on his desk stating the number of Americans killed in the war. Among Cofran's requirements was that every day fresh flowers be placed on the desks of all of his staff. He became embroiled in controversy with the mayor over the de–Nazification process and threatened to fire almost all city workers. He was transferred in September. He later was murdered for refusing a loan to the father of a fellow officer's mistress.[68]

Some military governors also created bad impressions in small places. Eichstatt, located halfway between Augsburg and Nuremberg, was just a town but also was a Land (county) seat and the center of a diocese. From the fall of 1945 until January 1947 it was ruled over by a Bostonian named Major Towle, who reported excellent progress in all aspects of administration during his tenure. Many local people took a different view of affairs. Recalled as a playboy and sometimes gangster, Towle often would slam his whip on his desk when his decisions were questioned by the inhabitants. Driving through the town he screamed at anyone in his way. A former mayor declared that Towle was surrounded by a coterie, both German and American, who were scoundrels and whores; they were housed in twenty-five commandeered houses. Towle shipped out hundreds of wooden boxes filled with confiscated goods and forged art work.

After he departed (leaving behind a stack of unpaid bills) there were no substantial problems between military government and the affairs of the town.[69]

A great improvement in the army-civilian relationship in the American zone occurred when in April 1946 Lucius Clay ordered military government to cease direct involvement in local administration and government.[70]

The Civil Affairs and Military Government division of the U.S. Army had the function of providing law, order and basic services in the immediate wake of military occupation; not, as it turned out in Germany, of providing extended periods of military government. Even if this division had been allowed to carry out its primary function, it was hardly ready to do it. Despite the fact that anyone from 1943 forward could anticipate American occupation in a part of Germany, there was little training in civil affairs. Most of those involved knew nothing about Germany and few of them learned the German language. Moreover, those who were drawn to this branch of the army rather than combat units, often were of a low caliber. It is difficult not to agree with the statement of George Shuster, who became Bavarian Land commissioner in 1950: "The United States was often represented by good men, but, alas, also by lechers, traffickers in women, manipulators of the black market, petty protagonists of illiteracy, and fools." A short-term military governor of Frieberg saw the job as a moral trap: "I decided to get out before I was completely demoralized by the rich life, the castles, the women, the drink and black market."[71]

The policy of non-fraternization ran into overwhelming opposition from the very moment blue-eyed blond Rhineland girls greeted invading Yanks with cries, "We have been waiting for you for three years!" This policy originated in a combination of political pressure on the home front, due to the usual excesses of war-time propaganda, vote pandering by politicians, including the great F.D.R., and almost total ignorance of German history and culture by military leaders who did not get to their elevated positions by studying Goethe and Hegal. The *Pocket Guide* to Germany, published by the army in late 1944, declared in effect that all Germans were Nazis and the Fräuleins would continue to be covert agents for a fallen regime, and so on. Confronted with the realities of occupation, however, the whole thing quickly crumbled. As Saul Padover observed, the no fraternization order "was about as effective as the late and unlamented Eighteenth Amendment" that banned the sale of alcoholic beverages.[72]

Problems began immediately. Some members of the Army Medical Corps declared that unless the policy was changed "the venereal disease rate would double within six months because if soldiers sought medical attention for this condition it would result in a $65 fine for fraternization." The policy would also result in increased GI alcoholism and crime. On June 4 the High Command dealt with the matter with an order: "Contraction of venereal disease or the facts concerning prophylactic treatment will not be used directly or indirectly as evidence of fraternization." Why, soldiers, of course, could have contracted the ailment in a variety of ways—contact with unclean beer steins, unsanitary latrines, etc.

Seeking to outfox MPs, some soldiers, *sans* uniform, wore the white armband of a displaced person and even French uniforms, while some German girls who put on a variety of deceptive garb, or were without uniforms, although German-speaking, claimed to be Allied nationals. DP armbands were sometimes provided to German women to allow them to attend army social events. GI humor had it that the German people were being shown that Americans were "engaged in the most widespread violation of their own laws since Prohibition."[73]

Even before the occupation began some army psychologists concluded "any soldier in the army of occupation must leave the non-fraternizing area every six weeks." One proposal that was considered was to establish "reservations for the wives of American soldiers in such cities as Bonn and Heidelberg." Other ideas were more letters from the girls back home and expanded athletic activities. The utility of cold showers was not mentioned.[74]

*Yank*, the army weekly, investigated the situation. It declared that "the German girls wore thin, tight dresses and they had a pleasant technique of walking down the streets so the sun would hit them just right." Moreover, "at beaches they wore swim suits about the size of a musette bag, without straps. They looked healthy. They looked good." Some of the young ladies were bold: "The girls winked at the GIs and smiled at them. Sometimes, when they walked down the streets, they would tap their backsides and say, 'Verboten.'" A similar story related that "one blond *Fräulein* with braided hair ... always walked past two MPs every day on her way to do shopping, swinging her hips from side to side even more noticeably than usual. As she passed she would look slyly at the MPs, tap one hip and utter the word 'Verboten.'"[75]

The attraction of American soldiers for German women became a staple of U.S. newspaper and magazine articles for the first year of the occupation. Non-fraternization also was the policy in the British zone, although the American troops were far better equipped with money, food, liquor, cigarettes and various luxuries than were their British counter-parts. Bernard Montgomery, not noted for his interest in women, declared that young German women were attempting to "sabotage" the official policy by wearing less and less clothes. Monty might not have noted that summer was coming on, but, in any case, he asserted that his men were "putting up a good show" in the face of such tantalizing behavior, which was jolly good of them.[76]

At the end of May the 12th Army Group headquarters announced the establishment of prophylactic stations. It declared that, "while Gen. Eisenhower's policy is being effectively followed by troops, there are cases of clandestine fraternizing." The stations were set up "for that reason, and for the health of other soldiers thus innocently exposed to diseased men." This action was followed by a poster campaign, with the title of "Hello Sucker," which in cartoon form showed the dire consequences of carnal contact with German females. *Stars and Stripes* commented: "An extensive observation shows the whole non-fraternization policy gradually is being undermined by that great irresistible natural force through which boy, for some centuries, has met girl." Saul Padover, an intelligence officer in Germany, had a succinct view of the matter: "Non-fraternization was wrecked on sex.... GI and Fräulein were magnet and steel." One army officer summed up the situation: "Soldiers are going to have their fling regardless of rules or orders. If they are caught they know what the punishment will be. However, that is not stopping them and nothing is going to stop them."[77]

As U.S. forces drove into Germany in February 1945, Claude Nair observed the early

effects of the non-frat policy: "Had we foreseen the inevitability of fraternization and prepared for it, instead of passing a law against it for everyone to laugh at, we might have turned
it to advantage by indoctrinating our men with positive ideas." But from all reports, soldiers disliked boring lectures on democracy and "the American way of life," and grim posters
warning of the penalties for fraternization had little or no effect. In an article in *Life* magazine at the beginning of July, Percy Knauth summed up the cross-gender encounter: "For
the GI it is not a case of policy or of politics or of going out with girls who used to go out
with the guys who killed your buddies. You don't talk politics when you fraternize. It's more
a matter of bicycles and skirts waving in the breeze and a lonesome, combat-weary soldier
looking warily around the corner to see if a policeman is in sight."[78]

After issuing a number of pious statements in May, Eisenhower declared that, of course,
not speaking to Germans did not apply to little children. Who did he think would be with
the children? In August, Eisenhower declared that U.S. soldiers could now have "normal
public contacts" with German people, including standing, walking and talking with them,
but that was all. Some restrictions remained in place until the end of 1946. In the area of
Bad Gastein in Austria, Col. Robert Sink, commander of the 506th PIR, noted in the summer of 1945 that the initial lessening of the non-frat policy "at first was construed by the
troops to mean an almost complete reversal of the policy." Moreover, he said, "With the
departure of many DPs it is becoming more difficult to enforce the policy." VD film had
been shown and "troops have been instructed that the taking of a prophylactic will in no
was be constructed or implied as a violation of anti-fraternization." 1st Lieut. Donald Zahn
of the 506th took a practical position on the matter: he informed his company, "[D]on't let
me see you" violating the ban on Fräulein contact.

The implementation of the shifting policy of non-fraternization was placed on subordinate commanders. In this matter, as in most other aspects of affairs in the American zone,
Eisenhower had little continuing interest or commitment. His primary mission done, he
clearly was looking ahead. In January 1947 the American military personnel were informed
they no longer needed to fear and shun the occupied people; U.S. soldiers would now serve
as "ambassadors of the American way of life."

Considering the bitter, racist-tinged war with the Japanese, as opposed to that with the
Germans, it seems strange that the non-fraternization policy was not employed in the American occupation of Japan, which began at the end of August 1945, possibly in reaction to
all of the problems caused by this measure in Germany. What was provided for almost all
of the first year of this occupation was government-organized houses of prostitution, a policy initiated by the Japanese government in anticipation of the arrival of a horde of American GIs. The U.S. Army established "prophylactic stations" adjoining these places.[79]

The arrival of dependants of army personnel in Germany only exacerbated critical
food, fuel and housing shortages. While many German people survived the bitter winter of
1945–46 without coal and with little food and miserable housing, the arrival of American
families in 1946 resulted in 65,000 more housing units being confiscated for their use. With
German people urgently needed for clearing rubble and rebuilding, the Military Government decreed that American families would be limited to three household servants. After
the hardships of the Depression and the rationing of the war, women, mostly of lower
middle-class backgrounds, in American military families in Germany were living in luxury
while surrounded by millions of people struggling to exist. Most of the expense of this program was paid for by the German people through payment of "occupation costs." It was the
view of spokesmen for the U.S. Army that American housing complexes, surrounded by

barbed-wire with warnings for the "indigenous population" to keep out, somehow was a good way to show the German people the virtues of democratic Middle America. A German joke made the rounds that the Americans made concentration camps and then put themselves in them.[80]

Few of the American dependents had substantial relationships with German people. "Through the unwarranted requisitioning of homes, hotels and restaurants," declared Hans Habe, "through the whole conquering attitude in peacetime, unnecessary hardships were inflicted upon our pupils in democracy." The diplomat George Kennan was stunned by what he observed: "Each time I had come away with a sense of sheer horror at the spectacle of this horde of my compatriots and their dependents camping in luxury amid the ruins of a shattered national community, ignorant of the past, oblivious to the abundant evidences of present tragedy all around them, inhabiting the same sequestered villas that the Gestapo and SS had just abandoned, and enjoying the same privileges, flaunting their silly supermarket luxuries in the face of a veritable ocean of deprivation, hunger and wretchedness, setting an example of empty materialism and cultural poverty."

Ute Frevert has painted a grim picture of conditions in Germany in the immediate post-war period: "The men's war was over, but the women's battle for bread and coal continued, growing ever more bitter and desperate as provisions and supplies became scarcer."[81]

Just before Eisenhower left Germany to become army chief of staff in November 1945 he declared that a "relatively small minority" of soldiers gave the occupation army "a lead reputation that will take our country a long time to overcome." Shortly thereafter a report of the Seventh Army's CIC was much more explicit: "The general opinion of the Germans is that ... American soldiers are men who drink to excess, have no respect for the uniform they wear, are prone to rowdyism, treat civilians with no regard for human rights and benefit themselves through the black market." The problem became more acute after the war with Japan ended. The historian Earl Ziemke has commented, "After V-J Day, what appeared to be almost an epidemic of unprovoked attacks on German civilians and robberies by U.S. soldiers had spread across the zone."[82]

## Alpine Wonderland

In the occupation of Germany, the story went, the Russians got the agriculture, the British the industry and the Americans the scenery. The Bavarian Alps are the epitome of mountain grandeur and were virtually untouched by the war. The people of Berchtesgadener Land suffered less of the hardships that defeat and occupation imposed on most German people. With the exception of the now notorious Nazi buildings on the Obersalzberg, not a single house was destroyed or even substantially damaged. The trauma of capture of the town lasted for but three days. What soon followed was routine American-style occupation, without conflict or opposition.

"The war is over. Germany lost it," Karl Jacob tersely reminded readers on the requisitioned pages of the *Berchtesgadener Anzeiger* in the second week of May 1945. The local paper was refashioned into the bi-lingual *Official Gazette* and its long list of "Notices" of the Military Government ushered in the formal occupation. For the next seven years Berchtesgaden and the Obersalzberg would be under military occupation; for the next fifty years U.S. servicemen would maintain a token military presence and a more considerable political and economic impact. The major U.S. Army activity in the area was its operation of recreation facilities for its members.[83]

The Berchtesgaden region was hardly a typical scenario of challenges and perils for its conquerors. Far from the ravaged battlefields and destroyed cities, war left its quaint Bavarian homes unblemished and its public services fully functional. Although its citizens initially were relatively well nourished, its major misfortune was an impending shortage of foodstuffs. Transportation breakdowns left only a five day basic food supply. Only the scars of the Obersalzberg bombing marred its postcard-perfect beauty. Lurking behind the pristine physical attractions of the area were complex and unresolved questions concerning the fate of the mountainous domicile of Adolf Hitler.[84]

These were matters for the future. The immediate concern was to try to quickly restore pre-war living conditions. The restrictions imposed by the military government were no more than would be expected and hardly onerous.

In his message to the people, Jacob declared, "If we obey the orders given by the Military Government strictly and prevent acts of sabotage by former Nazi leaders, we shall be able to survive these times." He urged the people to "keep an eye on well-known fanatic Nazis! Report all suspicious occurrences to the nearest police station or directly to the Military Government." Jacob need not have worried: there occurred only insignificant and random hostile acts.[85]

At first the town was jammed with evacuees from Munich and recuperating German soldiers, but with U.S. military moving into local housing, this number quickly was reduced. At that time, there were 600 displaced persons there, who were provided for in two camps, but there was a flood of them to follow. Many were young men whose only experience had been as soldiers in the German military and, therefore, lacked civilian skills. An area technical training program for them was soon initiated.[86]

The existing police force was maintained minus weapons and uniforms, but with identifying arm bands. The force consisted of eleven full-time members and forty-five reservists. Crime was almost unheard of—three cases of civilian looting in the first weeks of the occupation. Rationing was continued with "foreign workers and former prisoners of war receiv[ing] from now on the highest rations." Patricia Lochridge, an American journalist, recalled that an investigation revealed that there was only one Jew living in the land—"an attractive black-haired young woman who spoke fair English" and was then hired as an interpreter. Curfew hours were from 11 P.M. to 6 A.M. A sign of the return of normality is indicated in Notice No. 6: "The collection of garbage from households will be resumed"; it was to be supplied to area pigs. General Eisenhower had informed the people in the American zone that "coal will not be available for heating houses this winter," but in a heavily wooded area like Berchtesdagen this was not a problem. Thus, the people there were spared the pain and suffering that was present in much of the rest of Germany during the first two winters after the war.

As was done in other parts of Germany, Nazi literature and regalia was collected and destroyed; street names reverted back to their pre–Nazi designations. In Berchtesgaden, Adolf Hitler-Strasse once again became Maximilianstrasse, Horst Wesselweg once again was Weineldweg. Moreover, on Corpus Christus day "the traditional processions will again take place."[87]

There were few serious restrictions. Persons living outside the area during the war were, for a short time, prevented from returning. Civilians were ordered to report all government officials who were in hiding. There was a crack-down on the improper use of Red Cross armbands. Notice No. 24: "All civilians are strictly forbidden to loiter near any of the offices or similar institutions of the American Army." With the opening of the recreation area for

U.S. servicemen, a bathing area on the Königssee was restricted to American military personnel; apparently German girls were gathering there![88]

As has been seen, the most noted U.S. Army policy in its occupation zone was its non-fraternization order. This position did not last past the summer of 1945 and could hardly be effectively enforced in a recreation area such as Berchtesgaden. The Seventh Army command seemed to be in a dilemma. It reported that in its area there had been "an immediate and open mingling of soldiers and German civilians." Although non-fraternization soon fell by the wayside, the longer the U.S. military could project the image of the German people as being threatening and dangerous, the longer it could justify its presence and privilege. A 1946 troop orientation pamphlet stated the need to be on guard: "You are a soldier fighting a new war.... We've got to watch every German 24 hours a day.... The ragged German trudging along the street with a load of firewood may not look vicious, but he has a lot in common with a trapped rat."[89]

Efforts in the American zone to wipe out the vestiges of Nazism accelerated in September 1945. Persons with SS tattoos were prohibited from removing them. Because of the clothing shortage, former German soldiers were allowed to continue to wear military uniforms but were required to dye them in colors other than blue or olive drab. Most importantly, all members of the Nazi Party were ordered out of employment except in positions of "ordinary labor." A long list of those removed from their positions in *Landkreis* Berchtesgaden appeared in the *Official Gazette*.[90]

Every German adult in the American zone—thirteen million of them—was required to go through a de–Nazification process, the first step of which was to fill out a 131-question form—the *Fragebogen*. Because many people had been required to belong to Nazi-affiliated bodies as a requirement of employment and others were often only nominal members of party organizations, there was a wave of anxiety about the questionnaire. One response was, "You have to have been born in a concentration camp to be a good German today." As a result of the process, 3.7 million Germans were found to have been involved in some form of Nazi activity. After putting on trial 170,000 them by June 1946, the Military Government transferred the de–Nazification program to German tribunals, who carried on, in a less than determined fashion, until 1950.[91]

A few adamant Nazis had moved to Berchtesgaden after the war. Of the 38,000 people in the Land, about 10,000 had belonged to the Nazi Party or its many auxiliary organizations. Because the Nazis forced the consolidation of all kinds of groups into Nazi organizations, many people—postmen, teachers, doctors and others—were included in this total. With this factor in mind, de–Nazification in the area took place without incident.[92]

The local military government was also required to suppress black market sales of products of American origin, but with American servicemen already coming into the area for recreation, this order was most difficult to enforce. Gradually the many foreign workers left stranded in the area were repatriated. The German prisoner camp outside the town was closed.[93]

At the end of the war twelve million German people were driven out of eastern Europe, and Berchtesgadener Land received about 5000 of them, who were housed in 142 barracks and other facilities in the county. By 1949 thirty percent of the inhabitants of Berchtesgaden alone were uprooted *Deutsche* from the east. That non–Germans came into the area is seen by the fact that a Ukranian high school existed there from 1946 to 1950.[94]

Large numbers of American servicemen came to town and went up to the Berghof and the Kehlstein. The influx averaged about 3000 a day during the week and 10,000 on weekends. The high crime rate among the 500,000 American soldiers who remained in Germany reached down to Garmisch but rarely to cozy Berchtesgaden. By Christmas 1945 all was calm in Berchtesgadener Land.[95]

In the early years of the occupation there were, not unexpectedly, matters that irritated the locals. A colonel who commanded the Recreation Area took a high-handed approach. In all matters, it was "my reservation" and all questioning of his decisions were met with, "Well, who won the war?" Toilet facilities were segregated, with German employees directed to those for "indigenous personnel." U.S. Army regulations required that all water be chlorinated, so all of the people of the town found that their fresh, Alpine fluid now had a vile taste. There was substantial local opposition to a Recreation Area decision in early 1951 to build a bowling facility on the Triftplatz, a small plaza in the town center. This would require the chopping down of several "fine old Bavarian cooper beeches." Despite bitter protests, the trees came down and the bowling alley was built.[96]

Another source of complaint, certainly not limited to Berchtesgaden, was about the low cultural level of American servicemen. The post-war draftees were not of the same caliber as the war-time soldiers, and as the occupation wore on many German people now had the gumption to talk about it. As one Berchtesgadener declared of the U.S. soldiers, "So long as they continue to arrive so utterly unprepared for a foreign culture and comport themselves as Europeans have come to expect," Communist propaganda would have an appeal for at least many German people. He continued: American servicemen "sometimes seemed determined to prove, by their behavior, that the Germans are a superior race. The only constructive thing they have shown us, in the main, is the democratic relationship between them and their officers."[97]

In a book published in 1947, Wolfgang Friedmann noted, "The spontaneous generosity and bigheartedness of the Americans is notorious." Yet, "hardly less notorious is the sight of slovenly and drunken troops, their often repulsive attitude towards women and the general contrast of the deportment of a large proportion of the occupying troops with the democratic ideals and the values proclaimed on paper." Friedmann also observed that there had been a rapid reversal of German attitudes towards the British occupation: at first the British military were praised for their conduct, but with asset stripping and the impact of a colonial mentality among British administrators, German assessment of the British plummeted. Another factor, in common with American soldiers, was the arrival of young, untrained replacement troops.[98]

Whatever many Germans felt about American soldiers, the occupying troops had an overwhelmingly positive view of the "Krauts." A survey taken in November 1945 showed that an impressive eighty percent of GIs admired their hosts for their cleanliness, industry and resilience. Nor were there any recorded complaints about German food and beverages. If they preferred an exclusive diet of American cuisine, army-style, they could always remain on their base. On the other hand, during the "cigarette year" of 1945–46, they could leave the post and have anything they wanted. While GIs had almost unlimited supplies of them, at that time one pack of cigarettes cost almost a month's pay of the average German worker.[99]

From all appearances relations between the locals and American troops in Berchtesgaden were amicable. Most GIs were impressed by the physical attributes of the people, particularly the females. Capt. Laurence Critchell noted, "There are scores of children. Like the young women, they are almost all blond. The girls are tanned a rich gold-brown which makes you think of wheat fields in the summertime. They wear flowered skirts and loose blouses, and if you look at them directly they will meet your eye." In exchange for flour, housewives baked bread for the Amis. The army quickly supplied food, clothing and medical treatment for displaced people who were housed in the former SS Camp Dürreck on the Obersalzberg. In the town it provided hot school lunches and a youth center where the girl's activities consisted of "ballet, sewing and painting while the boys were able to work on crafts of all kinds." But there was real hunger in the land. As in other parts of Germany, 1945–46 was the cigarette year in the Berchtesgaden region, with people exchanging the cigarettes received from GIs as payment for farm produce. Some of the scanty harvest of 1946 was saved in part by the intervention of U.S. Army vehicles and soldiers. Malnutrition and related diseases were commonplace. Expedients—wood flakes from the beech tree—failed.

Apparently most children found the Yanks friendly and generous. One woman recalled that as a child the U.S. troops instilled in her "a feeling of well being because we all knew they were there to protect us. It was actually fascinating when we saw the self-assured military MPs riding around in their open jeeps, chewing gum—usually with one leg propped up on the door." Her sister "fondly remembers one particular Army officer (she recalls the impressive decorations of ribbons and bars) who wore the light khaki pants with an Eisenhower jacket. It was next to our house where the path led down to the bahnhof. He gave her a handful of candy and they had a snowball fight before he walked to the train station, calling to her in broken German 'Auf Wiedersehen.'"[100]

## Kleines Amerika im Land

### R and R at the Berchtesgaden Recreation Area

After the hubbub of activity in the immediate post-war years, Berchtesgadener Land returned to something like its old Alpine serenity. Scenery has always been Berchtesgaden's lure. The Hitler legend soon became an attraction for the hordes of Americans who descended on the area. In due time they would become a very subdued lot, conspicuous in their inevitable Bavarian hats, laden with pins from places visited, their cameras, loafers and Bermuda shorts. To the locals they were a bit amusing, sometimes irritating but always a welcome economic boost.

The town rarely suffered from the off-duty excesses of GIs as did Frankfurt, Kaiserslautern ("K-town") or Munich. Soldiers looking for more hedonistic attractions were ill-advised to seek out the Bavarian Alps, and if one insisted on partying in the mountains a rival recreation area in Garmisch was much more inviting.

The U.S. Army established the Berchtesgaden Recreation Area in October 1945. For the first two years a unit of the Women's Army Corps was in charge of the post exchange, snack bars, library and service club, after which the facilities were run by the Army Exchange Service. American military visitors changed considerably after the widespread introduction of dependents in 1947. At this juncture, grizzled combat behavior gave way to the softer lifestyle of an occupation army, complete with "permanent" housing facilities, schools, shopping complexes and other amenities of home. American military deployment in Europe surpassed 400,000 troops for well over thirty years, and when one adds dependents, Department of Defense civilians and military retirees, as well as welcomed Canadian and British forces, a "market" of almost one million customers could be lured to Berchtesgaden and its sister recreation areas—two lakeside hotels at Chiemsee and several sites at the larger and more lively Garmisch facility. The Berchtesgden Recreation Area attracted almost 150,000 visitors in 1947.[101]

Accommodation rates were most attractive. As late as the early 1960s, "Enlisted men and their dependents can have a room with bath for $1.25 a night ($1 without bath), officers $2.25 ($2 without) and civilians GS-6 and below $1.50 ($1.25). A good sirloin steak costs only a little more."[102]

For the small colony of Americans stationed in Berchtesgaden conditions bordered on the idyllic. There were, however, a few drawbacks. Running an Alpine recreation area was not the stuff of which ambitious officer resumes were made, and the area's wholesome outdoor pleasures left a few GIs longing for the rollicking and lusty attractions of Munich. For those seeking religious renewal, however, Berchtesgaden was the home of the U.S. Forces Alpine Inn Religious Retreat Center, where "thousands of servicemen take administrative leave to refresh themselves spiritually." It also possessed the General Walker Hotel, the largest hotel in the Armed Forces Recreation Center's network, which stood as the "American convention site of Europe."[103]

Like most U.S. military abroad, the American community remained somewhat cloistered around the command post at Stangass and Strub Kaserne on the outskirts of the town. Most of the troops were assigned to logistical and backup roles for the recreation area itself. There were a handful of military police, engineers and quartermaster personnel, as well as a small military intelligence unit and a rudimentary medical facility. A few lucky soldiers drew such taxing but temporary assignments as ski patrolmen at the Skytop facility or lifeguard or tennis instructor duty at the Berchtesgadener Hof at the same time many other soldiers were freezing in Korea or hacking through rainforests in Vietnam.[104]

The few dozen dependents had an even better existence, indulging in all the recreation area's inexpensive endeavors and capitalizing on a favorable exchange rate that was over four deutschmarks to the dollar until it tumbled in the 1970s.

The American elementary school at Stangass was a tiny, quaint, two room building. Around it existing Wehrmacht buildings were utilized and an apartment building was constructed. Little "Little America" was the result. For high school education, dependent children were boarded at the American complex in Munich. Of course, there was a full athletic program. Track meets for American schools in Germany were often held, without any concern, at the Nuremberg stadium, built for Nazi Party jamborees. The inevitable spoiler was the looming recognition that after a year or two, at most three years, it was back to a more conventional, and often unattractive, posting.[105]

## The Occupation of Occupation

On 16 May 1945 a Civil Affairs and Military Government unit of eight soldiers, specially trained for the area, arrived on the scene. It was led by Captain Michael E. DiPietro, who soon gained a positive reputation for his balanced and effective administration. When he was shortly promoted and transferred, comments in the local newspaper were testimony to the admirable conduct of his office. Already the current *Landrat* (governor) Karl Theodor Jacob, after initial removal and arrest by the CIC, was retained in office, with a Dr. Kollmann being appointed Berchtesgaden *Bürgermeister*. Because of his long service in office during the Nazi era, however, Jacob was again removed from office on July 16. He later returned to this position and served until the 1960s.[106]

Berchtesgadener Land was only a fragment of the American zone of occupation in Germany, but it was undoubtedly the most politically sensitive one. Not only was it notorious as the site of the Hitler sub-government, but after the war it attracted a range of unrepentant followers of the Führer.

A year after the occupation began the local Military Government unit reviewed events. It noted that in May 1945 most people in Berchtesgaden viewed the arrival of the Americans with relief—the war was over—but there also was "passivity mingled with fear," because they had been bombarded by Nazi propaganda to expect the worst. The next month it observed that "all past undercover Nazis are now bedecked with lamb's white virtues and are now strong anti–Nazis." There was another aspect as well: "Civilians [are] becoming more brazen in the realization that much 'wool can be slipped over the eyes'" of the American conquerors. Two months later the situation had worsened, with the MD detachment reporting, "More arrogance and resentment springing up in the civilian population towards Americans." It attributed these developments to three probable factors—"the too friendly fraternal relations of some military personnel," the realization that the Americans were "not as tough as they look," and the rising participation of soldiers in the black market.[107]

Yet during its first year the Military Government of the Land was successful in getting an almost complete response to the required *Fragebogen* (questionnaire). By February 1946, 5093 questionnaires had been processed without charges, while 742 were in the "mandatory removal" category, five had received "discretionary adverse" recommendations and 1300 were in the vague category of "discretionary, no adverse recommendation."[108]

This process having reached completion in April 1946, MG "decided to pass the burden of denazification into the hands of the German Ministry." Yet it warned that the de–Nazificiation tribunals "will malfunction unless closely observed." Friends of friends could well intercede: "It would be reckless to assume that some of these anti–Nazis, of tribunal-like vintage, would not sway the benches with wailing tears for led-astray friends, etc." Indeed, it believed, "There are still too many former leaders displaced temporarily by denazification axes straining at their artificial leashes to rebound into positions of influence—and that will occur as soon as MG and civilian authorities are weak enough or MG retires completely." A prophecy fulfilled.[109]

Another problem that arose was the continued increase of displaced persons into the Land. German soldiers had been rapidly dispatched from the area, with the POW camp at Bad Reichenall closing in November 1945 and Camp Nye in Berchtesgaden, which at its peak had 1100 SS members, closing in April 1946. Despite the protests of many local people that they could not subsist without tourists, the Land was closed to visitors for the summer of 1946. Nevertheless, the refugee commissioner reported that burgomasters "sabotage his work; they want summer guests, not refugees."[110]

The thousands of eastern European displaced persons pouring into the Land created a serious situation both in terms of accommodation and public order. MG did not understate the scope of the problem, declaring that it faced "increasing difficulties in accommodating refugees and expellees," which were accompanied by "armed robberies, black marketing, illicit dealing [and] thefts." Most of the offenses dealt with black market operations. In May 1946 MG warned displaced persons leaders and Polish guard officers that action would be taken to curb "the rising crime rate in the Landkreis," but the warning had "no great effect." The next month MG concluded that if the situation did not improve, the camps would be transferred to elsewhere in the U.S. zone. A year later the situation apparently was no better, with attention centering on the Bad Reichenhall camp, which had 6000 inhabitants. Threats and warnings were without effect, but the problem gradually resolved itself as the refugees drifted off to other places, with many of them migrating to the new state of Israel.[111]

At the end of the first year of occupation, the local detachment observed that American efforts at inculcating democracy had been totally ineffective. It declared that "Anti-Nazi, public-minded Germans consider American methods (or rather lack of methods) in this regard primitive and old-fashioned; criticisms are uttered of the amateur secret service plans of adolescent" members of the Counter-Intelligence Corps. MG supported the proposition that American professors and politicians be brought over "to teach German people of democracy." A cadre of American academics, many from rural institutions, eventually were employed for this purpose, but many Germans were not impressed by either their intellect or instruction. Stirring to eloquence, the author of the MG report provided urgent advice: "Now while the embers of war still smolder, while the metal of men's minds is still a malleable mass—now is the time to mould and stamp the ductile medium with sledge-hammer unremitting blows of an all-embracing propaganda of Goebbels-like efficiency and coin a new political currency for the German future."[112]

Kreis Berchtesgaden continued its supervision of the Land. In April 1946 it announced that all residents above the age of twelve "must be in possession of a valid registration card within 24 hours of their arrival in their assigned communities." This form was in addition to the CIC *Fragebogen*, which also had to be submitted when applying for a registration card. Information about discharged soldiers had to be included, the disposition of which had to be certified by local authorities and "any errors contained thereof (viz., testifying that a man was discharged when he is actually an escaped PW) will involve the official in severe disciplinary and court action."[113]

A month later MG sought to solicit voluntary statements about lurking remnants from the past: "This your opportunity to bring to the attention of Military Government those people that are not considered of high moral and political standing, and above all those who are Nazi activists who are today playing an influential role in the community life." The accusations were to be submitted by mail and supported "with proof." It was extremely doubtful that there was a considerable response.[114]

Meanwhile the transition from war to peace continued. Again in May 1946 the MG repeated its injunction that no civilians, including former prisoners of war and German police men, could wear undyed U.S. Army uniforms. At the same time, it declared that this order did not permit German policemen "to demand identity documents from persons they have reason to believe are civilian or Military Members of the U.S. Armed Forces." With "Off Limits" signs proliferating in the Land, the MG decided to call in all the existing signs and issue new ones. The order encompassed thirty-one locations.[115]

A long-standing problem came to the fore in September 1946 when the detachment reported on the matter of "women loitering about the streets." When MPs turned these women over to the local police "the women were generally released and again back on the streets the following day." According to existing law, "they can only be tried and imprisoned if there is evidence of prostitution." At the same time, the provost marshal at the Berchtesgaden Recreation Center reported a "sharp upturn in the VD rate since the middle of December."[116]

More ominously, the detachment noted a growing propensity of local authorities to obstruct the workings of military government: "Still under the cloak of suave obsequiousness and cringing readiness displayed to follow suggestions offered, contacts with the majority of German officials awaken a sense of masked hostility, of unwilling submissiveness to 'force majeure' that suggest the elements of hidden fires beneath the smooth surface."[117]

Almost a year later, in June 1947, the detachment reported that the Land "is a hot-bed of reactionary tendencies with Nazi undercurrents, more or less coming up to the surface," and repeated that "unceasing supervision is urgently required."[118]

The situation had not improved the next year. In March 1948 the detachment reported "many 'flares' of excitements that Edelweiss groups were operating in the area, SS men were roaming loose, subversive groups were operating for Russian agents, etc." Based on information "that a band of a few hundred Edelweiss and SS were staging" in the Königssee area, the CIC and the U.S. Constabulary launched a large scale sweep of the area that came up empty handed. At the same time a Dr. Lenz of the Christian Democratic Union, after a series of fiery speeches denouncing the operations of the military government, was banned from political activity in the Land. Noting that Lenz "is an arrogant, demagogic type who believes he has 'outsmarted' everyone," the report added that "attempts to apprehend him and imprison him have been without success thus far by CIC agents—as he outsmarts them and clings to strong protectorates somewhere!!!" Then there was the big picture. The detachment report declared, "It can be affirmatively said that the political barometer and horoscope in this area is a stormy and inclement one." The persistent problem, it stated, was that "perfectly clean, reputable (politically speaking) personalities in this area and administration are a 'rara avis' and Diogenes would have a difficult task to fulfill his mission here."[119]

## Up on the Berg

A large number of local people were employed in the recreation area, at wages that were above those for comparable work in the area. Although there were no signs pointing to its location, many people found their way to the Obersalzberg. Not only American servicemen but German vacationers toured the wrecked site, the result being that the tons of smashed marble and other stone from the Berghof soon were gone. Despite the presence of army guards, everything went. Tourists could view the remains of the houses of Göring, Bormann and Hitler and some smaller structures, but the huge tunnel system was sealed up. The demand for souvenirs was so great that a local manufacturer produced bathroom tiles that were passed off as being from the *Hitlerhaus*.

Adjacent to the Berghof, the Zum Turken guesthouse was bought by Therese Partner, the daughter of its original owner, Karl Shuster, in 1946. After a three-year struggle with local authorities, the original building was restored and reopened. Occasionally former members of the Obersalzberg staff would stay there and reminisce. It is now operated by a granddaughter, Ingrid Scharfenberg. For a small fee, tourists could explore a bit of the tunnel complex under its property.[120]

In 1947 the U.S. Army dispatched a demolition squad to get rid of the dangerous, blasted wreckage of buildings, but the Special Services objected. It derived considerable income from the admission tickets to the area. Its great boast had been that the network of military recreation facilities it operated did not cost the U.S. taxpayer one cent. The Nazi buildings remained.[121]

Just above the Berghof was the Platterhof, a hotel built in the 1930s for visiting Nazis, which had suffered some damage during on onslaught of April 25. According to one source, much greater internal damage was done by French soldiers during their brief occupation of the Obersalzberg and in the immediate period of the occupation, by local residents, who stripped away whatever was left inside. The building and adjacent facilities were put under army guard until 1953 when the complex was rebuilt for vacationing army families.[122]

Everyone who went to the Obersalzberg also had to go up to the spectacular tea house looming above on the Kehlstein. Built with Nazi funds as a gift for Hitler on his fiftieth birthday in 1939, it survived the war unscathed. At first American soldiers attempted to restore the elevator that reached the building from the last parking area. At length, Georg Mehr, unrepentant Nazi, was restored to his position of elevator maintenance man. Serving a sentence for falsifying the date he had joined the Party, he was sprung from prison and brought back to the Kehlstein. A crisis had occurred: without the elevator in operation, U.S. officers had to make the demanding climb to the top. Nevertheless, problems did occur. On one occasion the elevator broke down and a major general was trapped mid-way up for two hours. An all-points alert was sent out to find Mehr. In Salzburg at the time, he was accosted by an American officer who rushed him to the rescue.[123]

## Deutschland Erwacht

### 1951–2001

The establishment of the Federal Republic of Germany and the formation of the North Atlantic Treaty Organization in 1949 marked the restoration of self-government in West Germany and the effective end of the U.S. occupation.

Although a large U.S. Army presence remained, the military regime was over. The changed relationship was seen in Berchtesgadener Land in July 1951 when agreement was reached between the Bavarian government and the U.S. Land Commissioner for Bavaria concerning the Obersalzberg. The area was to be returned to nominal German control and the ruins of the building in the Berghof complex were to be demolished. But there was a trade-off—the Eagle's Nest on top of the Kehlstein would revert back to Bavarian control and the road leading up to it—closed to non-military vehicles since the war—would be reopened to civilian traffic.[124]

German government concern about clearing the Berghof area first arose at the beginning of 1951 with the rise of neo–Nazi activity in West Germany. There was a report that one of the tour guides on the Obersalzberg, a former Göring house manager, was providing a Nazi-inspired commentary. At a series of public meetings around West Germany a variety of old Nazis began to beat the drums about their interpretation of the Nazi years and Hitler, as well as to advocate the revival of militant nationalism. Among those involved were Col. Hans-Ulrich Rudek, the most decorated *Luftwaffe* pilot; Sepp Huber, a former Hitler Youth leader and Nazi propaganda leader of Berchtesgaden; and, after his release from prison in October 1952, Albert Kesselring. Even Alois Hitler emerged from obscurity at this time to make a few fiery super-nationalist speeches. Several small German groups became linked to Natinform, a coordinating organization formed by a tiny fascist splinter group in England. Out of this came a fantastic scheme to hold a World Aryan Congress in Dublin, Ireland, in January 1953. The assumption about holding the meeting there was that, as a neutral nation, the Republic of Ireland would not be adverse to allowing such a controversial conference on its territory. This assumption was never put to the test, as the various groups shortly engaged in bitter squabbling and apparently the result was a small gathering with little attention or significance. But the emergence of neo–Nazi activity in Germany got media attention and caused concern in various circles, and not just there.[125]

The leader of the movement in Berchtesgadener Land was Heinz Erich Krause, who used the name Hek Rau as editor of a mimeographed weekly called *Deutschland Brief;* his co-editor was Sepp Huber. A young man in his 30s who had served in a mountain division during the war, Krause had drifted in from Austria about six years before and, as an unskilled worker, for a while was employed in the American military motor pool. He was seen as an effective but nervous public speaker (one of many parallels with another Austrian blow-in). At a variety of public meetings—usually held in the train station restaurant—he denounced the American occupation as well as the new German government, but had only words of praise for the idealism and aspirations of the Nazi movement. Col. Rudel received a hero's welcome in Berchtesgaden on several occasions when he was guest speaker at Krause's meetings. In the town Frau W. Breinlinger distributed neo–Nazi material from Argentina and elsewhere.

Krause joined forces with a variety of local right-wingers, with a mouthpiece provided by the *Berchtesgadener Anzieger*, in opposing the wiping out of the Nazi remains on der Berg. After a disastrous performance at a public debate with a Social Democratic representative in October 1951, however, Hek Rau faded from public view. Publication of *Deutschland Brief* was shifted to Spain and soon ended. One Hitler was enough for Berchtesgaden and for Deutschland.[126]

## Berghof Blow-up

The deposition of the Nazi ruins on the Obersalzberg became a matter of growing concern in the early post-war years. Based on a military government directive of 27 December 1948, the commanding officer of a military post "has the authority to order the destruction" of any facility or structure under U.S. Army control. After extended negotiations and with the recommendation of George Shuster, Bavarian Land Commissioner, the U.S. High Commission in October 1951 "approved the de-requisitioning of the Obersalzberg properties on the condition that the buildings be razed completely and all structural evidences of their location erased." The authority to demolish was provided for five buildings—the houses of Hitler, Göring and Bormann, the SS barracks and the Hotel Platterhof. The Munich Military Post retained control of the Speer studio and the Hinterbrand ski lodge, while the disposition of the fantastic Kehlstein building "will be discussed in subsequent correspondence," but this too was shortly transferred to the Bavarian government. These actions did not apply to the Haus Turken (or Zum Turken) guest house which had been reacquired by the family of its original owner. In the event, the U.S. Army decided to keep the Platterhof hotel, which it had rebuilt as a resort for army officers under the name of the General Walker Hotel.[127]

One of the first things that the Bavarian government did when it assumed control of the area was to ban the collecting of souvenirs at the site. The Obersalzberg drew large numbers of visitors. In the period from July to October 1951 136,560 (110,000 of whom were non–Germans) toured the berg. Even before formal agreement had been reached with American authorities, the Bavarian government—on 25 October 1951—announced that demolition would take place.

The demolition plans roused controversy in the Land. The two Berchtesgaden newspapers saw the matter from different angles. The *Berchtesgadener Kurier* saw ominous signs in the series of political meetings which focused on German nationalism and the evils of the American occupation. The other paper, the *Berchtesgadener Anzeiger*, owned by an ex–Nazi, saw the meetings as insignificant, but demanded a referendum on the question of demolition. Local opinion was that the vote would have been heavily against demolition.[128]

Paul Moor, an American journalist who was there in both 1951 and 1952, described the public mood at the time: "Bavaria is traditionally a cranky and intransigent state, and generalizations applicable to it seldom hold for other parts of the nation; but the Obersalzberg controversy has moved the Berchtesgadeners to an unfettered self-expression which is not common in Germany." Moor saw the episode as an example of what John J. McCloy, American High Commissioner in Germany, once termed occupational fatigue.

Everett Schoning, the State Department representative on the scene, considered the significance of the action. He regretted that the army attempt to get rid of the structures five years before had been frustrated by the Recreation Area officials. "In a way it's too bad, considering it turned into such a pain in the neck for everybody. I'm frankly glad it's settled and I look forward to the day when there won't be anything up there but a grove of trees." Although he believed "the racket about the ruins will quiet down," he saw the agitation against the occupation as something that would continue.[129]

The agreement of November 1951 stated that the structures were to be demolished and the area planted in trees; then the grounds would be returned to the Bavarian government, as would be the "*Diplomat Haus*" on top of the Kehlstein. A demolition company agreed to pay $7143 to the Bavarian government to clear the site and take possession of the rubble, with the stipulation that nothing from the ruins was to be sold as a memento. Due to the heavy snow of that winter, demolition did not begin until April 30 1952, the anniversary of Hitler's death, with the event becoming a cover story in *Life* magazine. Almost everything above ground had been trucked away by the end of the summer, but the lower part of a small garage and the sections of the foundations of the Berghof remained.[130]

At first the Bavarian government decided to turn the Kehlstein building into a youth hostel, but then leased it to the Berchtesgaden branch of the Bavarian Alpine Association. Although the original excellent kitchen was not used, a restaurant was opened, along with a gift shop. A short distance from the building a crucifix was erected. Since then more than 300,000 tourists annually make the trip to Hitler's Alpine eyrie. Its spectacular views are often obscured by fog, but the structure screams of the horrors of history.[131]

On one occasion there was an incident by an American officer which revived memories of the Hitler era. In December 1968 a Lt. Col. Clark, head of the BRA, was responsible for recreating the Berghof scene, using models of Hitler, Eva Braun and others of the inner circle, in two rooms furnished in the style of that period in the tunnel system under the General Walker Hotel. The matter came to the attention of the German press, the exhibit was quickly closed and Lt. Co. Clark was transferred.[132]

Gradually hotels and other buildings taken by the U.S. Army in 1945 reverted back to civilian ownership. With the remarkable revival of the German economy came an increase of tourists, and American soldiers became less conspicuous. The outbreak of the Korean War brought more American troops to Germany, thus reversing the decline of the U.S. military presence. As long as the Cold War existed a large elements of the U.S. Army remained in Germany and the Berchtesgaden Recreation Area continued to serve its purpose.

When U.S. airbases in Germany were used in the 1990s as staging areas for military activity in Kuwait and Bosnia, for a few weeks there was a surge of American military to the area. For those short periods, it was like old times in Berchtesgaden.[133]

## *Amerika Goes Home*

The crumbling of the Soviet Union and the end of the Cold War in 1990–91 led to the gradual withdrawal of American armed forces in Germany. By 1995 the U.S. military was reduced to 100,000 personnel. The Heidelberg and Berchtesgaden recreation areas were closed, with only Chiemsee and Garmisch remaining open, both at much reduced scales. Now, at last, the Obersalzberg, with all its associations, would be back in Germany hands.[134]

Various German political leaders did not relish the prospect. Both the federal and Bavarian government wanted the U.S. military to retain control of the property there for ten more years, but financial terms could not be agreed upon. What the German government wanted was for the Americans to give up the Chiemsee recreation area, but remain on the Obersalzberg—to keep a lid on that area—with the German government providing funds to renovate the buildings there. The proposed deal required that the U.S. military remain there for a decade, but the best the Americans would offer was to remain there as long as U.S. military personnel in Germany remained at 100,00, so no agreement was reached. It was time to face the legacy of Hitler.[135]

When the U.S. Army closed the General Walker Hotel and other facilities in Berchtesgaden in 1995, the area around the site of the Berghof was well covered in trees. The only property that remained in U.S. military hands was the Winterbrand Lodge, which continued as an "adventure center" for the children of American servicemen. Then in 1996 things began to happen. Without any obvious indication of a change in the status of the location, a gravel path was installed leading to the Berghof site. The next year the area was cleared. Repairs were made to the hotel. Something was up, but what? Wolfgang Illner, a spokesman for the Bavarian government, recalled the situation: "After years we were suddenly handed a political hot potato, and it was very difficult to decide what to do with it."[136]

At the end of 1997 the Bavarian government announced that it proposed to build a "documentation center" beside the site of the Berghof and lease the Platterhof/Walker hotel together with two adjoining buildings. The "documentation center" was to be the first public recognition of the Nazi era. In announcing the project, the Bavarian government stretched credulity when it declared that the matter of the disposition of the Obersalzberg would have been addressed earlier but for the continued presence of the Americans. Munich, the "birthplace" of the Nazi movement, would have been more appropriate and had not been under U.S. control since 1949. However, the objective of the display facility was clearly stated: "The center should counteract the rather emotive, mystical portrayal of history. This cannot be done by destroying all traces of the past or by putting up a memorial."[137]

When there were no takers for the property, a year later the government came up with another plan: the whole 262 acres of the Obersalzberg, minus the Berghof area, would be sold to a corporation which would build a resort hotel on another part of the mountain, with the old hotel being demolished. At first, the Bavarian government retained overt control, however, as the corporation was owned by a bank in which the Bavarian government had a commanding interest.[138]

This two-fold plan quickly became a source of controversy. The debate centered on both location and content of the center. The Simon Wiesenthal Centre in Vienna opposed the plan, with the choice of location being "scandalous." It asserted that experts from Israel and the United States should have been involved in the planning. Moreover, the proposed center "will be perceived as a banalization of Nazi crimes and create a magnet for neo–Nazis from around the world." A Bavarian government spokesman responded, "The state remains owner of the entire property exactly for that reason: to prevent the mountain from becoming a pilgrimage site."

Martin Seidl, a Berchtesgaden councilor, declared that the facility should not be on the Obersalzberg but in Munich or Berlin. "Hitler was in Berlin as often as he was in Obersalzberg," he said, "and we don't want accusations that people here are earning money through Nazi tourism." Josef Renoth, another councilor, asserted, "We don't want to become another Dachau," adding, "We would rather the historical element w[as] played down."[139]

The center also had its advocates. Andreas Nachama, the leader of the Berlin Jewish community, who was involved in its planning, praised the center and its exhibits. He recalled when he visited the mountain six years before he was "strongly angered that there was no information—only souvenirs."[140]

The Institute for Contemporary History in Munich was given the responsibility of designing the building and, more importantly, deciding on its contents. The proposed building would incorporate the facade of a Nazi-era guest house and would link up to the tunnel system under the Platterhof hotel. An advisory committee of historians recommended that rather than display material that was largely about the region and its history, with some reference, of course, to Hitler, it should be about the whole Nazi era in Germany including the Hitler chapter on the Berg. This decision was made at the top; opinion in Berchtesgadener Land was not solicited.[141]

Many local people objected to the emphasis on the Nazi connection, noting that the Obersalzberg and Berchtesgaden had a long history before Hitler came along, and a half century had passed since his death. They further argued that a comprehensive treatment of the Nazi era would more appropriately belong in Munich, which was the "founding city" of the Nazi movement. Was this not an attempt of the Bavarian metropolis to evade this historical reality and saddle little Berchtesgaden with the stigma?

A spokesman for the institute did not address the matter of location, but declared that reproductions of Nazi posters and photographs of a smiling Hitler surrounded by happy children would make people aware of the insidious appeal of such propaganda.[142]

Another purpose of the center was to offset material on the Nazis era periodically being sold at the Zum Turken guest house at the other side of the Berghof site. In the late 1940s this building was returned to the family of its original owners. Since the property included part of the bunker system, tourists for an entrance fee could go down into it. The problem arose with its gift shop, which sometimes sold pictures and videos which presented an attractive view of Hitler and his associates, including Eva Braun. Local authorities had warned the Zum Turken proprietor about the illegal sale of this type of material but the problem persisted.[143]

The Obersalzberg was to undergo its third major transformation, the first two being, of course, the construction of the Berghof complex and the Allied bombing of April 1945. Construction began in 1999 and the center, which cost two million dollars, opened on 13 October 1999 without incident and with little ceremony. The occasion was conveniently well outside the summer tourist season. 2000 persons came to the center the first week, but visitors have averaged 125,000 annually since. Two years later the center produced a well-illustrated guide to the Nazi era, *Die tödliche Utopie* ("*The Deadly Utopia*"). The facility is not a documentation or research center, but a structure housing historical displays and a link to a section of the tunnel system. An admission price of five marks for adults probably is enough to discourage casual visitors. The Platterhof/Walker hotel was demolished and the area made into a parking lot for the center.[144]

Meanwhile, the hotel project went ahead. The government-controlled corporation sold the rights for the hotel to a British company—Six Continents Hotels. The Munich architect Herbert Kochta designed a horseshoe-shaped facility of 138 rooms and 12 suites. The location for the complex was not at a distant part of the mountain, but on the site of Hermann Göring's house, only about a quarter of a mile away from that of the Berghof. This raised objections from some Jewish groups and Social Democratic politicians. Michael Friedman, the deputy head of Germany's Central Council of Jews, commented that the use of the site as a hotel "masks the historical reality. Such places should be preserved and used for a totally different purpose." His proposal: "An international centre where young people could meet to talk about the dark past." Peter Renoth, the deputy mayor of Berchtesgaden, argued that the existence of the documentation center demonstrated that there was no attempt to evade the Nazi connection at the place. Launching the beginning of the hotel construction in the summer of 2001, Kurt Faltlhauser, the Bavarian finance minister, declared that "Bavaria is not forgetting the Nazi years. But tourism on the Obersalzberg goes back to a long time before the Nazi period." As well, the veteran Nazi hunter Simon Wiesenthal brushed aside objections: "Hitler traveled all over Germany and Austria. Can we say we can't build in places just because he was there?"

Almost inevitably, a press headline referred to the building as "Hotel Hitler." The International Resort Berchtesgaden opened at the beginning of March 2005 and employs about two hundred persons. A horse-shoe shaped wall of glass with mountain views for all rooms, it also has mineral baths, sauna and indoor and outdoor swimming pools. The American Bar reflects the fifty years of U.S. military occupation. Designed in a round, futuristic style, the structure looms over the site of the Berghof, only about three hundred yards away. In a hollow at the base of the hill is the surviving Göring staff building. The tangible link with the Nazis is evident. As well, it was to be expected that every guest at the hotel would want to see the Nazi-era museum, which would mean a stroll down the hill, past by the Zum Turken and then along the site of Hitler's villa. As well, everyone will be aware of the existence of the huge shelter and tunnel system sealed up under the berg. Although promotional material produced for the hotel makes no mention of Nazi connections with the neighborhood, referring rather to the facility as "an oasis of well-being," at least each of its 138 rooms is supplied with a copy of *Die tödliche Utopie*.[145]

In keeping with an almost unbroken record of political insensibility, the German political leadership blundered its way into a new episode of scorn and embarrassment.

In 1998 furniture confiscated by the U.S. Army from the chancellery building at adjoining Stangass was given to the German government, which had difficulty deciding what to do with unwelcome furnishings. In May 2000 the building, empty since the U.S. Army left five years before, was put under a preservation order. An obvious thing to do would be to put the furniture back in the building, but it is very doubtful that the authorities would want to create another attraction in "Hitlerland."[146]

The German government at last came to grips with the Nazi heritage at this time in other ways. A Jewish museum, the largest in Europe, was constructed in Berlin. During excavation of the site, part of an SS dungeon was unearthed and this was, appropriately, incorporated in the complex. The museum opened on 20 September 2001. After several years of heated debate about purpose, location and design, in June 1999 a plan was approved for a Holocaust memorial in the capital. The memorial, which opened in May 2005, is located near the Brandenberg Gate and almost directly above the site of the Führerbunker. Covering an area of four football fields, it consists of 2711 concrete rectangular slabs of different heights on sloping ground, "a design intended to make visitors uneasy, unsure of time and space." In Nuremberg, site of the massive Nazi rallies, construction was begun on a museum within the remains of the main rally meeting hall. In February 2001 the German government began a nation-wide program of historical preservation and recognition of structures that were important in the Nazi era.[147]

In April 2000, the government established a Web site listing unclaimed art works seized by the Nazis, principally of works from the "Linz List" of paintings and other art work assem-

**Documentation Center under construction on the Obersalzberg, July 2002. (Photograph by Arthur H. Mitchell)**

bled by Hitler for his planned Führer gallery in his hometown. That October the town government closed a Nazi memorabilia shop in Berchtesgaden. Following in the wake of various European film-makers, Tom Hanks and Steven Spielberg made a television series based on the war experiences of a company of soldiers in the 101st Airborne Division, culminating at Berchtesgaden; the series was shown in September–November 2001.[148]

At the same time as the Obersalzberg center opened, in Vienna a plain concrete, box-shaped Holocaust memorial, designed as shelves of books, was completed in the Judenplatz. At Branau on the Danube a local group announced that Hitler's birth house would be remodeled into a reconciliation center.[149]

After more than half a century, the painful but dramatic heritage of Hitler, the Nazis and the Obersalzberg has come full circle. The terrible question remains—will this kind of madness ever return, in this or some other form?

What transpired on the Obersalzberg from the late 1920s to the mid–1940s was a microcosm of the shift of power from Europe to America. The eruption of a wrathful but futile movement to dominate European by a single nation, generated and directed by Hitler from the Berghof, was followed, appropriately, by the occupation of that area by the new dominant power in European civilization—the young Colossus of the West.

# Notes

## Preface

1. Tonybee, *Survey of International Affairs*, vol. 1 (1938), 194.

## Chapter One

1. Ernst Hanisch, *Obersalzberg, the "Eagle's Nest" and Adolf Hitler*, 6–8; "description" <www.ns.aus.tm/propaganda/Adolf/07.html>; Josef Geiss, *Obersalzberg: History of a Mountain from Judith Platter Until Today*, 8–67.

2. Military Government, *Landkreis Berchtesgaden*, "First Annual Report of Military Government Activity," 5 May 1945–20 June 1946.

3. "Humboldt" Irmgard Hunt, *On Hitler's Mountain*, 29; Ulrich Chaussy, *Nachbar Hitler*, 196, 201, 204; Peter Gay, *Freud: A Life for Our Times*, 8–9, 158, 417, 543; "mushrooms" *New Statesman*, 8 January 2001, p. 37.

4. U.S. Army Counter Intelligence Corps interview with Paula Hitler, 5 June 1946; John Toland, *Adolf Hitler*, 629.

5. Werner Maser, *Hitler: Legend, Myth and Reality*, 42–43; August Kubizek, *Young Hitler*, 65–66; Walter Langer, *The Mind of Adolf Hitler* (here citing the typescript that later became the book published under that title), 114; Toland, *Hitler*, 20; "Dr. Bloch" U.S. Army, Office of Strategic Services, *Hitler Source Book*, 112–13; "piano" Frederic Spotts, *Hitler and the Power of Aesthetics*, 225; Hitler, *Mein Kampf* (1943 ed.), 18; Ronald Hayman, *Hitler and Geli*, 26; Brigitte Hamann, *Hitler's Vienna*, 133, 174–75.

6. Hamann, 184; 155–56, 182, 187; Hitler, *Hitler's Letters and Notes*, 107; *Mein Kampf*, 21; Maser, *Hitler's Mein Kampf: An Analysis*, 85–86; the Göring statement is according to Hjalmar Schacht in G.M. Gilbert, *Nuremberg Diary*, 263; Kuby, *The Russians and Berlin, 1945*, 176.

7. Hamann, 184, 142; *Mein Kampf* (1971 Houghton-Mifflin ed.), 21, also 25, 34; Hitler, *Speeches of Adolf Hitler* vol. 1, 862; Toland, *Hitler*, 554–55; David Schönbaum, *Hitler's Social Revolution*, 58–59.

8. Donald Welch, *The Third Reich: Politics and Propaganda*, 56.

9. Hitler, *Hitler's Table Talk, 1941–44* (27–28 Sept. 1941), 44; "proletarian" Hitler to Carl Burckhardt, League of Nations representative in Danzig, in Burckhardt, *Mein Danziger Mission, 1937–1939*.

10. Michael Burleigh, *The Third Reich: A New History*, 239.

11. Ignatius Phayre, "Holiday with Hitler"; Ley, "The Führer and the German Worker," in *Adolf Hitler: Bilder aus dem Leben des Führers* (Pictures and Life of the Führer); "hod carrier" Eduard Bloch, "My Patient Hitler," p. 69; see also Bloch, "My Patient Hitler: A Memoir of Hitler's Jewish Physician," *Journal of Historical Review* 14, no. 3 (May/ June 1994); Paula Hitler recalled that her guardian in Linz knew that Hitler was working as a laborer in Vienna (U.S. Army Counter Intelligence Corps interview, 12 July 1945); Office of Strategic Services, *Hitler Source Book*, part 2, 316; "Mussolini" Hitler, *Hitler's Secret Conversations, 1941–1944* (31 Jan. 1942), 218.

12. Hitler, *Speeches*, v. 2, 988; Hamann, 141–44, 182–84; "hod carrier" G. Ward Price, *I Know These Dictators*, 46; Hanisch, "I Was Hitler's Buddy," *New Republic*, April 1939, 5, 12, 19; Hamann, 184, 155–56; Franz Jetzinger, *Hitler's Youth*, 117–19, 130–33; Ian Kershaw, *Hitler: 1889–1936*, 53.

13. Albert Speer, *Inside the Third Reich*, 98; Gitta Sereny, *Albert Speer: His Battle with Truth*, 102.

14. "Housepainter" O.K. Werckmeister, "Hitler the Artist," *Critical Inquiry*, Winter 1997, v. 23, no. 2, p. 270; "paperhanger" R. MacEachen, "Paperhanger Makes Good," poem, *Commonweal*, 8 April 1938.

15. Ludecke, *I Knew Hitler*, 52; A.P. Laurie, *The Case for Germany*, 1; "Churchill" Richard Grunberger, *A Social History of the Third Reich*, 339; Fry, *Hitler's Wonderland*, 104.

16. Robert Payne, *The Life and Death of Adolf Hitler*, 582–83; Ludecke, 52.

17. Hitler, *Mein Kampf*, 51–65; "W.P. Hitler" U.S. Army, Office of Strategic Services, *Hitler Source Book*, 928; Hamann, 166–68; Kubizek, 185–87.

18. Hanisch, "I Was Hitler's Buddy," *New Republic*, 5 April 1939.

19. Hanisch, "I Was Hitler's Buddy"; Spotts, 140–42.

20. Speer, *Spandau: The Secret Diaries*, 28; "A personal thing" Toland, *Hitler*, 62; 698; Emmy Göring, *My Life with Göring*, 62–63; Steven Beller, *Vienna and the Jews: 1867–1938: A Cultural History*; "rumor" Bella Fromm, *Blood and Banquets: A Berlin Social Diary* (15 Aug. 1934), 178, and Fritz Thyssen, *I Paid Him*, 159–60.

21. Kershaw, *Hitler, 1889–1936: Hubris*, 31–36; Joachim Fest, *The Face of the Third Reich*, 9–10; "Hitler and Wagner" Robert Waite, *Adolf Hitler: The Psychopathic God*, 99–110, and Peter Viereck, *Mega-politics: The Roots of the Nazi Mind*, 126–43; Kubizek, 185–87; Hanisch, "I Was Hitler's Buddy."

22. Waite, 389; Alan Bullock, *Hitler: A Study in Tyranny*, 47; Jetzinger, 144–59; Hamann, 395–401.

23. "Cleaner" Oskar Tolz account in James Bunting, *Adolf Hitler*, 40; "landlady" Laurie, 13, 19; Hans Baur, *Hitler's Pilot*, 78; Toland, *Hitler*, 73.

24. Toland, *Hitler*, 79–97; Lothar Machtan, *The Hidden Hitler*, 68–69, 236; Stig Hornshoj-Moller, "The Führer Myth," ch. 2, p. 4, <holocaust-history.org/fuhrer-myth>.

25. Mayr, "I Was Hitler's Boss," *Current History* v. 1, no. 3 (November 1941), 193–97.

26. "Erlanger" Heinz, *Germany's Hitler*, 276–77; Ernst Hanfstängl, *Hitler: The Missing Years*, 47, 66, 161.

27. Truman Smith, *Berlin Alert: The Memoirs and Reports of Truman Smith*, 46, 72–73.

28. "Hanfstängl" Flood, *Path to Power*, 169, 170.

29. Flood, *Path to Power*, 169, 170.

30. Payne, 224; Huss, 168; "accents of Hitler and Stalin" Alan Bullock notes that Stalin spoke Russian with a Georgian accent, but says nothing about Hitler's Austrian accent (*Hitler and Stalin: Parallel Lives*, 4). On Hitler's accent see also Hanfstängl, *Missing Years* (1994 ed.), 34.

31. Flood, *Path to Power*, 480–81; Toland, *Hitler*, 192–93.

32. "Eckart" Robert S. Wistrich, *Who's Who in Nazi Germany*, 49; Flood, *Path to Power*, 379; Konrad Heiden, *Hitler: A Biography*, 192.

33. Hitler, *Hitler's Table Talk*, 16 Jan. 1942, 211–13; Hayman, 100; Hanfstängl, 82–83. Anton Drexler, a co-founder of the forerunner to the Nazi Party, claimed it was he who introduced Hitler to Obersalzberg (Heinz, *Germany's Hitler*, 167).

34. Edgar Mowrer, *Germany Puts the Clock Back*, 253; Flood, 380–81, 568–69; "renounces citizenship" Oran Hale, "Adolf Hitler: Taxpayer"; J.H. Brennan, *Occult Reich*, 25, 55, 111; "Haushofer" Gerald Suster, *Hitler: Black Magician*, 100, 120–25.

35. William Carr, *Hitler: A Study in Personality and Politics*, 24, 27–28; "Austria" Flood, 598; Hitler, *Table Talk*, 215; Hanisch, *Obersalzberg*, 11–12; Waite, 223–25; Kershaw, *Hitler, 1889–1936: Hubris*, 284–85; Nerin Gun, *Eva Braun: Hitler's Mistress*, 76.

36. In Percy Schramm, *Hitler: The Man and the Military Leader*, 37.

37. Hale, "Adolf Hitler: Taxpayer," 830–42.

38. Bullock, 133–34.

39. Hitler, *Table Talk* (26 July 1942), 595; Hanisch, *Obersalzberg*, 12; Speer, *Inside the Third Reich,*, 46–47; Freidline Wagner interview, *OSS Source Book*, 191; Florian Beierl, *History of the Eagle's Nest*, 7; Jochem von Lang, *The Secretary: Martin Bormann*, 93.

40. Hitler, *Table Talk* (2 Jan. 1942), 164–65; "no sportsman" Phayre, "Holiday with Hitler"; Langer, 132; "hunting" Hitler, *Hitler's Secret Conversations* (28 Oct. 1941); "lederhosen" Hitler, *Hitler's Secret Conversations* (12 Aug. 1942), 511, (17 Feb. 1942), 258; Hanisch, *Obersalzberg*, 7–8.

41. Hitler, *Table Talk* (9 Feb. 1942), 306–07; Hitler, *Table Talk* (5 Feb. 1942), 240; Harry Sions, "Berchtesgaden."

42. Speer, *Inside Third Reich*, 47, 86; Kershaw, *Hitler, 1889–1936: Hubris*, 534, 387; William Russell, *Berlin Embassy*, 271–72; Phayre, "Holiday with Hitler"; Dietrich, *The Hitler I Knew*, 161–62; Emmy Göring, *My Life with Göring*, 67; Felix Kersten, *The Kersten Memoirs, 1940–1945*, 165–171; "Wotan" Frederick Öchsner, *This Is the Enemy*, 77.

43. ; Hanfstängl, 65; Speer, 47; Klaus Fischer, *Nazi Germany*, 286; Carr, 51; Sions, "Berchtesgaden."

44. Speer, *Inside*, 47; *Hitler's Secret Conversations* (19 Feb. 1942), 259; Kurt Georg Ludecke, *I Knew Hitler*, 94–95.

45. Dietrich, 193–94; Hayman, 92; Speer, *Inside*, 46; Ludecke, 97, 428.

46. Ludecke, 347, 371; Dietrich, 194–95.

47. At least through the mid–1920s Hitler also resumed painting: Maser, *Hitler: Legend, Myth and Reality*, 53, 65.

48. Ludecke, 94–95, 97, 438, 347, 371.

# Chapter Two

1. Peter Labanyi, "Images of Fascism," 155–56.

2. Burleigh, 264–66; Labanyi, 173; "dog and stove" Rainer Zitelmann, *Hitler: The Policies of Seduction*, 159.

3. Geiss, *Obersalzberg*, 132; Payne, 352; Speer, *Third Reich*, 295; Kershaw, *The "Hitler Myth,"* 60.

4. Ernest Bramsted, *Goebbels and National Socialist Propaganda, 1925-1945*, 210.

5. Peter Hoffmann, *Hitler's Personal Security*, 180–81, 126; Hanisch, *Obersalzberg*, 16; Sereny, 431; *Eagle's Nest: Obersalzberg in an Historical View*, 72; Langer, 70–73.

6. Pierre J. Huss, *Heil! and Farewell*, 14–16; "pistol" Kuby, 177; John G. Hughes, *Getting Hitler into Heaven*, 30.

7. "Commuted" Kershaw, *Hitler, 1889–1936*, 370, 380; <www.n.s.aus.tm'propaganda/Adolf/07.html>; "The Hitler No One Knows"; Bruckner, "The Private Life of the Führer"; "Hitler in the Mountains," German Propaganda Archive, Randall Bytwerk, editor.

8. Huss, 13.

9. Claudia Koonz, *The Nazi Conscience*, 78.

10. Phayre, "Holiday with Hitler," 50–58; Phayre, "Hitler's Mountain Home"; "Holocaust Scholars Protest Attempt by *Home and Gardens* to Suppress Hitler Article," USNewswire, 23 Oct. 2003.

11. Bramsted, 205.

12. Speer, *Third Reich*, 131; Heiden, *Der Führer: Hitler's Rise to Power*, 379; Heiden, *Hitler: A Biography*, 316. Fritz Wiedemann, Hitler's long-time aide, also noted Hitler's casual routine. Kershaw, *Hitler, 1889-1936*, 534; James Stern, *The Hidden Damage*, 131–32.

13. Dietrich, 136, 214; "Speer" Richard Overy, *Interrogations*, 230.

14. [Dohring interview] Tilman Remme, "Life with Hitler and His Mistress"; Dohring and Lohse, *U.S. News and World Report*, 22 Sept. 1997; Speer, *Inside the Third Reich*, 88; Albert Krebs, *The Infancy of Nazism*, 161.

15. Speer, *Inside*, 88; "Jung" Toland, *Hitler*, 682; Dietrich, 144–45.

16. Krebs, 196; Sefton Delmer, *Trail Sinister*, 156; "haircut" Gun, *Eva Braun*, 208; T.R. Ybarra, "Hitler on High"; Burckhardt; Bullock, *Hitler: A Study in Tyranny*, 411–12.

17. "One idea" Dietrich, 136; "three days" Arvid Fredborg, *Behind the Steel Wall: A Swedish Journalist in Berlin, 1941-43*, 87; Kirkpatrick, *The Inner Circle: Memoirs of Ivone Kirkpatrick*, 98–99.

18. Ernest Pope, *Munich Playground*, 145–46, 3–4; Bruckner, "Private Life of Führer."

19. Heiden, *Hitler*, 314.

20. Payne, 353–53; Speer, 85–86; von Lang, *The Secretary*, 94.

21. *Ibid.*, 95; Payne, 352; Gun, *Eva Braun: Hitler's Mistress*, 116; Phayre, "Holiday with Hitler," 54; Timothy Ryback, "Hitler's Forgotten Library."

22. Pauline Kohler, *The Woman Who Lived in Hitler's House*, 71–75, 60–63; Florian Beierl, interview with author. The claim that Rudolf Ossietz was Hitler's resident astrologer was made by Walter Tschuppik in a German language newspaper in London shortly after Rudolf Hess, a confirmed believer in astrology, made his quixotic

flight to Scotland in May 1941. There is no evidence that Hitler believed in astrology (Ellic Howe, *Astrology and Psychological Warfare during World War II*, 159–60, 196–97).

23. Karl Wiegand, "Hitler foresees his end," *Cosmopolitan* magazine, April 1939; H. Hoffmann, *Hitler Was My Friend*, 135–36; Schirach, *The Price of Glory*, 156.

24. Toland, *Hitler*, 198, 807, 1088, 1180; "books" Timothy Ryback, "Hitler's Forgotten Library"; Fromm, 75–76, 102; Pope, 144–45; Bridget Hitler, *Memoirs*, 161; Kurt Krüger, *I Was Hitler's Doctor*, 114–17; Emmy Göring, *My Life with Göring*, 99; R. Manvell and H. Fränkel, *Hess*, 131; "British astrologer" Kenneth Strong, *Intelligence at the Top*, 94; Goebbels, *Final Entries* (29 March 1945), 270; Joachim Fest, *Face of Third Reich*, 60; Hugh Trevor-Roper, *Last Days of Hitler*, 129, 140–41.

25. Sions, "Berchtesgaden"; Paul Moor, "The Old Order"; "Junge" Kate Haste, *Nazi Women*, 77; Leon Degrelle, "The Enigma of Hitler"

26. Geiss, 68.

27. Sydney Morrell, "Hitler's Hiding Place," 486–88; "new railway station" David Harper, *Berchtesgaden Guide*, 109.

28. Hitler, *Table Talk* (16–17 Jan. 1942), 210–11; Schirach, 178; Fest, 526; Stephen Goode, "Dutch Master from Delft," *Insight on the News*, 24 Sept. 2001; Speer, 86.

29. Gun, *Eva Braun: Hitler's Mistress*, 117; James Leasor, *Rudolf Hess: The Uninvited Envoy*, 99.

30. Elisabeth von Stahlenberg, *Nazi Lady: The Diaries of Elisabeth von Stahlenberg, 1933–1938*, 132–33.

31. "Dohring" Remme, "Life with Hitler and His Mistress."

32. Von Lang, *The Secretary*, 97; Dietrich, 208; Toland, *Hitler*, 1012; Kershaw, *Hitler 1889–1936*, 534.

33. Florian Beierl, interview with author.

34. "Farm" Geiss, 93, 96, 100–02; von Lang, 97–98.

35. Speer, *Third Reich*, 86–87; Dietrich, 180, 196; Hale, "Adolf Hitler: Taxpayer"; *Times* (London), 17 Oct. 1998; Steven Erlanger, "Hitler, It Seems, Loved Money and Died Rich"; Reuters report, 17 Dec. 2004; Ladislas Farago, *Aftermath: Martin Bormann and the Fourth Reich*, 32.

36. Traudl Junge in Pierre Galante and Eugene Silianoff, eds., *Voices from the Bunker*, 63; Hanisch, *Obersalzberg*, 15; Geiss, 100.

37. Von Lang, *The Secretary*, 94; Hanisch, *Obersalzberg*, 14–15; Toland, 537–38; Bernhard Frank, *Hitler, Göring and the Obersalzberg*, 66, 70, 72; "in Bormann's name" James McGovern, *Martin Bormann*, 128.

38. Harper, *Your Complete Guide to Berchtesgaden*, 118–19; Sereny, 120.

39. Von Lang, 94, 103; Speer, 84; "87 buildings" McGovern, *Martin Bormann*, 128; Dietrich, 10.

40. Dietrich, 197.

41. Speer, 85; Hitler, *Table Talk*, 316; von Lang, *The Secretary*, 103.

42. Pope, 142–43; Morrell, "Hitler's Hiding Place," 488.

43. Speer, *Spandau: The Secret Diaries*, 129–30.

44. Stahlenberg, 203–04; Baur interview, in Boone, "Oberz," 56.

45. Dietrich, 145. Leon Degrelle recalled this experience: "At one or two o'clock in the morning he would still be talking, untroubled, close to his fireplace, lively, often amusing. He never showed any sign of weariness. Dead tired his audience might be, but not Hitler" ("The Enigma of Hitler").

46. Bullock, *Hitler and Stalin: Parallel Lives*, 374, 382; Alexander Solzhenitsyn, *The First Circle*.

47. Wolfgang Wagner, *Acts: The Autobiography of Wolfgang Wagner*.

48. "Geli" Haste, *Nazi Women*, 40–49, 52–53; Friedelind Wagner, *Heritage of Fire*, 128.

49. "Magda" Haste., 66–71; 232–33; Anja Klabunde, *Magda Goebbels*, 141–46.

50. Huss, 29; "Eva's perfume" Kohler, 175–76, Krüger, 227; Stahlenberg, 139–40, 188; Sions, "Berchtesgaden."

51. Baur, *Hitler's Pilot*, 56–59.

52. Huss, 72; Leni Riefenstahl, *Leni Riefenstahl: A Memoir*, 143–166, 175–76, 179–80, 184–200, 209–11, 257–61, 304–05; Fromm, 131; Richard D. Mandell, *The Nazi Olympics*, 271; American intelligence report, 30 May 1945, in *Film Culture* 55 (Fall 1992), 35–38.

53. "Wisbar and Zeissler" U.S. Army, Office of Strategic Services, *Hitler Source Book*.

54. "Jenny Jugo" Kohler, 168–73; Beierl, interview with author; Ian Sayer and Douglas Botting, *The Women Who Knew Hitler*.

55. Krüger, 227–28; "Jenny's contribution" Rudolph Semmler, *Goebbels: The Man Next to Hitler*, 160; Dietrich, 218–19; Gun, 186.

56. "Hasselbach" U.S. Army Counter Intelligence Corps history, v. 14, *Man Named A.H.*, 160.; "Werner" *Berliner Kurier*, 6 Aug. 1996; H. Hoffmann, *Hitler Was My Friend*, 191.

57. "Inge Ley" George Duncan, "Women of the Third Reich," 8.

58. "Pistol" Öchsner, 107; Riefenstahl, *Leni Riefenstahl*, 228; "reported" Pope, 133, see also 136–37; Stahlenberg, 106, 123; Friedelind Wagner, *Heritage of Fire*, 141–42, also 205–06.

59. Fromm, 255; Jan Dalley, *Dianna Mosley: A Biography*; Toland, *Hitler*, 807–08, 836–37; Richard Griffiths, *Fellow Travellers of the Right: British Enthusiasts for Nazi Germany, 1933–9*, 171–75; H. Hoffmann, 164–66; Dietrich, 188–89.

60. Speer, *Spandau*, 106; Pope, 3, 6–7, 137–38; Friedelind Wagner, *Heritage of Fire*, 138, 144. Frederick Öchsner was told that in 1939 Hitler "had had young women, three or four at a time to dance for him in very sparse attire at Berchtesgaden. His fascination at these times seems to have been partly outright erotic and partly the 'It's the art of the thing that interests me' rationalization" (*This is the Enemy*, 109–10; see also William D. Bayles, *Caesars in Goose Step*, 51–52).

61. Gun, 186–87; U.S. Army Counter Intelligence Corps history, v. 14, *Man Named A.H.*, 143; "Brandt" Overy, 262.

62. Charles de Gaulle, *The War Memoirs of Charles de Gaulle: Salvation, 1944–1946*, 86–88.

63. Toland, *Hitler*, 533; Bullock, *Hitler and Stalin: Parallel Lives*, 383, 407, 385.

64. "Bormann house" Von Lang, *The Secretary*, 96, Geiss, 80–87; "Göring" Geiss, 114–15; "Speer" Speer, *Third Reich*, 84; "Keitel and Jodl" Geoff Walden, "Third Reich in Ruins"; "Ribbentrop" *Trial of the Major War Criminals* ("Nuremberg Trials"), v. 10 (30 March 1946); "Himmler" Wilhelm Wulff, *Zodiac and Swastika*, 100.

65. "Goebbels" Ralf Reuth, *Goebbels*, 236–40, 242–44; " house staff" Florian Beierl, interview with author.

66. Dietrich, 181–82; Riefenstahl, *Leni Riefenstahl*, 178; Emmy Göring, *My Life with Göring*, 64; "Eva's pine boughs".

67. Dietrich, 182; Baur, *Hitler's Pilot*, 109.

68. "New Year's Eve" Boone, "Oberz," 56–58, in Gun, 103–05; H. Hoffmann, 143–44.

69. Beierl, *History of the Eagle's Nest*; Lochner, *What About Germany?* 75–76; "elevator" Julian Bach, Jr., *America's Germany: An Account of the Occupation*, 47–48; von Lang, *The Secretary*, 97, 101–05.

70. Beierl, *Eagle's Nest*, 93–97, 103; Moor, 63.

71. Toland, *Hitler*, 680; Silkirk Panton, "Hitler's New Hiding Place," London *Sunday Express*, in *Current History* 50, no. 71–2 (April 1939). According to Frederick Öchsner, on Hitler's first use of the elevator it stopped halfway up for four hours (*This Is the Enemy*, 75–76). "visits" "Pages from my Scrapbook."

72. Panton, "Hitler's New Hiding Place"; Öchsner, 76–77; Bach, 4; Hamburger, "Letter from Berchtesgaden."

73. Andre Francois-Poncet, *The Fateful Years: Memoirs of a French Ambassador in Berlin, 1931-38*, 280–81; "Hitler's Palace in the Clouds," Amsterdam *Telegraaf*, in *Living Age*, 1939 (n. 356), 32–33; Price, *I Know These Dictators*.

74. Huss, 163–65.

75. "Hitler's Palace in the Clouds," Amsterdam *Telegraaf*, in *New Age*, March 1939, 32–33; Hanisch, 18; Langer, 38, 169.

76. "Gretl reception" Beierl, 126; Toland, 1208–09; "lunch and photos" Hans Baur, in Boone, "Oberz," 68; "Eberstein" *A Man Named Hitler* v. 14, p. 143, history of the U.S. Army Counter Intelligence Corps in W.W.II.; Gun, 228; Irmgard Hunt, *On Hitler's Mountain*, 167; "Munich bombing" Dietrich, 220.

77. "Platterhof" Geiss, 132–41.

78. *Ibid.*, 99–100.

79. Andrew Roberts, *The "Holy Fox": A Biography of Lord Halifax*, 65.

80. David Dutton, *Anthony Eden: A Life and Reputation*, 35; "Lloyd George" Thomas Jones, *A Diary with Letters, 1931-1950*, 244–52; Kershaw, *Hitler, 1936-1945: Nemesis*, 29, 854, n. 135; Hanisch, *Obersalzberg*, 26–27, 32.

81. "Windsors" Ralph G. Martin, *The Woman He Loved*, 384–401; 424–36; Jones, *Diary*, 374–75; Toland, *Hitler*, 1056.

82. "Halifax" Roberts, *Halifax*, 65–73; John Lee, *A Soldier's Life: General Sir Ian Hamilton.*

83. Alfred Duff Cooper, *Old Men Forget*, 228–29, 235; Pope, 192.

84. Kurt von Schuschnigg, "Summons to Berchtesgaden," *Commonweal*, 3 Jan. 1947, 294–98; *ibid.*, *Austrian Requiem*; "Toynbee" John Ray, *The Night Blitz, 1940-1941*, 46.

85. Boone, "Obersalzberg," 110–14, 117–19, 142; Harper, *Your Complete Guide to Berchtesgaden*, 124.

86. Toland, *Hitler*, 1016; David Irving, *Hitler's War*, 251; "house above Linz" James P. O'Donnell, *The Bunker*, 14.

87. Karl Billinger, *Hitler Is No Fool*, 171.

88. Toland, 732–38; Louis P. Lochner, *What About Germany*, 1–4; E.L. Woodward and R. Butler, eds., *Documents on British Foreign Policy, 1919-1939*, v. 7, 258–59.

89. Speer, *Inside*, 162–63; Remme, "Life with Hitler and His Mistress." While in Spandau prison in 1946, Albert Speer recalled Hitler's statement about the forthcoming flow of blood: "How odd that none of us was shocked by this remark.... I distinctly recall that when Hitler made this remark I did not think of the endless misfortunes it meant, but of the grandeur of the historical hour" (*Spandau: the Secret Diaries*, 301).

## Chapter Three

1. Speer, *Inside Third Reich*, 167–68, 176–77, 181.

2. *Ibid.*, 215–17.

3. Von Lang, *The Secretary*, 279–80.

4. Geiss, 152–61; Dietrich, 223.

5. Harper, *Your Complete Guide to Berchtesgaden*, 18; Beierl, interview with author.

6. Dietrich, 251; Speer, *Inside*, 391, 217, 538n; Irving, *Hitler's War*, 661; "East European workers" Fest, *Plotting*, 261.

7. O'Donnell, *The Bunker*, 58–60; Goebbels, *Goebbels Diaries, 1942-1943* (29 July 1943), 421, (26 Nov. 1943), 530; "ground to air missile, code name Waterfall" Speer, *Inside*, 364–66.

8. *New York Times*, 12 May 1945.

9. Geiss, 164–73; Public Records Office, London, *Operation Foxley*, 100, 106; "facilities" Beierl, interview with author; 1999 bunker tour; "first section" Bernhard Frank, *Hitler, Göring and the Obersalzberg*, 53; "honey" Bormann, *Bormann Letters*, 191; Hanisch, *Obersalzberg*, 35.

10. Harper, *Your Complete Guide to Berchtesgaden*, 61–65; Chaussy, 142–159; Beierl, *History of the Eagle's Nest.*; "Bormann's bricks" Beierl, interview with author.

11. Geiss, 177; Toland, *Hitler*, 1070, 1154; Irving, *Hitler's War*, 640; "paintings" Anni Winter statement, report dated 27 Oct. 1947, National Archives, U.S. Army, Record Group 260, Ardelia Hall Collection.

12. Bernhard Frank, *Obersalzberg*, 50, 10, 20, 29, 82–83, 86–88; 34–40, 55; Ingrid Scharfenberg, interview with author.

13. "smoke" Hanisch, *Obersalzberg*, 35; Morell, *Adolf Hitler, the Medical Diaries*, 156–57; "steps" Toland, 1070, and Irving, *Hitler's War*, 640.

14. Beierl, interview with author; *New York Times*, 26 April 1945; Morell, 149; Peter Hoffmann, 195–96; Walden, "*Third Reich in Ruins*," see "miscellaneous buildings."

15. Wesley F. Craven and James L. Cate, *The Army Air Forces in World War II*, 638, 894 n. 7; Lt. Col. Jack Nicholas to Col. Barr, 25 April 1945, in HQ, 15th Air Force, Analysis Reports, March 1944–June 1945; William Breuer, *Feuding Allies*, 198; Henry Arnold, *American Airpower Comes of Age*, John Huston, ed., vol. 2, 166. For an account of an aborted mission by the 763rd Bomber Squadron of the 15th Air Force to attempt to kill Hitler at a different location that coincided with photo-reconnaissance flights see Leroy W. Newby, "Your Mission: Kill Hitler" (*American Heritage*, Oct. 1998, 26–29).

16. "Policy of AAF and Eisenhower" Craven and Cate, 284; "Roosevelt's position" Michael BeschlU.S. Army, Office of Strategic Services, *The Conquerors*; Ronald Schaffer, *Wings of Judgement: American Bombing in World War II*, 89, 91, 103–06; Hanisch, 35–36.

17. Allen Dulles, *From Hitler's Doorstep*, 341.

18. *Ibid.*, "target plan" facing p. 25; "airdrop" Cornelius Ryan, *The Last Battle*, 125.

19. Craven and Cate, 638; Nicholas to Barr.

20. Nicholas to Barr.

21. Nicholas to Barr.

22. *New York Times*, 22 Feb. 1945; U.S. Army Air Force, 15th Air Force, MAAF War Room mission report, 20 February 1945.

23. *Life*, 19 March 1945; *Newsweek*, 5 March 1945.

24. P. Hoffmann, *Hitler's Security*, 194–95; Kit Carter and Robert Mueller, *U.S. Army Air Forces in World War II: Combat Chronology, 1941-1945*, 488.

25. Foxley documents, from AD/A, undated, late 1944, HS6/ 623, UK Public Records Office, London.

26. *Ibid.*, from X, 9 Oct. 1944; A/CD, 28 June 1944, HS 6/623.

27. *Ibid.*, L/BX, 31 Oct. 1944, HS 6/625; Public Record Office, London, *Operation Foxley: The British Plan to Kill Hitler*, 21, 108–13; HS 6/623, HS 6/624, HS 6/626, Public Record Office, London; Bernie Ross, "The Foxley Report: Plotters Against Hitler."

28. Public Records Office, *Operation Foxley*, 14; Kershaw, x; Denis Rigdon, *Kill the Führer: Section X and Operation Foxley*, 10–49; London *Times*, 23 July 1998; *Irish Times*, 23 July 1998; "Alfred Dorner" account of Mark Dorner, "Stories from WWII" Web site.

29. "Foxley" Public Records Office, London, HS 6/626; "Goebbels" L/BX, 4 Dec. 1944, HS 6/623 and L/BX, 16 March 1945, HS6/626; from Capt. Joll, 22 Feb. 1945, HS 6/623. One planner suggested employing Rudolf Hess, "either through persuasion or hypnosis" to get at Nazi leaders (X/Plans, 18 Dec. 1944, HS 6/623).

30. L/BX, 12 Feb. 1945, HS 6/623; "Skorzeny" L/BX, undated, early 1945, HS 6/626 .

31. A/CD, 6 April 1945, HS 6/623; from Capt. Jolly, 22 Feb. 1945, HS 6/623.

32. Stanley P. Lovell, *Of Spies and Stratagems*, 81–85, 89–91.

33. Military Attaché, Bern, Report No. 4222, 20 March 1942, U.S. Military Intelligence Reports, Germany, 1941–1944, microfilm; Joachim Fest, *Plotting Hitler's Death*, 193–95, 238, 243.

34. Irmgard Hunt says that with the Berchtesgadener Land filled with evacuees it became known as "Germany's air-raid shelter." *On Hitler's Mountain*, 186. Ryan, 196; "proclamation" Fest, 732; Irving, *Hitler's War*, 724–25, 779; O'Donnell, *The Bunker*, 110.

35. "Montgomery Doppelgänger" Clifton James, *I Was Monty's Double*; "Eisenhower Doppelgänger" *New York Times*, 22 May 1945.

36. SOE, *Operation Foxley*, 101, 104; Kohler, 99–102.

37. "Baur" Boone, "Obersalzberg," 172; also Baur, *Hitler's Pilot*, 210; "two Hitlers in Berlin" Glenn Infield, *Hitler's Secret Life*, 282, 284; "mid–1930s proposal" O'Donnell, *The Bunker*, 366–67.

38. "Brückner" U.S. Army Counter Intelligence Corps history, v. 14, 141; "Smersh" Lev Bezymenski, *The Death of Adolf Hitler*, 32–33.

39. "servant" *New York Times*, 9 May 1945; Ada Petrova and Peter Watson, *The Death of Hitler*, 52–53, 90, 93, 136; Peter Hoffmann, interview with author, 12 October 1999. Hoffmann's *Hitler's Personal Security* says nothing about Doppelgänger: David Irving e-mail, 9 Dec. 1999; see also Michael Musmanno (*Ten Days to Die*, 236), Dietrich (214), and Glenn Infield's speculation that Hitler used a double to cover his escape from Berlin (*Hitler's Secret Life*, 261–63, 278–85).

40. Walter Ansel, *Hitler Confronts England*, 126–247; Leasor, *Rudolf Hess*, 82–103. Leasor has come to the conclusion that Hitler knew about Hess's flight beforehand (*ibid.*, 172–73). John Harris and Mei Trow (*Hess: The British Conspiracy*) also believe this. See Hess article, *History Today*, Jan. 2000; Speer, *Third Reich*, 247; Speer, *Spandau*, 212–13.

41. Goebbels, *Goebbels Diaries, 1942–1943* (27 April 1942), 192; Anton Joachimsthaler, *The Last Days of Hitler*, 168; "uniform and bombers" Irving, *Hitler's War*, 506.

42. Emmy Göring, *My Life with Göring*, 38; David Irving, *Göring: A Biography*, 380–81, 385, 397, 404–05, 419; Roger Manvell and Heinrich Fränkel, *Hermann Göring*, 261–64, and 278–79, 298–300; Goebbels, *Final Entries, 1945*, 197.

43. Peter Padfield, *Himmler*, 419.

44. Kershaw, *Hitler, 1936–1945*, 631–32; Goebbels, *Goebbels Diaries: Final Entries*, 279; Fest, *Hitler*, 762–74; Morell, 157.

45. Kersten, 165–67, 171; Bernhard Frank, *Obersalzberg*, 78, 88; "OSS informant" Foxley papers, HS 6/623; von Lang, *The Secretary*, 302.

46. "Eva" Infield, *Eva and Adolf*, 238–40, 250, 252, 330–31; Toland, *Hitler*, 1129–35; "award, microscope to Morell" Morell, *Adolf Hitler, the Medical Diaries*.

47. "Zabel" Morell, 120, 127, 154, 163; "Winter" *ibid.*, 162; "Exner" *ibid.*, 133, 143n., "Brandt" Emmy Göring, *My Life with Göring*, 66–67; Toland, *Hitler*, 1019, 1067.

48. "Swerin" U.S. Army Counter Intelligence Corps history, v. 14, *Man Called A.H.*, 173.

49. Hans Ulrich Rudel, *Stuka Pilot*, 143–44.

50. Goebbels, *Goebbels Diaries, 1942–1943* (2 March 1943), 262; (14 April 1943) 328; see also 192, 198.

51. Toland, 1010–19; Hanisch, 22–23; Riefenstahl, *Leni Riefenstahl: A Memoir*, 294–95. Earlier in the month, on March 7, Leni was given a physical examination by Theo Morell, Hitler's doctor, in Salzburg (Morell, 151).

52. Speer, *Third Reich*, 340–41, 354, 358–59; "D-Day" Kershaw, *Hitler*, 640; Toland, *Hitler*, 1075–76; Fest, *Plotting Hitler's Death*, 238; David Fraser, *Knight's Cross: A Life of Field Marshall Erwin Rommel*, 504.

53. Hanisch, 32–33; H. Hoffmann, 192; Dietrich, 202.

54. Kershaw, *Hitler, 1936–1945*, 581–82.

55. Dietrich, 216; "Henriette" Toland, *Hitler*, 1016; H. Hoffmann, 191; Davidson, *The Trial of the Germans*, 305–06; "dogs and reconstruction" Traudl Junge, *Until the Final Hour*, 138; Gun, 220–21; "Dachau" 209; Schirach, 185–89, 174; Irving, *Hitler's War*, 529–30, 874; Leon Goldensohn, *The Nuremberg Interviews*, 250; Emmy Göring, *My Life with Göring*, 90–91.

56. Karl von Eberstein in U.S. Army Counter Intelligence Corps history, vol. 14, *Man Called A.H.*, 142.

57. Douglas Kelley, *22 Cells in Nuremberg*, 222, 230.

58. Langer, 165.

59. SOE, Section X, HS 6/694; "Operation Casement," SOE Records, Public Record Office, London; Eunan O'Halpin, SOE plans, *Irish Times*, 26 Feb. 2005; Allen Dulles, *From Hitler's Doorstep: The Wartime Intelligence Reports of Allen Dulles, 1942–1945*, 328; "Commons question" *New York Herald Tribune*, 16 May 1945; Timothy Maier, "Adolf Hitler's secret FBI files," *Insight on the News*, 22 March 1999; "Arans" Ian Sayer and Douglas Botting, *America's Secret Army*, 306.

60. Speer, *Spandau*, 170; Rigdon, 142–43, 145; London *Times*, 23 July 1998; Sefton Delmer, *Black Boomerang*, 244; Marvin Meek, "ULTRA and the Myth of the German 'National Redoubt,'" 37.

61. "Brandt" Kelley, 212; Dr. Hans Hasselbach, U.S. Army Counter Intelligence Corps history, v. 14, *Man Called A.H.*, 162; "Dohring" Remme, "Life with Hitler..."; "Speer" Sereny, 193; Schirach, 19.

62. Emmy Göring, *My Life with Göring*, 64–66.

63. SOE, *Operation Foxley*, 48, 105, 108.

64. "Gretl" Brandt in Overy, 261–62.

65. *Ibid.*, 262.

66. Gun, 211, 238, 208–09. According to Gertrud

Weisker, when an aunt of Eva's, a nun whose convent had been occupied by the military, asked for help in allowing the nuns to remain there, Eva replied, "Let your hair grow," meaning make preparation to leave the facility (Linda Grant, "My Cousin, Eva Braun," *The Guardian*, 27 April 2002).

67. Simon Finch, "Eva and Me" (interview with "Elizabeth Winkler," cousin of Eva Braun), *The Guardian*, 28 Dec. 1999; "meeting with Gertrude Weisker" Grant, "My Cousin."

68. *Ibid.*; H. Hoffmann, 160; "Winter" Musmanno, *Ten Days to Die*, 153; "Eva's house and Winter's reputation" Lee Miller, *Lee Miller's War*, 198–99, 193; Friedrich Karl von Eberstein, "National Redoubt" transcript, 142–43; Hasselbach, *Man Called Hitler*, v. 14, 162; Gun, 114.

69. "Dohring" Remme, "Life with Hitler..."; Sereny, 193; Musmanno, 153.

70. Hasselbach, 160; Dietrich, 215; Tradl Junge, *Voices from the Bunker*, 63.

71. H. Hoffmann, *Hitler Was My Friend*, 195; Beierl, interview with author; von Lang, *The Secretary*, 281; Joseph E. Persico, *Piercing the Reich*, 289; Nicholas to Barr.

72. Irving, *Hitler's War*, 656, 886.

73. Morell, 233; Fest, 708; "Below" Kershaw, *Hitler, 1936-1945*, 650; Bernhard Frank, *Obersalzberg*, 79, 91; Christa Schröder, one of Hitler's secretaries, in Kelley, 233. Schröder later said that the day before the assassination attempt Hitler told her that "he had a very bad feeling. He said that nothing must be allowed to happen to him now because he did not have any successor" (ibid.). "Göring remained" Hamburger, "Letter from Berchtesgaden."

74. Von Lang, *The Secretary*, 278, 309.

75. Trevor-Roper, 95; Louis Kilzer, *Hitler's Traitor*, 186–88; Reinhard Dörries, *Hitler's Last Chief of Foreign Intelligence*, 107, 115–16; Anthony Cave Brown, *The Last Hero: Wild Bill Donovan*, 530; Anthony Read and David Fisher, *The Fall of Berlin*, 221.

76. Toland, *Hitler*, 1113, 1116; "wives along" Jacques Nobecourt, *Hitler's Last Gamble*, 34; "Stauffenberg" P. Hoffmann, *Hitler's Personal Security*, 191; "avoidance, given up, Berlin bombing" Giesing, U.S. Army Counter Intelligence Corps history, v.14, *Man Called A.H.*, 153.

77. United Press report in *New York Times*, 5 Feb. 1945.

78. "Swiss open secret world of anti-Hitler defenses," *International Herald Tribune*, 26 July 1999; Stephen Ambrose, *Eisenhower and Berlin, 1945: The Decision to Halt at the Elbe*, 73; Wilhelm Höttl, *Hitler's Paper Weapon*, 148–49; Peter Black, *Ernst Kaltenbrunner*, 235.

79. Perry Biddiscombe, *Werwolf!: The History of the National Socialist Guerilla Movement, 1944-46*, 179.

80. Timothy Naftali, "Creating the Myth of the Alpenfestung," 206–10; Helms to OSS Special Intelligence staff, 10 Aug. 1944, N.A. RG, Entry 92, Other OSS Records: COI/ OSS Central Files (1942–1946), (1) Box 564/ Folder 10: X-32,299; J.F.C. Fuller, "Hitler's Plan: Victory Through Chaos"; Donovan to F.D.R., N.A., RG 226, microfilm MI1642, roll 30, frames 1070–73.

81. George Axelsson, "Götterdämmerung—by Hitler."

82. Hofer, "The Alpine Fortification," pp. 2–4; Hofer, "The National Redoubt"; Stephen Fritz, *Endkampf: Soldiers, Civilians and the Death of the Third Reich*, 5–6.

83. Frank H. Hinsley, *British Intelligence in the Second World War*, 711.

84. Other articles about the Redoubt: J. Scott, "Inside the Reich; Desperate Nazis Prepare a Wagnerian Tragedy,"

*Life*, 21 Aug. 1944; V. Schiff, "Last Fortress of the Nazis; in the Alps East of Switzerland," *NYT Magazine*, 11 Feb. 1945; "Germans Gather Men, Forge Weapons, for Last Stand in the Heart of Europe," *Newsweek*, 2 April 1945.

85. *Stars and Stripes*, 17 April 1945, 4; Ambrose, *Eisenhower and Berlin*, 74–76.

86. Ryan, 212.

87. OSS report, 3 March 1945, Charles Cheston, Acting Director, to Joint Chiefs, N.A., RG 226, microfilm, roll 30, frames 235–36; Rodney G. Minnott, *The Fortress That Never Was*, 86–87; G-2 report, 7th Army, 25 March 1945. A hand-written note is at the bottom of the report: "Nothing in this report should be construed to indicate the enemy capable of effecting an impregnable defensive set-up—only stubborn delay of termination of resistance" (note in William W. Quinn Papers, MHI; N.A., RG 226, microfilm, roll 52, frames 252–63).

88. Persico, *Piercing the Reich*, 289.

89. Bradley F. Smith, *The Shadow Warriors*, 279; Dulles, 400–01, 430, 433, 447–48, 450–51, 472, 475–76, 485, 492–93, 504–05; Neal Petersen, "The OSS Around the Globe," in George C. Chalou, ed., *The Secrets War*, 286, 293, ref. 54.

90. Ryan, 212.

91. De Gaulle, *The War Memoirs*, 179–89.

92. Hinsley, *British Intelligence in World War II*, 716; Churchill, *The Second World War: Triumph and Tragedy*, 457. The shifting of scarce German forces to western Hungary in early 1945 probably was designed to retain control of its last significant sources of oil and bauxite (Ronald Zweig, *The Gold Train*, 76–78). "Churchill cable" W.C. to Stalin, 21 March 1945, Churchill Archive, 20/213A, in John Nichol and Tony Rennell, *The Last Escape*, 199, ref. 481.

93. SHAEF Joint Intelligence Committee to Combined Intelligence Committee, 19 April 1945, N.A., RG226, microfilm, roll 11, frames 621–25; "Bad Gastein" Carl Boyd, *Hitler's Japanese Confidant: General Oshima Hiroshi and MAGIC Intelligence*, 171; "fascist retreat" Jochen von Lang, *Top Nazi: SS General Karl Wolff, the Man Between Hitler and Himmler*, 260–61.

94. Bernhard Frank, 56–57, 80, 57.

95. Hofer, "The Alpine Fortification," 6–7; Hofer, "The National Redoubt," 5–11, 22.

96. Wilhelm Höttl, *The Secret Front*, 294–98; Marie Vassiltchikov, *The Berlin Diaries, 1940-1945, of Marie "Missie" Vassiltchikov*, 276, 278.

97. Hofer, "Alpine Fortification"; Hofer, "National Redoubt"; Höttl, *The Secret Front*, 286; Hinsley, *British Intelligence in the Second World War*, 735.

98. Albrecht Kesselring, *Kesselring: A Soldier's Record*, 327; Ernst von Salomon, *Fragebogen*, 319, 333; Biddiscombe, *Werwolf!*, 180.

99. Ryan, 213–14; Bruce Lee, *Marching Orders*, 406–07, 411–12; Eberstein, "National Redoubt"; Ludwig Muhe, "Wehrkreis VII Police (National Redoubt)"; August Marcinkiewicz, "National Redoubt"; Strong, *Intelligence at the Top*, 255–56; "wind" Kershaw, *Hitler, 1936-45: Nemesis*, 781.

100. Ryan, 405; "70 sites and Ultra" Biddiscombe, *Werwolf!*, 178, 267; Dennis Piszkiewicz, *The Nazi Rocketeers*, 199–200, 208–10, 219–21; Dulles, 508; *Stars and Stripes*, 4 April 1945; Nichol and Tony Rennell, *The Last Escape, 1944-45*, 42, 52–58, 178–185, 254–56.

101. Glenn Infield, *Skorzeny: Hitler's Commando*, 111, 114–15; Strong, *Intelligence at the Top*, 235.

102. Persico, *Piercing the Reich*, 160, 254–59, 290; Richard Dunlop, *Donovan: America's Master Spy*, 466. Christof Mauch declares that the assertion of the OSS that it effectively penetrated Germany in the last months of the war was a self-serving myth (*The Shadow War Against Hitler*, 182).

103. William Casey later said that the two OSS agents in Munich, as well as other operatives in the area, found no evidence of a build-up of a national redoubt (Casey, *The Secret War Against Hitler*, 200, 205–08). 1944 OSS report on economic conditions in southern Germany; Gerald Schwab, *OSS Agents in Hitler's Heartland: Destination Innsbruck*; Mauch, *Shadow War Against Hitler*, 182; Nelson MacPherson, *American Intelligence in War-time London: The Story of the U.S. Army, Office of Strategic Services*, 106–119.

104. SOE Records, Public Records Office, London.

105. "Ultra" David Eisenhower, *Eisenhower: At War, 1943–1945*, 729; Bennett, *Behind the Battle*, 274.

106. Naftali, "Myth of Alpenfestung," 212–13.

107. Omar Bradley, *A General's Life*, 418–18, 431; Sherman W. Pratt, *Autobahn to Berchtesgaden*, 516, 565; Paul Gallagher, interview with author; Ambrose, *Supreme Commander*, 623.

108. Bradley, *A Soldier's Story*, 536; Carlo D'Este, *Eisenhower*, 641; Russell Weigley, *Eisenhower's Lieutenants*, 715–16.

109. Hinsley, *British Intelligence*, 717; Dwight Eisenhower, *Crusade in Europe*, 415.

110. Ike to Stalin: Antony Beevor, *The Fall of Berlin: 1945*, 141, 144–47; Read and Fisher, 283, 295.

111. Naftali, "Myth of Alpenfestung," 203–04; Ike to FDR, *Stars and Stripes*, 6 April 1945.

112. Harry C. Butcher, *My Three Years with Eisenhower*, 799, 804, 809, 812; "radio stations" Gernter d'Alquen statement, in Michael Musmanno, *Ten Days to Die*, 107 .

113. John Ehrman, *Grand Strategy: October 1944–August 1945*, 147–48.

114. "Study of War Department on Probable Developments in German Reich," in Forrest C. Pogue, *George C. Marshall: Organizer of Victory*, 557, 568–69.

115. Ambrose, *Eisenhower and Berlin*, 77–78; "April 16 statement" Jean de Lattre de Tassigny, *The History of the French First Army*, 482n; "Smith" Butcher, 810, 814; "SHAEF memo" U.S. Army, *Official Diary for the Commanding General, 7th Army*, v. 3, 680.

116. Hinsley, *British Intelligence*, 719, 733; Ehrman, *Grand Strategy*, 134.

117. Lionel Ellis, *Victory in the West: The Defeat of Germany*, v. 2, 302; Bradley, *General's Life*, 421; Ambrose, *Supreme Commander*, 624; Weigley, *Eisenhower's Lieutenants*, 703.

118. Toland, *Last Hundred Days*, 439, 311–12; Dulles, 328, 466; Dietrich, 225.

119. Toland, *Hundred Days*, 385–86.

120. Ambrose, *Supreme Commander*, 76–77; Toland, *Hundred Days*, 307–08, 470–74; Forrest C. Pogue, "Why Eisenhower's Forces Stopped at the Elbe"; Chester Wilmot, *The Struggle for Europe*, 797.

121. Höttl, *Hitler's Paper Weapon*, 148–49; Lyman Kirkpatrick, *Captains Without Eyes*, 148–49; Minnott, 23–25, 27, 35–37, 86, 94, 172n. Charles Whiting, *Werewolf: The Story of the Nazi Resistance Movement*, 66; Naftali, "Myth of Alpenfestung," 215–21; "Nazis report underground terror group," *Stars and Stripes*, 3 April 1945; Meek, 17; Goebbels, *Final Entries, 1945*, 269, 289, 294, 296, 304, 311.

122. Dörries, *Hitler's Last Chief of Foreign Intelligence*, 292–94; Strong, 256.

123. Nichol and Rennell, *The Last Escape, 1944–45*, 466, 199–200.

124. "Prominente" *Ibid.*, 266–68, 367; Giles Romilly and Michael Alexander, *The Privileged Nightmare*, 220–31.

125. Nichol and Rennell, 281, 488 refs. 28, 29.

126. Mark Boatner, *Biographical Dictionary of World War II*, 129–130; Baldwin, "Our Generals in the Battle of Germany," *New York Times Magazine*, 22 Oct. 1944; Michael A. Markey, *Jake: The General from West York Avenue*, 8–77; Devers, *Diary*, 13 Dec. 1943; Jacob Devers oral history transcript, 100, 113–14, 127–28, 138.

127. Bradley, *General's Life*, 217; Martin Blumenson, ed., *The Patton Papers*, 413.

128. Charles MacDonald, *The Mighty Endeavour: American Armed Forces in the European Theater in World War II*, 408; see comment of Geoffrey Perret, *There's a War to be Won*, 431; "Devers's system" Guy Salisbury-Jones, *So Full of Glory*, 198; Jeffrey Clarke and Robert Smith, *Riviera to the Rhine*, 577.

129. Devers, *Diary*, 21, 25 Aug. 1944.

130. *Ibid.*, 25 Aug. 1944.

131. Devers, "Operation Dragoon: The Invasion of Southern France," *Journal of Military History* 10, no. 2, 3–41; Markey, *Jake*, 77.

132. Clarke and Smith, 39–40.

133. Blumenson, *Patton Papers*, 552, 444; Bradley, *General's Life*, 210, 390; Ambrose, *The Supreme Commander*, 313, 499; "ranking" *Eisenhower Papers*, IV, 2466–69; "Colmar" D'Este, *Eisenhower*, 669; Devers oral history, 119, 128.

134. Clarke and Smith, 576.

135. *Ibid.*, 437–39, 444.

136. *Ibid.*, 439–40, 563.

137. Blumenson, *Patton Papers*, 21 Sept. 1944, p. 552, 12 Feb. 1944, p. 414; Bradley, *A General's Life*, 210, 217, 390, 403–04, 421; Devers, *Diary*, 26 Nov. 1944.

138. Blumenson, *Patton Papers*, 583; Clarke and Smith, 437–45, 576–76.

139. "Rhine" *Ibid.*, 440; D'Este, 801, ref. 24; Devers, *Diary*, 24 Nov. 1944.

140. "Strasbourg" Franklin L. Gurley, "Policy Versus Strategy: The defense of Strasbourg in Winter 1944–1945," *Journal of Military History* 53, no. 8, 486–88; Devers, *Diary*, 27, 28 Dec. 1944, 1 Jan. 1945; Clarke and Smith, 496–97, 511, 576–77.

141. Whiting, *Forgotten Army*, 106–10, 131, 196; Weigley, *Eisenhower's Lieutenants*, 550–54, 580; U.S. Army, *Official Diary for Commanding General, Seventh Army*, v. 3, 478–79, 486–88; D'Este, 659; Devers, *Diary*, 27 April 1945.

142. D'Este, 668–70; see Crosswell, *Chief of Staff*, 306; Clarke and Smith, 576–77.

143. Blumenson, *Patton Papers*, 84, 170–71, 177, 413, 414, 417, 552–53, 557, 558, 588, 625, 627, 635–36, 798.

144. D'Este, 483; Chester Hansen diary, 24 April 1945, MHI.

145. D'Este, 404, 766 ref. 45, 548, 641, 670; Murray and Millett, *A War to Be Won*, 418.

146. "Bradley, Patton and Eisenhower" D'Este, 441, 402–03; Clarke and Smith, 576.

147. De Lattre, *French First Army*, 23, 355, 413–14; "French-speakers" Markey, *Jake*, 70–72.

148. Patch Papers, U.S. Military Academy Archives.

149. Hanson W. Baldwin, *Tiger Jack*, 55, 141.

150. "Wedemeyer, etc." Keith Eiler, ed., *Wedemeyer on War and Peace*, 62, 66; James Parton, *"Air Force Spoken Here": General Ira Eaker and the Command of the Air*, 262,

also 276; Bendetson, Truman Library Oral History Transcript; "Hoge" "Engineer Memoir," <us.army.mil>.

151. Ernie Pyle, *Brave Men*, 306–12; D'Este, 404, 766 ref. 45, 670; Murray and Millett, *A War to Be Won*, 418.

152. "Stuttgart" De Lattre, *French First Army*, 490–91; De Gaulle, *Complete Memoirs*, 859–63; U.S. Army, *Official Diary for the Commanding General, Seventh Army*, 677–80.

153. "Ulm" De Lattre, 544–63; MacDonald, *Last Offensive*, 430–32.

154. "Alsos" W.H. Allison, "Colonel Boris Pash," Stadt Haigerloch Web site; Boris Pash, *The Alsos Mission*, 139; photo following p. 32, 200–18; Samuel Goudsmit, *Alsos*, 88–112; Whiting, *Forgotten Army*, 204–06. Rainer Karlsch, in *Hitlers Bombe* (Munich, 2005), has speculated that German scientists exploded a crude nuclear devise on 3 March 1945 (AP report, 15 March 2005).

155. Franklin Gurley, "Policy Versus Strategy," *Journal of Military History* 58, no. 3, 486–87; Hansen diary, 16 April 1945. Thomas Griess of the West Point history department began a biography in the 1970s but this has not appeared in print (Devers oral history transcript, 68); alone among World War II four-star generals, there is not a scholarly article on Devers.

156. Reuben E. Jenkins, "The Battle of the German National Redoubt—Planning Phase," *Military Review*, Dec. 1946, 3–6.

157. *Ibid.*, 6–8.

158. Reuben E. Jenkins, "The Battle of the German National Redoubt: Operational Phase," Jan. 1947, 16–26.

159. *Ibid.*; Hinsley, *British Intelligence in World War II*, 614.

160. Helmut Kleikamp, "36th Volks Grenadier Division"; Otto Hofmann, "National Redoubt."

161. Clarke and Smith, 32–34.

162. Charles Corlett, *Cowboy Pete: The Autobiography of Major General Charles H. Corlett*, 88–93; D'Este, 482–83.

163. "Patch" Whiting, *Forgotten Army*, 54; William K. Wyant, *Sandy Patch*, 2–3, 149, 173–74, 205; Boatner, *WW II Biographical Dictionary*, 411–12; "Tactician's Dream," *Time*, 28 Aug. 1944; Patch to Julia Patch, 14 Sept. 1944, Patch Papers, USMA Archives; Hansen diary, 16 April 1945; Lucian Trusott, *Command Missions*, 383; William W. Quinn, oral history transcript, MHI; De Lattre, *French First Army*, 53, 57; Denis Johnston, *Nine Rivers to Jordan*, 390.

164. Devers oral history transcript, 181.

165. "Guadacanal" *Time* article, 1943, in Strobridge and Nalty, "From the South Pacific to the Brenner Pass"; *Time* cover story, 28 Aug. 1944; *Time* cover story, 4 Sept. 1944; Bill Mauldin, *Up Front*, 193–95; Strobridge and Nalty, "From the South Pacific to the Brenner Pass," 41–49.

166. Wyant, 173–74, 205; Strobridge and Nalty, 46; Bradley, *A General's Life*, 396–97.

167. Boatner, 302–04, 130; Liddell Hart, "An Appreciation," De Lattre, *French First Army*, 11–12.

168. Weigley, *Eisenhower's Lieutenants*, 551; "De Gaulle" Devers oral history transcript, 168–69.

169. Devers oral history transcript, 173; Devers, *Diary*, 7, 25 November 1944. At the time of the invasion of southern France, de Lattre "launched into a tirade" directed at Lucian Prescott, C. O. of the Third Infantry Division, for inspecting French units without de Lattre's permission, although Truscott had been invited to do so by the unit commanders (Truscott, *Command Missions*, 403–04).

170. Devers, *Diary*, 7 No. 1944; de Lattre, *French First*, 158n., 194, 75, 175; Henry Maule, *Out of the Sand*, 260.

171. Devers oral history transcript, 173.

172. Fritz, *Endkampf*, 178–80; G-2 Periodic Report, no. 212, 3rd Inf. Div., 11 April 1945, no. 217, 16 April 1945, N.A. Record Group 407, 303–2.15; Russ Cloer, "The Final Days of the War"; Robin Cross, *Fallen Eagle: The Last Days of the Third Reich*, 195.

173. G-2, 3rd Inf. Div., no. 218, 17 April 1945.

174. *Ibid.*; and 23 April 1945; U.S. Army, *Official Diary*, *7th Army*, v. 3, 665; David Daub, interview with author; John H. Toole, *Battle Diary*, xxxi; Trevor Ravencroft, *The Spear of Destiny: The Occult Power Behind the Spear Which Pierced the Side of Christ*; "swastika" Hugh A. Scott, *Blue and White Devils*, 168; United States Army, Information and Education Services, *Blue and White Devils*, 2–4.

175. G-2 Periodic Report, no. 219, 3rd Inf. Div., 18 April 1945; 7th Army U.S. Army Counter Intelligence Corps summary, 1–30 April 1945, William Quinn Papers, MHI.

176. Cloer, "Final Days of the War," 16–17.

177. G-2 Periodic Report, XXI Corps, 15 April, N.A. Record Group 407, 303–2.1. Gerhard Boldt, part of the *Führerbunker* staff, dismissed the possibility of effective Werwolf action (*Hitler: The Last Ten Days*, 90–92).

178. G-2 intelligence report, 7th Army, 2 May 1945, N.A. Record Group 407, 303–3.2; "Innovative weapons" G-2 bulletin, no. 23, 3rd Inf. Div., 22 April 1945, N.A., R.G. 407, 303–2.1; HDQS, 7th Army, 2 May 1945, N.A., R.G. 407, 303–3.2; "Radio Werwolf" Whiting, *Werewolf*, 144–46. See also Naftali, "Myth of the Alpenfestung," 205.

179. 7th Army U.S. Army Counter Intelligence Corps summary, 1–30 April 1945, Quinn Papers, MHI; "sheep" Col. McDonald in Denis Johnston, *Nine Rivers from Jordan*, 428.

180. Harold Zink, *The U.S. Army in Germany, 1944–1951*, 472.

181. Pratt, *Autobahn to Berchtesgaden*, 565–66.

182. G-2 Periodic Report, no. 224, 3rd Inf. Div., 28 April 1945; "O'Daniel" John Turner and Robert Jackson, *Destination Berchtesgaden*, 171; "Furst" Marguerite Higgins, *News Is a Singular Thing*, 86–88; United States Army, Information and Education Services, *Blue and White Devils*, 4.

183. 3rd Inf. Div., 29 April 1945; *ibid.*, 25 April; Earl Ziemke, *U.S. Army in the Occupation of Germany*, 253; William J. Kunz, narrative, April–May 1945, 77; "Dachau" Scott, *Blue and White Devils*, 169; United States Army, Information and Education Services, *Blue and White Devils*, 5; "Pullach" Nathan White, *From Fedala to Berchtesgaden*, 275; Toland, *Hundred Days*, 469–474; Wyant, *Sandy Patch*, 198.

184. Intelligence report, 7th Army in G-2, 3rd Inf. Div., 31 March 1945, N.A., R.G. 407, 303–2.15.

185. G-2 Periodic Report, no. 219, XXI Corps, 15 April 1945, R.G. 407, 303–2.15.

186. G-2 report, no. 219, 12th Army Group, G-2 report, XII Corps, no. 246, in 3rd Inf. Div. G-2 report, 18 April 1945, R.G. 407, 303–2.15.

187. Musmanno, 31; Persico, *Piercing the Reich*, 288; Minnott, 18–23; Toland, *100 Days*, 262–63.

188. Speer, *Inside the Third Reich*, 465, 477; O'Donnell, *The Bunker*, 137.

189. Von Lang, *The Secretary*, 180–81.

190. "South America" Farago, *Aftermath*, 122, 125, 129; William Stevenson, *Bormann Brotherhood*, 109; "U.S. State Dept." Isabel Vincent, *Hitler's Silent Partners: Swiss Banks, Nazi Gold and the Pursuit of Justice*, 188–91; "claims of flights to Argentina" Odessa network program, The Learning

Channel, 24 Feb. 1998; Ronald C. Newton, The "Nazi Menace" in Argentina, 1931-1947, 354, 468 n.65, 358, 260–61, 172, xv.

191. O'Donnell, The Bunker, 249, 27–28; Goebbels, Final Entries, 1945, 245; "Beermann" CrU.S. Army, Office of Strategic Services Fallen Eagle, 201; "Jodl" Gerhardt Herrgeselle statement, New York Herald Tribune, 16 May 1945.

192. Gun, 239–40; Beever, Fall of Berlin, 75.

193. Ibid., 241; "Who else…" Traudl Junge to Otto Skorzeny, Infield, Skorzeny, 109; Infield, Eva and Adolf, 266; Jack Fleischer, "Dateline: A. Hitler's Munich Love Nest," PM, 4 May 1945; O'Donnell, The Bunker, 108; Semmler, Goebbels, 188. Eva obviously made another trip out of Berlin, most probably to Munich, as Bormann's diary on March 7 noted, "In the evening Eva Braun left for Berlin with a courier train" (Beever, Fall of Berlin, 155).

194. Goebbels, Final Entries, 1945, 270.

195. Toland, 100 Days, 100, 271–72; von Lang, 320, says Feb. 24.

196. Trevor-Roper, 111 (p. 148 in 1962 bkb. ed.); von Lang, 320; "Other departments" Georg von Hengl, "Report on the Alpine Fortress."

197. O'Donnell, The Bunker, 140, 296–97, 308–09; Baur, Hitler's Pilot, 188.

198. "Russian media" New York Herald Tribune, 2 May 1945; "Reitsch" Gun, 262, Reitsch book…; Yelena Rzhevskaya in "Hitler's trail leads to Moscow," World Press Review, July 1995; Toland, Adolf Hitler, 1223; Speer, 474. Cross, Fallen Eagle, 221.

199. Ibid., 475; Irving, Göring, 455–57, 459 (in his book Hitler's Pilot, Baur said that this meeting took place on April 17); Bernhard Frank, 103; "Reitsch" U.S. Army Counter Intelligence Corps, Man Named, 304.

200. U.S. Army, Office of Strategic Services, Art Looting Investigation Unit, the Göring Collection, Consolidated Interrogation Report No. 2, 15 Sept. 1945, part XI.

201. "Himmler" Wulff, Zodiac and Swastica, 164–65, 189; Trevor-Roper, 126; Hinsley, British Intelligence, 736–37; Kershaw, Hitler, 1936-1945, 816–19.

202. Toland, Hitler, 1192–93; Fest, Hitler, 739; Junge, Until the Final Hour, 161; "Keitel" Ryan, 435; "Berger claims he urged Hitler to remain in Berlin" Trevor-Roper, 126–27; "Reitsch" U.S. Army Counter Intelligence Corps history, v. 14, 303–04; Robert E. Work, "Last Days in Hitler's Air Raid Shelter," Public Opinion Quarterly 10, no. 4 (Winter 1946–47), 565–81; W. Byford-Jones, Berlin Twilight, 104; "Saur" Irving, Hitler's War, 792, 798.

203. Emmy Göring, My Life with Göring, 116; Joachimsthaler, 68, 100; Irving, Hitler's War, 804–05; Morell, 272; Baur, Hitler's Pilot, 189.

204. Von Lang, 321; "two secretaries" Toland, 1186; "Schröder" Ib Melchior and Frank Brandenburg, Quest: Searching for Germany's Nazi Past, 100–01; "Eva" ibid., 1192; "Magda" Reuth, Goebbels, 356; H. Hoffmann, Hitler Was My Friend, 228; Fritz Redlich, Hitler: Diagnosis of a Destructive Prophet, 215; "Morell" interview by Tania Long, New York Times, 22 May 1945, Baur, Hitler's Pilot, 181; Riefenstahl, Leni Riefenstahl, 302.

205. Bezymenski, The Death of Adolf Hitler, 11–13; "Catastrophe" Robert Harris, Selling Hitler, 32; "Trevor-Roper" Margueritte Johnson, "Black ink and red swastikas," Time, 2 May 1983; O'Donnell, The Bunker, 97–98, 116–18; Ian Sayer and Douglas Botting, Nazi Gold, 40. 2000 passes were issued for those who composed this evacuation group (Beever, Fall of Berlin, 261).

206. For the "Hitler Diaries" see Robert Harris, Selling Hitler; for a summary of this caper, see pp. 1–2. Some contemporaries have asserted that German intelligence officers shortly recovered crates of material from near the crash site and after the war the "Bormann group" had them transported to safe keeping in Spain (Melchior and Brandenburg, Quest, 177–78, 185, 289–92).

207. "Eva" U.S. Army Counter Intelligence Corps history, v. 14, 368–69, 448–49, 407, 366; "Herta" Frank, Eva Braun, 286–87; Kershaw, Hitler, 1936-1945, 1031, ref. 52.

208. O'Donnell, The Bunker, 124n; "Mata O'Hara" O'Donnell, 177–215, 33n. Neither ULTRA intercepts nor a claim by a captured German general that Hitler would remain in Berlin were conclusive evidence that he would do so (Meek, 68–69).

209. Ralph Bennett, Ultra in the West, 199–200; Jeff Korte, "Eisenhower, Berlin and the National Redoubt," Gateway: An Academic History Journal on the Web, 26–27, 32; "very end of April" Hinsley, British Intelligence in the Second World War, 734–35. General Ritter von Hengl later estimated that ninety percent of the 250,000 German military personnel, including about 460 generals, who piled into the Alps, were non-combatants (Meek, 80).

210. Von Lang, 321; "military" Beierl, 195; "Herrgesell" Jack Fleischer report, 16 May 1945, New York Herald Tribune; complete article, Jack Stenback, ed., Typewriter Battalion, 360; "Schmidt" New York Herald Tribune, 14 May 1945.

211. "Families" Sayer and Botting, Nazi Gold, 88; "Himmler mistress" Speer, 216; Toland, Hitler, 1190, 1208; von Lang, The Secretary, 324–25; Sayer and Botting, America's Secret Army, 304–05.

212. Infield, Skorzeny, 116; Sayer and Botting, Nazi Gold, 27–36, "11 boxes" 63–64, 114, 215–16; "Jacob" 87, 276; "2200 gold coins" McGovern, Martin Bormann, 120, 200.

213. Ibid., 26, 41–47; Infield, Skorzeny, 97–98; "Toplitzsee" The Guardian, London, 25 Jan. 2000.

214. Other organizations, art collections: Merkers; Ian Sayer and Douglas Botting, Nazi Gold, 12–15; see also Lynn H. Nicholas, The Rape of Europa: The Fate of Europe's Treasures in the Third Reich and the Second World War.

215. Zweig, The Gold Train, 73, 79, 83, 96–100, 119–20. "U.S. Government compensation" AP report, 11 March 2005.

216. E.H. Cookridge, Gehlen: Spy of the Century, 112–18; Reinhard Gehlen, The Service: The Memoirs of General Reinhard Gehlen; Heinz Höhne and Hermann Zolling, The General Was a Spy: The Truth About General Gehlen and His Spy Ring.

217. Harris, Selling Hitler, 32–35. O'Donnell (The Bunker, 44) says Schaub was bringing some important Hitler records to the Obersalzberg. "Puttkamer" Kershaw, Hitler, 1936-1945, 800; "Eva material" U.S. Army Counter Intelligence Corps history, v.14, Man Named A.H., 273, 283–84; "Gohler and Konrad" David Irving, Action Report online, 8 July 2002; "U.S. Army Counter Intelligence Corps files" David Irving, Hitler/ Robert Gutierrez material, David Irving summary, 1983, "Real History and the search for Hitler's papers," Irving Web site.

218. Von Lang, 321; Bernhard Frank, Obersalzberg, 95; Sayer and Botting, Nazi Gold, 76.

219. Reuth, Goebbels, 356; O'Donnell, The Bunker, 122–23.

220. Irving, Hitler's War, 798 (and refs. p. 898), 809–10 (and refs. p. 900); Joachim Fest, Speer: The Final Verdict.

221. O'Donnell, The Bunker, 122–23.

222. Hofer, "The National Redoubt," 10–11, 22; Hinsley, British Intelligence, 732, 735.

223. Hengl, "Report on the Alpine Fortress," 2–7, 11–12, Hengl, "The Alpine Redoubt," 9–11; "300,000 surrendered" see Chapter 4, pp. 1–4.

224. Minnott, 100–01, 103–05; Moor, "The Old Order."

225. Toland, 100 Days, 440–41, 582; Minnott, 87, 101–02.

226. Black, Kaltenbrunner, 235–39, 257–58.

227. Ibid., 242–45; "Skorzeny" U.S. Army Counter Intelligence Corps history, v. 14, Man Named A.H., 550, 558.

228. James Lucas, World War II through German Eyes, 182–84.

229. Toland, 100 Days, 427–32; "Galland" Manvell and Fränkel, Göring, 299; Irving, 14–19, 455–57, 461; Leonard Mosley, The Reich Marshal, 314–16; Irving, Göring, 456–57, 461; Petrova and Watson, Death of Hitler, 78.

230. "Ovation" Kuby, 101; "Sudetengau" Gen. Brauchitsch in Trial of the Major War Criminals ("Nuremberg trials") transcript; "Herrgesell" Jack Fleischer dispatch, New York Herald Tribune, 16 May 1945; complete Fleischer article "All is 'Kaput' for Adolf," in Jack Stenback, ed., Typewriter Battalion, 358. Pierre J. Huss also interviewed Herrgesell and reported that Hitler had given the same vague mandate to Göring, but Herrgesell believed that Hitler was being sarcastic in stating that the discredited Göring would be an effective successor (International News Service, 15 May 1945, in Louis L. Snyder, ed., Masterpieces of War Reporting, 455–59). "Koller" Report of events of April 22–23, 1945, HQ, 7th Army, G-2 Documents Section, in William W. Quinn file, MHI; "next day" Kershaw, Hitler, 1936-1945, 805.

231. Göring claimed he telephoned Hitler on April 24 to propose that he take over the leadership (New York Herald Tribune, 10 May 1945). "Göring already knew" Toland, 100 Days, 429; "Koller" Trevor-Roper, 128–31; Joachim Fest, Inside Hitler's Bunker, 83–85; Emmy Göring, My Life with Göring, 122, 127–28; Toland, Hitler, 1148; Kuby, 116.

232. Bernhard Frank, 98–107, 110; Speer, Inside Third Reich, 482–83; Baur, Hitler's Pilot, 182.

233. Hinsley, British Intelligence, 739.

234. Musmanno, 132–34; Baur, 108–09; "Speer assumption about Bormann, A.H. Göring insults" Speer, Third Reich, 478–79, 482–83.

235. "Target information sheet" Beierl, History of the Eagle's Nest, 137–38, sheet, 139; Bernhard Frank, 110–20; Martin Middlebrook and Chris Everitt, The Bomber Command War Diaries, 701. 98 P-51s went on the mission but only 88 arrived on the site (Roger Freeman, Mighty Eighth War Diary, 496). Lt. Clifford J. Price (397th Fighter Squadron, 9th U.S. Air Force) recalled that he fired a rocket into the picture window of the Berghof ("Stories from WWII" Web site). "Massive tonnage" Beierl, Eagle's Nest, 183. Local people recall that the first attack was led by American planes, followed an hour later by British bombers; "Giant bombs missed Berghof" Ingrid Schartenberg and Florian Beierl interviews in White, From Fedala to Berchtesgaden, 268n. The four Allied witnesses were Lt. David Daub and Sgt. Isadore Valenti and Lt. Sherman Pratt, all of the 3rd Infantry Division, and Lt. Laurent Touyeras of the French 2nd Armored Division.

236. Berchtesgadener Anzeiger, 30 April 1945; Beierl, interview with author; Toland, 100 Days, 439–40; Hanisch, Obersalzberg, 37. Fest, in Hitler (732), says 318 Lancaster bombers took part in the attack, while Eisenhower (Crusade in Europe, 420) said the bombing was by the U.S. Eight Air Force, with no mention of the RAF. Irving, Hitler's War, 17; New York Times, 26 April, 7 May

1945; Gun, 261. A New York Times report (8 May 1945) declared, "The walls are cracked and sagging in some spots but the building itself withstood the tremendous blasting by 350 Lancaster bombers." "Eighth Air Force area bombing" Freeman, Mighty Eighth War Diary, 496.

237. Harper, Your Complete Guide to Berchtesgaden, 111; Beierl, 195–96.

238. Ibid., 190–96.

239. Bernhard Frank, 118–21; Irving, Göring, 19–20.

240. Military Government Berchtesgaden, "First Annual Report," 5 May 1945–20 June 1946, p. 5, OMGB 10/77/115.

241. Robert E. Work, "Last Days in Hitler's Air Raid Shelter," Public Opinion Quarterly 10, no. 4 (Winter 1946–47), 565–81.

242. Baur, Hitler's Pilot, 187.

243. "Marriages" Baur, Hitler's Pilot, 184; Musmanno, 173; "Junge" Gerald McKnight, The Strange Loves of Adolf Hitler, 23; Infield, Eva and Hitler, 281–84; "Schenck" O'Donnell, The Bunker, 162; "Flegal" Man Called A.H., 357. "Führerbunker" Irving, Hitler's War, 822; Trevor-Roper, (1962 ed.), 242; Joachim Fest (Inside Hitler's Bunker, p. 101), says the other weddings took place after the Adolf-Eva nuptials.

244. "Posters" Joseph Persico, Nuremberg: Infamy on Trial, 360–61; "search" Thomas Elliott, interview with author; "fate of Bormann" Farago, 122, 125, 129; Stevenson, Bormann Brotherhood, 109; O'Donnell, The Bunker, 296–309; Beierl, interview with author; Denis Staunton, "Bormann's Ashes Are Dumped in the Baltic," The Guardian, 29 Aug. 1999.

245. Nigel West, MI5, 81, 89n.; "Giesler" David C. Lodge, Where Ghosts Walked, 343; Sayer and Botting, Nazi Gold, 87, 60; James S. Plaut, "Hitler's Capital: Loot for the Master Race," Atlantic Monthly, Oct. 1946, 75.

246. Trevor-Roper, 127; Alexander in Romilly and Alexander, Privileged Nightmare, 220–31; Nichol and Rennell, 364–71.

247. Hinsley, British Intelligence (abridged ed.) 614–15.

248. Geiss, 196; "Göring's freight load of art" Harper, Your Complete Guide to Berchtesgaden, 109, 112; Bernard Taper, "Investigating Art Looting for the MFA & A," 136–37; "Frank's permission" Bernhard Frank, 129–30; "25,000 bottles of wine" Goebbels, Goebbels Diaries, 262n; Beierl, interview with author; U.S. Army, Office of Strategic Services, Art Looting Investigation Unit, Göring Collection, part XI.

249. Sayer and Botting, 77; Kesselring, Kesselring, 332; Geiss, 186–87, 194; "Goehler statement to U.S. Army Counter Intelligence Corps" A Man Called A.H., 529–31; "Konrad" ibid., 548, 409, 271–80, xiii.

250. Kershaw, Hitler Myth, 223; Marlis Steinert, Hitler's War and the Germans, 253, n. 273, 282; "no response" Haste, Nazi Women, 227; Eberstein, "National Redoubt"; Hofmann, "National Redoubt"; Berchtesgadener Anzeiger, 25 April–4 May 1945.

251. "Jacob agreement" Bernhard Frank, 121, 129–30; Harris, 34–35; Beierl, interview with author; Hanisch, Obersalzberg, 30.

252. Geiss, 186–87; Military Government Berchtesgaden, "Report of Military Government: Berchtesgaden," 5 May 1945–20 June 1946," p. 5–6.

253. Hengl, "Report on the Alpine Fortress," 8; Sayer and Bottling, Nazi Gold, 77; Moor, "Old Order." Major Richard Winters said he found General Kastner's body in the Luftwaffe officers' club on the road to the Königssee

(Ambrose, *Band of Brothers*, 277). White, *From Fedala to Berchtesgaden*, 280; Reiss, *Chicago Daily News*, 11 May 1945.

254. United States Army, Information and Education Services, *Blue and White Devils*, 1–2; O'Daniel: de Lattre, *French First*, 355–56; Higgins, *News Is a Singular Thing*, 86; Prescott, *Command Missions*, 548; R.M. Ancell, *Biographical Dictionary of World War II Generals and Flag Officers*, 342; "son" Whiting, *Forgotten Army*, 94.

255. Toole, *Battle Diary*, xxvi, xxix; Scott, *Blue and White Devils*, 165.

256. Ambrose, *Band of Brothers*; Leonard Rapport and Arthur Norwood, Jr., *Rendezvous with Destiny: A History of the 101st Airborne Division*, 730–31; David K. Webster, "We Drank Hitler's Champagne," *Saturday Evening Post*, 3 May 1952; Moor, "The Old Order."

257. Maule, *Out of the Sand*; Alain Godec, interview with author; Blumenson, ed., *Patton Papers*, 511; Presidential unit citation, War Department, General Orders no. 44, 6 June 1945; Maule, 259–62, 266, 269, 271.

258. David Webster, *Parachute Infantry: An American Paratrooper's Memoir of D-Day and the Fall of the Third Reich*, 186–87; "rear-guard attacks on French" Biddiscombe, *Werwolf!*, 172–77.

259. Kuntz, narrative, 77, 79.

260. U.S. Army, *The Seventh United States Army in France and Germany, 1944–1945: Report of Operations*, v. 2, 852, 855; "506th to be first" Donald Burgett, *Beyond the Rhine*, 127–28; Pratt, *Autobahn to Berchtesgaden*, 592–93.

261. *Ibid.*, 570–71, 576–81, 586–90.

262. "Skorzeny" Ibid., 591, who was captured on May 17. *New York Times*, 22 May 1945; G-2 Periodic Report, 3, 4 May 1945, N.A., RG 94, 303–2.1.

263. Kuntz, narrative, 79.

264. U.S. Army, *Seventh United States Army in France and Germany*, v. 2, 852; Whiting, *Forgotten Army*, 216–18.

265. U.S. Army, *Seventh United States Army in France and Germany*, v. 2, 855; Hq., 7th Inf., 4 May 1945, N.A. R.G. 407, 303–3.2; Girard, "Temoignage de l'Aide de Camp du General Leclerc de Hauteclocque"; Pratt, 565–66.

266. Lloyd Ramsey, correspondence with author; John A. Heintges, oral history transcript, 378–83.

267. Rapport and Northwood, 731–32; Webster, *Parachute Infantry*, 186; "not apprehensive" Jack Agnew, interview with author; *New York Times*, 5, 7 May 1945.

268. 506th PIR After Action report, 1–10 May 1945; Pratt, 592–93.

269. Webster, "We Drank Hitler's Champagne," *Saturday Evening Post*, 3 May 1953, 134–39.

270. Girard, "Temoignage de l'Aide de Camp"; "Fray" Whiting, *Forgotten Army*, 213.

271. Heintges, oral history transcript, 381; Maule, 276–77; White, *From Fedala to Berchtesgaden*, 279; William B. Rosson, oral history transcript, 136–37.

272. Ramsey, correspondence with author.

273. Cloer, "The Final Days of the War"; Lloyd Ramsey, correspondence with author; Whiting, *Forgotten Army*, 213–14; "everybody" U.S. Army, *Seventh United States Army in France and Germany*, v. 2, 855.

274. Pratt, 594–95.

275. Hanisch, *Obersalzburg*, 38; Geiss, 191, 196; Military Government Berchtesgaden, "Report of Military Government: Berchtesgaden, 5 May 1945–20 June 1946," 6.

276. Pratt, 596; 506th Parachute Infantry Regiment, After Action Report, 1–10 May 1945, Summary Report, 1945; Heintges, 388–89.

277. Pratt, 595–96; Rosson, oral history transcript, 138; Heintges, 385; "booby-trapped" 3rd Inf. Div. report, 4 May 1945; 7th Inf. Regt. report, 5 May 1945.

278. Marguerite Higgins report, *New York Herald Tribune*, 5 May 1945.

279. Devers said, "I am convinced that until I can turn the First French Army back to the French Government, I will have lots of annoying details to put up with. However, this does not bother me at all" (*Diary*, 6 May 1945). Weigley, *Eisenhower's Lieutenants*, 714; de Lattre, *French First Army*, 495–501.

280. Daub letter, *Watch on the Rhine*, February 2002; David Daub, interview with author, 22 Feb. 2003.

281. HQ 7th Inf. Regt. report, 5 May 1945; "Rachicle" Third Infantry Division, *Front Line*, 12 May 1945; Pratt, 596–602, 608–10; Heintges, 394.

282. Isadore Valenti, *Combat Medic*, 235–36; Isadore Valenti, interview with author.

283. Donald Straith, correspondence with author; Webster, *Parachute Infantry*, 189.

284. "Agreement with French" U.S. Army, *Seventh United States Army in France and Germany*, v. 2, 855; Pratt, 592; White, *From Fedala to Berchtesgaen*, 280. Donald Zahn declared that the French force on the Obersalzberg was there "illegally," the area being outside its zone of occupation (Zahn, interview with author). Heintges, 394.

285. Maxwell Taylor, *Swords and Ploughshares*, 106; Ambrose, *Band of Brothers*, 272–73. The television production was vague about the capture of Bergchtesgaden and the Obersalzberg but left the impression that the 101st were there without any other units being there before it. Television, including the History channel, is entertainment. Several veterans of the Third Inf. Div. have written to Ambrose stating that their division was first to Berchtesgaden, but Ambrose did not respond to their letters (James Tubman letter, *Watch on the Rhine*, veterans of 3rd Inf. Div. newsletter, Aug. 2000).

286. "French looting" Cloer, "The Final Days of the War," 18; Taylor, *Swords*, 107; "manure" Beierl, interview with author; "reputation" Jack Agnew, interview with author; Daniel Gren, "Up into the Eagle's Nest," London *Financial Times*, 7 April 1990; "American looting" Ambrose, *Band of Brothers*, 272–75; "Heintgas" Beierl, interview with author; "Americans also looting" Hershel V. Mayo account, in Larry Mayo, <shawkids/wwii/stories> Web site; Morrell, 161n. During her long service as a stretcher bearer in the French First Armored Division, Anita Leslie says she only knew of one case of attempted rape, this by a north African soldier (*A Story Half Told*, 168); "brick/book" Godec, correspondence with author.

287. Raymond Dronne, *L'Hallali de Paris a Berchtesgaden*.

288. Godec, interview with author; "La Lettre du 40e RANA," bulletin of veterans association of a artillery unit of French Second Armored Division, no. 9, 15 April 1997.

289. Beierl, interview with author; Biddiscombe, *Werewolf!*, 172, 259–63; Wyant, *Sandy Patch*, 193.

290. Hershel Mayo account; Godec, correspondence with author.

291. Girard, "Temoignage de l'Aide de Camp"; Touyeras, "Berchtesgaden"; Alain De Boissieu, *Pour Combatte avec de Gaulle*, 313–17; French Army, Excerpts from daily log book of Group du 64 RADB (artillery battalion) of Second Armored Division, 4–5 May 1945; "Dutch flag" Godec interview with author, citing *The Longest Path*. "Missing SS officers" Bernhard Frank's account jumps

from the arranged surrender to his capture (*Hitler, Göring and the Obersalzberg*, 129, 132–37).

292. "Argument" Godec interview with author, citing Jean-Julien Fonde, *Leclerc's Wolves*; Girard, "Temoignage de l'Aide de Camp"; "two French soldiers to Eagles' Nest" Georges Esnault, "The Conquest of Berghof: Berchtesgaden," The flag was given to Raymond Dronne by a French woman while he was in hospital in Alexandria, Egypt, with Dronne promising to raise it on German territory (Godec, correspondence with author).

293. Touyeras, "Berchtesgaden"; Girard, "Temoignage de l'Aide de Camp"; "French damage to Platterhof" Georg Mehr account, in Moor, "Old Order."

294. Girard, "Temoignage de l'Aide de Camp"; Mark Bando, *101st Airborne: From Holland to the Eagle's Nest*; Beierl, *History of the Eagles Nest*, 140, Beierl, interview with author; "watches" *PM*, 15 May 1945.

295. Heintges, 395–99; "Lively discussion" Touyeras, "Berchtesgaden"; Ramsey, correspondence with author; Pratt, 611–113; "French troops participated" photograph provided by Florian Beierl.

296. The 7th Inf. Regt. report recorded that on May 5 "a flag raising ceremony was held in the afternoon..." without mentioning the French presence (Daily report, 6 May 1945, N.A., R. G. 407, 303–3.2). Donald G. Taggart, ed., *History of the Third Infantry Division in World War II*, 370–73, 367; Beierl, interview with author.

297. White, *Fedela to Berchtesgaden*, 281; Heintges, oral history transcript, 385–87.

298. Daub, interview with author.

299. Report Military Government—Berchtesgaden, pp. 6, 28.

300. Jacques de Guillebon, account of artillery battalion of French Second Armored Division, in D. Roudeau and R. Stephane, eds., *Des Hommes Libre: La France Libre par Ceaux Quil'ont Faite*, 385; Beierl, *History of the Eagle's Nest*, 141; de Boissieu, *Pour Combatte Avec de Gaulle*, 316.

301. De Guillebon account, in Roudeau and Stephane, 383; memoir in *Le Chemin Le Plus Long* ("The Longest Road").

302. Jacques Beal, *Marechal Philippe Leclerc de Hautecloque*, 43, 52–53; "Les Editions du Port-Glaive," in *Figures de l'Historie Nr 2* (August 1991); Godec, interview with author; Jean Mabire, *La Brigade Frankreich*.

303. William Heller, 3rd Inf. Div. Web site; Hamburger, "Letter from Berchtesgaden"; French Army, Excerpts from daily log book of Group du 64 RADB (artillery battalion) of Second Armored Division,

304. Rapport and Northwood, 73–32.

305. Webster, *Parachute Infantry*, 190–96.

306. Miller, *Lee Miller's War*, 199–200. The first woman journalist to arrive on the scene probably was Evelyn Irons of the London *Standard* (*Los Angeles Times*, 2 May 2000).

307. Higgins, "U.S. Flag Flies Over Ruins of Berchtesgaden," *New York Herald Tribune*, 7 May 1945. "Negatives" The soldier brought them home to Michigan (Statement of Harold Deutsch, *Captured German and Related Records*, p. 114).

308. Webster, 196–99.

309. Knauth, *Germany in Defeat*, 125–26.

310. "Walton" Nancy C. Sorel, *The Women Who Wrote the War*, 370.

311. Avalon Project, Nuremberg Trial Proceedings, vol. 2, p. 273.

312. Zahn, who said the French unit was illegally on the Obersalzberg, the area being outside its zone, was

assisted by French-speaking Sgt. Leroy Gros of New Iberia, Louisiana (Zahn, interview with author). Girard, "Temoignage de l'Aide de Camp"; U.S. Army, *Official Diary, 7th Army*, 691; Mark Bando interview; Godec, correspondence with author.

313. Toole, *Battle Diary*, 153.

314. "Tourists" Wyant, *Sandy Patch*, 199, 205; Florian Beierl in Ryback, "Hitler's Forgotten Library." 3000 of Hitler's books, representing an estimated ten percent of his collection, were shipped to the U.S.A., with 1200 of them ending up in the Library of Congress (*ibid.*).

315. Heintges, oral history transcript, 390, 394.

316. Clay, *Decision in Germany*, 81–82; 7th Inf. Regt. daily report, 6 May 1945, N.A. Record Group 407, 303–3.2. On his first visit Lt. Kay Summersby, U.S.A., rode around with him in his jeep (Beierl, *Eagle's Nest*, 141). "guides" Richard Elliott, interview with author; White, 281.

317. Bahlau, interview with author; Burgett, *Beyond the Rhine*, 146.

318. Pratt, 613–14; Heintges, oral history transcript, 399–407.

319. Higgins, *News Is a Singular Thing*, 96–97.

320. "From Chad to Berchtesgaden you have prevailed. In the name of France I ask you and demand from you that you show in the service of your country the same energy tomorrow in peace that you have given yesterday in war" (*Journal de Marche du 1/3e R.A.C.* ["Journal of March of 1/3 Colonial Artillery Regiment, of French Second Armored Division"], 95).

321. Reuben E. Jenkins, "The Battle of the National Redoubt: Operational Phase," 16–26 .

322. Burgett, *Beyond the Rhine*, 134, 139; Ambrose, *Band of Brothers*, 273–74.

323. Burgett, 135, 152–53.

324. Bahlau, interview with author.

325. *New York Times*, 8 May 1945; London *Times*, 9 May 1945.

326. *PM*, 20 May 1945.

327. John F. Kennedy, *Prelude to Leadership*, 73–74, and Hugh Sidey note, xliii.

# Chapter Four

1. *New York Times*, 5 May 1945; Charles Marshall, *A Ramble Through My War*, 270; Webster, *Parachute Infantry*, 196–97; David A. Foy, *For You the War Is Over*.

2. Webster, 197–99.

3. Rapport and Northwood, Jr., 757; Knauth, *Germany in Defeat*, 167–68.

4. Webster, 197; Rapport and Northwood, 757; Higgins, "500,000 Nazis Trek to Munich Unguarded and in Battle Array," *New York Herald Tribune*, 29 May 1945.

5. Reuben Jenkins typescript, p. 21, MHI; Martin Gilbert, *The Day the War Ended*, 256–57.

6. Rapport and Northwood, 737–740; Ambrose, *Band of Brothers*, 274–75.

7. *Chicago Daily News*, 8 May 1945.

8. Karl Hugo Pruys, *Kohl: Genius of the Present*, 7–8.

9. Ernst von Salomon, *Fragebogen*, 323, 393, 403–04, 416–45.

10. "Snipers" Al Hassenzahl interview, Heintges, oral history transcript, 388; "minor problems" Military Government Berchtesgaden, "First Annual Report," 5 May 1945—20 June 1946; 506 Parachute Infantry Regiment,

After Action Report, 1–10 May 1945, Historical Record, 11–31 May 1945; London *Times*, 28 May 1945; Toole, *Battle Diary*, 151–52; "minor sabotage" Rapport and Northwood, 756; Biddiscombe, *Werwolf!*, 186–87.

11. Bernhard Frank, 122–23, 128; Irving, *Göring*, 19–22; Robert E. Conot, *Justice at Nuremberg*, 32.

12. Stack, "Capture of Göring," 36th Infantry Division Web site.

13. "Baton" Patch Papers, Patch to Dow Richardson, 16 Oct. 1945; Julia Patch to G.X. Lester, 4 June 1947; "emeralds" *Official Diary for the Commanding General, Seventh Army*, 9 May 1945, p. 696; "Truman" *Richmond Times-Dispatch*, 17 June 1945.

14. Conot, 467–69, 542; G.M. Gilbert, *Nuremberg Diary*, 198–99; Nicholas, *Rape of Europa*, 345; *New York Herald Tribune*, 12, 15 May 1945; Eisenhower order, 8 May 1945, in William Quinn Papers, MHI; Irving, *Göring*, 471–72.

15. Kesselring, *Kesselring*, 333–43; *Chicago Tribune*, 10 May 1945.

16. Third Infantry Division, Operations Report, May 1–10, 1945, National Archives; Whiting, *Forgotten Army*, 216–18.

17. Kesselring, 290–91; Rapport and Northwood, 741; Taylor, *Swords and Plowshares*, 108; Knauth, *Germany in Defeat*, 102; "Kesselring capitulation" ibid., 92–102; *Stars and Stripes*, 18 May 1945; "most surprised" AP report, *Chicago Daily News*, 10 May 1945.

18. Earl Ziemke, *U.S. Army in the Occupation of Germany*, 322.

19. Kesselring, 343–44; Wistrich, *Who's Who in Nazi Germany*, 138–39.

20. Turner and Jackson, *Destination Berchtesgaden: The Story of the United States Seventh Army in World War II*, 180.

21. 395th U.S. Army Counter Intelligence Corps Detachment, HQ 7th Army, report, 5 July 1945; Infield, *Skorzeny*, 97–124; *New York Herald Tribune*, 18 May 1945; *New York Times*, 22 May 1945; Charles Foley, *Commando Extraordinary*, 200–01; Boatner, 507.

22. Black, *Kaltenbrunner*, 248–49, 253, 255–59; Sayer and Botting, *Nazi Gold*, 88–89; Robert Matteson, "The Last Days of Ernst Kaltenbrunner," *Studies in Intelligence* 4, no. 2 (Spring 1960), A11–A29; "Höttl" CIA History Staff, "Wilhelm Höttl: International Man of Mystery"; Höttl testimony at Eichmann trial, www.nizkor.org; Naftali, "Myth of the Alpenfestung," 227.

23. Charles Messenger, *Hitler's Gladiator ... Sepp Dietrich*, 171–73.

24. Sayer and Botting, *Nazi Gold*, 88; Rapport and Northwood, 745.

25. Padfield, 606–611.

26. "Ley" *New York Herald Tribune*, 17, 18 May 1945; Conot, *Justice at Nuremberg*, 7–72; Rapport and Northwood, 741–4; Speer, *Spandau*, 424; Ronald Smelser, *Robert Ley: Hitler's Labor Front Leader*, 291–93.

27. "Streicher" *New York Herald Tribune*, 24, 26 May 1945; Rapport and Northwood, 744–45; Conot, *Nuremberg*, 32.

28. Sayer and Botting, *Nazi Gold*, 86–87, 108–10.

29. Toland, *100 Days*, 430; Wistrich, *Who's Who in Nazi Germany*, 20; Public Relations Office statement, 22 May 1945, in 101st After Action Report, May 1945.

30. William R. McMahon, interview with author; "posters" Persico, *Nuremberg*, 360–61.

31. "Swartz" Rapport and Northwood, 743; "Morell" ibid., 749; *New York Herald Tribune*, 24 May 1945; *Chicago Daily News*, 5 May 1945; Wistrich, *Who's Who in Nazi Germany*, 65–66, 4–5.

32. "Kannenberg" Higgins, *News is a Singular Thing*, 103–04; see also Irving, *Hitler's War*, 169; "Sauckel" Goldensohn, 211.

33. *New York Herald Tribune*, 22 May 1945; Sayer and Botting, 88; "Luise Jodl" Persico, *Nuremberg*, 95.

34. George Allen, foreword to *Hitler Directs His War*, Felix Gilbert, ed., ix–xii; Allen, "The Discovery of the Hitler *Lagebesprechunger*," 53–62; *The Library Chronicle*, University of Pennsylvania, 1957, 53–62.

35. "Paula's detention" *New York Herald Tribune*, 28 May 1945; "U.S. Army Counter Intelligence Corps interview 16 May 1945" B. Hammon, *Hitler's Vienna*, 414, n. 199; "5 June 1946 interview" National Archives, R.G. 631, 31/57/05, box 87a; *Stars and Stripes*, 29 May 1945.

36. "Angela" Christa Schröder, *Er war mein Chef*, 154, 296–97 n.34, 364–46 nn. 280–82; U.S. Army Counter Intelligence Corps transcript, "The Very Uninteresting Life of Hitler's Half-sister," George Allen Papers; "death" *Wikipedia s.v.* "Angela Hitler."

37. "Alois" Wulf Schwarzwaller, *The Unknown Hitler*, 164; Beierl, interview with author; "death" *Wikipedia s.v.* "Alois Hitler, Jr."

38. John M. Taylor, *General Maxwell Taylor*, 139. Donald Straith, who was there, has said the Japanese diplomats were placed under guard and not evicted (Straith, correspondence with author). *Stars and Stripes* report dated 28 May 1945.

39. Michael Smith, *Station X: Decoding Nazi Secrets*, 224–25.

40. Rapport and Northwood, 748–49; Higgins report, *New York Herald Tribune*, 21 May 1945; Records Concerning Central Points, R.G. 260. 390/45, National Archives; Patricia Lochridge, "I Governed Berchtesgaden," *Women's Home Companion*, Aug. 1945, 4, 100. Taylor, 108; Nicholas, *Rape of Europa*, 344.

41. Plaut, "Hitler's Capital; Loot for the Master Race," *Atlantic Monthly* 178, no. 4 (Oct. 1946), 73–78.

42. Bando, *101st Airborne*, 150.

43. *Berliner Zeitung*, 9 April 1994.

44. Nicholas, 342–44; Rapport and Northwood, 748; Thomas C. Howe, *Salt Mines and Castles*, 190–911.

45. Nicholas, 345–46. The baton was presented to Gen. Patch, who donated it to the West Point museum (Wyant, *Sandy Patch*, 204); Kenneth Alford, *The Spoils of World War II*, 123–24.

46. Nicholas, 346, 351, 429; Irmgard Hunt, *On Hitler's Mountain*, 205–217; Taper, "Investigating Art Looting for the MFA & A," 135–38.

47. Taylor, 109; Nicholas, 429; "amber room" *Berliner Zeitung*, 9 April 1994; "Castle's art collection faces Nazi loot probe," *Irish Examiner*, 10 March 2005.

48. "Kaltenbrunner gold" Sayer and Botting, 89; "Berger currency" Patricia Lochridge, "I Governed Berchtesgaden"; Rapport and Northwood, 749.

49. Alford, *Spoils of World War II*, 80–84.

50. Russell Hill report, *New York Herald Tribune*, 21 May 1945; Alford, *Spoils of World War II*, 14–16.

51. Beierl, *History of the Eagle's Nest*, 190–91; Leonard E. Vierling, correspondence with author.

52. "V-2 experiments" *Stars and Stripes*, 18 June 1945; Arthur L. Smith, *Hitler's Gold: The Story of the Nazi War Loot*, 99–100; Kate Connolly, "Submarines to dredge lake for Nazi gold," *Guardian*, 25 Jan. 2000; Michael Leidig, "Mini-sub to hunt for Nazi secrets," London *Times*, 16 Jan. 2000; Melissa

Eddy, "Salvage Crew Seeks Nazi Treasures," Associated Press, 4 July 2000; CBS News, "Hitler's Lake—Part II: The Search For Answers," 3 July 2002, <CBSNews.com>.

53. "Stangass" Seymour Korman report, Chicago Tribune, 8 May 1945; "Walker Hotel" R.G. 260.4.9, National Archives; Joseph Siren, interview with author; U.S. Lady, Oct. 1961.

54. HQ 506 Parachute Infantry Regiment, After-Action Report, 1–10 May 1945, Historical Record, 11–31 May 1945; 502 Unit History, <WW2-airborne.us/units>; "501 PIR" "Overview of 101st in WW2," <WW2-airborne. us/units>; Ambrose, Band of Brothers, 295–96; Bando, 101st Airborne, 150–51; James McDonough and Richard Gardner, Skyriders: History of the 327/401 Glider Infantry, 133.

55. 506 Parachute Infantry Regiment, Historical Record, 11–31 May, 1–30 June, 1 July–2 Aug. 1945; Ambrose, Band of Brothers, 284–290.

56. Agnew, interview with author; Hans Georg Zabel, interview with author.

57. Rapport and Northwood, 755.

58. "wrecks, polo, planes" ibid., 755–56; Webster, 205–39; Richard Elliott and William McMahon, interviews with author; William Kunz manuscript, Military History Institute; Ambrose, Band of Brothers, 276–77.

59. Paul R. Miller, interview with author; <currahee.hispeed>.

60. "Aug. 1" Rapport and Northwood, 761; Hugh C. Daly, 42nd Rainbow Infantry Division History: World War II.

61. Edward N. Peterson, The American Occupation of Germany: Retreat to Victory, 351–52.

62. Marshall Knappen, And Call It Peace, 180–85.

63. Some examples of this criticism: Drew Middleton, "Failure in Germany" Colliers, 17 Feb. 1946; Edward P. Morgan, "Heels Among the Heroes," Colliers, 18 Oct. 1946; and John Dos Passos, "Americans Are Losing the Victory," Life, 7 Jan. 1946. Bud Hutton and Andy Rooney, Conqueror's Peace: A Report to the American Stockholders; "Collins appeal" ibid., 34.

64. John Willoughby, Remaking the Conquering Heroes, 12–13, 16–22; Truscott, Command Missions, 514; Russell Hill, Struggle for Germany, 113, 115.

65. James P. Warburg, Germany: Bridge or Battleground, 82–83; Peterson, 87–91, 157, 259, 162–65; Harold Zink, American Military Government in Germany, 28–30; Hill, Struggle for Germany, 121.

66. Kenneth W. Hechler, "The Enemy Side of the Hill: The 1945 Background on Interrogation of German Commanders," in Donald S. Detwiler, ed., World War II: German Military Studies, vol. 1, pp. 135–36; "five cents" Franklin Davis Jr., Come as a Conqueror, 138.

67. Stars and Stripes, 21 March 1945.

68. Peterson, 272–75, 325.

69. Ibid., 306–13, 334.

70. Ibid., 176, 236, 244.

71. Ibid., 31–34, 89–90, 96–97, 175–76; Shuster, The Ground I Walked On, 195; Peterson, 301.

72. Eisenhower announced the non-fraternization policy on 12 Sept. 1944—the date U.S. forces first entered German territory (Davis, 142, see also 143); Zink, American Military Government in Germany, 238–39; U.S. Army, Special Service ed., Pocket Guide No. 10: Germany, 4–10; Padover, "Why Americans Like German Women," American Mercury, Sept. 1946.

73. Ziemke, 324–25, 332, 421; "armband" Bahlau, interview with author; "armbands for German women" Ambrose, Band of Brothers, 289.

74. Delbert Clark, Again the Goose Step, 230–32; New York Herald Tribune, 14 May 1945.

75. Yank staff correspondents, "Fraternization," Yank, 31 Aug. 1945; Percy Knauth, "Fraternization: The word takes on a brand-new meaning in Germany," Life, 2 July 1945. GI attraction to German females was sometimes called "frauleinization."

76. James P. O'Donnell, "Do the Fräuleins Change Our Joe?" Newsweek, 24 Dec. 1945; Padover, "Why Americans Like German Women"; John Willoughby, "The Sexual Behavior of American GIs During the Early Years of the Occupation of Germany," Journal of Military History 62 (Jan. 1998), 155–74; "Monty" Knauth, "Fraternization."

77. Stars and Stripes, 30 May, 11 June 1945; Eugene Davidson, The Death and Life of Germany, 55; Saul K. Padover, Experiment in Germany, 263; Ziemke, 324.

78. Nair, "The Blind Spots of Capt. Springer," Aachen, 19 Feb. 1945, in Cedric Belfrage, Seeds of Destruction, 66; Knauth, "Fraternization."

79. Peterson, 154–55; Davis, 145, 194–95; Davidson, 55–56; 506th Parachute Infantry Regiment, Historical Record, 11 May–2 Aug. 1945; Zahn, interview with author; John W. Dower, Embracing Defeat: Japan in the Wake of World War II, 124–132.

80. Hill, Struggle for Germany, 143; Peterson, 122, 156, 171, 296; "3 servants" Paul W. Gulgowski, American Military Government, 378; Ziemke, 325.

81. Hans Habe, Our Love Affair with Germany, 22; Ute Frevert, Women in Germany History: From Bourgeois Emancipation to Sexual Liberation, 258.

82. Ziemke, 421.

83. Official Gazette, 14 May 1945.

84. Knauth, Germany in Defeat, 164; Patricia Lochridge, "I Governed Berchtesgaden," Women's Home Companion, Aug. 1945, 4, 100.

85. Official Gazette, 14 May 1945; Rapport and Northwood, 756.

86. Patricia Lochridge, "I Governed Berchtesgaden"; Moor, "The Old Order"; Official Gazette, 24 Nov. 1945.

87. Official Gazette, 14 May, 11 Aug. 1945; Patricia Lochridge, "I Governed Berchtesgaden."

88. Official Gazette, 26 May, 2 June 1945.

89. Ibid., 16, 2, 9 June 1945; Ziemke, 332.

90. Ibid., 322–23, 326; Peterson, 90; Davidson, 127–30, 277–78.

91. Official Gazette, 16 June, 6, 20 Oct., 15 Dec. 1945; "concentration camp" W.L. White, Report on the Germans, 137; Irmgard Hunt, On Hitler's Mountain, 242–43.

92. Zink, American Military Government in Germany, 130–46; Habe, Our Love Affair with Germany, 27–32; Douglas Botting, From the Ruins of the Reich, 261–62; Gulgowski, American Military Government, 333–38; "influx of ex–Nazis" Moor, "The Old Order"; "10,000 of 38,000 in Nazi organizations" ibid.

93. Official Gazette, 15 Dec., 24 Nov. 1945.

94. Harper, Your Complete Guide to Berchtesgaden, 112; "Ukranians" Ihor Lysyj, The Ukranian Weekly, 1 June 1997.

95. "3000 a day" Rapport and Northwood, 747; "GI crime rate" Sayer and Botting, Nazi Gold, 311; Gulgowski, 236–38. For an example of the trouble an occupation soldier could get into, see Finn McMahon (Post Bellum Blues), 196–237.

96. Moor, "Old Order"; Gulgowski, 236.

97. Moor, "Old Order."

98. Wolfgang Friedmann, Allied Military Government of Germany, 43–46.

99. Gulgowski, 244–52, 260–64; Dagmar Barnouw, *Germany 1945: Views of War and Violence*, 61.

100. Laurence Critchell, *Four Stars of Hell*, 308; "bread" Beierl, interview with author; Irmgard Hunt, *On Hitler's Mountain*, 224, 232–34, 247–50; "girls" Barbara Ulrich Cherish and her sister Antje Wagenführ in Barbara Ulrich Cherish, interview with author; Irmgard Hunt, *On Hitler's Mountain*, 225–26.

101. N. von Wurzbach, *Berchtesgaden: Mountains, Customs and Legends*, 97–99; Joseph Siren, interview with author.

102. *U.S. Lady*, Oct. 1961; Wurzbach, *Berchtesgaden*, 99–105.

103. *U.S. Lady*, Oct. 1961.

104. Siren, interview with author.

105. *Ibid.*

106. [DiPietro] Military Government Berchtesgaden, "First Annual Report," 5 May–20 June 1945; *Berchtesgadener Anzeiger*, 18 July 1945; Siren, interview with author. The members of this MG unit, training together for this assignment since September 1944, consisted of Capt. DiPietro, 1st Lt. William Gibson, 2nd Lt. Arvo Nappa, Cpl. James Seevers, Cpl. Robert Vollbehr, Pfc. Leo Shargel, Pfc. John Wahlberg and Pfc. Joseph Mathews; "Jacob" Military Government Berchtesgaden, "First Annual Report"; Moor, "Old Order." Jacob was removed from office in the 1960s after being involved in the illegal disposition of property used by the Berchtesgaden Recreation Center (Beierl, interview with author).

107. Military Government Berchtesgaden, Detachment 311, "First Annual Report," 5 May 1945–30 June 1946.

108. Military Government Berchtesgaden, Detachment 311, monthly report, Feb. 1946, OMGB 10/77, 115–17.

109. Military Government Berchtesgaden, Detachment 311, First Annual Report, 5 May 1945–20 June 1946.

110. *Ibid.*

111. *Ibid.*; second annual report, 1 July 1946–30 June 1947.

112. Military Government Berchtesgaden, Detachment 311, "First Annual Report," 5 May 1945–20 June 1946.

113. *Official Gazette*, 13 April 1946.

114. *Ibid.*, 18 May 1946.

115. *Ibid.*, and 1 May 1946.

116. Berchtesgaden Military Government Berchtesgaden, monthly report, 20 Aug.–20 Sept. 1946.

117. *Ibid.*

118. *Ibid.*; 2nd annual report, 1 July–30 June 1946.

119. *Ibid.*, quarterly report, 1 Jan.–31 March 1948.

120. Goerg Mehr in Moor, "Old Order"; "tiles" Norbert Muhlen, *Return of Germany*, 31; Rapport and Northwood, 441; "Zum Turken" Moor, "Old Order"; Walden, "Third Reich in Ruins"; Ingrid Scharfenberg, interview with author; Zum Turken Web site.

121. Everett Schoening, U.S. State Dept. resident officer in Berchtesgaden, in Moor, "Old Order."

122. Georg Mehr statement, in Moor, "Old Order."

123. *Ibid.*

124. *New York Times*, 22 Feb. 1951, 21 July 1951, editorial 9 Aug. 1951; Beierl, *History of the Eagle's Nest*, 150–52.

125. Muhlen, *Return of Germany*, 33; Kurt P. Tauber, *Beyond Eagle and Swastika*, 197, 1078–79; "Natinform" Tauber, 244, 249–50, 323, 1120, 1154; "World Aryan Congress" Tauber, 1154, n. 178. There is no record of this meeting being held in Dublin.

126. Tauber, 193, 251, 1074–75, 1079, 629.

127. "demolition authority" Memorandum of Maj. Gen George Hay, 11 Feb. 1949, Military Government Berchtesgaden 17/162–63/13; Shuster to Hans Ehard, Minister President of Bavaria, 1 Nov. 1951, Bavarian State Archives, Munich, StK 114/ 105; Ingrid Scharfenberg, interview with author.

128. *New York Times*, 27 July 1951; Muhlen, *Return of Germany*, 32; *Life*, 2 June 1952; Geiss, 200–01; Moor, "The Old Order," 57–67.

129. *Ibid.*

130. American High Commission for Germany to Land Commissioner for Bavaria, 1 Nov. 1951, letter of agreement concerning transfer of building sites, Bavarian State Archives; Moor, "The Old Order"; *Life*, 2 June 1952; author's observation, 1995.

131. *New York Times*, 12 May 1952; American High Commission for Germany, letter of agreement.

132. "Recreate Berghof," *TZ Munich*, 17 Dec. 1968, 4 Jan. 1969; Beierl, interview with author.

133. "Kuwait and Bosnia" David Harper and Beierl, interview with author.

134. Beierl, interview with author; Iris Melcher, interview with author.

135. *Los Angeles Times*, 3 Feb. 1995; *Baltimore Sun*, 20 Feb. 1995.

136. Author's observation, 1996 visit; George Böhmer, "Americans returning Alpine property to reluctant Germans," Associated Press, 19 Feb. 1995; Tony Patterson, "Furor in the Eagle's Nest," *The European*, 31 March–6 April 1995; *Berchtesgadener Anzeiger*, 27 March 1995; "Alpine view, legacy of demons," *New York Times*, 13 Sept. 1995; Elizabeth Moser, "Business comes before morality...," *Burgerliste der Stadt Salzburg*, 27 Dec. 1995.

137. *Berchtesgadener Anzeiger*, 13 Dec. 1996; London *Sunday Telegraph*, 24 Oct. 1999. Until the area around the Berghof was cleared some unknown person or persons maintained a circle of white stones, regularly decorated with flowers, in front of the site (author's observation, 1995 visit; and Beierl, interview with author).

138. *Berchtesgadener Anzeiger*, 11 April, 9 Dec. 1997; Fiona Fleck, "Bavarians face legacy of Hitler retreat," Reuters, 1 Feb. 1998; "advisory board appointed" Bavarian Finance Ministry press release, 5 June 1997; Louise Potterton, "Hitler home ... for sale," London *Telegraph*, 27 Sept. 1998.

139. "German State finds investor...," Reuters, 19 Nov. 1998; Michael Leidig, "Hitler hotel faces demolition," London *Telegraph*, 5 Dec. 1998; "Arabian bankers sue...," Associated Press, 22 Nov. 1998.

140. Fascism Watch Web site, vol. 1.4, Oct. 1997; "Outrage at Third Reich museum," London *Sunday Telegraph*, 24 Oct. 1999; Patterson, "Furor in the Eagle's Nest."

141. "Town puts Nazi past on display," Associated Press, 21 Oct. 1999.

142. Beierl, interview with author; Roland Losch, "New documentation center...," Associated Press, 21 Oct. 1999.

143. "Ingrid Scharfenberg, owner of Zum Turken" Nada Weigelt, "What next when the Americans leave the Führer's vacation retreat?," *Deutsche Presse-Agentur*, 8 Feb. 1995; Fleck, "Bavarians face legacy of Hitler retreat."

144. "Hitler's mountaintop retreat gets new information center," Associated Press, 22 Oct. 1999; Horst Moller, Volker Dahm and Hartmut Mehringer, eds., *Die todlich Utopie*. Obersalzberg Documentation Center Web site.

145. Peter Finn, "Memory and Renewal Clash at Hitler's 'Lair'," *Washington Post*, 4 September 2001; "Hotel

Hitler" *Newsweek International*, 16 July 2001; Kate Connolly, *The Observer* (London), 5 August 2001; Mitchell
Symons, "The Hitler Hotel Has No Room for a Sense of
Shame," *Daily Express* (London), 6 Sept. 2002; "Hitler's
former Alpine retreat site of new luxury hotel," AFP, 28
Feb. 2005; Brian Boyd, *Irish Times*, 5 March 2005; Timothy Ryback, "The Hitler Shrine," 131–34; Reuters report,
1 March 2005.

146. "Stangass" *Chicago Tribune*, 8 May 1945; "furniture" *Deutsche Presse-Agentur*, 3 Jan. 1998; London *Independent*, 3 Dec. 2000; "building" London *Times*, 29 May 2000.

147. "German government program" London *Sunday
Telegraph*, 11 Feb. 2001; Jane Kramer, "The Politics of Mem-
ory," *New Yorker*, 14 Aug. 1995; Stephen Greenblatt,
"Ghosts of Berlin," *New York Times*, 28 April 1999; "Berlin
Jewish museum" T.J. Reed, "Unplayable History," *Times
Literary Supplement*, 5 Oct. 2001; "Bundestag approves

Holocaust memorial," BBC online, 25 June 1999; John
Hooper, "Monumental hassles in Berlin," *Guardian* (London) 26 Sept. 2000, Knight Ridder Newspapers, 11 May
2005; "Nuremberg" Finn, "Memory and Renewal Clash
at Hitler's 'Lair'."

148. "Web site" ABC News, 6 April 2000; "Linz
gallery" U.S. Army, Office of Strategic Services, "Linz:
Hitler's Museum and Library"; "Linz museum" R.G.
260.390/45, National Archives; "shop" *Scottish Daily
Record*, 13 Oct. 2000; "TV series" London *Daily Telegraph*,
5 Aug. 2000.

149. "Vienna memorial" ABC News, 25 Oct. 2000;
"Braunau" Muhlen, *The Return of Germany*, 32–33; "Hitler
House: Old Walls, New Ideas," *Braunauer Rundschau*, 4
May 2000; Paul Watson, "Austrian town of Hitler's
birth...," *Los Angeles Times*, 13 Jan. 2000; "Hitler birth-
place...," *The Scotsman*, 10 Feb. 2000.

# Selected Bibliography

## Primary Sources

### Interviews and Correspondence

Agnew, Jack. 506 P.I.R., 101st. Telephone interview with author, 10 Nov. 2004, and correspondence. Huntington Valley, Pa.

Allen, Ralph. Interview with author, May 2001. Sycamore, South Carolina.

Bahlau, Fred. 506th Inf. Regt. Telephone interview with author, 6 October 2003, and correspondence. Irish Hills, Onstad, Michigan.

Bando, Mark. Telephone interview with author, 13 Jan. 2006. Detroit, Michigan.

Beierl, Florian. Interviews with author, summer 2001 and 2003, and correspondence. Berchtesgaden, Bavaria, Germany.

Bergin, Donal. Interview with author, 5 Aug. 2003. Tallaght, County Dublin, Ireland.

Callan, Charles. Interviews with author, summers 2003–05. Dublin, Ireland.

Cherish, Barbara Ulrich. Telephone interview with author, 16 June 2003, and correspondence. Lake Hughes, California.

Cloer, Russell. 7th Infantry Regt., 3rd Infantry Division. E-mail to author, 28 July 1998.

Daub, David. 3rd Signal Company, 3rd Infantry Division. Telephone interviews with author, 5, 11, 23 September 2002, and correspondence.

Duggan, John P. Lt. Col. (ret.) Irish Army. Interview with author, 17 July 2002. County Dublin, Ireland.

Elliott, Richard. 506th Inf. Regt. Telephone interview with author, 11 April 2003. Eagleville, Missouri.

Gallagher, Paul. U.S. Army, mountain infantry, Italy, 1943–45. Interview with author, 10 Dec. 2002. Quincy, Mass.

Godec, Alain. Interviews with author, 12–15 July 2003, and correspondence. Paris, France.

Harper, David. Interview with author, 9 Aug. 2001. Berchtesgaden, Bavaria, Germany.

Hassinger, Ted. Telephone interview with author, 10 July 2003. Bad Reichenhall, Bavaria, Germany.

Hoffmann, Peter. Telephone interview with author, 14 Feb. 2004. McGill University, Montreal, Canada.

McMahon, William R. 101st. Telephone interview with author, 18 May 2003. Hickory, North Carolina.

Melcher, Iris. Interviews with author, summer 2001, 2003. Berchtesgaden, Bavaria, Germany.

Miller, Paul R. 506 P.I.R., 101st. Telephone interview with author, 8 June 2003. Elizabethtown, Pa.

Mitchell, Arthur. U.S. Army, France, Belgium, 1944–45. Interview with author, 24 June 2004. Westwood, Mass.

Parks, Robert L. 506th P.I.R. Telephone interview with author, 20 January 2006. Buchanan, Tennessee.

Parris, Albert. Interview with author, 1 Aug. 2002. Tallaght, County Dublin.

Pratt, Sherman. 7th Regiment, 3rd Inf. Div. Telephone interviews with author, 9 Oct. 2002 and 18 April 2003, and correspondence. Arlington, Virginia.

Ramsey, Lloyd. 7th Regiment, 3rd Inf. Div. Telephone interview with author, 12 April 2003, and correspondence. Salem, Virginia.

Sademach, Ingrit. Interview with author, 16 July 2001. Berchtesgaden, Bavaria, Germany.

Scharfenberg, Ingrid. Interview with author, 22 July 2003. Obersalzberg, Bavaria, Germany.

Siren, Joseph. Interviews with author, 2000–05. Allendale, South Carolina.

Siren, Mary. Interview with author, 18 March 2001. Orlando, Florida.

Straith, Donald B. Telephone interview with author, 19 June 2004, and correspondence. Warren, Michigan.

True, William M. 101st. Telephone interview with author, 9 April 2003, and correspondence. Port Hueneme, California.

Valenti, Isadore. 3rd Inf. Div. Telephone interview with author, 13 June 2004, and correspondence. Pittsburg, Pennsylvania.

Vierling, Leonard E. Telephone interview, 17 March 2003. Lake Elsinore, California.

Williams, Joseph. Interview with author, 5 Aug. 2003. Clondalkin, County Dublin, Ireland.

Williams, Thomas. Telephone interview with author, 30 April 2002. Temperance, Michigan.

Zabel, Hans Georg, Interview with author, 11 July 2001. Berchtesgaden, Bavaria, Germany.

Zahn, Donald. 506th PIR. Telephone interview with author, 18 Jan. 2006. Littleton, Colorado.

## Documents

Allen, George. CIC activity and interrogation transcripts, in Berchtesgaden, May 1945. University of Pennsylvania Archives.

Bradsher, Greg. *Holocaust-Era Assets: A Finding Aid to Records at the National Archives at College Park, Maryland.* Washington, D.C.: NARA, 1999.

Devers, Jacob L. Diary, 1943–45. York County Historical Trust, York, Pennsylvania.

Eberstein, Friederich Karl von. "National Redoubt (Battle sector VII, SS and Police; 1944–45)." MS. # B-136. Military History Institute, Carlisle Barracks, Pennsylvania.

French Army. Excerpts from daily log book of Group du 64 RADB (artillery battalion) of Second Armored Division, May 1945. Archiv Leclerc, Paris.

_____. Excerpts from daily log book of 31e Batterie du 64 RADB of Second Armored Division, May 1945.

Hansen, Chester. Diary, 1944–45. Military History Institute.

Hengl, Georg von. "Report on the Alpine Fortress." MS. #B-459, 1–13, in Donald Detwiler, ed., *World War II German Military Studies*, vol. 24. New York: Garland, 1979.

_____. "The Alpine Redoubt: Final Historical Survey of this 'Spectre.'" MS. #B-461, 1–15, in Donald Detwiler, ed., *World War II German Military Studies*, vol. 24. New York: Garland, 1979.

Hobe, Cord von. "Panzer Kampfgruppe XIII (6 April–5 May 1945)." MS. #B-772, Military History Institute.

Hofer, Franz. "The Alpine Fortification and Defense Line: A Report on German and U. S. Views of the 'Alpine Redoubt' in 1944." MS. #B-457, 1–26, in Detwiler, ed. *World War II German Military Studies*, vol. 24. New York: Garland, 1979.

_____. "The National Redoubt." MS. #B-458, 1–36, in Detwiler, ed. *World War II German Military Studies*, vol. 24. New York: Garland, 1979.

Hofmann, Otto. "National Redoubt." MS. #B-140, Military History Institute.

Kleikamp, Helmut. "36th Volks Grenadier Division (28 March–3 May 1945)." MS. #B-616, Military History Institute.

Kunz, William J. Narrative, April–May 1945, 39th Field Artillery, 3rd Inf. Div. Military History Institute.

Marcinkiewicz, August. "National Redoubt." MS. #B-187, Military History Institute.

Memorial du Marechal Leclerc de Hauteclocque. 23 Allee de la 2e DB, Dalle-Jardin Atlantique courvant la gare Montparnasse.

Muhe, Ludwig. "Wehrkreis VII Police (National Redoubt)." MS. #B-130, Military History Institute.

Muller, Walter J. Reports as military governor of Bavaria, 1946. Hoover Institution, Stanford.

O'Daniel, John W. Brief biography. Dept. of Defense, Office of Public Information, 1956. The Citadel Archives, Charleston, S.C.

Skubik, Stephen J. Report on death of Martin Hammitzsch. Hoover Institution, Stanford University.

Supreme Headquarters Allied Expeditionary Force. *Counter Intelligence Handbook, Germany, Revised April 1945.* Washington, D.C.: Government Printing Office, 1945.

United States Army. *Official Diary for the Commanding General, Seventh Army.* Vol. III. 1 December 1944–2 June 1945.

_____. *Proclamation, Berchtesgadener Land,* May 1945.

_____. *Report of Operations (Final After-Action Report).* Wiesbaden, Germany, 1945.

_____. *The Seventh United States Army in France and Germany, 1944–1945: Report of Operations.* 2 vols. Nashville, Tenn.: Battery Press, 1998.

_____. *United States Army in the Occupation of Germany, 1944–46.* Washington, D.C.: Government Printing Office, 1975.

_____. Counter Intelligence Corps. 5 June 1946. N.A., Record Group 319 IRR XE575580.

_____. _____. Leni Riefenstahl interrogation.

_____. _____. National Archives. *A Man Called Adolf Hitler.* Vol. 14 of CIC in WWII. In *Covert Warfare,* John Mendelsohn, ed. 18 vols. New York: Garland, 1989.

_____. _____. Paula Hitler interrogation. 12 July 1945. Eisenhower Library.

_____. Office of Special Services. *Pocket Guide, No. 10: Germany.* Washington, D.C., 1944.

_____. Office of Strategic Services. *Hitler Source Book.*

_____. _____. Operations and Reports. National Archives, Record Group 226.

_____. _____. Report on Hitler, 1943.

_____. _____. *South Germany: An Analysis of the Political and Social Organization, the Communications, Economic Controls, Agriculture and Food Supply, Mineral Resources, Manufacturing and Transportation Facilities.* Report no. 232, 22 September 1944.

_____. _____. Art Looting Investigation Unit. "The Göring Collection." Consolidated Interrogation Report No. 2, 15 September 1945.

_____. _____. _____. "Linz: Hitler's Museum and Library." Consolidated Interrogation Report No. 4, 15 December 1945. National Archives, Record Group 260.390/45.

_____. Office of the Military Government, Bavaria. National Archives. Record Group 260.

____. Office of the Military Government, Germany. *Reports of the Military Government for Germany, U.S. Zone, 1945-53.*

____. 101st Airborne Division. 506th Parachute Infantry Regiment. After Action Report for May 1-10, 1945. National Archives, Record Group 260.390.9/7-3.

____.____.____. Historical Record. May 11-31, 1945; June 1-30, 1945; July 1-August 2, 1945. National Archives, Record Group 260.390/9/7-3.

____. Third Infantry Division. National Archives. Record Group 407.

U.S. Army Air Force. HQ, 15th Air Force. Analysis Reports File, April 1944-June 1945, Lt. Col. Jack Nicholas to Col. Barr, 25 April 1945, proposals to bomb Obersalzberg area. Air Force Historical Research Agency, Maxwell Air Force Base.

____. ____. MAAF War Room, mission report, 20 February 1945.

Woodward, E.L., and Butler, Rohan, eds. *Documents on British Foreign Policy, 1919-1939.* 3rd series. Vol. vii. London: H.M. Stationary Office, 1954.

ORAL HISTORY TRANSCRIPTS

Devers, Jacob. Only to mid-1944. Eisenhower Library, Abilene, Kansas, 1974-75.
Heintges, John A. Military History Institute.
Quinn, William. Military History Institute.
Rosson, William B. Military History Institute.

NEWSPAPERS AND PERIODICALS

Associated Press. Reports on Obersalzberg documentation center. Nov. 1998, Oct. 1999.
Associated Press. Conservation order for Reichskanzlei building at Stengass. 29 May 2000.
*Berchtesgadener Anzeiger.* 1945, 1995-2005.
*Chicago Daily News.* April-May 1945.
*Chicago Tribune.* April-May 1945.
*Frankfurter Allgemeine Zeitung.* 1990-2000.
*New York Herald Tribune.* May 1945.
*New York Times.* 1943-46, 1951-52, 1995-.
*PM* (New York). April-May 1945.
*Stars and Stripes.* German edition. April-October 1945.
*Times* (London). 1945.
*Yank: The Army Weekly.* 1943-45.

## Works by Contemporaries

### Articles

Allen, George. "The Discovery of the Hitler *Lagebesprechunger.*" *The Library Chronicle* (University of Pennsylvania), v. xxiii, no. 2 (Spring-Summer 1957), 53-62.
Axelsson, George. "Götterdämmerung—by Hitler." *New York Times Magazine,* 30 July 1944.

"Berchtesgaden." *New Yorker,* 16 May 1945.
Bloch, Eduard. "My Patient Hitler." *Colliers,* 15 March 1941, pp. 11, 35-37; 22 March 1941, pp. 69-72.
Boehmer, George. "Americans Returning Alpine Property to Reluctant Germans." Associated Press, 19 Feb. 1995.
Boyes, Roger. "Hitler's Alpine Lair revives Bitterness Buried in the Past." *Times* (London), 18 Feb. 1995.
Bruckner, Wilhelm. "The Private Life of the Führer." Berlin Web site, no date.
Campbell, Christy. "Bavaria Cashes in on Hitler's House." *Sunday Telegraph* (London), 11 Jan. 1998.
Cloer, Russell. Army Service Experiences Questionnaire, Military History Institute.
____. "The Final Days of the War." *The Watch on the Rhine* (Society of 3rd Infantry Division) 80, no. 2 (October 1998), 16-18.
Connolly, Kate. "British to Revive Hitler's Favorite Holiday Spot." *The Observer* (London), 5 August 2001.
De Guillebon, Jacques. Account of artillery battalion of French Second Armored Division in Berchtesgaden, May 1945. In Daniel Roudeau and Roger Stephane, eds., *Des Hommes Libres: La France Libre Par Ceaux Quil'ont Faite.* Paris: Bernard Grasset, 1997.
Degrelle, Leon. "The Enigma of Hitler." *Journal of Historical Review* 14, no. 3 (May/June 1994).
Devers, Jacob. "Operation Dragoon: The Invasion of Southern France." *Journal of Military History* 10, no. 2, 3-41.
Drummond, Roscoe. "A Soldier's General" (Jacob Devers). *Christian Science Monitor,* 19 June 1943.
Esnault, Georges. "The Conquest of Berghof: Berchtesgaden." *Caravane* (publication of veterans of French Second Armored Division association), issue no. 408, 3rd quarter 2000.
French Second Armored Division. Artillery battalion log book.
____. "40e Rana." Veterans' association of one of three artillery units, "La Lettre du 40e Rana"—"En Allemagne." Bulletin, 15 April 1997.
Finn, Peter. "Memory and Renewal Clash at Hitler's 'Lair.'" *Washington Post,* 4 September 2001.
Foss, Kendall. "Berchtesgaden Revisited." *New York Post,* 5 June 1946.
"Fraternization." *Yank: The Army Weekly,* 31 August 1945.
Fuller, J.F.C. "Hitler's Plan: Victory Through Chaos." *Newsweek,* 4 Sept. 1944.
Girard, Christian. "Temoignage de l'Aide de Camp du General Leclerc de Hauteclocque" (war diary). *Journal de Guerre, 1939-1945.* Paris: Editions L'Harmattan, October 2000.
Hamburger, Philip. "Beauty and the Beast." *New Yorker,* 1 May 1995.
____. "Letter from Berchtesgaden." *New Yorker,* 9 June 1945.

Higgins, Marguerite. May 1945 articles, *New York Herald Tribune*.

Hitler, Alois. "Adolf Hitler by Alois Hitler." *New York American*, 30 Nov. 1930.

"Hitler's Palace in the Clouds." Orig. in *Telegraaf*. Amsterdam: New Age, March 1939. 32–33.

Jenkins, Reuben E. "The Battle of the National Redoubt—Operational Phase." *Military Review* 26, no. 10 (Jan. 1947), 16–26.

_____. "The Battle of the National Redoubt—Planning Phase." *Military Review* 26, no. 9 (Dec. 1946), 3–8.

Johnson, Richard. "Champagne at the Eagle's Nest." *New York Times*, 7 May 1945.

Junge, Traudl. "Recollections." In P. Galante and E. Silianoff, eds., *Voices from the Bunker*. New York: Putnams, 1989.

Lang, Tania. "Hitler as Wotan." *Current History*, Feb. 1940, 50–51.

Lessner, Erwin. "Hitler's Final V Weapon." *Collier's*, 27 Jan. 1945.

Ley, Robert. "The Führer and the German Worker." In *Adolf Hitler: Bilder aus dem Leben des Führers*. Hamburg: Publisher unknown, 1936.

Lockridge, Patricia. "I Governed Berchtesgaden." *Women's Home Companion*, August 1945.

Losch, Roland. "New Documentation Center Explains History of Hitler's Mountain Retreat." Associated Press, 21 Oct. 1999.

Matteson, Robert. "The Last Days of Ernst Kaltenbrunner." *Studies in Intelligence* 4, no. 2 (Spring 1960), A11–29.

Mayr, Karl. "I Was Hitler's Boss." *Current History* 1, no. 3 (November 1944), pp. 193–99.

Moor, Paul. "The Old Order: Berchtesgaden Seven Years Later." *Harpers*, Dec. 1952, pp. 57–67.

Morrell, Sydney. "Hitler's Hiding Place." Orig. in *Sunday Express*, London, New Age, August 1937, 486–88.

"Nazis Feather Their Nest." Orig. in *Deutsche Revolution*. Prague: New Age, May 1937. 212–14.

Newby, Leroy W. "Your Mission: Kill Hitler." *American Heritage*, Oct. 1998, 26–29.

Padover, Saul K. "Why Americans Like German Women." *American Mercury* 357 (Sept. 1946), 354–57.

Paterson, Tony. "Furor in the Eagle's Nest." *The European* (London), 31 March–6 April 1995.

Phayre, Ignatius. "Hitler's Mountain Home." *Home and Gardens* (British), November 1938, pp. 193–95.

_____. "Holiday with Hitler." *Current History* 44 (1936), pp. 50–58.

Plaut, James S. "Hitler's Capital; Loot for the Master Race." *Atlantic Monthly* 178, no. 4 (October 1946), 73–78.

Pogue, Forrest. "Why Eisenhower's Forces Stopped at the Elbe." *World Politics* 4, no. 3 (1952), 356–68.

Reed, T.J. "Unplayable History." *Times Literary Supplement*, 5 Oct. 2001.

Reitsch, Hanna, and Robert E. Work. "Last Days in Hitler's Air Raid Shelter." *Public Opinion Quarterly*, Winter 1946–47, pp. 565–81.

Riefenstahl, Leni. "American Intelligence Report on Leni Riefenstahl—May 30th, 1945." *Film Culture* 77 (Fall 1992), pp. 35–38.

Rzhevskaya, Yelena. "Hitler's trail leads to Moscow." *World Press Review*, July 1995. Extract from *Jerusalem Report*, 4 May 1995.

Sions, Harry. "Berchtesgaden." *Yank: The Army Weekly*, 22 June 1945.

"Tactician's Dream." (Patch cover story.) *Time* magazine, 28 August 1944.

Taper, Bernard. "Investigating Art Looting for the MFA & A." In Elizabeth Simpson, ed., *The Spoils of War: World War II and Its Aftermath: The Loss, Reappearance and Recovery of Cultural Property*. New York: Harry Abrams, 1997.

Touyeras, Laurent. "Berchtesgaden." His account of French troops at the Obersalzberg and the Kehlstein on 4–5 May 1945. Bulletin of French Second Armored Division veterans' association, 1970.

Trevor-Roper, Hugh. "All in the Family." Review of *Memoirs of Bridget Hitler. New York Review of Books*, 28 June 1979.

Tubman, James. "First to Berchtesgaden? Yes." Letter. *Watch on the Rhine*, (publication of 3rd Infantry Division Society), August 2000.

United States Army, Information and Education Services. *Blue and White Devils: The Story of the Third Infantry Division*. Paris, 1945, 32 pages.

Vodder, Harry. "Hitler's Hideaway." *New York Times*, magazine section, 12 Nov. 1944, p. 36.

Webster, David K. "We Drank Hitler's Champagne." *Saturday Evening Post*, 3 May 1952, 134–39.

Weigelt, Nada. "What Next When the Americans Leave the Führer's Vacation Retreat?" *Deutsche-Press-Agentur*, 8 Feb. 1995.

Work, Robert E. "Last Days in Hitler's Air Raid Shelter." Hanna Reitsch interview. *Public Opinion Quarterly* 10, no. 4 (Winter 1946–47), 565–81.

Ybarra, T.R. "Hitler on High." *Collier's*, 4 Sept. 1937.

## Books

Association des Français Libre. *Revue de la France Libre*. Paris, 1990.

Bach, Julian, Jr. *America's Germany: An Account of the Occupation*. New York: Random House, 1946.

Baldwin, Hanson W. *Tiger Jack*. (Short biography of John W. Wood.) Ft. Collins, Colorado, 1979. Old Army Press.

Baur, Hans. *Hitler's Pilot*, London: Frederick Muller, 1958.

Belfrage, Cedric. *Seeds of Destruction*. New York: Cameron and Kahn, 1954.

Bernadotte, Folke. *The Curtain Falls: Last Days of the Third Reich*. New York: Knopf, 1945.

Billinger, Karl. *Hitler Is No Fool*. New York: Modern Age Books, 1939.

Blumenson, Martin, ed. *The Patton Papers: 1940–1945*. Boston: Houghton Mifflin, 1974.

Boldt, Gerhard. *Hitler: The Last Ten Days*. New York: Coward, McCann and Geoghegan, 1973 (original 1947).

Bormann, Martin. *The Bormann Letters*, H. Trevor-Roper, ed. London, 1954.

Bradley, Omar N. *A General's Life*. With Clay Blair. New York: Simon and Schuster, 1983.

_____. *A Soldier's Story*, New York: Henry Holt, 1951.

Burgett, Donald R. *Beyond the Rhine: A Screaming Eagle in Germany*. Novato, California: Presidio, 2001.

Butcher, Harry C. *My Three Years with Eisenhower: The Personal Diary of Captain Harry C. Butcher, USNR*. New York: Simon and Schuster, 1946.

Byford-Jones, W. *Berlin Twilight*. London: Hutchinson, 1947.

Casey, William. *The Secret War Against Hitler*. Washington, D.C.: Regnery Gateway, 1988.

*Le Chemin le Plus Long* ("The Longest Road"). Compilation of memoirs of members of 1st Company of 501st Tank Regiment (501e R.C.C.) of French Second Armored Division.

Corlett, Charles, H. *Cowboy Pete: The Autobiography of Major General Charles H. Corlett*. Santa Fe, New Mexico: Sleeping Fox, 1974.

De Boissieu, Alain. *Pour Combatte Avec De Gaulle*. Paris: Plow, 1981.

De Lattre de Tassigny, Jean. *The History of the French First Army*. London: George Allen and Unwin, 1947.

Delmer, Sefton. *Black Boomerang*. New York: Viking, 1962.

_____. *Trail Sinister: An Autobiography*. London: Secker and Warburg, 1961.

*La 2e [Deuxième] D.B. e, France, General Leclerc, Combattants et Combat*. Paris, 1946.

Dietrich, Otto. *The Hitler I Knew*. London: Methuen, 1957.

Dronne, Raymond. *L'Hallali de Paris a Berchtesgaden* ("The March from Paris to Berchtesgaden"). Paris: Editions France-Empire, 1985.

Dulles, Allen. *From Hitler's Doorstep: The Wartime Reports of Allen Dulles, 1942–1945*. Neal H. Petersen, ed. University Park, Pa.: Pennsylvania State University Press, 1996.

Eisenhower, Dwight D. *Crusade in Europe*. New York: Doubleday, 1948.

_____. *Dear General: Eisenhower's Wartime Letters to Marshall*. Joseph Hobbs, editor. Baltimore: Johns Hopkins Press, 1971.

_____. *The Eisenhower Diaries*. New York: W.W. Norton, 1981.

_____. *The Papers of Dwight David Eisenhower: The War Years*. Alfred Chandler, ed. 5 vols. Baltimore: Johns Hopkins Press, 1970.

Fonde, Jean-Julien. *Les Loups de Leclerc* ("Leclerc's Wolves"). Paris: Editions Plon, 1982.

Frank, Bernhard. *Hitler, Göring and the Obersalzberg*. Berchtesgaden: Anton Plenk, 1989.

Francois-Poncet, Andre. *The Fateful Years: Memoirs of a French Ambassador in Berlin, 1931–38*. London, 1949.

Fry, Michael. *Hitler's Wonderland*. London: John Murray, 1934.

Gehlen, Reinhard. *The Service: The Memoirs of General Reinhard Gehlen*. New York: Popular Library, 1972.

Gilbert, G.M. *Nuremberg Diary*. New York: New American Library, (orig. 1947) 1961.

Goebbels, Joseph. *Final Entries, 1945: The Diaries of Joseph Goebbels*. New York: G.P. Putnam's Sons, 1978.

_____. *The Goebbels Diaries, 1939–1941*. London: H. Hamilton, 1982.

_____. *The Goebbels Diaries, 1942–1943*. Garden City, New York: Doubleday, 1948.

Habe, Hans. *Our Love Affair with Germany*. New York: G.P. Putnam's Sons, 1953.

Hanfstängl, Ernst. *Hitler: The Missing Years*. New York: Arcade, 1994 (orig. 1957).

Hauser, Heinrich. *The German Talks Back*. New York: Henry Holt, 1945.

Heiden, Konrad. *Der Führer: Hitler's Rise to Power*. Boston: Houghton Mifflin, 1944.

_____. *A History of National Socialism*. New York: Alfred A. Knopf, 1935.

_____. *Hitler: A Biography*. New York: Alfred A. Knopf, 1936.

Heinz, Heinz A. *Germany's Hitler*. London: Hurst and Blackett, 1934.

Higgins, Marguerite. *News Is a Singular Thing*. Garden City, N.Y.: Doubleday, 1955.

Hill, Russell. *Struggle for Germany*. London: Victor Gollancz, 1947.

Hinsley, Frank H. *British Intelligence in the Second World War: Its Influence on Strategy and Operations*. Vol. 3, part II. New York: Cambridge University Press, 1988.

Hitler, Adolf. *Hitler's Letters and Notes*. Werner Maser, ed. London: Heinemann, 1973.

_____. *Hitler's Secret Book*. Salvator Attanasio, trans. New York, 1961.

_____. *Hitler's Secret Conversations, 1941–1944*. New York: Farrar, Straus and Young, 1953.

_____. *Hitler's Table Talk, 1941–1945*. London: Weidenfeld and Nicolson, 1973.

_____. *Mein Kampf*. New York: Stackpole Sons, 1939.

_____. *The Speeches of Adolf Hitler*. Norman H. Baynes, ed. 2 vols. New York: Howard Fertig, 1969.

Hitler, Bridget. *The Memoirs of Bridget Hitler*, Michael Unger, ed. London, 1979.

Höttl, Wilhelm. *Hitler's Paper Weapon*. London: R. Hart-Davis, 1955.

_____. *The Secret Front: The Story of Nazi Political Espionage*. London: Weidenfeld and Nicolson, 1953.

Hoffmann, Heinrich. *Hitler Was My Friend*. London: Burke, 1955.

Howe, Thomas C., Jr. *Salt Mines and Castles: The Discovery and Restitution of Looted European Art.* Indianapolis: Bobbs-Merrill, 1946.

Huss, Pierre J. *Heil! and Farewell.* London: Herbert Jenkins, 1943.

Hutton, Bud, and Rooney, Andy. *Conqueror's Peace: A Report to the American Stockholders.* Garden City, N.Y.: Doubleday, 1947.

Ingersoll, Ralph. *Top Secret.* New York: Harcourt Brace, 1946.

James, Clifton. *I Was Monty's Double.* London: Popular Book Club, n.d.

Junge, Traudl. *Until the Final Hour: Hitler's Last Secretary.* London: Weidenfeld and Nicholson, 2003.

Kelley, Douglas M. *22 Cells in Nuremberg: A Psychiatrist Examines the Nazi Criminals.* New York: Greenberg, 1947.

Kennedy, John F. *Prelude to Leadership: The European Diary of John F. Kennedy, Summer 1945.* Introduction by Hugh Sidey. Washington, D.C.: Regnery, 1995.

Kersten, Felix. *The Kersten Memoirs: 1940–1945.* London: Hutchinson, 1956.

Kesselring, Albrecht. *Kesselring: A Soldier's Record.* Westport, Conn.: Greenwood, 1953.

Knappen, Marshall. *And Call It Peace.* Chicago, Illinois: University of Chicago Press, 1947.

Knauth, Percy. *Germany in Defeat.* New York: Alfred A. Knopf, 1946.

Kohler, Pauline. *The Woman Who Lived in Hitler's House.* New York: Sheridan House, 1940. Excerpts in *Liberty* magazine, 15 June–July 1940.

Krebs, Albert. *The Infancy of Nazism: The Memoirs of Ex-Gauleiter Albert Krebs, 1923–1933.* W.S. Allen, ed. New York: Franklin Watts, 1976.

Krüger, Kurt. *I Was Hitler's Doctor.* New York: Biltmore, 1943.

Langer, Walter C. *The Mind of Adolf Hitler: The Secret Wartime Report.* New York: Basic Books, 1972.

Laurie, A.P. *The Case for Germany: A Study of Modern Germany.* Berlin: Internationaler Verlag, 1939.

Lochner, Louis P. *What About Germany.* New York: Dodd, 1942.

Lovell, Stanley P. *Of Spies and Stratagems.* Englewood Cliffs, New Jersey: Prentice-Hall, 1963.

Ludecke, Kurt Georg, *I Knew Hitler.* London: Jarrolds, 1938.

MacMahon, Finn. *Post Bellum Blues.* New York: New American Library, 1965.

Marshall, George C. *The Papers of George Catlett Marshall.* 4 vols. Baltimore: John Hopkins University, 1981.

Miller, Lee. *Lee Miller's War: Photographer and Correspondent with the Allies in Europe, 1944–45.* Antony Penrose, ed. Boston: Little, Brown, 1992.

Morell, Theodor. *Adolf Hitler, the Medical Diaries: The Private Diaries of Dr. Theo Morell.* David Irving, ed. London: Sidgwick and Jackson, 1983.

Mowrer, Edgar A. *Germany Puts the Clock Back.* London: Bodley Head, 1933.

Muhlen, Norbert. *The Return of Germany: A Tale of Two Countries.* Chicago: Henry Regnery, 1953.

Musmanno, Michael. *Ten Days to Die.* Garden City, New York: Doubleday, 1950.

Öchsner, Frederick. *This Is the Enemy.* Boston: Little, Brown, 1942.

Padover, Saul K. *Experiment in Germany: The Story of an American Intelligence Officer.* New York: Duell, Sloan and Pearce, 1946.

Parton, James. *"Air Force Spoken Here": General Ira Eaker and the Command of the Air.* Bethesda, Maryland: Adler and Adler, 1986.

Pope, Ernest. *Munich Playground.* New York: G.P. Putnam's Sons, 1941.

Pratt, Sherman W. *Autobahn to Berchtesgaden: A Combat Soldier's View of His Role in World War II.* Baltimore: Gateway Press, 1992.

Price, G. Ward. *I Know These Dictators.* London: George G. Harrap, 1937.

Public Records Office. *Operation Foxley: The British Plan to Kill Hitler,* Introduction by Mark Seaman. London: PRO Publications, 1998.

Riefenstahl, Leni. *Leni Riefenstahl: A Memoir.* New York: Picador, 1995.

Romilly, Giles and Alexander, Michael. *The Privileged Nightmare.* London: Weidenfeld and Nicholson, 1954.

Rudel, Hans Ulrich. *Stuka Pilot.* Dublin: Euphorion Books, 1953.

Salomon, Ernst von. *Fragebogen.* Garden City, N.Y.: Doubleday, 1955.

Schmidt, Paul. *Hitler's Interpreter: The Secret History of German Diplomacy, 1935–45.* London: Heinemann, 1951.

Schramm, Percy. *Hitler: The Man and the Military Leader.* Chicago: Academy Chicago, 1981.

Schröder, Christa. *Er War Mein Chef.* Munich: Langen Muller, 1985.

Schuman, Frederick. *The Nazi Dictatorship.* New York: Knopf, 1936.

Scott, Hugh A. *The Blue and White Devils: A Personal Memoir and History of the Third Infantry Division in World War II.* Nashville, Tennessee: Battery Press, 1984.

Semmler, Rudolph. *Goebbels: The Man Next to Hitler.* London, 1947.

Shaw, George Bernard, *The Matter with Ireland,* Dan H. Laurence and David H. Greene, eds. Letter to London *Times,* 18 May 1945. New York: Hill and Wang, 1962.

Shirer, William L. *Berlin Diary: The Journal of a Foreign Correspondent, 1934–1941.* New York: Knopf, 1941.

Skorzeny, Otto. *Skorzeny's Secret Missions.* New York: E.P. Dutton, 1950.

Smith, Truman. *Berlin Alert: The Memoirs and Reports of Truman Smith,* Robert Hessen, ed. Stanford: Hoover Institution, 1984.

Speer, Albert. *Inside the Third Reich*. New York: Macmillan, 1970.

———. *Spandau: The Secret Diaries*. New York: Macmillan, 1976.

Stahlenberg, Elisabeth von. *Nazi Lady: The Diaries of Elisabeth von Stahlenberg, 1922–1948*. London: Blond and Briggs, 1978.

Taggart, Donald G., ed. *History of the Third Infantry Division in World War II*. Washington, D.C.: Infantry Journal Press, 1947.

Taylor, Maxwell. *Swords and Plowshares*. New York: W.W. Norton, 1972.

Thyssen, Fritz. *I Paid Hitler*. New York: Farrar and Rinehart, 1941.

Toole, John H. *Battle Diary*. Missoula, Montana: Vigilante Press, 1978.

*Trial of the Major War Criminals: Proceedings of the International Military Tribunal Sitting at Nuremberg, Germany, 20 November 1945 to 1 October 1946* (referred to as "Nuremberg trials"). Vols. 1–23. London: H.M. Stationary Office, 1946–51.

Truscott, Lucian. *Command Missions: A Personal Story*. New York: E.P. Dutton, 1954.

Valenti, Isadore. *Combat Medic*. Pittsburgh: Word Association, 1998.

Wagener, Otto. *Hitler: Memoirs of a Confidant*. New Haven, Conn.: Yale University Press, 1985.

Wagner, Friedelind. *Heritage of Fire: The Story of Richard Wagner's Granddaughter*. New York: Harper, 1945.

Warburg, James P. *Germany: Bridge or Battleground*. New York: Harcourt, Brace, 1947.

Webster, David. *Parachute Infantry: An American Paratrooper's Memoir of D-Day and the Fall of the Third Reich*. Baton Rouge: Louisiana State University Press, 1994.

White, Nathan. *From Fedala to Berchtesgaden: A History of the Seventh Infantry Regiment*. Brockton, Mass.: Kent Print, 1947.

White, W.L. *Report on the Germans*. New York: Harcourt, Brace, 1947.

Wulff, Wilhelm. *Zodiac and Swastika: How Astrology Guided Hitler's Germany*. New York: Coward, McCann and Geoghegan, 1973.

Wurzbach, N.V. *Berchtesgaden: Mountains, Customs and Legends*. Berchtesgaden Recreation Area, Munich Military Post, U. S. Army, 1949.

Zink, Harold. *American Military Government in Germany*. New York: Macmillan, 1947.

———. *The U.S. in Germany, 1944–1951*. New York: Van Nostrand, 1957.

## Later Works

### Articles

"Berchtesgaden." *After the Battle*, no 9. Winston G. Ramsey, ed. London, 1975.

Berlin, R.H. "United States Army World War II Corps Commanders: A Composite Biography." *Journal of Military History* 53, no. 2, 147–167.

Catle, Stephen. "Hitler's Mentally Ill Relative Was Sent to Gas Chamber." *Independent* (London), 19 Jan 2005.

CIA History Staff. "Wilhelm Höttl: International Man of Mystery." Center for the Study of Intelligence *Bulletin* no. 12 (Fall 2001).

Cloer, Russ. "The Final Days of the War." *Watch on the Rhine*, Oct. 1998, 16.

Connolly, Kate. "Submarines to Dredge Lake for Nazi Gold." *The Guardian* (London), 25 Jan. 2000.

Erlanger, Steven. "Hitler, It Seems, Loved Money and Died Rich." *New York Times*, 9 Aug. 2002.

Finch, Simon. "Eva and Me" (interview with "Elizabeth Winkler," cousin of Eva Braun). *The Guardian* (London), 28 Dec. 1999.

Gardner, David. "The Last of the Hitlers." *Irish Independent*, 21 Oct. 1998.

Gatzke, Hans W. "Hitler and Psychohistory." *American Historical Review* 78, no. 2 (April 1978), 394–401.

Gordon, Linda. "My Cousin Eva." *The Guardian*, 27 April 2002.

Green, Daniel. "Up into the Eagle's Nest." London *Financial Times*, 7 April 1990.

Griffin, Roger. "Party Time: The Temporal Revolution of the Third Reich." *History Today* 49, no. 4 (April 1999), 43–47.

Gurley, Franklin L. "Policy Versus Strategy: The Defense of Strasbourg in Winter 1944–1945." *Journal of Military History* 58, no. 3, 481–514.

Diver, Krysia. "Lodt file reveals Hitler's paranoia." *The Guardian*, 21 March 2005.

Hale, Oron J. "Adolf Hitler, Taxpayer." *American Historical Review* 60, no. 4 (July 1955), 830–42.

Labanyi, Peter. "Images of Fascism: Visualization and Aestheticization in the Third Reich." In M. Laffan, ed., *The Burden of German History, 1919–45*. London: Methuen, 1988. 151–77.

McAually, James. "Hitler's Brother and the Girl from Tallaght." *Sunday Press* (Dublin), 16 April 1989.

McCarthy, Tony. "Hitler: His Irish Relatives." *Irish Roots* 1 (Spring 1992), 30–33.

McManus, John. "The Eagle's Nest: The Last Great Prize." *World War II* magazine, May 2005.

Melcher, Iris. "A Scientific Look at the "Big Pond" in Obersalzberg." *Berchtesgadener Anzieger*, July 16 1996.

Naftali, Timothy. "Creating the Myth of the Alpenfestung: Allied Intelligence and the Collapse of the Nazi Police-State." In G. Bischof and A. Pelinka, eds., *Austrian Historical Memory and National Identity*. New Brunswick, N.J.: Transaction, 1997.

Pascal, Julia. "Unbanning Hitler." *New Statesman*, 25 June 2001.

Remme, Tilman. "Life with Hitler and His Mistress." London *Telegraph*, 27 September 1997.

Ryback, Timothy W. "The Hitler Shrine." *Atlantic Monthly*, April 2005.

_____. "Hitler's Forgotten Library: The Man, His Books and His Search for God." *Atlantic Monthly*, May 2003.

_____. "Hitler's Lost Family." *New Yorker*, 17 July 2000.

Strobridge, Truman, and Nalty, Bernard. "From the South Pacific to the Brenner Pass: General Alexander M. Patch." *Military Review* LXI (June 1981), 41–49.

"To Disenchant the Mountain: Historical Exhibit on the Obersalzberg." *Frankfurter Allgemeine Zeitung*, 23 October 1999.

## Books

Alford, Kenneth. *The Spoils of World War II: The American Military's Role in the Stealing of Europe's Treasures*. Secaucus, N.J.: Carol, 1994.

Ambrose, Stephen E. *Band of Brothers: E Company, 506th Regiment, 101 Airborne: From Normandy to Hitler's Eagle's Nest*. New York: Simon and Schuster, 1992.

_____. *Eisenhower and Berlin: The Decision to Halt at the Elbe*. New York: W.W. Norton, 1967.

_____. *The Supreme Commander: The War Years of General Dwight D. Eisenhower*. Garden City, N.Y.: Doubleday, 1970.

Bacque, James. *Crimes and Mercies: The Fate of German Civilians under Allied Occupation, 1944–1950*. Toronto: Little, Brown, 1997.

Bando, Mark. *The 101st Airborne: From Holland to Hitler's Eagle's Nest*. Osceola, Wisconsin: Motorbooks International, 1995.

_____. *Vanguard of the Crusade: The 101st Airborne Division in World War II*. Bedford, Pa.: Alberjona Press, 2003.

Baudot, Marcel; Bernard, Enri; Brugmans, Hendrik; Foot, Michael; and Jacobson, Hans-Adolf, eds. *Historical Encyclopedia of World War II*. New York: MJF Books, 1989.

Beever, Antony. *The Fall of Berlin, 1945*. New York: Viking, 2002.

Beierl, Florian. *History of the Eagle's Nest*. Berchtesgaden: Verlag Plenk, 1998.

_____. *Hitler's Berg: Licht ins Dunkel der Geschichte. Geschichte des Obersalzbergs und seiner geheimen Bunkeranlagen*. Berchtesgaden, Germany: Verlag Beierl, 2005.

Bezymenski, Lev. *The Death of Adolf Hitler: Unknown Documents from Soviet Archives*. London: Michael Joseph, 1968.

Biddiscombe, Perry. *Werwolf!: The History of the National Socialist Guerrilla Movement, 1944–1946*. Toronto: University of Toronto, 1998.

Binion, Rudolph. *Hitler Among the Germans*. New York: Elsevier, 1976.

Black, Peter R. *Ernst Kaltenbrunner: Ideological Soldier of the Third Reich*. Princeton, N.J.: Princeton University Press, 1984.

Blair, Clay. *Ridgway's Paratroopers: The American Airborne in World War II*. Garden City, New York: Dail Press, 1985.

Bonn, Keith. *When the Odds Were Even: The Vosges Mountains Campaign, October 1944–January 1945*. Novato, California: Presidio, 1994.

Brennan, J.H. *Occult Reich*. Aylesbury, Bucks, England: Futura, 1974.

Breuer, William B. *Feuding Allies: The Private Wars of the High Command*. New York: John Wiley, 1995.

_____. *Operation Dragoon: The Allied Invasion of the South of France*. Novato, California: Presidio, 1996.

Bullock, Alan. *Hitler: A Study in Tyranny*. New York: Harper and Row, 1964.

_____. *Hitler and Stalin: Parallel Lives*. New York: Alfred A. Knopf, 1992.

Burleigh, Michael. *The Third Reich: A New History*. New York: Hill and Wang, 2000.

Carr, William. *Hitler: A Study in Personality and Politics*. New York: St. Martin's Press, 1979.

Carter, Kit, and Mueller, Robert. *U.S. Army Air Forces in World War II: Combat Chronology, 1941–1945*. Washington, D.C.: Center for Air Force History, 1991.

Chalou, George C., ed. *The Secrets War: The Office of Strategic Services in World War II*. Washington, D.C.: National Archives and Records Administration, 1992.

Chaussy, Ulrich. *Nachbar Hitler: Führerkult und Heimatzerstörung am Obersalzberg*. Berlin: Ch. Links Verlag, 2001.

Churchill, Allen. *Eyewitness Hitler: The Nazi Führer and His Times as Seen by Contemporaries, 1930–1945*. New York: Walker, 1979.

Clarke, Jeffrey, and Smith, Robert. *Riviera to the Rhine*. Washington, D.C.: U.S. Army Center of Military History, 1993.

Conot, Robert E. *Justice at Nuremberg*. New York: Harper and Row, 1983.

Corbonnois, Didier, with Alain Godec. *L'Odyssee de la Colonne Leclerc*. Paris: Histoire & Collections, 2003.

Craven, Wesley F., and Cate, James L. *The Army Air Forces in World War II*. Vol. 3, *Europe: Argument to V-E Day, January 1944 to May 1945*. Chicago: University of Chicago Press, 1951.

Critchell, Laurence. *Four Stars of Hell*. New York: Ballantine Books, 1947.

Croswell, Daniel. *The Military Career of General Walter Bedell Smith*. Westport, Conn.: Greenwood, 1991.

Davidson, Eugene. *The Death and Life of Germany: An Account of the American Occupation*. New York: Knopf, 1959.

Davis, Franklin, Jr. *Come as a Conqueror: The United States Army's Occupation of Germany*. New York: Macmillan, 1967.

D'Este, Carlo. *Eisenhower: A Soldier's Life*. New York: Henry Holt, 2002.

Dörries, Reinhard. *Hitler's Last Chief of Foreign Intelligence: Allied Interrogations of Walter Schellenberg*. London: Frank Cass, 2003.

Dronne, Raymond. *L'hallali de Paris a Berchtesgaden*. Paris: Empire, 1985.

Dzwonchyk, Wayne M. "General Jacob L. Devers and the French First Army." M.A. thesis, University of Delaware, 1975.

Ellis, Lionel F. *Victory in the West: The Defeat of Germany*. Vol. 2. London: H.M. Stationary Office, 1968.

Ehrman, John. *Grand Strategy: October 1944–August 1945*. Vol. 6 of J.R.M. Butler, editor, *History of the Second World War*. United Kingdom Military series. London: HMS Office, 1956.

Farago, Ladislas. *Aftermath: Martin Bormann and the Fourth Reich*. New York: Simon and Schuster, 1974.

Fest, Joachim C. *Hitler*. New York: Harcourt, Brace, Jovanovich, 1974.

Flood, Charles B. *Hitler: The Path to Power*. Boston: Houghton Mifflin, 1989.

Friedmann, Wolfgang. *The Allied Military Government of Germany*. London: Stevens and Sons, 1947.

Fritz, Stephen G. *Endkampf: Soldiers, Civilians and the Death of the Third Reich*. Lexington, Kentucky: University of Kentucky, 2004.

Galante, Pierre and Eugene Silianoff, eds. *Voices From the Bunker. Recollections of Traudl Junge*. New York: G.P. Putnams, 1989.

Geiss, Josef. *Obersalzberg: History of a Mountain from Judith Platter until Today*. Berchtesgaden: Anton Plenk, 1989 (orig. 1951).

Gilbert, Martin. *The Day the War Ended: May 8, 1945—Victory in Europe*. New York: Henry Holt, 1995.

Gimbel, John. *The American Occupation of Germany: Politics and the Military, 1945–1949*. Stanford, California: Stanford University Press, 1968.

Gulgowski, Paul W. *The American Military Government of United States Occupied Zones of Post-World War II Germany*. Frankfurt/Main: Haag and Herchen, 1983.

Gun, Nerin. *Eva Braun: Hitler's Mistress*. New York: Meredith, 1968.

Hamann, Brigitte. *Hitler's Vienna: A Dictator's Apprenticeship*. Oxford: Oxford University Press, 1999.

Hanisch, Ernst. *Obersalzberg: The "Eagle's Nest" and Adolf Hitler*. Bad Reichenhall, Bavaria: Berchtesgaden Landesstifung, 1996.

Harper, David. *Your Complete Guide to Berchtesgaden*. Berchtesgaden: D. Harper and Ch. Dundas-Harper, GdbR, 1997.

Harris, Robert. *Selling Hitler: The Extraordinary Story of the Con Job of the Century—the Faking of the Hitler "Diaries."* New York: Pantheon Books, 1986.

Hoffmann, Peter. *Hitler's Personal Security*. Cambridge, Mass.: MIT Press, 1979.

Howe, Ellic. *Astrology and Psychological Warfare during World War II*. London: Rider and Company, 1972.

Hutter, Clemens M. *Hitler's Obersalzberg*. Berchtesgaden: Berchtesgadener Anzeiger, 1997.

Hymoff, Edward. *The OSS in World War II*. New York: Ballantine Books, 1972.

Infield, Glenn B. *Hitler's Secret Life: The Mysteries of the Eagle's Nest*. New York: Stein and Day, 1979.

_____. *Skorzeny: Hitler's Commando*. New York: St. Martin's Press, 1981.

Irving, David. *Göring: A Biography*. New York: William Morrow, 1989.

_____. *Hitler's War*. New York: Viking Press, 1977.

Jetzinger, Franz. *Hitler's Youth*. Westport, Conn.: Greenwood, 1976.

Joachimsthaler, Anton. *The Last Days of Hitler: The Legends, the Evidence, the Truth*. London: Arms and Armour Press, 1998.

Katz, Barry M. *Foreign Intelligence: Research and Analysis in the Office of Strategic Services*. Cambridge, Mass.: Harvard University Press, 1989.

Kershaw, Ian. *The "Hitler Myth": Image and Reality in the Third Reich*. Oxford: Clarendon, 1987.

_____. *Hitler, 1889–1936: Hubris*. New York: W.W. Norton, 1998.

_____. *Hitler, 1936–1945: Nemesis*. New York: W.W. Norton, 2000.

_____. *Popular Opinion and Political Dissent in the Third Reich: Bavaria, 1933–1945*. New York: Clarendon, Oxford University Press, 1983.

Kilzer, Louis. *Hitler's Traitor: Martin Bormann and the Defeat of the Reich*. Novato, California: Presidio, 2000.

Kirk, Tom. *The Longman Companion to Nazi Germany*. London: Longman, 1995.

Kuby, Erich. *The Russians and Berlin, 1945*. London: Heinemann, 1965; New York: Hill and Wang, 1968.

Lang, Jochen von. *The Secretary: Martin Bormann, the Man Who Manipulated Hitler*. New York: Random House, 1979.

Large, David C. *Where Ghosts Walked: Munich's Road to the Third Reich*. New York: W.W. Norton, 1997.

Lee, Bruce. *Marching Orders: The Untold Story of World War II*. New York: Crown, 1995.

Lehrer, Steven. *Hitler Sites: A City-by-City Guidebook (Austria, Germany, France, United States)*. Jefferson, North Carolina: McFarland, 2002.

Lucas, James S. *World War II through German Eyes*. London: Arms and Armour Press, 1987.

MacDonald, Charles B. *The Last Offensive*. Washington, D.C.: Center of Military History, U.S. Army, 1984.

Machtan, Lothar. *The Hidden Hitler*. New York: Basic Books, 2001.

Madden, Paul. *Adolf Hitler and the Nazi Epoch: An Annotated Bibliography of English-Language Works on the Origins, Nature and Structure of the Nazi State*. Lanham, Maryland: Scarecrow Press, 1998.

Manvell, Roger, and Fränkel, Heinrich. *Hermann Göring*. London: Heinemann, 1962.

Markey, Michael A. *Jake: The General from West York Avenue.* Historical Society of York County, Pa., 1998.

Maser, Werner. *Hitler: Legend, Myth and Reality.* New York: Harper and Row, 1973.

_____. *Hitler's Mein Kampf: An Analysis.* London: Faber and Faber, 1970.

Mauch, Christof. *The Shadow War Against Hitler: The Covert Operations of America's Wartime Secret Intelligence Service.* New York: Columbia University Press, 2003.

Maule, Henry. *Out of the Sand: The Epic Story of General Leclerc and the Fighting Free French.* London: Oddhams Books, 1966.

McDonough, James L., and Gardner, Richard S. *Skyriders: History of the 327/401 Glider Infantry.* Nashville, Tenn.: Battery Press, 1980.

McGovern, James. *Martin Bormann.* New York: William Morrow, 1968.

McKale, Donald M. *Hitler: The Survival Myth.* New York: Stein and Day, 1981.

McRandle, James H. *The Track of the Wolf.* Evanston, Illinois: Northwestern University Press, 1965.

Meek, Marvin. "ULTRA and the Myth of the German 'National Redoubt.'" M.A. thesis. Fort Leavenworth, Kansas: U.S. Army And General Staff College, 1999.

Middlebrook, Martin, and Everitt, Chris. *The Bomber Command War Diaries: An Operational Reference Book, 1939–1945.* London: Penguin, 1990.

Minnott, Rodney G. *The Fortress That Never Was.* London: Longmans, 1964.

Mommen, Hans, ed. *The Third Reich Between Vision and Reality.* New York: Berg, 2000.

Moller, Horst; Dahm, Volker; and Mehringer, Hartmut, eds. *Die tödliche Utopie: Bild, Texte, Dokumente, Daten zum Dritten Reich.* Munich: Institute of Contemporary History, 2002.

Mosley, Leonard. *The Reich Marshal: A Biography of Hermann Göring.* Garden City, N.Y.: Doubleday, 1974.

Muhlen, Norbert. *The Return of Germany: A Tale of Two Countries.* Chicago: Henry Regnery, 1953.

Newton, Ronald C. *The "Nazi Menace" in Argentina, 1931–1947.* Stanford, California: Stanford University Press, 1992.

Nicholas, Lynn H. *The Rape of Europa: The Fate of Europe's Treasures in the Third Reich and the Second World War.* New York: Alfred A. Knopf, 1994.

Nobecourt, Jacques. *Hitler's Last Gamble: The Battle of the Bulge.* New York: Schocken, 1967.

Overy, Richard. *Interrogations: The Nazi Elite in Allied Hands, 1945.* New York: Viking, 2001.

Paul, Barbara Dotts. *The Germans After World War II: An English-Language Bibliography.* Boston: G.K. Hall, 1990.

Payne, Robert. *The Life and Death of Adolf Hitler.* New York: Praeger, 1973.

Perret, Geoffrey. *There's a War to Be Won: The United States Army in World War II.* New York: Ballantine, 1991.

Persico, Joseph E. *Piercing the Reich: The Penetration of Nazi Germany by American Secret Agents During World War II.* New York: Viking Press, 1979.

Peterson, Edward N. *The American Occupation of Germany: Retreat to Victory.* Detroit: Wayne State University, 1977.

Petrova, Ada, and Watson, Peter. *The Death of Hitler: The Full Story with New Evidence from Secret Russian Archives.* New York: W.W. Norton, 1995.

Piszkiewicz, Dennis. *From Nazi Test Pilot to Hitler's Bunker.* New York: Praeger, 1999.

_____. *The Nazi Rocketeers: Dreams of Space and Crimes of War.* Westport, Conn.: Praeger, 1995.

Pogue, Forrest C. *George C. Marshall: Organizer of Victory.* New York: Viking Press, 1973.

Rapport, Leonard, and Northwood, Arthur. *Rendezvous with Destiny: A History of the 101st Airborne Division.* Madelia, Minnesota: House of Print, 1965 (orig. 1948).

Redlich, Fritz. *Hitler: Diagnosis of a Destructive Prophet.* New York: Oxford University Press, 1999.

Reuth, Ralf Georg. *Goebbels.* New York: Harcourt, Brace, 1993.

Rigdon, Denis. *Kill the Führer: Section X and Operation Foxley.* Gloucestershire, England: Sutton, Thrupp-Stroud, 1999.

Ryan, Cornelius. *The Last Battle.* New York: Simon and Schuster, 1966.

Sayer, Ian, and Botting, Douglas. *America's Secret Army: The Untold Story of the Counter Intelligence Corps.* New York: Franklin Watts, 1989.

_____, and _____. *Nazi Gold: The Story of the World's Greatest Robbery—and Its Aftermath.* London: Panther Books, 1984.

Schaffer, Ronald. *Wings of Judgment: American Bombing in World War II.* New York: Oxford University Press, 1985.

Schwab, Gerald. *OSS Agents in Hitler's Heartland: Destination Innsbruck.* Westport, Conn.: Praeger, 1996.

Schwarzwaller, Wulf. *The Unknown Hitler.* New York: Berkley Books, 1990.

Sereny, Gitta. *Albert Speer: His Battle with Truth.* New York: Alfred A. Knopf, 1995.

Smith, Arthur L. *The War for the German Mind: Reeducating Hitler's Soldiers.* Providence, Rhode Island: Berghahn Books, 1996.

Smith, Bradley F. *Adolf Hitler: His Family, Childhood and Youth.* Stanford, California: Hoover Institution, 1967.

_____. *The Shadow Warriors: OSS and the Origins of the CIA.* New York: Basic Books, 1983.

Smith, Michael. *Station X: Decoding Nazi Secrets.* New York: TV Books, 1999.

Spotts, Frederic. *Hitler and the Power of Aesthetics.* London: Hutchinson, 2002.

Steinert, Marlis G. *Hitler's War and the Germans:*

*Public Mood and Attitude During the Second World War*. Athens, Ohio: Ohio University Press, 1977.

———. *Twenty-three Days: The Final Collapse of Nazi Germany*. New York: Walker, 1969.

Stierlin, Helm. *Adolf Hitler: A Family Perspective*. New York: Psychohistory Press, 1976.

Suster, Gerald. *Hitler: Black Magician*. London, 1996.

Tabori, Paul, ed. *The Private Life of Adolf Hitler: The Intimate Notes and Diary of Eva Braun*. London: Aldus, 1949. Fiction.

Tauber, Kurt P. *Beyond Eagle and Swastika: German Nationalism Since 1945*. 2 vols. Middletown, Conn.: Wesleyan University Press, 1967.

Toland, John. *Adolf Hitler*. New York: Ballantine Books, 1976.

———. *The Last Hundred Days*. Toronto: Bantam Books, 1985.

Trevor-Roper, Hugh. *The Last Days of Hitler*. Chicago: University of Chicago Press, 1992.

Turner, John, and Jackson, Robert. *From Fedala to Berchtesgaden: The Story of the U.S. Seventh Army in World War II*. New York: Scribner's, 1975.

Vigneras, Marcel. *Rearming the French*. Washington, D.C.: Office of the Chief of Military History, Dept. of the Army, 1957.

Vincent, Isabel. *Hitler's Silent Partners: Swiss Banks, Nazi Gold and the Pursuit of Justice*. New York: William Morrow, 1997.

Waite, Robert. *Adolf Hitler: The Psychopathic God*. New York: Basic Books, 1977.

Weigley, Russell F. *Eisenhower's Lieutenants: The Campaigns of France and Germany, 1944–1945*. Bloomington, Indiana: Indiana University Press, 1981.

Whiting, Charles. *America's Forgotten Army: The Story of the U.S. Seventh*. New York: St. Martin's, 1999.

———. *Werewolf: The Story of the Nazi Resistance Movement, 1944–1945*. London: Leo Cooper, 1972.

Willett, Ralph. *The Americanization of Germany, 1945–1949*. London: Routledge, 1989.

Willoughby, John. *Remaking the Conquering Heroes: The Social and Geopolitical Impact of the Post-War American Occupation of Germany*. London: Palgrave, 2001.

Wilmot, Chester. *The Struggle for Europe*. London: Fontana/Collins, 1974.

Wilt, Alan F. *The French Riviera Campaign of August 1944*. Carbondale, Illinois: Southern Illinois University Press, 1981.

Wyant, William K. *Sandy Patch: A Biography of Lt. General Alexander M. Patch*. Westport, Conn.: Praeger, 1991.

Wyden, Peter. *The Hitler Virus: The Insidious Legacy of Adolf Hitler*. New York: Arcade, 2001.

Ziemke, Earl. *The U.S. Army in the Occupation of Germany*. Washington, D.C.: Office of Military History, 1975.

Zitelmann, Rainer. *Hitler: The Policies of Seduction*. London: London House, 1999.

Zweig, Ronald W. *The Gold Train: The Destruction of the Jews and the Looting of Hungary*. New York: William Morrow, 2002.

## Web Sites

Avalon. (For Nuremberg trials.) <www.yale.edu/lawweb/avalon/imt/>.

Bytwerk, Randall, ed. and trans. German Propaganda Archive. <www.calvin.edu/academic/CAS/gpn>.

German Propaganda Archive, Randall Bytwerk, editor and translator. <www.calvin.edu/academic/CAS/gpn>.

Duncan, George. "Women of the Third Reich." <members.iinet.net.au/~gduncan/women.html>.

Federal Bureau of Investigation. Hitler sightings files. <www.paperlessarchives.com/hitler>.

Hanfstängl, Ernst. Files. <foia.fbi.gov/foiaindex/haufstan>.

Feldgrau, German Armed Forces, 1919–1945. <feldgrau.com>.

Frank, Walter S. "Adolf Hitler: The Making of a Führer." <smoter.com/hitler>.

Heller, William, and Third Infantry Division. <warfoto.com>.

Hornshoj-Moller, Stig. "The Führer Myth." <holocaust-history.org/fuehrer-myth/>.

Irving, David. Action Report online. <ActionReport.com>.

Korte, Jeff. "Eisenhower, Berlin and the National Redoubt." *Gateway: An Academic History Journal on the Web*. Spring 2002. <grad.usask.ca/gateway/index.html>.

National Socialism. <ns.aus.tm/propaganda/Adolf/o7.html>.

Obersalzberg Documentation Center. <www.obersalzberg.de/cms_d>.

Office of Strategic Services. *Hitler Source Book*. <www.nizkor.org/hweb/people/h/hitler-adolf/oss-papers/text/>.

"Pages from my Scrapbook." <Scrapbookpages.com/Kehlsteinhaus>.

Ross, Bernie. "The Foxley Report: Plotters Against Hitler." <bbc.co.uk/history/war/wwtwo/_the plotters_print.html>.

Walden, Geoff. "Third Reich in Ruins." <Thirdreichruins.com>.

Wiesenthal, Simon. <SimonWiesenthalCenter.com>.

# Index

Afghanistan 160
Agnew, Jack 126, 159–60
Alexander, Michael 119
Allen, George 153
Allied Combined Chiefs of Staff 79
Allied intelligence 54, 68, 75, 77
Allied prisoners of war 54, 73, 74–75, 82, 112, 119, 145, 159; Moosburg camp 76, 82
Alpenfestung *see* National Redoubt
Alsos mission 91
Altaussee 74, 110, 111, 157
Amann, Max 33
Ambrose, Stephen 131
Amsterdam 62
Anderson, Harry 155
Andrews, Frank 83
Anschluss 46
Antonescu, Ion 61
Ardennes offensive 69, 75, 78, 86, 87, 102
Argentina 62, 81, 103
Arnold, Henry (Hap) 51–52
Art recovery 155–57; Amber room 155, 157; Salzburg coin collection 157
astrology 30–31
Augsburg 100, 151, 162
Austria 1, 18, 79, 103, 113; gold in 110; nationalism revived 113, 121, 151
Axelsson, George 69
Axmann, Arthur 147, 153

Baarova, Lida 41
Bad Gastein 73, 109, 154, 160
Bad Reichenhall 111, 121, 126, 127, 128, 139, 172
Bahlau, Fred 141–42
Baille-Stewart, Norman 119
Baldwin, Hanson 83
Barker, Harry 146
Barnson, McFarlan 146
Bastonge 125, 126
Baur, Hans 16, 27, 37, 42, 56, 104–5, 117, 118–19
Bayreuth festival 29, 36, 46
Beck, John I. 53
Beck, Josef 46
Beermann, Helmut 103
Beierl, Florian 117, 134, 157, 158
Belgium 109

Bendetson, Karl 90
Berchtesgaden 1, 3, 6, 7, 18–19 31–32, 34, 79, 156, 167, 169; Recreation Area 166–68, 169, 170–71, 177
*Berchtesgadener Anzeiger* 166, 176
*Berchtesgadener Kurier* 176
Berchtesgadener Land 8–10, 20, 49, 56, 62, 75, 119, 120, 144, 158–60, 166, 167, 174, 177
Berger, Gottlob 59, 106, 119, 152, 157
Berghof 6, 27, 30-31, 44-46, 55-57, 58, 60, 61, 129, 174, 175, 176, 177; *see also* Obersalzberg
Bernadotte, Folk 106
Bernstein, Victor 142
Berlin 46, 67, 71, 73, 80–81, 102, 104; bunker 49
Biddiscombe, Perry 188
Bielenberg, Christobel 132
Billinger, Karl 46
Bischofswiesen 117
Black Forest 86, 92, 129
Blanda, Elizabeth 63
Blank, Arnold 75
Blitt, Henry 152
Bloch, Edward 10, 12
Bloomberg, Werner von 27
Blumenson, Martin 86
Boris, King of Bulgaria 46, 61
Bormann, Albert 116
Bormann, Martin 33, 34, 39, 41, 44, 48, 50, 51, 54, 57, 59–60, 61, 62, 65, 66, 74, 100, 102–3, 104, 109, 111, 114, 115, 117, 118–19, 148, 150, 153
Bouhler, Philip 153, 159
Bowen, William 146
Bradley, Omar 77, 78, 85, 86, 88, 89, 93, 95
Branau 181
Brandt, Karl 40, 59, 63, 64, 65, 66, 102
Braun, Eva 19, 20, 23, 36, 39, 40, 41, 44, 50, 54, 59, 61, 63, 64, 65, 67, 102, 103–4, 106, 107, 108, 111, 116, 117, 118, 120, 137, 179
Braun, Ilse 64
Braun, Margarete (Gretl) (later Fegelein) 44, 674, 108, 111, 120
Brauschitz, Col., von 148
Brecht, Bertolt 13
Bredow, SS leader 115

Breinlinger, W., Frau 176
Breitenbach, Edgar 156
Brennero 128
Brettel, Jack 129
British Army 169; intelligence 31, 72, 79, 80, 117
Brooke, Alan 80
Bruck, Austria 141, 147, 155, 159
Bruck, Dorothy van 40
Brückner, Wilhelm 26, 27, 56
Bruskin, Sydney 151
Burckhardt, Carl 29
Burgett, Donald 140, 141

Carol, King of Rumania 46
Casey, William 76
Catholic Church 46
Chamberlain, Neville 32, 45
Charlemagne Division 135
Christian, Gerda 104
Churchill, Winston 13, 54, 57, 63, 72, 84, 88
Ciano, Galeazzo 46
Cofran, Major 162
Clark, Lt. Col. 177
Clark, Mark 84, 140
Clarke, Jeffry 86
Clay, Lucius 140, 157, 163
Cloer, Russell 97, 99, 131, 136
Collins, Joseph Lawton 161
Colmar pocket 85, 124
Cooper, Alfred Duff 54
Corlett, Charles 93
Critchell, Laurence 169
Czechoslovakia 45, 109, 139

Dachau 61, 100, 178
Danat, Elly 23, 31
Daub, David 98, 129, 135
de Boissieu, Alain 135
de Castellane, Capt. 133
de Gaulle, Charles 40–41, 72, 88, 90, 96, 135, 141
Degrelle, Leon 31
de Guillebon, Lt. Col. 131, 133
de Lattre deTassigny, Jean 88, 89, 90, 91, 94, 95–96, 97, 122, 124, 128–29
Delmer, Sefton 63
Depression 5, 20
D'Este, Carlo 88
DeValera, Eamon 63

Devers, Jacob 83, 85; commander 86, 89, 91; relations with French 96–97, 128–29
Dickey, Douglas 129
Diebner, Kurt 91
Diessen 139
Dietrich, Otto 23, 28, 29, 33, 34, 36, 38, 49, 61, 81
Dietrich, Sepp 35, 151
DiPietro, Michael 135
Dohring, Herbert 28, 32, 47, 63, 65
Dönitz, Karl 106, 113, 117, 118, 120, 152
Donovan, William 63, 68, 76, 78
Doppelgängers 56–57
Dorner, Alfred 54
Dorsky, Louis 146
Dowley, Bridget 154
Dragoon (formerly Anvil) Operation 84
Dronne, Raymond 131
Dulles, Alan 52, 63, 71–72, 81, 113

Eaker, Ira 84, 90
East Prussia headquarters 49, 55, 58, 60, 66, 67
Eberstein, Friedrich von 75, 121
Ebertin, Elisbeth 30
Ebertin, Karl von 40, 44
Eckart, Dietrich 17, 18, 158
Edelweiss 174
Eden, Anthony 44, 45
Eichmann, Adolf 103, 151, 159
Eichstatt 162
Eigruber, August 74
Eisenhower, Dwight 52, 56, 77–78, 80; relations with Devers 84, 85, 87, 88, 91, 92, 93, 95, 112, 114, 123, 125, 140, 148–49, 164, 166, 167
Elbe River 81
Elliott, Richard 160
Erlanger 16
Esser, Hermann 17, 21
Exner, Marlene von 59–60
Eyster, George 161

Falthauser, Kurt 180
Farago, Ladislas 118
Fegelein, Hermann 56, 63, 105, 108
Fest, Joachim 5
Fischhorn 74, 111, 120, 153, 155
Flegal, Erna 118
Förtsch, Gen. 141, 149
Foxley 53–54
France 109; government 88
François-Poncet, André 43
Frank, Bernhard 56, 59, 66, 73, 111, 114, 115, 117, 120, 121, 128, 132, 148
Frankreich Brigade 135
French, Edward 146
French Second Armored Division 121, 123–24, 125, 127, 130–31; in Berchtesgaden 131–32; to Obersalzberg 132–34, 135, 136, 139
Freud, Sigmund 10
Frevert, Ute 166
Frick, Wilhelm 153
Friedmann, Wolfgang 169
Fromm, Bella 37, 40
Fry, Michael 13

Führermuseum, Linz 110, 155, 180
Fuller, J.F.C. 68
Funk, Walter 109–10, 119, 150, 152–53, 157
Furst, Peter 100

Galland, Adolf 113
Garmisch-Partenkirchen 111, 157
Gehlen, Reinhard 111, 150
Geiss, Josef 31, 44, 120
Gerlach, Walther 91
German gold, shipment of 109–10, 150; in Berchtesgaden 141, 153; search for 145, 153, 157–58
German government 7, 31
German prisoners of war 125, 127, 128, 135, 140, 141, 144, 145–46, 168, 172, 173
Gilmore, William 150
Gloaguer, Paul 132
Goebbels, Joseph 25, 27, 31, 35, 36, 38, 39, 41, 44, 29, 54, 57, 58, 60, 62, 82, 86, 103, 104, 111, 112, 113, 116, 117
Göhler, Johannes 110, 120
Gontard, Hans 69
Gördeler, Carl 66
Gore, Albert 162
Göring, Emmy 41, 64, 141, 142, 156
Göring, Fritz 128
Göring, Hermann 1, 6, 22, 22, 34, 38, 41, 50, 55, 58, 64, 66, 103, 105, 106, 109, 111–12, 113–14; art collection 156
Gottsch, Werner 113
Goudsmit, Samuel 91
Grand Mufti of Jerusalem 160
Grethlein, Ingenieur 128
Guderian, Heinz 135, 152
Gun, Nerin 65
Günsche, Otto 103

Habe, Hans 166
Hahn, Otto 91
Haislip, Wade 124, 127–28
Halifax (Edward Wood) 45
Hallein mine 157
Hamberger, Philip 43
Hamilton, Ian 45
Hanfstängl, Erna 66
Hanfstängl, Ernst 16, 17, 18, 22
Hanisch, Reinhold 12, 13, 14
Hanson, Chester 89, 92, 94
Hapsburgs 46
Hart, B.H. Liddell 96
Hasselbach, Hans 39, 63
Hatherway, Calvin 156
Haushofer, Karl 18
Hearst, William R. 44
Hechler, Kenneth 162
Heidelberg 162
Heiden, Konrad 17, 28, 29
Heinrici, Gotthard 110
Heintges, John 101, 126, 128, 130–31, 134, 135, 139, 140
Heisenberg, Werner 91
Helms, Richard 68
Hengl, Georg Ritter von 112, 121
Hentschel, Johannes 56

Herrgeselle, Gerhard
Hess, Rudolph 31, 34, 57
Hewel, Walter 63
Heydrich, Reinhard 53
Higgins, Gerald 149, 150
Higgins, Marguerite 123, 137, 141
Hill, Russel 161, 162
Himmler, Heinrich 41, 54, 55, 66, 68, 69, 102, 105–5, 109, 115, 119–20, 149, 152, 153
Hintersee 116
Hitler, Adolf: Arbeiter 11–14; to Berchtesgaden 17–24, 109, 112, 114–15, 149; building projects 48; family 10, 11, 15; finances 33, 35; mountains and 25, 26; in Munich 15; politician 16; soldier 16; threats to 56; in Vienna 11–15; work routine 28–29
Hitler, Alois, Jr. 10, 154, 175
Hitler, Angela Rabual 10–11, 20, 34, 36, 37, 154
Hitler, Hans 154
Hitler, Paula 10–11, 19, 154
Hitler, William Patrick 14, 15, 154
Hitlerjugend (Hitler Youth) 125, 147
Hofer, Franz 69, 73, 74, 102, 109, 112, 150
Hofer, Walther 155
Hoffmann, Heinrich 27, 30, 39, 44, 67, 107
Hoffmann, Peter 53, 57
Hofmann, Otto 92, 121
Hoge, William 90
Horthy, Miklos 41, 61
Horton, Robert 125
Hummel, Helmut von 110, 119
Hungary 72, 109; gold train 110, 157
Huss, Pierre 25, 27, 37, 43

Illner, Wolfgang 178
Institute of Contemporary History (Munich) 179
Ireland 4, 62, 63, 151, 175
Irving, David 57, 131
Israel 172, 178
Italy 81, 84, 103, 109

Jacob, Karl Theodor 110, 121, 128, 166, 167, 171
James, Clifton 56
Japan 81, 101; diplomats 154, 165
Jaschko, Gen. 74
Jenkins, Reuben 92, 141
jet aircraft 125, 159
Jews 14–15, 37, 56, 57, 61; Hungarian Jews 110, 178, 179; Jewish museum, Berlin 180
Jodl, Alfred 66, 103, 106, 111, 114, 153
Johnston, Denis 94
Johnston, Richard 142
Jugo, Jenny 38–39
Jung, Carl 28
Junge, Traudl 32

"K, Major" 162
Kaltenbrunner, Ernst 55, 74, 102, 110, 113, 115, 119, 150, 1512, 157, 158
Kannenberg, Arthur 153

Kastner, Gustof 121, 141
Keannelly, Thomas 3
Kehlstein 42–43, 44, 51, 116, 117, 133, 137, 140, 142, 174, 176, 177
Keitel, Wilhelm 106, 109, 114, 142
Kellmann, Dr. 171
Kempka, Erich 104, 152
Kennan, George 166
Kennedy, John F. 142–43
Kershaw, Ian 13, 54
Kersten, Felix 59
Kesselring, Albert 72, 74, 112, 121, 125, 134, 146, 149–50, 175
Khan, Aga 44
Kharkov 61
Kirkpatrick, Helen 139
Kleikamp, Helmut 93
Klessheim castle 49, 61
Knappen, Marshall 161
Knauth, Percy 120, 137, 149
Knyphausen, von 68
Kochta, Herbert 179
Kohl, Helmut 147
Kohler, Pauline 30, 37, 56
Koller, Karl 114, 115
Königssee 117, 147, 168
Konrad, Franz 111, 120
Korean War 177
Kraft, James 140
Krause, Heinz Erich 175–76
Kubizek, August 14, 15
Kuby, Erich 11
Kunz, William 124, 125, 160

Labanyi, Peter 25
Laffert, Sigrid von 40
Lammers, Hans 49, 107, 114, 131
Landerk 129
Langbehn, Karl 66
Langer, Walter 21
Laurie, A.P. 13
Laval, Pierre 61
Leasor, James 32
Leclerc, Philippe 123–24, 127, 133, 135, 139, 141
Lend, Austria 140, 154
Lenz, Dr. 174
Leopold, King of Belgium 75
Lewin, Ronald 117
Ley, Inge 39
Ley, Robert 12, 45, 103, 152
*Life* 53, 165, 177
Linge, Hans 26, 50, 63
Lloyd George, David 45
Lochner, Louis 43
Lockridge, Patricia 167
Lodge, Henry C. 97
London *Sunday Times* 108
London *Times* 70, 142, 147
Lovell, Stanley 55
Ludecke, Hans Georg 13
Ludecke, Kurt 14, 24
Lueger, Karl 14, 15
Luftwaffe 58, 99, 114, 120

MacDonald, Charles 84, 92
Marcinkiewicz, August 75
Marshall, George 78, 79, 83, 84, 85, 86, 91, 97, 123, 148

Matteson, Robert 151
Mauterndorf, Schloss 115, 117, 148
Mayr, Karl 16
McCloy, John 177
Mecklenburg estate 48
Mehr, Georg 131, 175
Mend, Hans 16
Mengele, Josef 103
Menninger, Karl and William 55
Messiah, Albert 133
Milburn, Frank 124, 139
Milch, Erhard 58
Millar, George 153
Miller, Lee 136
Minford, Unity 39–40
Mittelwald 109, 157
Mittersill 159
Mohnke, Brigadeführer 57
Montgomery, Bernard 56, 80, 86, 88, 164
Moor, Paul 176–77
Morrell, Theodor 51, 59, 61, 65, 107, 153
Muauch, Ludwig 75
Müeller, Rene 38
Muhe, Ludwig 75
Mulhouse 87
Munich 2, 50; bomb shelter 49, 65, 93, 94, 100–1; German POWs to 145–46; Munich-Salzburg autobahn 125, 126
Murphy, Audie 98
Murphy, Robert 17
Mussolini, Benito 12, 41, 55, 61, 65

Nachama, Andreas 179
Nair, Claude 164–65
Natinform 175
National Redoubt 1, 68–82, 101, 102, 104, 106, 111, 141, 148, 150, 151
Nazis 3, 5, 2, 18, 20, 25, 54, 79, 82, 97; gauleiters 58
The Netherlands 79
Neumann, Josef 14
*New York Times* 70, 116
*Newsweek* 70, 108
Newton, Roland 103
Nicholas, Lynn 156
Nietzsche, Friedrich 3
Nordwind, Operation 87–88
Normandy invasion 61, 66, 68, 124
Norway 79
Nuremberg 93, 98

Oberg, Karl 152
Obersalzberg 1, 2, 4, 7, 18, 25, 65, 67; bombing of 115, 129; complex 29, 32–33, 34, 48, 66; demolition 174; documentation center 178–79; hotel 179–80; last days 104–5; military visitors 140; politicians visit 140; staff 31, 32, 65; tourists 176; tunnels 50; *see also* Berghof
Öchsner, Frederick 43
O'Daniel, John 98, 122–23, 125, 126, 127–28, 134, 140, 141
Odessa escape route 118
O'Donnell, James 108
Office of Strategic Services (OSS) 38,

44, 55, 59, 62, 63, 66, 68, 69, 71–72, 76–77, 103, 108, 111
*Official Gazette* 166
Öser, Oskar 117
Ossietz, Karl 30
Overlord, Operation 84

Padover, Saul 163, 164
Panton, Silkirk 43
Patch, Alexander 81, 86, 88, 90, 94–95, 100, 126
Patton, George 81, 84, 86, 87, 88, 92, 148, 159
Partner, Therese 174
Pash, Boris 91, 94
Paul, Prince Regent of Yugoslavia 46
Pavelic, Ante 61
Petain, Philippe 75
Peterson, Edward 161–62
Phayre, Igatius 12, 27, 30
Platterhof Hotel 134, 142, 159, 174, 176, 178
Poland 29, 46–47, 139, 147; Polish guards 172
Pongan, Markt 119
Pope, Ernest 29, 35, 40
Pratt, Sherman 77, 125, 126, 128, 129, 134
Price, G. Ward 43
Priebke, Erich 103
Prützmann, Otto 81
Puttkamer, Karl-Jesko von 11
Pyle, Ernie 89

Quant, Magda (later Goebbels) 36–37, 41, 107, 117
Quinn, William 94
Quisling, Vidkun 61

Rachicle, Fred 129
Rado, Emmy 68
Ramsey, Lloyd 100, 126, 127, 134, 140–41
Raubal, Friedl 20
Raubal, Geli 17, 19, 36
Reich Security Main Office (RSHA) 74, 77
Reichbank 109, 151
Reiss, Curt 121
Reiter, Maria 19
Reitsch, Hanna 105, 106, 117–18
Renoth, Josef 178
Renoth, Peter 180
Rhine 86
Ribbentrop, Joachim von 73, 106, 152
Riefenstahl, Leni 36, 39, 41, 60
Rohm, Ernst 22, 31
Roimer, Robert 156
Rommel, Erwin 61
Roosevelt, Franklin 31, 52, 69, 78
Rosenberg, Alfred 152
Rosson, William 127, 128
Rothschild family 131
Royal Air Force (RAF) 51, 57, 115–16
Rundstedt, Gerd von 150

Saalfelden 149
Salisbury-Jones, Guy 96

Salzburg 78, 113, 125
Sandrock, Mayor of Berchtesgaden 128
Sarcelet, Sgt. 133
Sauckel, Fritz 153
Saur, Karl-Otto 106
Scharfenberg, Ingrid 174
Schaub, Julius 21, 108, 111
Schellenberg, Markt 120–21
Schellenberg, Walter 66, 84
Schenck, Ernst-Gunther 118
Schiff, Victor 69
Schirach, Baldor von 20, 62
Schirach, Henriette 20, 30, 61–62, 63
Schmidt, Paul 109
Schneider, Herta 63, 111
Schönemann, Marion 40, 63, 64
Schonerer, Georg von 15
Schöning, Everett 177
Schorner, Ferdinand 113
Schröder, Christa 57, 62, 65, 104, 107
Schultze, Ada 62
Schuschnigg, Kurt von 46
Schuster, Karl 16, 34, 174
Schutzstaffel (SS) 54, 66, 67, 69, 70, 71, 73, 74, 119, 120, 126, 146, 149, 151, 176
Schwaiger, Hans 50
Schwarz, Xavier 153
Seckenheim 162
Seidl, Martin 178
Semmler, Rudolph 104
Senkowsky, Hermann 159
Seraglio, Operation 107–8
Shuster, George 163, 176
Siegsdorf 147
Sink, Robert 123, 137, 140, 141, 159, 165
Six Continents Hotels 179
Skorzeny, Otto 55, 76, 81, 110, 113, 125, 150–51
SMERSH (Russian counter-intelligence) 56, 57
Smith, Baldwin 56
Smith, Truman 16–17
Smith, Walter B. 79, 85, 88, 93
Soldatensender Calais 63
Solomon, Ernst von 147
Soviet Union 46, 47, 48, 56, 78, 81, 102, 104, 113, 118, 120, 142, 177
Spaatz, Carl 51
Spain 62, 81, 110, 151
Special Air Service (SAS) 53
Special Operations Executive (SOE) 51, 53–55, 56, 62, 64, 77, 108
Speer, Albert 13, 14, 20, 21, 22, 25, 28, 30, 32, 33, 41, 46, 47, 48, 49, 57, 58, 61, 63, 102, 105, 109, 111, 114–15, 152, 153, 158
Stack, Robert 148
Stahlenberg, Elizabeth von 32, 35, 39
Stalin, Josef 3, 6, 12, 17, 36, 40–41, 47, 48, 56, 57, 72, 78
Stalingrad 58
Stangass 29, 50, 142, 159, 171
Stars and Stripes 70, 78, 100, 140, 161
Stauffenberg, Claus von 55, 61, 67
Steiner, Gen. 107

Der Stern 158
Stimson, Henry 91
Strasbourg 86, 87, 88
Stredele, Berchtesgaden Nazi leader 120, 121
Streicher, Julius 152
Strobl, Austria 151
Stuttgart 90–91, 132
Sudentenland 45
Summersby, Kay 140
Supreme Headquarters, Allied Expeditionary Force (SHAEF) 55; intelligence 72–73, 75, 79, 86, 92
Swerin, Gerhard von 60
Switzerland 68
Syladek, Frank 129

Taper, Bernard 156
Taylor, Maxwell 131, 137, 141, 149, 150, 154, 156, 159
Tchad (Chad) 141
Templar, Gerald 63
Thorn, Theresa von 37
Thule Society 18
Tiso, Joseph 61
Die tödliche Utopia (The Deadly Utopia) 180
Tolsdorf, Theodor 146
Toole, John 98, 122–23, 139, 147
Toplitzsee 110, 158
Touyeras, Laurent 132–33
Towle, Major 163
Toynbee, Arnold 1, 41, 46
Trevor-Roper, Hugh 107, 108
Truman, Harry S 148
Truscott, Lucian 94, 122, 161
Tyrol, gold in 109, 110, 112

Ulm 91, 97
Ultra 75, 77, 80, 108, 117, 154–55
United States Army 1, 2, 6, 49; Sixth Army Group: 82, 84–85, 87, 90, 91, 92, 93, 125; Seventh Army Intelligence 71, 81, 86, 90, 91, 92–93, 96, 100, 124, 125, 140, 162; Third Infantry Division 97, 98, 100, 121, 125, 126, 127, 132–34 (war's end 135, 136, 139, 149, 154, 157, 160); Seventh Infantry Regiment 98, 100, 116, 125, 128, 129, 130; Thirty-sixth Infantry Division 148; Forty-second Infantry Division 142, 160; Forty-fifth Infantry Regiment 100; Eighty-fifth Infantry Division 128; One hundred-first (Airborne) Infantry Division 135 (on Obersalzberg 136, 139, 140, 141, 145, 146, 147, 149, 157, 160, 181; 502nd Regiment 136; 506th Regiment 121, 123, 125, 126, 136, 147, 153, 154, 158, 159, 160; 327th Glider Regiment 136, 139, 140, 159); One hundred-third Infantry Division 128; Twelfth Army Group: 88, 92, 101, 164; Fifth Army 132
United States Army Air Force 51–52, 66; bombing 58, 115, 116
United States Civil Affairs/Military Government 160–66, 163, 164,

168, 169; constabulary 174; denazification 168, 171; dependent housing 165–66; displaced persons 168, 172; Fragebogen 168, 171; non-fraternization 163–65
United States Counter Itelligence Corps 109, 111, 145, 147, 151, 153, 154, 166, 171, 173, 174
United States Federal Bureau of Investigation 63, 103
United States Joint Chiefs of Staff 68, 71
United States Military Government 117, 166–70; American academics in 173; in Berchtesgaden 117, 144
United States War Department 70, 79
Untersberg mountain 69

Valenti, Isadore 129
Vatican 67
Versailles, Treaty of 45
Volkssturm (People's Storm) 97, 98, 121, 145
Vosges campaign 86, 87
Vosser, Harry 69
V2 rocket 67, 75, 101, 135, 158

Wagner, Freidlind 40
Wagner, Richard 12, 21, 36, 75
Wagner, Siefried 36
Wagner, Winifred 36
Wagner, Wolfgang 36
Walton, Bill 139
Waneck, Wilhelm 113
Warburg, James 161
Weber, Richard 59
Webster, David 124, 126, 130, 136
Wedemeyer, Alfred 90
Wehrmacht (German Armed Forces) 66, 75, 78, 92–93, 98, 100, 112, 113, 116, 145
Weisker, Getraud 64–65
Werwolfs 67, 69, 78, 81–82, 99, 99, 124, 147, 150
Wiegand, Karl von 21, 30
Wiesenthal, Simon 180; Center 178
Wilmot, Chester 81
Winbar, Frank 38
Windsor, Duke and Duchess 45
Winter, Anny 50, 59, 65
Winter, August 74, 112
Winterbrand Lodge 178
Winters, Richard 141
Wood, John 90
Wulff, Wilhelm 41, 105

Yank 164

Zabel, Hans-Georg 160
Zahn, Donald 165
Zebel, Werner 59
Zeissler, Adolf 38
Zell am See 141, 147, 151, 153, 159, 160
Ziemke, Earl 166
Zink, Harold 100
Zum Turken hotel 10, 26, 36, 51, 176, 179